OXFORD BIBLE SERIES

General Editors
P. R. Ackroyd and G. N. Stanton

OXFORD BIBLE SERIES

General Editors
Peter R. Ackroyd and Graham N. Stanton

BIBLICAL INTERPRETATION

ROBERT MORGAN
with
JOHN BARTON

OXFORD UNIVERSITY PRESS

Oxford University Press, Walton Street, Oxford OX2 6DP

Oxford New York Toronto
Delhi Bombay Calcutta Madras Karachi
Kuala Lumpur Singapore Hong Kong Tokyo
Nairobi Dar es Salaam Cape Town
Melbourne Auckland Madrid

and associated companies in
Berlin Ibadan

Oxford is a trade mark of Oxford University Press

Published in the United States by
Oxford University Press Inc., New York

British Library Cataloguing in Publication Data

Morgan, Robert, 1940–
Biblical interpretation.
1. Bible. Interpretation
I. Title II. Barton, John, 1948–
220.6
ISBN 0-19-213257-1 (pbk.)

Library of Congress Cataloging in Publication Data
Data available
ISBN 0-19-213257-1 (pbk.)

5 7 9 10 8 6 4

Printed in Great Britain
on acid-free paper by
Biddles Ltd., Guildford and King's Lynn

GENERAL EDITORS' PREFACE

There are many commentaries on individual books of the Bible, but the reader who wishes to take a broader view has less choice. This series is intended to meet this need. Its structure is thematic, with each volume embracing a number of biblical books. It is designed for use with any of the familiar translations of the Bible; quotations are normally from RSV, but the authors of the individual volumes also use other translations or make their own where this helps to bring out the particular meaning of a passage.

To provide general orientation, there are two volumes of a more introductory character: one considers the Old Testament in its cultural and historical context, examining ways of approach to its complex ancient material; the other, on the New Testament, discusses the origins of Christianity. These two volumes point forward to the four which deal with different kinds of material in the Old Testament: narrative, prophecy, poetry/psalmody, wisdom and law; and to the three which handle different aspects of the New Testament: the Gospels, Paul and Pauline Christianity, the varieties of New Testament thought. The present volume looks at the nature of biblical interpretation, covering both Testaments. This is designed both to draw together some of the many themes touched on in the other volumes, and also to invite the reader to look further at the problems of understanding an ancient literature in the very different cultural context of the present time.

The authors of the individual volumes write for a general readership. Technical terms and Hebrew or Greek words are explained; the latter are used only when essential to the understanding of the text. The general introductory volumes are designed to stand on their own, providing a framework, but also to serve to raise some of the questions which the remaining volumes examine in closer detail. All the volumes, with the exception of the two general ones and that on biblical interpretation, include discussion of selected biblical passages in greater depth, thus providing examples of the ways in which the interpretation of the text makes possible deeper understanding of the wider issues, both historical and theological, with which the Bible is concerned. Select bibliographies in each volume point the way to further discussion of the many issues which remain open to fuller exploration.

P.R.A.
G.N.S.

PREFACE

This book was commissioned and begun as a joint project by an Old and a New Testament specialist. As work progressed we became convinced that a subject in which such difference of opinion and perspective was possible would be better served by one of us giving the book its essential character. A joint statement would run the risk of blandness. Since some of John Barton's views on the theme have appeared in *Reading the Old Testament* (Darton, Longman and Todd, 1984), and because our Christian theological interests in the theme involved giving the New Testament side greater emphasis, the lot fell my way. The Old Testament sections on Wellhausen, Gunkel, von Rad, and Lowth in Chapters 3, 4, 5, and 7 are substantially John Barton's work, the rest of the book mine. But like the editors, whose encouragement and suggestions have been much valued, and Anne Ashby and George Tulloch at OUP, John Barton has read through and commented constructively on the whole manuscript at various stages, and the result therefore remains the product of a happy collaboration. It is also a pleasure to acknowledge with gratitude the cheerful help and support provided by Mrs Doreen Abrams and Mrs Jane Pusey in the Faculty Centre, and Mrs Wilma Minty in the Faculty library.

R.M.

Oxford 1987

CONTENTS

Interpretation and Biblical Interpretation

What is interpretation?

Interpretation is an intermediary task performed by rational human beings to make human communication possible in difficult cases. In interpreting we first understand the human utterance and then elucidate it for ourselves or someone else. Whereas mechanical transmitters pass on messages by relaying sounds or transcribing them into a more permanent form, interpreters often say something quite different in order to get across the *meaning* of an utterance. Unlike the proverbial horse and mule, or the products of modern technology (artificial intelligence is a borderline case), interpreters have *understanding*.

The medium of human communication is normally language. Even where meaning takes non-linguistic forms it calls for articulation in words. Silence is sometimes meaningful, but only where its meaning could in principle be expressed. Non-verbal human expressions or forms of communication such as works of art or music are 'interpreted' because they too bear a meaning or meanings, intended by rational agents and/or discerned by rational receivers.

Borderline cases underline the human and linguistic character of interpretation. If we interpret the whine of a pet dog we are crediting it with more or less rational behaviour as it alerts us to its natural needs. If we speak of computer language and interpret computer data, this is because they represent the language and thought of rational agents.

A different kind of boundary is found in religious discourse.

Those who interpret oracles or speaking in tongues assume that through these a rational divine being is in communication with them. Any such unverifiable claims to interpret the word or will of God or the gods are evidently difficult and disputed matters. They will complicate our discussions of biblical interpretation. But in the context of these introductory reflections on interpretation as such, all that needs to be noted is that, like all religious discourse, talk of 'interpreting' the 'word' or 'will' of God uses the analogy of humans communicating with other humans. The complications ahead stem mainly from the biblical texts being both human communications to humans and (say some) divine communication to humans. On both scores there is wide scope for disagreement about the meanings of the messages, not to mention confusion between the two levels.

As well as borderline cases, negative examples also help to clarify what interpretation is. Again the decisive criterion is the presence or absence of meaning. That is what interpretation aims to clarify. Only the presence of human intentionality, or something analogous to that, makes interpretation an appropriate activity. Unlike symphonies, the noise of motor bikes is 'explained' rather than 'interpreted'—except where the next-door neighbour is saying something by revving up at midnight. The same is true of robots—unless, like computers, their makers are acting through them. Natural phenomena are also explained rather than interpreted—unless the earthquake is seen as an act of God's judgement. Whether we interpret or merely explain a riot depends upon the degree of intentionality and rationality judged to be present in any particular instance.

As the example of the non-verbal musical score which is 'interpreted' by a musician shows, neither the matter to be interpreted nor the manner of interpreting it has to take linguistic form. But human thought, emotion, and language are always implicit and provide the baseline for interpretation. That does not mean that this is simple. On the contrary, the word 'interpretation' is usually reserved for difficult cases where some form of intermediary activity is necessary.

The most obvious case is with foreign languages. At least until the advent of recent technology translation has always been a particular form of interpretation. Where speaker and hearer use the same language and share many assumptions, and the speaker does not mumble and the hearer is not deaf, there is usually no problem about understanding. We do not then make an issue of it by talking about 'interpretation', even though this is constantly taking place. The word is reserved for more difficult cases, where some conscious decoding is necessary or where misunderstanding or failure to understand is present or threatened. Foreigners need interpreters if they do not understand our language—and vice versa.

Conversation usually provides the simplest tasks for human understanding because the context provides a solid basis; facial expressions and tone of voice offer additional aids, and instant correction is possible. Even those speaking different languages can communicate and understand one another face to face. We do not need a degree in modern languages to know when someone is being unkind about our driving in Paris. Where we cannot see the eyes of a speaker, and the range of voice modulation is reduced, as on the telephone, misunderstanding is more probable.

Ignorance of the language is a serious barrier to human communication, but it is not the only source of misunderstanding. The Frenchman commenting on the mad Englishman's driving in Paris might have been drawing attention to the local custom of driving on the right hand side of the road. Unaware of this, the Englishman might have grasped the Frenchman's desperation without understanding the precise nature of the problem. Foreign cultures need interpreting to those unfamiliar with the alien customs or modes of thought. Language is the necessary vehicle here, but the heart of the problem lies in understanding the *subject-matter* being discussed. In biblical interpretation also, learning the languages is a first step, but the major difficulties arise over the subject-matter.

What makes the bad-driving example relatively straightforward, even were the Englishman ignorant of local customs as well as of the French language, is that here there is no time-gap to be overcome and further correction remains possible. Written texts from the distant past pose greater difficulties, and the risks of misunderstanding are much greater. Knowledge of the language is always incomplete, since languages develop and there is only limited evidence available from any period. But these deficiencies are aggravated by problems connected with the particular text under consideration. Lack of knowledge of the author's background assumptions may also hinder understanding. In addition, we often do not know the context or purpose of a text and have to reconstruct these hypothetically before we can understand. Above all, the interpreter of texts has to manage without any response from the author. In ordinary conversation misunderstandings are usually recognized and corrected. Correction in textual interpretation has to be self-correction, based on further reading of these fixed expressions from the past or on further reconstruction of the author's aims and background.

Despite these difficulties, we do read and expect to understand ancient texts. Some tell of matters with which we are at least partly familiar, and the writers communicate across the centuries. Others are more obscure, and we may wonder how much we are understanding. A religious ritual may be largely unintelligible from a surviving literary fragment. Or we may be completely baffled, an experience not unfamiliar to readers of modern poetry also.

It is not only the language and cultural assumptions which render some texts difficult. Literary conventions must also be understood. It is important to recognize what kind of text one is reading and what literary devices are being employed. How we classify it (the literary 'genre') will decide how we read it. Satire is misunderstood if it is not recognized as such, and metaphors are misunderstood if they are taken literally. *Gulliver's Travels* is crassly misunderstood if read as history, geography, or travel, and is only very partially understood when read by children. The full meaning of this political satire is now available only through literary and historical scholarship.

In that example scholarly information enables a modern reader to overhear much of what was heard and understood by Swift's original readers. Here the language is still plain and the story is enjoyable, perhaps even instructive, without any knowledge of the political allusions. But scholarly efforts remain necessary for a fuller understanding of the text.

Interpretation has long involved these different planes—the linguistic, the literary, and the historical. Strategies and techniques for analysing languages and literature were developed by classical grammarians and rhetoricians, and rules or procedures for classifying texts were codified. These were recovered and elaborated in the Renaissance, and since the eighteenth-century Enlightenment revolutionary advances have been made in the study of language and history. But the rules for interpreting all texts, which is where biblical interpretation begins, are 'simply' an extension and formalization of what happens unconsciously in ordinary conversation and reading the newspapers.

Or not so simply—as the word 'unconsciously' hints. The most significant developments in the art or science of interpretation during the nineteenth and twentieth centuries have been the emergence of the social sciences, especially psychology and sociology. These have affected the study of both history and literature. Even conversation may be as complicated as the individuals involved and the situations disclosed—or disguised. The possibilities of concealment, deceit, and double meaning which complicate some conversations also complicate some texts. Interpreters need to be sensitive to the wide range of human motivation and the depths of human sensibility. In the modern Western world Marx, Nietzsche, Freud, and latterly social anthropologists have alerted us to hidden dimensions in texts and other cultural 'scripts', and have thus uncovered further aspects of the interpretative task of decoding.

One person never fully knows another and may therefore never fully plumb the depths of a highly personal verbal communication. But we ordinarily understand as much as the other person intends, and we take this grasping of the author's or speaker's intentions as the norm for understanding. There are important cases where this is not what matters most, and biblical interpretation may be among them, but the natural starting-point for thinking about interpretation is the common-sense observation that most speakers and writers aim to be understood. Interpretation is the process by which this occurs and the intellectual discipline which makes it possible in difficult cases.

The aims of interpreters

The difficulties in human communication which interpretation overcomes are usually difficulties in the texts. Since most texts communicate the same message to different interpreters, it is natural to think that this is where meaning resides, that it was put there by the author and is dug out by interpreters, whether for themselves or others. Even if meaning is better seen as the product of an interaction between two or more people, the secondary or intermediary role of interpreters suggests that they are subordinate to the text or the author or speaker. They merely understand and elucidate the message. This impression is often made explicit where the texts have some special authority, as scriptures and laws have for those under them. Some theologians call themselves 'servants of the divine word'; lawyers and civil servants stand under their constitution.

That common-sense view of the privileged status of the text, whose interpreter can only mediate its meaning, is confirmed by the fact that we usually want to understand a text because we think the author is worth hearing, not because we think we can do something creative with it. The author's intention is usually the meaning sought, and the interpreter's skills are directed to recovering that. Interpreters develop methods which are appropriate to the material under consideration and can be trusted to yield its true meaning. The exception proves the rule: sometimes a text fails to express the author's intention. Writers may express themselves carelessly. But if we think we see what they mean we correct what they say in the light of that. As in conversation, the author's intention remains the norm of meaning. This is what interpreters seek, and it seems to subordinate them to the author or text.

But conversation is a misleading example, however useful for showing that interpretation is fundamentally all about understanding human utterances. It is untypical in one important respect. In the case of conversation or personal communication we are bound to the author's intention because the author is alive and has some moral right to be understood as intended.

For most texts in the public realm, such as books, laws, legends, or songs, this is not the case. The balance of power and moral rights then shifts to the interpreters. They are the masters or judges of meaning now, for better or worse. The interpreters are never mindless servants of the text, or midwives at the birth or communication of meaning. They are human agents with their own aims, interests, and rights.

Texts, like dead men and women, have no rights, no aims, no interests. They can be used in whatever way readers or interpreters choose. If interpreters choose to respect an author's intentions, that is because it is in their interest to do so. They want to know what the author meant. They are reading a particular text on the assumption that the author is worth hearing and therefore respect authorial intention.

There are other reasons for interpreters making authorial intention, or (better) the grammatical meaning which is assumed to represent the author's intention, into the norm for the text's meaning. In the privacy of their minds or studies individual interpreters can do what they like with a text and make it mean what they like. But it is important for a community to reach agreement about the meaning of such shared texts as its laws. Authorial intention or grammatical meaning provides a norm which makes possible both a determinate meaning and a rational argument between conflicting interpretations.

The importance of this for biblical interpretation will become apparent shortly. Religious communities need some measure of agreement over the interpretation of their scriptures. But the present point is that in all cases it is the interests or aims of the interpreters that are decisive, not the claims of the text as such. Any suggestion that a text has rights is a deception concealing someone else's interests. Where texts are accepted as authoritative within a community it is the community's authority that is invested in them. Religious communities may be responding to a higher authority in doing this, and may bind themselves by so doing, but even a scripture which binds a Church owes its authority to that Church's acknowledgement of a higher authority.

Interpreters interpret. It is they who are the active subjects in the act of interpretation. The texts are inert objects. Contrary to the impression given by ordinary conversation, where listening seems more passive than speaking, interpretation is not a matter of passive minds being hit by signals from external agents. In interpretation an active mind picks up the signals, then sorts and makes sense of them. The text itself is passive, whatever it reveals to the interpreter about the agent who composed it, and whatever its potential for activating the interpreter.

In contrast to conversation or contemporary communication, where another living person is present or represented by his or her letter, the interpreters' interests are decisive in textual interpretation. The text exercises some control over interpretations—but only because this is in the interests of the interpreters. The notion of validity in interpretation stems as much from the needs of interpreters as from the rules of the language used, and not at all from the rights of texts or their departed authors.

It follows that a book about interpretation (as opposed to a book containing interpretations) must attend to the aims and interests of the interpreters. But most books on interpretation focus on the character of the texts concerned and the methods appropriate for decoding them. This is because there is usually in fact a close correspondence between the nature of the texts and the interpreters' aims. People usually use texts which suit their purposes. But sometimes interpreters have little choice about which texts to interpret. Laws, scriptures, and classical literature are inherited and 'given'. At other times interpreters use texts in different ways from those intended by the author, as in historical research. In all cases where the relationship between the reader and the text or author is not straightforward the problems of interpretation are complex. Where there is scope for differing aims it is as important to attend to the aims of the interpreters as to the character and content of the texts. Some disagreements about what the Bible means stem not from obscurities in the texts, but from the conflicting aims of the interpreters.

The different aims of interpreters can be illustrated by considering three different disciplines, all based on interpreting texts: history, literary criticism, and law. This will sharpen our questions about biblical interpretation, because the Bible itself contains history, literature, and law. The character of the material has some bearing on how it is interpreted, but the aims of the interpreters are decisive, as is clear when one text is interpreted in different ways. The Book of Leviticus, for example, is read differently by Jews, Christians, historians, and anthropologists, on account of their different aims or interests.

However, aims and interests are themselves complex matters. Religious and theological aims are especially complex, involving historical elements and moral dimensions which may be expressed through literature or legal codes. It is therefore worth considering these three secular disciplines in their own right before turning to their application to the interpretation of the Bible.

This will enlarge our introductory account of what interpretation is by placing on the agenda the question of the interpreters' aims. It will also show how the importance of authorial intention varies in different contexts.

1. One aim in interpreting texts is to understand and write *history*. The historian's chief aim is to reconstruct, or rather represent, the human past as accurately and illuminatingly as possible, to set the human record straight. But despite the high ideals of objectivity and respect for 'how it actually happened', the subjectivity of the historian is operative in various ways. Understanding the past involves a constant interaction between the available material and the variety of aims and interests to be found in any human being. Despite the value set on objectivity, which is higher here than elsewhere in the humanities, and the methods developed to achieve reliable knowledge, the historian's imagination has a place too.

It is worth asking historians exactly why they want to know about the human past. If the study of history is more than a hobby, and is thought to offer guidance for the present, and to destroy false beliefs, we are already deep into personal political and moral judgements. This may not be obvious in much of the detailed technical work of establishing facts, but becomes clearer in the construction of larger historical narratives. Both involve interpretation, i.e. putting a construction on data, but whereas individual judgements can be right or wrong in a straightforward sense, the way these are arranged in a larger picture may be only more or less illuminating. Here the historian's choices about what is significant are crucial, and they may reflect wider interests than simple accuracy of portrayal.

The kind of history being written also offers scope for historians' values to affect their interpretations. Any political, social, economic, or religious history is likely to be coloured by the historian's own views of politics, society, economics, or religion. Provided the evidence is not distorted to serve the interpretation, this is legitimate and even salutary. The past can and should be viewed from different perspectives, and debate between historians contributes to human understanding.

What is finally illuminated through historical investigation of a portion of the human past is the human situation itself, and some historians aim that high. Their particular skill in setting the record straight makes a contribution to this, even though the facts they establish do not lead directly to such insight without the infusion of their own wider human sensibilities. The way in which these larger issues can arise out of more limited research is suggestive for the religious uses of historical study of the Bible. But the historian's primary contribution here remains at the level of concrete results achieved by specialized and detailed research.

The historian's initial search for information from texts and other data provides one case where the interpreter is helped by understanding the author's intentions. Historians may not believe the information a source intends to provide, and may draw from it information which the source did not intend to yield. But they ask what the author intended, if only to get through this to the information they themselves require. To bypass the author would be to risk misreading a source.

Quite apart from the religious and theological interests of Jews and Christians, which call for historical information about Israel, Jesus, and the early Church, historical questions are provoked by the character of the biblical material itself. But the material also invites other approaches, aims, and methods. If the Bible plainly contains history, it is even more plainly a collection of literature. The aims of literary interpretation are therefore also relevant to our problem.

2. In the interpretation of *literature* it is the text itself which is the focus of attention, not the content distilled from it. The aim of interpretation is no longer to obtain information, and the author's intention declines in importance. One mark of great literature is its capacity to illuminate and enlarge the experience of successive

readers in new social contexts. It thus evokes interpretations which the author, writing in a quite different world, could not have had in mind. Some interpretations are better, some worse; some more and some less illuminating. Some can be said to do violence to the text, and since that is a negative judgement it seems that even here the author's intention or the text itself may provide some kind of criterion and control. But it is a much looser control, allowing and even welcoming a variety of interpretations. If every production (non-verbal interpretation) of *King Lear* were the same, Shakespeare would soon become boring.

The individual literary or artistic case is thus different from the individual historical judgement about matters of fact, which can be right or wrong, but similar to the larger historical syntheses, where a variety of interpretations of (say) the Renaissance is desirable. One reason for this is that the aims of literary interpretation and of large historical syntheses include both enjoyment (which places a premium on variety) and a deepened understanding of our human condition, which cannot be given definitively but only probed from various perspectives.

The question that is emerging is: Why do people read the Bible? i.e. What are the aims of its interpreters? Do they read it to obtain information (of whatever sort), or for enjoyment or inspiration or instruction? Is there room for similar diversity in the interpretation of the Psalms, or even the Gospels, as in *King Lear*?

The literary and artistic parallel also draws attention to a dimension of biblical interpretation easily forgotten in a theoretical discussion. Dramatic performance is the natural mode in which some texts are interpreted. The clearest example is the musical score, but the interpretation of drama (which has religious origins) is equally suggestive for biblical interpretation. The religious contexts in which the Bible is interpreted include liturgical contexts in which it is 'performed', and these are significant for the meanings it yields to the assembled community.

3. The community dimension in biblical interpretation can be further clarified by a third sphere in which interpretation reigns, the *law*. But the community dimension is also present in historical and literary interpretation, and this again underlines the importance of

the interpreters' aims. We saw how in both these cases some variety in interpretation is desirable. A community's intellectual life would be impoverished if only one interpretation of its past or only one reading of its literature were available. On the other hand, there are limits to what a community will tolerate. Its identity is to some extent bound up with its history and literature, and can be damaged by outrageous interpretations. Novelty is sometimes rejected at first, only gradually gaining acceptance among scholars and by the wider community.

Eccentric interpreters of Shakespeare or Churchill or (in some countries) Marx lose nothing worse than their money, reputation, and academic promotion. This stands in sharp contrast to our third realm of interpretation, the law, where it is important that there be one and only one generally accepted understanding of a text within the community. Eccentric and incompetent judges cannot (in principle) be tolerated. A thousand interpretations of *Lear* may be enriching, even two of the *Highway Code* disastrous. A single agreed interpretation of legal statutes is necessary for the life of a society.

It often does not matter whether this corresponds to the original author's intention. Old laws remain relevant to new situations only through being applied afresh, and their meaning thus constantly expanded. What matters is how the community agrees to understand it now, and that means in practice how the judiciary interprets it. What the original author meant cannot always be known with certainty and therefore provides insufficient basis for the clarity and certainty which the community needs. The plain sense of a statute remains important because it provides the best basis for agreement about its meaning. But if this is ambiguous the grammatical sense must be supplemented by precedent, i.e. the history of its interpretation. The correct interpretation in this context is not simply identifiable with the original author's intention because this is insufficient to satisfy the interpreters' interests. Only a single agreed interpretation tells the community what to expect from the courts. In contrast to historical research, where the interpreter wants to know the author's intentions, and literary criticism, where a variety of interpretations is permissible, legal interpretation aims at a single meaning, regardless of the intentions of those who originally framed the statute.

Contrasting these three realms of interpretation shows that questions about what the Bible means are not straightforward. The Bible contains history, literature, and law. But the interpretation chosen does not depend on the nature of the texts alone. Genre is normally important, but here takes second place. Interpretation depends more on the interests of the interpreters. Leviticus is read as religious law by Jews, as a source of religious history by historians and anthropologists, and by Christians maybe as typology or outdated theology coupled with some moral exhortation.

The aims and interests of the interpreters are decisive here. But these are not easy to pin down. They vary even more than the biblical material does. One and the same person may read different parts of the Bible with different aims, or even the same passage with different interests at different times. It seems impossible to generalize about 'what the Bible means', or even what a particular text means. It means different things to different people at different times. The threat of chaos is never far from the surface in biblical interpretation. It has forced theologians to look for ways of restricting interpretations, saying which are admissible and which are to be rejected. A Bible that can mean anything means nothing.

Whether the legal example provides a true parallel to biblical interpretation depends on whether one uses the Bible in a legal way. This in turn depends on a prior theological decision. The legal example in fact provides a closer parallel to Jewish uses of their Bible (and Islamic uses of the Koran) than to most Christians' uses of their Bible. The literary and historical examples provide a more obvious analogy for some Christian theological uses of the Bible because (and this itself is a Christian theological judgement) Christianity does not centre on legal texts but on a person whose history can be narrated and whose significance has been interpreted by metaphors and other literary means. Nevertheless, the legal parallel contains some instructive points of contact with the uses of canonical texts in all religions which have scriptures, including Christianity.

First, societies have laws because they need them, and the needs determine how they are used or interpreted. The same is clearly true of religious societies and their scriptures.

Secondly, the social function of legal texts requires a single interpretation which can be known with sufficient certainty and consistency to allow some confidence about how the courts will decide particular cases. How far, if at all, this applies to a religious community's use of its scriptures varies according to how the religion is understood, and especially how revelation is understood within it. These matters are currently disputed in Western Christianity. Believers who draw doctrinal and moral information direct from their scriptures, and identify this with divine revelation, will want a single meaning. Those who believe that the process is more complex may not be so anxious for a single meaning, though even they will be unwilling to allow an anarchy of interpretations, since the identity of their religious group depends on a measure of agreement about the meaning of its scriptures. How much agreement about this is necessary will depend on the character of the religion and on what other norms are contributing to its unity or cohesion.

Thirdly, the need for a single interpretation of the laws is so important that societies give institutions the power to adjudicate between competing interpretations and to authorize new developments. Some similarity with the Roman Catholic magisterium is apparent. The embarrassment of Churches which lack any such arbitrator is instructive, as is the embarrassment of those who claim too much for their arbitrators. Judges can instantly create valid interpretations; theologians aiming at faithfulness to a revelation tacitly known within their community have to wait and see whether their proposals are accepted.

Fourthly, these authorized interpretations of a law need not correspond to the original author's intentions. How far this is true of the religious case depends on one's view of revelation, and that (as noted above) varies even within a particular religion.

Fifthly, even where authorial intention is not the norm for correct interpretations, it tends to reappear as an ideal point of reference where interpreters need to agree and have no other norms outside the text. That is why biblical scholarship was a matter of greater urgency to Protestants than to Roman Catholics.

Sixthly, the place of precedent in law, the history or tradition of the interpretation of a statute, offers some analogy to the Church's interpretation of its Bible. Judges are partly bound by precedent, not because it guarantees truth (it does not) but because it reduces uncertainty. How important certainty is in religion, and its relation to other values (such as rationality and tolerance), are debated. Certainty about salvation has been highly valued in some forms of Christianity. But how far this depends upon certainty about the meaning of scripture, whether as a whole or in parts, is again a further question involving one's view of how knowledge of God is mediated through the Bible.

The analogy between this aspect of law and the case of religion also depends in other ways on where believers suppose that true knowledge of God is to be found. If it is found in the common mind of the community reflecting on its scripture and living the mystery, then the tradition of interpretation will be important for more substantial reasons than simply for securing agreement, as in law. The more weight one attaches to corporate Christian experience, the more one will be disposed to look sympathetically on pre-critical and even pre-Protestant interpretation of the Bible. St Augustine and Origen lacked modern historical-critical instruments but did not lack understanding of the Bible.

This final point takes us into an area quite unlike anything found in law or history. It also happens to be the area which contains the chief aims and interests of many who engage in biblical interpreta-tion. The Jewish and Christian Bibles are scripture for those religious communities, and believers read their scriptures with a view to knowledge of God. They did so long before modern historical-critical methods were available, and they often do so today without making much use of these. It is not obvious what relevance such aims and methods could possibly have to discerning the mystery of God in Christ. If (as we think) they do have some relevance to this, the burden of proof lies on the modern theologians who make this claim. On the surface the aims of biblical historians seem quite remote from those of Jews and Christians who interpret the Bible in the expectation of religious insight.

Biblical interpretation and biblical scholarship

The problem

Our introductory reflections on interpretation have shown that it is no simple matter. Not only are texts often obscure and their distant authors hard to understand, but their modern interpreters have aims and interests of their own. These have to be considered too. An enormous range of possibilities emerges when different people with different aims interpret such a diverse collection of ancient texts as the Bible. Yet we have up to now only touched on the issue which has quietly haunted much biblical interpretation in the modern world.

The previous section's discussion of the aims of interpreters became increasingly remote from the realities of contemporary biblical scholarship. Our brief discussions of history and literary criticism echoed some of the things that biblical scholars do, but the legal example did not. That was brought in to illuminate part of the Church's use of its scripture, and this is a subject which biblical scholarship scarcely acknowledges as its proper concern. It is for theologians to decide how to use the Bible; biblical scholars simply say what it means. That at least is a commonly held view.

But that view illustrates rather than solves the issue at the heart of biblical interpretation today. This is the problem of interpreting religious texts, which some but not all interpreters accept as normative for their own religious belief and practice, in a culture whose rational procedures are no longer in harmony with traditional religion and do not speak of God directly in religious ways. The reason why a discussion of the Church's use of its scripture seems remote from the aims of biblical scholarship is that the latter's tasks stem from contemporary culture rather than from the religious uses of scripture. Scholarship is guided by such apparently non-religious aims as historical reconstruction and literary appreciation, not by the religious quest for God.

The situation is in fact more complicated than that, because the aims of interpreters are complex. Some historians have religious interests, and many biblical scholars are also believers. Some of the latter have integrated their religious faith and their critical reason. Later chapters will introduce a few of the giants in biblical scholarship who were also Christian theologians. The difficult dovetailing involved in combining religious aims and rational methods can best be clarified by some prominent historical examples.

The history of modern biblical scholarship has much in common with the history of classical scholarship. New techniques have yielded new knowledge and changed our understandings of some significant human and cultural monuments. But there is a major difference. Biblical scholarship has developed in a continuing and sometimes painful relationship with the religious communities whose self-understanding is at stake in the ways the Bible is understood. If the tensions are less in evidence today than formerly, that is not because they have been resolved, but because fewer biblical scholars are theologians.

The roots of the problem

Modern biblical scholarship arose in Western Europe as the old order crumbled in the late seventeenth and eighteenth centuries. The terrible consequences of religious divisions had helped discredit religious authorities, and the intellectual avant-garde felt free to investigate the Church's title-deeds. The old religious culture had centred on an unquestioned acceptance of the Judaeo-Christian understanding of God, but this was losing its self-evident character under the pressure of rationalist criticism. Enlightened human reason emancipated itself from the authority of religious traditions and no longer took for granted that the Bible spoke reliably about God and the world. The biblical picture of the world was challenged by natural science, and the biblical story further undermined by moral criticism and historical study. It was coming to be seen as a fallible human record which spoke unevenly of human religion and history.

The long and complex relationship between changing views of the Bible and the transition from the medieval to the modern world cannot be explored here. Distrust of the biblical record, and revulsion against warring religious groups that made appeal to its intolerant attitudes and behaved accordingly, were contributory factors in the emergence of modernity. The main point, to be illustrated in the next chapter, is that modern historical scholarship on the Bible is rooted in the eighteenth-century rationalist attacks upon Christianity. There is thus some justification for the hostility to it within religious circles.

But biblical studies today are also heir to a succession of theological attempts to combine what seemed true in the rationalists' observations with the inherited Christian faith. Biblical scholarship and religious faith could neither confirm nor destroy, neither absorb nor ignore, each other. It has been an uncomfortable but inescapable relationship.

The key term in this relationship will be found in the concept of 'religion'. But before seeing how this concept has offered nineteenth- and twentieth-century theology a way of combining the commitments of faith with the observations and judgements of reason, the size and shape of the gulf which divides much biblical scholarship from the practice of religion has to be recognized. Only then can it be bridged, and the motivations of religion continue to cultivate scholarship and the fruits of scholarship continue to nourish religious faith. Not all religion will welcome this nourishment: rational truth is disturbing as well as wholesome. But it is indispensable in a balanced religious diet.

It is often thought that the gulf can be bridged simply by popularizing scholarly methods and results. This has its place, and need not involve watering them down. But it does not solve the problem because the difference between the two sides is one of kind, not degrees, of knowledge. Scholars and worshippers are responding to different questions. Both the question of God and the question of Israelite, early Jewish, and early Christian religion are legitimate, but the question of the relationship between them cannot be answered simply by popularizing either side.

The subject-matter of the Bible

First consider biblical scholarship. It divides into the separate disciplines of Old and New Testament studies. They use similar methods, but in studying texts written in different languages and cultures they form separate specialisms. Both require a wide range of linguistic, literary, and historical knowledge and skills, and this has resulted in further specialization.

Faced with such formidably technical disciplines, anyone wanting to understand the Bible should inevitably, it seems, defer to the experts. But who *are* the experts at saying what the Bible means? The languages are important, but are not everything. Understanding a text also requires some understanding of its subject-matter. This is where our modern problems begin, because at their root lie some concealed disagreements about how this is to be defined. There is today a far-reaching dispute over what the Bible is essentially *about*, and the disagreements are connected with conflicting judgements about its truth and value. Some call the Bible superstition, others the word of God.

The obvious answer to the question of what the Bible is about is *religion*—specifically Israelite, early Jewish, and early Christian religion. But this introduces two complications. First, religion itself is defined in different ways, competing definitions sometimes reflecting differing opinions about its truth and value. Secondly, and more seriously, religious people do not usually describe the subject-matter of their scripture as 'religion'. For Jewish and Christian believers the subject-matter of the Bible is the living God.

The phrase 'the living God' distinguishes the believer's view from that of non-believing historians or philosophers who might also say that the Bible is about 'God'. There the inverted commas identify the biblical writers' beliefs without committing the modern investigators. On the other hand, those who say that the Bible is about 'the living God' or 'God whom we worship' claim to share some of the writers' most significant convictions. This is evidently important to them, for, as such phrases also indicate, what believers mean when they speak of God includes the dimension of personal involvement and commitment. Their disagreement with non-believers is not merely about the existence of a defined and agreed biblical subject-matter, but also about what the subject-matter truly is, or how it can be adequately specified.

It seems that the word 'God' means different things, even different kinds of things, to different people. It is therefore unhelpful as a description of the biblical subject-matter. The word 'religion', on the other hand, provides a more stable category. No one disputes the existence of religion in general or biblical religion in particular, and arguments about their definition can be conducted by reference to available data. Those who believe that the Bible is a true witness to the ultimate reality which they call God, and which they worship, will want to say more than that it is about religion. But even they can accept the term 'religion', provided that it is defined in a non-reductive way. To say that the Bible is about religion is correct as far as it goes.

The category 'religion' also provides the best way of explaining what the biblical writers and their successors have meant by 'God'. If religions can be understood (more or less) by any sympathetic observer, and can also be seen to point to the transcendent reality to which they refer, then they offer the only satisfactory guides to how the word 'God' is to be understood in religious contexts. Instead of weighing philosophical definitions and arguments, enquirers should look first at religion itself to see how the word is used. This would improve their understanding of the Bible.

Participation in a religion, with all that this implies for a person's own intellectual, moral, and spiritual life, is a further step not required of anyone undertaking the scientific study of religion. On the other hand, participation is what matters most to believers, and that explains their unease about the purely historical, philosophical, and social scientific study of religion, including the biblical scholarship which made many pioneering contributions to it. Such a detached and disinterested study of the Bible seems alien to their concerns. The roots of the problem lie in the terms in which scholarship perceives and describes the biblical subject-matter: as human religion claiming to mediate the transcendent, not (as believers prefer to say) the living God.

Later chapters will show how biblical scholars have made themselves expert in the study of religion. They have become historians of religion as well as linguists, and are steeped in religious literature. But for those who acknowledge the same ultimate reality as the biblical writers and accept their testimony, such expertise is not enough. For them it is knowledge of God rather than 'understanding religion' which enables one to say what the Bible means. The true experts here are the spiritual, rather than the purely intellectual, heavyweights.

This conviction—that religious engagement and theological insight are at least as important in biblical interpretation as historical and philological learning—lies behind many Christians' reservations about modern biblical scholarship. They suspect that it is missing the main point by restricting itself to matters on which believers and non-believers can in principle agree. They insist on doing justice to that other level, on which the Bible is of decisive importance for their own lives. This further dimension is not primarily a property of the text itself but a matter of how it is read. It is therefore best described not in terms of the inspiration or authority of the Bible, but in terms of its use in religious contexts where its subject-matter is defined as 'the living God' or 'God whom we worship'.

The uses of the Bible

The relationship between biblical scholarship and religious belief and practice is the underlying theme of all that follows. The story of modern biblical scholarship will be told in a way that highlights the often hidden persistence of this issue. Its continuing presence is scarcely surprising since this is what gives the Bible and its interpretation their cultural importance. Biblical interpretation is a serious matter, not primarily because it is academically respectable, but because it helps shape many people's religion, and so affects whole societies, including those in which religious practice has declined or is changing. When, in past centuries, particular interpretations were banned or burnt and their authors silenced, the reason was that the subject aroused stronger passions than most other academic debate. Modern secular societies are more tolerant, but the potential for conflict remains. It is the price exacted by the religious importance of the Bible.

These wider cultural dimensions of biblical interpretation have always been present and often discussed, but the discussion has been clouded by two centuries of warfare between traditional Christianity and modern Western rationalism. In their determination not to be deflected from their proper questions and insights by the traditional religious framework which they were threatening, biblical scholars have sometimes pursued their literary and historical goals without much regard for the different kinds of significance which the Bible has for believers. Those theological questions about 'the use of the Bible' are often in consequence treated as an appendage to biblical scholarship, rather than being seen to constitute some of its contexts. Far from providing theological afterthoughts in ministerial training, reflection on the various uses of the Bible and on one's aims in interpreting it should precede biblical study and determine the choice of methods by which these texts are to be analysed.

The danger that religious interests might distort historical research justifies, and even gives theological value as well as cultural significance to, the relative independence of biblical scholarship from the pressure of religious interests. But in fact the study of texts is always undertaken within some larger framework, whether this is recognized or not. The larger framework, constituted by inter- preters' interests, determines what questions are considered important, what methods are found appropriate, and what explanations are deemed satisfying.

The peculiar problems of biblical interpretation with which this book is concerned arise from the tensions between the two different kinds of framework of interpretation within which the Bible is read today. It is read in terms of its own and subsequent believers' religious framework. This allows it to speak of 'the living God'. But it is also read within the secular rational frameworks of modern scholarship, which do not use normative (i.e. believing) language about God. Both frameworks are legitimate. Both are appropriate to particular contexts, and serve particular aims or goals. The Bible can be read and used in different ways. It is used in various ways even within the framework of religious practice; it is also used as a collection of sources for historical research, or as a collection of literary artefacts.

It is possible to keep these different uses of the Bible separate, but not for long. Understanding of the Bible gained by historical study either must be denied or must influence those religious beliefs which are based on older understandings. Most believers are rightly cautious about changing well-tried beliefs to suit prevailing intellectual fashions, but theologians are committed to relating faith to reason. They are therefore bound to relate the two kinds of framework within which they read the Bible: both as a source of knowledge about human religion, and as a source of their own personal and communal knowledge of God. Their struggles to relate these two frameworks can be traced through the modern history of biblical interpretation because this has itself been part of the history of modern theology.

There is in any academic discipline a constant interaction between the interpretative frameworks and the results of research done within them. The tensions are particularly acute in biblical interpretation because the frameworks themselves are heavily contested. Some believers want a traditional religious framework, some scholars a purely secular one, and different theologians construct different hybrids. While theologians agree to give scholarly methods and results their due, some of these results are sufficiently disputed to allow for a variety of theological syntheses between faith and scholarship or reason.

Even within a secular biblical scholarship there is disagreement whether history or literature offers the more appropriate framework for research, as we shall see in Chapter 6. The historical paradigm discussed in Chapters 2, 3, and 4 has dominated much biblical, especially New Testament, research. But this was itself established partly in response to religious and theological interests, and bears the marks of its origins. Recognition of these relativizes but does not discredit the historical paradigm. Any framework can blind researchers to some of the evidence, but will also contribute to the discovery or production of meaning and stimulate further research. Some awareness of the religious interests present in much past biblical scholarship, and a sense of the legitimate interaction between religious aims and scholarly methods, may suggest what relationships between religious belief and the rational investigation of the Bible are appropriate today.

Some analogies
The problem of the interpreters' personal involvement in understanding cultural texts which touch human life most intimately is not unique to the study of religion or the Bible. It arises in one form or another throughout the humanities and social sciences. Recent debates about philosophy, history, and literature reveal increasing interest in this aspect of interpretation. Politics and psychology offer analogies: Marxists and psychoanalysts form tight-knit groups and claim that an understanding of their subject is closely related to a particular political or clinical practice. Neither here nor in religion does this mean that these subjects cannot be investigated by non-practitioners, but all three cases can look rather different to the committed, and in each case the differences touch on matters of truth, value, and reality.

It is possible to lay one's commitments aside for certain

intellectual purposes, but anyone who does so is bound to be looking for reintegration. As committed Marxists need a theory of politics and an anthropology to combine their faith and their reason, so biblical scholars who are also believers need a theory of religion and some metaphysics to connect the religion which they study with the reality they perceive in it and worship. But that is the conclusion of another chapter (Chapter 6).

The dependence of Marxists and Freudians on classical texts, their commitment to certain beliefs, myths, and rituals, their claim to bring human wholeness or salvation, all offer analogies with religions. Also comparable, despite the differences of scale, is their minority status in a pluralist society. For all their pretensions to scientific method, universality, and truth, these ideologies are whole-heartedly believed only by devotees, some of whom are heretics within their own institutions.

Allowing for the powerful Judaeo-Christian heritage in Western culture and the pervasive, if residual, Christian ethos, something similar can be said about religion. A full-blooded Jewish or Christian belief in God, with all that this implies, is today shared only by minorities. The claim is universal, but present realities mock it. In speaking of 'the living God' or 'God whom we worship', believers are taking a revolutionary stand against the norms of contemporary culture. The culture at large speaks of 'religion' in a more detached way, just as it prefers to speak of politics, psychology, and medicine, rather than to express Marxist and Freudian beliefs and engage in their corresponding rituals.

If the stand taken by religious commitment looks less than revolutionary this is because the dominant culture is tolerant and makes space for most minority groups. By classifying themselves as religions Christianity and Judaism find a place in the culture, and even qualify for tax exemptions. But their unconditional allegiance to God whom they worship also contains a threat to the consensus. At any moment, over any issue, true believers might go into opposition and be prepared to face martyrdom.

Against separation

The problem for biblical interpretation in a secular society, identified with the help of these political and sectarian analogies, is the relationship between the believer's 'insider' talk of 'God whom we worship' and the more neutral view of the biblical subject-matter reflected in its description as 'religion'. Biblical scholarship, like all scholarship, takes its norms of rational investigation and argument from the wider culture and therefore speaks in the latter idiom. But many biblical scholars are also believers, and therefore speak in both languages. The question is how, or whether, these are to be related. We have identified different aims and different contexts. But how far should believers' talk of God, modelled on and fuelled by the Bible, be influenced by their historical research? How far, if at all, might historical judgement be legitimately affected by the religious beliefs and values of the historian?

The constructive aim of this book is to make explicit a model for bridging the gulf between critical scholarship and religious faith. The model has been present throughout the 150-year triumphal march of historical study in modern biblical interpretation, and it is adaptable to the new interest in literary study of the Bible. But it has not often been made explicit in English-language discussion, and where recognized has sometimes been resisted.

There are many who say that the two sides should be kept firmly apart, because bridging the gulf would lead to confusion. If scholars do their own work with integrity (it is said), they will shed enough light to illuminate those on the other side of the gulf. It is not their business what use theologians make of their work.

It is true that individual biblical scholars cannot and should not be forced to take an interest in theology. Specialization allows them other bolt-holes where there is also work to be done. But if ever the biblical disciplines were defined so narrowly as to transfer all theological questions to the systematic theologians, the disciplines would lose their rationale and would shrink into insignificance. Scholars generally live off the interest that their work holds for others, and the biblical disciplines owe their very existence and shape primarily to religious interests. Even the cultural significance of the Bible is largely parasitic upon its scriptural status within Christianity. While biblical scholarship, like any other, must be free to pursue truth in whatever ways seem promising, it can hardly afford to ignore the challenges to its value from the religious majority of those most interested in the Bible.

The relationship between faith and scholarship is also threatened on the other side by the indifference or hostility of believers. Religious faith sometimes seems to flourish best unhampered by the complications introduced by biblical scholarship. But most responsible religious teachers recognize its importance. Their proper concern is sometimes expressed in two contrasting complaints. One is that biblical scholarship is too remote from religious interests, the other that it impinges upon them in damaging ways. These complaints might seem to cancel each other out, but both contain some validity, and their contradictory character highlights the problem. It can be solved neither by insulating scholarship from belief nor by conflating them. Any such attempt to answer either complaint would aggravate the other. Both sides must retain their integrity, but the relationship between them needs to be clarified.

The concordat in modern theology

The main problem for biblical interpretation today has now been identified as the contrasting frameworks within which the Bible is interpreted—by the historian on the one hand and the believer on the other. Relating these two ways of understanding the subject-matter of the Bible is a problem only for 'theologians', i.e. for believers who want to relate their faith to their rational knowledge, which now includes historical knowledge. Other believers can ignore scholarship, and other scholars can ignore religious faith. The resulting interpretations of the Bible will not satisfy thoughtful believers and may be thought superficial, but they are not illegitimate.

The problem of interpreting the Bible in a theologically responsible way, i.e. in a way that is answerable to both faith and reason, is one aspect of the wider problem of speaking intelligibly of 'God whom we worship' in a culture whose rational norms have no obvious place for such language. The solutions offered within theologically interested interpretation of the Bible will therefore be found to correspond to those offered within modern theology generally.

This parallel between biblical interpretation and Christian theology must appear suspect. It implies a risk of scholarly judgement being corrupted by religious interests. Histories of biblical scholarship are accordingly sometimes presented as the progressive elimination of religious influence. Progress in historical research has certainly involved reducing illegitimate bias. But it has involved other kinds of advances too. More importantly for our theme, historical aims are not the only legitimate ones. Biblical interpretation is about the whole range of interaction between interpreters and these texts.

Contrasting this with biblical scholarship marks some shift of perspective. Scholarship focuses on the texts, and the methods used and results achieved. Interpretation includes all that, but takes a step back and also considers the scholars and other interpreters themselves. It aims to clarify the motives which lead them to read the Bible in one way rather than another. The character and content of the texts are factors in this, but the aims and interests of interpreters who approach a text with definite expectations are also important.

Historians expect to obtain historical information from the texts. But Jews and Christians also read their Bibles in the context of their communities' faiths, with some expectation of their knowledge of God being reinforced, developed, or challenged. This has led theologians in the modern world, as in earlier generations, to try to do theology in and through their biblical interpretation. Even while engaging in the necessary historical research as objectively and honestly as possible, some have been seeking to understand and where necessary restate their religion in new social and intellectual contexts.

The main difference between modern Western and older styles of biblical interpretation lies in the use of the new rational methods. But these historical methods in particular are themselves the product, and in part the expression, of a more hostile cultural climate which makes possible and even encourages non-theological interpretations of the Bible. However, so long as religious communities continue to use the Bible as their scripture, non-theological interpretations will be accompanied by theological ones, i.e. attempts to define the Bible as speaking not simply of human history and religion but of 'God whom we worship'.

The relationship between these two kinds of aim and perspective has played a part in the history of modern biblical scholarship. The subtle combinations of history and theology produced over the past 150 years remain instructive because it was during this period that historical-critical biblical scholarship took its present shape. In recent years the monolithic structure has been challenged and biblical interpreters have been freed to explore new approaches. But the linguistic and historical disciplines remain foundational, and the well-tested relationship between these and theological reflection provides a possible model for theology's relationship to other rational methods and approaches, notably those of the social sciences and literary criticism.

The word 'scholarship' evokes the linguistic and historical disciplines, even when the focus is upon literature rather than history. In secular literary criticism 'scholarship' implies texts, editions, and the historical and biographical background information which is now accorded its legitimate but subordinate place (see below, p. 217).

'Biblical interpretation', by contrast, suggests a greater emphasis upon the ways interpreters relate their wider understandings of reality to the texts. In the past such biblical interpretation has been almost exclusively theological interpretation, relating the texts to the respective religious community's belief and worship. The way in which this confessional theological domination of biblical interpretation is at present having to make room for other interpretative possibilities is a fascinating aspect of the Bible in the modern world. As the most important text in Western culture, its interpretation cannot be restricted to the religious communities that use it as scripture. Now that religion in the West is no longer restricted to the Judaeo-Christian tradition it is even possible to take a religious interest in the Bible without belonging to a church or synagogue.

By taking its bearings from the recent history of biblical scholarship the following investigation will avoid the 'way-out' religious fringes of biblical interpretation, attractive though some of them may be. It aims instead to throw light on the relationship between the scholarship introduced in the other books in the Oxford Bible Series and the religious faith of the Christians (mainly

Protestants) who pioneered these developments. This will yield suggestions for those of all denominations who follow in the tracks of the pioneers.

If such an investigation also contributes to the new interest in theology outside the churches, that will be just tribute to those who developed the new methods in the teeth of ecclesiastical opposition. But despite opposition, most of these biblical scholars were conscious of contributing to their Churches' theology as they persuaded their co-religionists to face and assimilate the new literary and historical truth they were discovering. The struggles which ensued were part of the perennial struggle between conservatives and progressives in any great religious institution.

Theology in every age uses whatever current methods will help it to understand its community's classic texts. Understanding these scriptures with the help of the rational instruments, methods, or techniques of the day forms part of the interface it constructs between contemporary culture and its inherited faith and tradition. But that traditional accommodation of faith and reason came under strain in the eighteenth century when critical reason was turned against the traditional faith, and a world emerged which no longer took its bearings from the idea of God.

As belief in God became optional and religion marginal, theology itself had to change. When the Bible was no longer generally accepted as an infallible source of revelation, a theology responsive to the intellectual climate could no longer proceed by making deductions from its revealed data. An inductive approach was necessary. Believers began to reflect on the knowledge of God they believed they possessed in their own religious consciousness and community, and to read scripture in the light of that.

This involved a change from seventeenth-century Protestant scholasticism, but it was not very different from what creative theologians such as St Paul, St Augustine, and Luther had done, and what thoughtful Christians do today. Theology has always been the theology of some religious community, and theologians have always reflected on its tradition in the light of their own experience, and on their own experience in the light of the tradition. At moments of historical crisis this has led to strikingly new formulations. What changed during the eighteenth century in

Europe was not the nature or task of theology, but the state of scientific knowledge, and (gradually) the relationship of the Christian religious community to the wider culture. They were no longer virtually identical.

This did bring some change in theological method, because, as a rational activity, theology is responsive to the rational norms of the day. As the Bible came to be rightly seen as a collection of fallible human documents, theology bowed to this truth of human reason— and sought to combine it with the conviction that through the Bible the community was given a saving knowledge of God.

The chief way in which modern theology has combined its recognition of the human character of the Bible with its conviction of divine revelation has been through the concept of human 'religion'. Religion is undeniably a human phenomenon, and as such both imperfect and historically conditioned. But it can also be held to mediate some true awareness of God. Theology was therefore able to accept the man-centred thinking of modernity expressed in Alexander Pope's line that 'the proper study of mankind is man', and yet insist (*a*) that this study ought to include the study of religion; and (*b*) that the truth about human existence, especially human morality and self-transcendence, is only grasped when the essential truth contained in religion is understood, and the reality of God acknowledged.

Atheists disagreed, and arguments about the necessity of religion and the reality of its transcendent referent have continued to the present day. Even where this apologetic starting-point is accepted there is a need for theological discrimination concerning the adequacy of particular expressions of religion. But starting with religion gives theology an empirical and experiential base to replace its older metaphysical foundations. In this way religious studies, including the historical study of biblical religion, could provide a new natural theology, i.e. a rational basis for believers' talk of revelation.

Modern theology's insistence that all true human existence must include religious talk (including worship) of God is a variation on a Reformation theme. Luther, Calvin, and Zwingli all insisted that knowledge of God and knowledge of 'man' are inseparable. Their emphasis upon theology's human existential aspect, made vivid by the Bible (especially by St Paul), was a protest against the scholasticism of late medieval theology. What distinguished the eighteenth-century protests against scholasticism (now Protestant) was their new human-centred concepts of religion, the religion of the heart in pietism, and 'natural religion' in the theology of rationalism.

The 'natural religion' of Enlightenment philosophy and theology represented a massive theological break with traditional Christianity, while remaining within the institution. Its anti-supernatural faith, based on a deist conception of God and the moral teaching of Jesus understood in modern terms, was able to draw religious life from the traditional faith while generating little religious power of its own. Since Protestantism does not usually expel heresy, this drastic innovation, breaking with every book in the New Testament, every Father, and every Reformer, has continued to exist on the cultured fringes of Christianity. But it was decisively answered and the breach, in principle at least, repaired by 'the father of modern theology', Friedrich Schleiermacher (1768–1834).

Drawing much from the devout pietism of his youth, and more than his opponents realized from the Reformers, Schleiermacher resisted the 'natural religion' of the Enlightenment, its deist understanding of God, and its novel reduction of Jesus' status. As a philosopher with a sharp eye for realities, he replaced the modern abstraction 'natural religion' with actual 'positive' religions, and as a theologian he took seriously and sought to express the faith of his own existing religious community. This needed restatement in a new intellectual milieu, and that involved theological corrections of some past formulations, but Schleiermacher preserved continuity with the past. The essence of Christianity, he said, was to be apprehended by studying its history, especially its origins. Christian theology must be true to its tradition as well as compatible with modern thought. It must therefore include a biblical interpretation which is both rational in its methods and theological in its aims.

The details of Schleiermacher's *Brief Outline on the Study of Theology* (1811, 1830²; ET 1966), his posthumously published manuscripts on *Hermeneutics* (ET 1977), his *Speeches on Religion*, addressed in 1799 to its 'cultured despisers' (ET of 3rd edn. 1894), and his restatement of *The Christian Faith* (1821–2, 1830–1²; ET

1928) do not concern us here. What mattered for biblical interpretation was that this reorientation of Christian theology to history and the religious consciousness both demanded a theologically oriented biblical interpretation and provided the necessary model for combining subsequent biblical scholarship with a modern Christian theology. Once Christian beliefs were grounded experientially in the believer's religious consciousness it was possible to describe the biblical religion historically or phenomenologically, and at the same time identify with it religiously. The religion of the Bible rang true even if its doctrines seemed hard to justify in isolation. Doctrines make sense only in the context of a functioning religion or total system of symbols.

Schleiermacher's turn to 'religion', and to Christianity as a particular historical religion, makes him the key figure in modern biblical interpretation, as well as the father of modern theology and a great-uncle of religious studies. Despite the special importance of Hegel's religious philosophy of history for biblical scholarship in the 1830s (see Chapter 3), it is Schleiermacher's reorientation of theology which provides the key to our later discussions. Even Baur (below, pp. 62 ff.), who preferred Hegel, and Rudolf Bultmann (below, pp. 104 ff.), who partially accepted Karl Barth's reaction against nineteenth-century liberal theology and biblical interpretation, are heirs to Schleiermacher. Bultmann preferred the existentialist categories of Kierkegaard and Heidegger, and the Pauline tones of Luther, to the terminology of either Schleiermacher or Hegel. But he stood closer to both than many have recognized. He stood firmly within the tradition of both the Reformation and the Enlightenment when he asserted in 1924 that 'theology speaks of God because it speaks of man as he stands before God'.

This reorientation of much modern theology since Schleiermacher (Roman Catholic as well as Protestant), towards reflection on religion and human existence, has provided the basis for most modern attempts to interpret the Bible theologically. It has enabled biblical scholarship to be combined with and contribute to Christian theological speaking of God. Biblical scholars can study the human religion disclosed in these texts by whatever historical, literary, and social scientific methods are available, without either asserting or denying the believers' claims that their tradition mediates a knowledge of God. The human reality of religion which scholarship discloses may or may not mediate the ultimate, non-empirical reality acknowledged by believers on the basis of their full participation in the life of a religious community. Scholarship leaves open that question of God because its rational procedures cannot settle it. But it leaves the question genuinely open, allowing believers to affirm it on other grounds.

Prospects

Problems

The Schleiermacherian concordat or 'eternal covenant' between faith and modern thought remains an ideal which nineteenth-century theology rarely achieved in practice. Few theologians were as successful as Schleiermacher in combining loyalty to the tradition with openness to new knowledge. After his death in 1834 the historical research on the Gospels (to be reported in Chapters 2, 3, and 4) placed additional strains on the relationship by seeming to destroy orthodox belief in the incarnation. Schleiermacher's own restatement of an incarnational Christology needed revision, and some of the Hegelian revisions were rightly anathema to the orthodox. Equally problematic, the philosophical climate of German idealism which had encouraged restatements of Christian belief gave way to a positivism that was hostile to all religion. When the climate is bad most theologians remain indoors; conservative theologies prevail.

Biblical scholarship made great advances in the century following Schleiermacher's death, but specialization took its toll. Few of the scholars had the theological breadth to keep up with their historical advances. Their theological interpretations of the Bible were (with notable exceptions) inferior to their technical scholarship. A gulf developed between systematic theology and biblical studies in the late nineteenth century and it was not satisfactorily bridged by the simplistic kinds of 'biblical theology' which followed in the 1940s and 1950s in the wake of the Barthian reaction against liberal scholarship. It was partly bridged by some of the classic German figures discussed in later chapters, but their syntheses proved precarious too.

In recent years this gulf has been deepened by institutional factors. Until recently most biblical scholars have taught in contexts which required them to relate their rational work to the faith of their religious communities. This remains the case in German and Swiss university theological faculties geared to ministerial training, but elsewhere is now less common. A number of biblical scholars now work in secular contexts. The secularization of biblical scholarship which took place in the nineteenth century when biblical historians partly freed their discipline from theological presuppositions is being followed by a more radical secularization, in which contact with the Jewish and Christian religious communities is much weaker.

A secular biblical scholarship can contribute to religious life through the stimulus of unexpected insights and even unwelcome information. The boundaries are in any case difficult to draw with precision in a culture still permeated by the Judaeo-Christian tradition, as will become clear when we consider the Bible as literature (Chapter 7). But before this initially helpful separation of historical and religious interests in the Bible becomes an impoverishing divorce, the theological reconciliation tribunal has bridging work to do.

The need for a better relationship between the two sides is underlined by the present state of popular religious publishing. Like every specialist field, Old and New Testament scholarship communicates its discoveries to a wider readership. But popularizations of biblical research are unusual in serving a dual interest. The religious-book market is created and sustained more by people's religious needs than by their intellectual curiosity. The most widely read works are those which adapt the results of research to satisfy these needs, not always those which report the research most scrupulously.

There has always been plenty of genuine religious use of the Bible that is not directly informed by biblical scholarship beyond the use of translations. Discipleship does not depend on learning. But it may then miss sources of nourishment and correction, and those who value the Bible for their religion ought surely to value truth from whatever quarter to assist in its interpretation. Any such truth, however, will support religious aims only if the two sides are set in a right relationship.

It is always possible for a religious or any other group to develop its own methods of interpretation which will reinforce its own shared understanding of its authoritative texts. Within the closed circle communication would still be possible. That would be an extension of the licence already noted for any individual to do what he or she likes with texts in private. But there are strong reasons why Christians and Jews resist this tactic, at least outside the private realm of religious devotion. The Christian community is not a closed society with private standards of truth and reality, and the Bible functions in important ways in the religious community's necessary communication with the world outside, as well as evoking thought, worship, and private devotion within the community.

Besides, believers are themselves part of the 'world outside', living most of their lives on assumptions shared with their contemporaries and yet claiming that God is the reality on which everything depends. It is therefore in their interests as believers to cultivate methods of interpretation and standards of rationality which will be acknowledged outside, rather than to form a ghetto.

It has accordingly always been a central task of theology to forge connections between believers' religious knowledge of God and the rational knowledge of the world they share with others. Believers have to be able to give reasons for their faith, to themselves as well as to others, and some of these will include appeal to the biblical evidence. For this to be persuasive it is again important that the Bible is interpreted by methods considered rational in the wider culture.

Religious readings

If rational methods are equally important for some religious and some non-religious readings of the Bible, the distinction between them cannot be located in the methods used. A consequence of this religious commitment to rationality is that the distinction is not best drawn, either, between those who see the Bible as a collection of human documents and those who assert its divine inerrancy. This division between rational and irrational interpretations of the Bible is not in itself interesting. More significant than its irrationality is the fact that fundamentalism is one striking attempt to use the Bible religiously. The significant divide is between all attempts to read the Bible religiously (on the assumption that it speaks of God) and non-religious readings.

There is then in fact a further division in the religious camp between those who read the Bible rationally (but with religious aims) and those who read it irrationally. Rather than scold the latter, theologians should consider (*a*) where this matters and where it does not, and (*b*) what elements of truth or justified protest are contained in it. But their chief responsibility is to insist that the religious presupposition that the Bible somehow mediates God is compatible with seeing it as a collection of human documents to be interpreted by the same methods as are applied to other ancient documents.

That leads us back to the question of how this can be done, and to the solution adumbrated in the previous section. But before returning to the concept of 'religion', it is necessary to touch on another issue raised by our insistence on the use of rational methods in religious interpretation of the Bible: What is distinctive about religious readings, or reading the Bible religiously?

The answer lies not in a method, nor in the immediate aim of discovering what the author was saying, but in a context. The Bible is assumed to inform and sustain a knowledge and love of God within the religious communities whose identity and relationship to God is constituted through these foundational documents. How this is understood varies in different forms of Christianity and Judaism. But such differences of theological opinion, which lead to different interpretative strategies, are secondary to the division between religious and non-religious contexts and goals in interpretation.

This division is often invisible, not only because both sides can use the same methods, with a view to understanding what the human authors were saying, but also because religion can be said to embrace the whole range of human concerns. Thus a literary reading of the Bible might well evoke feelings which could be called religious. Inspiration is a term used in both literary and religious contexts. Or again, Marxist and psychoanalytic interpretations of the Bible, developed for the sake of human salvation or well-being, have some claim to be called religious. The boundaries are fluid, and this helps theology to speak meaningfully of God as the reality that determines everything, and in particular human existence. But it is within the Jewish and Christian religious communities that the Bible is claimed to mediate a knowledge and experience of God. If outside these contexts it still has some religious power, that is largely a by-product of its past and present uses within religious institutions. The cultural history of the West means that our two sides are intertwined in ways which are important for literary criticism, law, and history, as well as for religion and theology. But the distinction between the two contexts is clear in principle.

The religious uses of the Bible are diverse, and its uses in Christian (or Jewish) theology only a part of these. The Bible provides the vocabulary of praise, and the stories which shape the community's identity, before ever it provides concepts for rational thought and argument. It contains more symbols than arguments. But symbols give rise to thought, and while theologians may 'murder to dissect', their reflection on the tradition, especially the foundational texts, is central. Much patristic, medieval, Reformation, and modern theology has therefore been done as interpretation of scripture. Despite their modern emphasis upon the human authors, the tradition of theological interpretation of the Bible has been continued by such twentieth-century theologians as Barth, Bultmann, Dodd, Theissen (below, p. 150), Via (below, p. 258), and Roman Catholic scholars such as R. E. Brown and H. Schürmann. They have all illuminated the faith of their religious communities by expounding these normative texts by whatever rational methods were currently available to them.

But when the Bible is expounded or assimilated with a view to communicating or deepening the religious community's faith and love there is a possibility of tension between this aim and the desire to be true to what a particular text is actually saying. There is rarely any simple or complete correspondence between the text being read and the reader's own religion. Links have to be forged. Theological interpretation of the Bible seeks to relate the ancient text to the religious questions of the modern reader, without doing violence to either.

Allegorical interpretation is one form of this which lacks credibility today because it can make the text say something far removed from the grammatical meaning or what the author intended. One shrewd critic of theology at the end of the last century (Overbeck) thought that all theological interpretation of the Bible was tarred with the same brush. That would be indignantly denied by most Christian theologians today, after more than two centuries of historical exegesis. But Overbeck was right to imply that religious interpretation of the Bible is guided by interests external to the text, and interests which in part differ from those of 'profane' historians such as himself. How the Bible is read in religious contexts, including theological interpretation (which is a religious as well as an intellectual activity), is partly shaped by interpreters' prior understandings of their religion.

Christians understand their faith in differing ways, and this may affect how they understand the Bible, both as a whole and in its various parts. The interplay of varying religious aims and different rational methods results in a kaleidoscope of possible readings. Since 'reading the Bible' means in fact reading a part of it, questions also arise about what is central and what peripheral, and the relation of the parts to the whole. A variety of invisible filters operate here. There is, strictly speaking, no such thing as 'scripture alone' in religious contexts. It is always already interpreted in a provisional way from the perspective of some prior understanding of one's religion. This perspective may be modified as a result of reflection on writings deemed authoritative, but theological positions are involved from the outset when the Bible is read as scripture, i.e. under the presupposition that it speaks of the God who is worshipped.

A way forward

The central problem for biblical interpretation identified in this chapter could be described as combining and relating believers' interests in hearing what they call 'the word of God' in scripture with their use of rational methods that make no such assumptions and provide no vocabulary for this religious task. We have distinguished between religious and non-religious aims in interpretation, while recognizing that the same methods may be used and some of the same results valued on both sides. Both may be further subdivided, and the two sides will frequently overlap. There are historical, literary, social scientific, and other aims and methods in non-religious interpretation, but any of these may be taken over and subordinated to religious aims. The latter subdivide also. There are several different legitimate uses of the Bible in theology, ethics, worship, and spirituality. There are also some illegitimate ones in these and other areas, such as ecclesiastical administration. In each case methods of interpretation are chosen for their efficacy in fulfilling the interpreter's aims and their appropriateness to the text being interpreted.

The concordat between faith and reason by which this combination of rational methods and religious interests has been achieved hinges on the concept of 'religion'. This human phenomenon can be described and evaluated in various rational ways (historical, sociological, psychological, philosophical) without either affirming or denying the believers' convictions that their participation mediates a true knowledge of God which is not available in any other way.

This type of solution was initiated by W. M. L. de Wette (1780–1849) when he was a student of Fries, but was placed on the agenda of modern theology by Schleiermacher. After his death in 1834 the philosophical and theological climate deteriorated, and when the scientific study of religion made its decisive advances around the turn of the century it was in a philosophical context of positivism which offered little hope for theological appropriation. Despite the efforts of Ernst Troeltsch (1865–1923) it was not until the 1960s that both the philosophical and the theological conditions were right for renewing Schleiermacher's theological programme in a more radically pluralist culture, supported by a now more mature science of religion. The possibilities this offers biblical interpretation have been hindered by the reaction against theological interpretation in contemporary biblical scholarship, but some pointers will be introduced in Chapters 5–7.

The scientific study of religion, which includes the 'non-religious' or secular study of the Bible, Koran, *Bhagavadgita*, etc., observes that participants speak of 'revelation', in reference to foundation events, present experiences, and even (derivatively) sacred texts. It can neither confirm nor deny the truth of such claims. Secular scholars and believing theologians (there is overlap but not identity here) can agree only in their descriptions. The conviction of religious truth comes to some immediately and intuitively, to others through participation over a long period, and to others not at all. Defining the subject-matter of the Bible as 'religion' rather than 'God' leaves a door open both for believers' claims and for whatever rational methods and approaches seem likely to illuminate it.

In addition to leaving a door open for theological claims, understanding the subject-matter of the Bible as 'religion' allows the texts themselves to be illuminated in new ways. Historical and linguistic study helps interpreters to bridge the distance in time and culture that separates them from the Bible. But it is no substitute for some prior understanding of the biblical subject-matter. Every reader needs some foothold in the text being studied, some preliminary grasp of what it is about, before understanding can take place. Nobody understands a scientific paper, however lucid its English prose, without knowing what the subject is and knowing something about it.

In the same way it is possible to read Greek and Hebrew fluently, but have little understanding of the Bible. What one understands it to be remains decisive. To understand Genesis 1–3 as natural science is to misunderstand it. To understand the Bible as literature or as history offers some understanding. Understanding it as religious literature or history of religion offers more—but only if the interpreter already knows what religion is. Understanding it as 'religion' embraces both the historical and literary perspectives, and also opens the door to social scientific descriptions which are not given due weight when the emphasis falls on history or literature.

The very success of historical scholarship in the nineteenth century gave it a prominence in modern biblical scholarship which some would question today. What are the reasons for investing so much effort in these tasks and neglecting the others? Historians have good professional reasons for concentrating upon historical research, but those whose interests in the Bible are primarily religious need to ask how important this is relative to other kinds of interpretation.

Their answers will turn on how historical study contributes to religious readings of the Bible. There are several reasons for insisting upon the importance for religions of a historical and grammatical understanding of their classical texts. Religions need to exclude some interpretations of their scripture, and one way of doing so is by arguing linguistically that the text 'cannot' mean this, or historically that the author cannot have meant that. More generally, a historical dimension is rarely absent from the understanding of any ancient text.

It can, however, be argued that literary interpretation takes priority in religion, relegating historical, textual, and linguistic scholarship to a necessary but subordinate and preparatory role. Both history and literature may explore human experience, with which religion is also concerned. But history has other, more immediate, aims. When it takes on the larger issues it usually becomes literature. This natural alliance between literary study and the theological interpretation of the Bible will be explored in Chapters 6 and 7.

Editors and translators of Shakespeare or Euripides have their necessary place, and commentators are indispensable in a world where not everyone has the time, the ability, or even the inclination to become knowledgeable about Elizabethan England or classical Athens. Some Shakespearian tragedies also have a historical subject-matter about which specialists will be better informed than the author. But neither form of historical expertise equips the scholar to interpret Shakespeare. The capacity to fathom the tragedies requires an understanding of human existence, not merely knowledge of the past and techniques for researching this. Literary appreciation depends upon a resonance with the reader's experience. An actor or theatre-goer may understand a play 'better' than a narrowly textual scholar.

The point here is not to suggest that a worshipper might have a better intuitive grasp of what the Bible is most importantly about than a successful scholar, though that is not inconceivable. The point is rather that defining the Bible's subject-matter as 'religion', which embraces the whole of human reality, opens the interpreter to insights from different sides, as well as opening a door to the believer's theological interpretation.

There is a convergence between a participant's or believer's theology which starts from a theory of religion and an observer's scientific study of religion that is open to theological claims. This compatibility between the believer's 'insider' stance and the 'outsider' stance of the historian or social scientist allows theology to study Israelite, Jewish, and early Christian religion by every available rational method, but without abandoning its own rather different aim of deepening and correcting contemporary religious faith.

One consequence of this concordat between faith and reason is that biblical scholarship can, if it wishes, go its own way without reference to the religious interests of most readers of the Bible. Historical, literary, or sociological study can be pursued from a purely academic interest. Even the study of biblical religion, involving all these approaches, can be carried out without much thought of relating the results to one's own religious understanding. It is often not clear whether a piece of biblical scholarship has been undertaken out of a purely historical interest, or in the hope of clarifying, or even in the hope of discrediting, Christianity or Judaism by close attention to an important part of their tradition.

Most of the interpreters to be considered in the following chapters made their aims clear and, as one would expect from innovators, their respect for the truth as they saw it outweighed their respect for inherited opinions. All expressions of religious faith are historically conditioned and ultimately inadequate. The identity and continuity of religious traditions depends more on the same scriptures being interpreted than on the interpretations themselves being identical. But that insight was born of historical study, and the midwives were not popular. The most famous and least popular of all was prevented from taking up his professorial appointment. David Friedrich Strauss was instead compelled to take very early retirement, as the next chapter relates.

Further reading

BARR, J., *The Bible in the Modern World* (London, 1973).
—— *Explorations in Theology 7* (London, 1980).
CHILDS, B. S., *Biblical Theology in Crisis* (Philadelphia, 1970).

FARLEY, E., *Theologia: The Fragmentation and Unity of Theological Education* (Philadelphia, 1983).

FERGUSON, D. S., *Biblical Hermeneutics: An Introduction* (Atlanta, 1986; London, 1987).

GADAMER, H.-G., *Truth and Method* (London and New York, 1975).

GEERTZ, C., *The Interpretation of Cultures* (New York, 1973).

GERRISH, B. G., *Tradition in the Modern World* (Chicago and London, 1978).

HARVEY, VAN A., *The Historian and the Believer* (New York, 1966; London, 1967).

HIRSCH, E. D., *Validity in Interpretation* (New Haven, 1967).
—— *The Aims of Interpretation* (Chicago and London, 1976).

JAMESON, F., *The Political Unconscious: Narrative as a Socially Symbolic Act* (London, 1981).

KELSEY, D., *The Uses of Scripture in Recent Theology* (London, 1975).

MORGAN, R. and PYE, M. *Ernst Troeltsch: Writings on Theology and Religion* (London, 1977).

NIETZSCHE, F., 'On the Uses and Disadvantages of History for Life' (1874), in *Untimely Meditations* (Cambridge, 1983).

NINEHAM, D. E., *The Use and Abuse of the Bible* (London, 1976).

PALMER, R. E., *Hermeneutics: Interpretation Theory in Schleiermacher, Dilthey, Heidegger, and Gadamer* (Evanston, 1969).

PYE, M. and MORGAN, R., *The Cardinal Meaning: Buddhism and Christianity in Comparative Hermeneutics* (The Hague, 1973).

REVENTLOW, H. GRAF, *The Authority of the Bible and the Rise of the Modern World* (London, 1984).

RICOEUR, P., *Freud and Philosophy: An Essay on Interpretation* (London, 1970).

ROGERSON, J., *Old Testament Criticism in the Nineteenth Century: England and Germany* (London, 1984).

SMART, J. D., *The Past, Present, and Future of Biblical Theology* (Philadelphia, 1979).

STENDAHL, K., *Meanings* (Philadelphia, 1984).

TAYLOR, C., *Philosophy and the Human Sciences*, ii (Cambridge, 1985).

THISELTON, A. C., *The Two Horizons* (Exeter, 1980).

WOOD, C. M., *Toward Christian Understanding* (Philadelphia, 1982).

2

Criticism and the Death of Scripture

History, myth, and theology: D. F. Strauss

The most dramatic theological event of a century prone to religious controversy occurred in 1835, when a junior lecturer at the Protestant seminary of Tübingen University in southern Germany published a book which shook the European Churches. *The Life of Jesus* by David Friedrich Strauss was seen as a massive assault upon the central tenets of Christianity. The time had passed when a theological work could unleash the political and social consequences of Luther's ninety-five theses. The Church was no longer locked into the institutions of society to the extent that it had been in the religious culture of Europe before the eighteenth century. But the Christian faith still commanded sufficient respect for an attack upon its title-deeds to be considered an outrage. Protestantism had neither the machinery nor the stomach for excommunicating heretics, but Strauss lost his post in Tübingen, and when in 1839 a liberal government in Zurich offered him a professorship the people rebelled, the government fell, and the young offender was pensioned off before he arrived.

Strauss might have guessed that his *Life of Jesus* would cause offence, and that few of his readers would remain cool long enough to appreciate his concluding dissertation, a *tour de force* in which a new version of Christianity rose like a phoenix from the ashes of his critical bonfire. This dissertation, appended to 1,400 pages of devastating analysis of the Gospel history, begins:

The results of the inquiry which we have now brought to a close have apparently annihilated the greatest and most valuable part of that which the Christian has been wont to believe concerning his Saviour

Jesus, have uprooted all the animating motives which he has gathered from his faith, and withered all his consolations. The boundless store of truth and life which for eighteen centuries has been the aliment of humanity, seems irretrievably dissipated; the most sublime levelled with the dust, God divested of his grace, man of his dignity, and the tie between heaven and earth broken. Piety turns away with horror from so fearful an act of desecration . . . (1972 edn., p. 757)

Piety did not turn away; it hit back hard and forced him out of his seminary post even before this dissertation was published in the second volume, a few months after the first. Yet Strauss thought he was vindicating true religion. The passage goes on to show that it is his *own* piety that turns away in horror from the critical bonfire,

and strong in the impregnable self-evidence of its faith, pronounces that, let an audacious criticism attempt what it will, all which the Scriptures declare and the Church believes of Christ, will still subsist as eternal truth, nor needs one iota of it to be renounced. Thus at the conclusion of the criticism of the history of Jesus, there presents itself this problem: to re-establish dogmatically [i.e. at the theological level] that which has been destroyed critically [i.e. at the historical level]. (Ibid.)

This combination of critical destruction of the Gospel history and theological reconstruction of Christian belief opened a new era in Western religious thought. Karl Marx judged in 1844 that 'the criticism of religion [which] is the beginning of all criticism' had been adequately performed by Strauss and other young Hegelians, opening the way for the criticism and revolutionary change of society itself. Strauss had no such ambitions. Like many radical theologians he was quite conservative in his politics and ethics. And he was confident that the Christian religion would continue when educated people (including the clergy) understood its doctrinal content in less literalistic ways.

As with many classics, the significance of *The Life of Jesus* has been seen differently at different times. In his brilliant survey of modern historical research on the life of Jesus, first published in 1906 and translated into English with the arresting title *The Quest of the Historical Jesus* (1910), Albert Schweitzer praised Strauss for recognizing the central importance of eschatology in Jesus' thinking. Contemporary biblical scholars are more impressed by the way he anticipated twentieth-century history of traditions research (see below, Chapter 4). In 1835 a few theologians at once realized its epoch-making significance for the shape of Christology. But for most it was not its implications for this central citadel of faith which caused alarm but its destruction of the outer ramparts. For most Protestants, even in Germany, the truth of Christianity depended to an extent now difficult to imagine on a belief in an inspired holy scripture, free of all error. Strauss revealed that this view was no longer generally held in university theology and among the educated: in some sense the Bible might still be called inspired; inerrant it evidently was not. This is what caused the shock, together with the impression that the credal beliefs about Jesus were being denied by being deprived of their supposed historical basis.

But for academic theology the significance of Strauss lies in the other three areas just mentioned. The two major historical issues, eschatology and the history of the Gospel tradition, have dominated twentieth-century New Testament criticism; and the central theological issue of Christology remains the crucial issue raised for the Christian Church by biblical scholarship.

Historical and theological claims are closely intertwined in Christian belief, though in ways that are not entirely clear. Belief in Jesus as God incarnate has, from the end of the first century, been nourished by the more than human picture of Jesus provided by the four Gospels, and Christians have echoed the appreciation of the editor of the Fourth Gospel for 'the disciple who bears witness of these things and wrote these things: and we know that his witness is true' (John 21: 24). As the greatest English biblical scholar of the nineteenth century, Bishop Lightfoot, wrote in response to radical Gospel criticism, 'I cannot pretend to be indifferent about the veracity of the records which profess to reveal him whom I believe to be not only the very Truth but the very Life.' Because he thought of the Gospels as 'the records of the divine life' it seemed to him important that they were historically accurate, and not simply true in a less tangible sense. The outstanding critical historians of the English Church, Thirlwall, Lightfoot, and Stubbs, had all learned much from German historical research, but were all 'pre-critical' in their attitudes to the Gospels. While that soon changed, it is hard to find much English appreciation for Strauss himself before the reissue of George Eliot's 1846 translation in 1972.

There was not much that was original in Strauss's assault on the historicity of the Gospels, and he himself did not see the significance of his work there. His presentation of the contradictions between the four Gospels was for him merely a preliminary to unfolding the theology sketched out in the concluding dissertation. This was to be worked out in a later volume, but was never in fact written. Considered as constructive historical research the book was defective, as the next chapter will explain. But despite his short title, Strauss was not in 1835 interested in reconstructing a 'Life of Jesus'. That project only became popular in 1863 with Renan's *Vie de Jésus*. Unlike some of his successors, Strauss was a good enough theologian to know that a biography of Jesus could never bear the weight of Christian theological claims. His critical aim of demolishing the historicity of the Gospel records was a first step in the programme of a theologian who had learned from Kant that the historical could serve only for illustration, from Lessing that there was a 'big, ugly ditch' between truths of history and truths of reason, and finally from Hegel how to get theological truth from these largely unhistorical Gospel records. Strauss's philosophical theology found no support, but much of his critical analysis was unanswerable.

Strauss showed in a piece-by-piece analysis of each Gospel incident that these stories were not history, but something else. If traditional supernaturalism depended upon the historicity of the Gospels, its fabric was relentlessly unpicked by Strauss's analysis. Never again (it seemed) could the Gospels be used as historical evidence for traditional belief.

Strauss argued that the Gospels must be judged unhistorical, both on account of the contradictions between them, and because heirs to a modern scientific (mechanistic) view of the world do not believe in angels, demons, voices from heaven, walking on water, and other interferences with the laws of nature. Traditional beliefs about the historicity of the Gospels had become incredible to many: Strauss anchored that intuition in scholarly argument. In the process he showed the sorry state of contemporary theology in its attempts to answer the intellectual challenge of modern rationalism.

The brittle theologies of the day cracked under the pressure of this massive exposure of their inherent weaknesses. Conservative attempts to harmonize the Gospels were bankrupt, and 'rationalist' theologians' attempts to give a non-supernatural account of the Gospel stories were without basis in the texts themselves. They confirmed that miracle-stories were unacceptable to modern sensibilities, but failed to solve the problem they had recognized.

This 'problem of miracle' was far from new. It received its classic formulations in the eighteenth century, for example from David Hume. But much more than the contradictions between the Gospels (which had been discussed in the early Church), this was a point at which traditional confidence about the Bible began to founder. The reason, as Strauss observed, was that here the biblical record came into direct collision with modern scientific apprehensions of truth and reality. That required theological reconstruction, but the repairs offered by contemporary theology only revealed the extent of the damage. Neither Strauss nor the rationalist theologians of his time believed in miracles. The supposedly closed system of nature brooked no such divine interventions. Jesus doubtless performed some psychosomatic healings, but these could not be called miracles in the sense of suspending the laws of nature. The difference between Strauss and the 'naturalist' interpreters was that he was prepared to reject the historicity of these stories outright, whereas they rejected the miraculous element but sought to retain the general reliability of the records. Their approach is still popular and may even provide the most plausible explanation of some passages in the Gospels. Strauss's point was simply that it had no basis in the text.

In *The Quest of the Historical Jesus* (pp. 52–3), Albert Schweitzer provided some examples of the rationalist interpretation of the miracle-stories from a work published in 1828 by a respected Heidelberg professor, H. E. G. Paulus:

The nature miracles suggest their own explanation. The walking on the water was an illusion of the disciples. Jesus walked along the shore, and in the mist was taken for a ghost by the alarmed and excited occupants of the boat. When Jesus called to them, Peter threw himself into the water, and was drawn to shore by Jesus just as he was sinking.

Immediately after taking Jesus into the boat they doubled a headland and drew clear of the storm centre; they therefore supposed that he had calmed the sea by his command. It was the same in the case where He was asleep during the storm. When they waked him he spoke to them about the wind and the weather. At that moment they gained the shelter of a hill which protected them from the wind that swept down the valley; and they marvelled among themselves that even the winds and the sea obeyed their Messiah. . . .

The feeding of the five thousand is explained in the following way. When Jesus saw the multitude an-hungered, he said to his disciples, 'We will set the rich people among them a good example, that they may share their supplies with the others', and he began to distribute his own provisions, and those of the disciples, to the people who were sitting near them. The example had its effect, and soon there was plenty for every one.

The explanation of the transfiguration is somewhat more complicated. While Jesus was lingering with a few followers in the mountainous district he had an interview upon a high mountain at night with two dignified-looking men whom his three companions took for Moses and Elijah. . . .

In dealing with the raisings from the dead the author is in his element. Here he is ready with the unfailing explanation taken over from Bahrdt that they were only cases of coma. These narratives should not be headed 'raisings from the dead', but 'deliverances from premature burial'. In Judaea, interment took place three hours after death. How many seemingly dead people may have returned to consciousness in their graves, and then have perished miserably!

Even if such speculations were correct in individual cases, Strauss pointed out, the historian could never know. The rationalists' solution to the problems faced by critical modern readers of the Bible left them worse off than ever. Supernaturalism was intellectually unconvincing but (for some) still religiously powerful. The rationalist attempt to rescue the Gospel narratives by removing this miraculous element was still rationally unconvincing, and religiously unsatisfying as well. It was a move in the wrong direction. Rescuing a historical core saved the wrong part of the religious apple. It was the narrative fruit, not the historical core which Strauss preserved for fermenting and distilling into a philosophical-theological truth acceptable to modern (Hegelian) educated people.

Strauss thus advocated a new kind of interpretation which took the Gospels as they stood, recognizing the unhistorical character of their miraculous element, but finding religious significance precisely in this unhistorical material. He extended to all the supernatural material the category of 'myth', which others had already applied to the stories of the virgin birth and Ascension. Legendary material grows up around the memory of a religious hero. Strauss thought that several of these unhistorical Gospel stories reflected Old Testament prototypes, especially the Elijah and Elisha cycles. Belief in Jesus as Messiah encouraged unhistorical stories about him as the fulfilment of scripture. 'Myth' was simply the form in which a true religious content was expressed in the childhood of the human race. These mythical narratives only needed interpreting to bring out what modern people could recognize as their philosophical truth.

In a Church which still clung to the traditional doctrine of scripture, it was Strauss's negations that caused the storm that swept him out of Tübingen. In retrospect, now that many of his negative judgements are widely taken for granted, it is his positive proposals which are most interesting. More than anyone else it was Strauss who drew explicit attention to the task of theological interpretation. Whatever was wrong with his actual proposal, his understanding of the task makes him a central, almost symbolic, figure in modern biblical interpretation.

Strauss's application to the human race of the 'idea' of the unity of God and man failed to persuade the Christian community of its continuity with past interpretations of the Bible and Christian tradition. Unlike Bultmann's demythologizing in the twentieth century (below, p. 110), Strauss's translation of the mythic material into a development of Hegel's philosophy was a theological novelty. He not only saw that the mythic material expressed the early Christians' evaluation of Jesus as divine; he also transferred their apprehension of God from the crucified and risen Christ (which is where Christian orthodoxy continues to find it) to the human race as a whole.

The reason Strauss proposed such a startling innovation was his philosophical conviction, derived from Schelling, that the idea of God embraces all reality. It follows that 'the idea' is 'not wont to lavish all its fulness on one exemplar', namely Jesus of Nazareth (p. 779). In a straight clash between what he thought philosophically true and traditional Christian belief Strauss unhesitatingly preferred the former. A theologian's first loyalty is to truth, not to tradition. His new theology failed to convince others and he was left a sad theological outsider. But his combination of historical criticism and religious philosophy had a certain elegance. By supposedly destroying the classical Christological dogma, whose fate was thought by friend and foe to hinge on the historical evidence for it furnished by the Gospels, Strauss neatly made room for his new theory.

Despite the attractions for anyone influenced by German idealism of finding God in the universal process of Spirit through history as a whole, rather than in the particularity of a historical individual, Strauss's novel suggestion that the idea of a union of the human and the divine applied to the human race rather than to Jesus was plainly not acceptable to orthodox Christians. But the tendency to separate the Christ idea, or Christ of faith, from the Jesus of history has continued to bedevil liberal theology. Modern historical study of the Gospels predisposes students in this heretical direction by requiring them (rightly) to distinguish between the Jesus of history and the evangelists' (and their predecessors') theological evaluations of him. This methodological distinction made by the historian is disastrous when carried over into Christology. It drives a wedge between the 'Jesus of history' and the 'Christ of faith', seen by believers as one.

But this unfortunate consequence of making the legitimate procedures of Gospel criticism into the basis of Christology was not immediately apparent to many. The furore caused by Strauss stemmed from the points at which he was right in his critical reasoning, not where he was unorthodox in his theological speculations. This modern historical reasoning was for Strauss merely a negative preliminary to his partly positive description of the religious language of the Bible as 'myth'. But that is beside the point. His historical negations were dynamite, the explosion of which opened the way to subsequent New Testament scholarship.

The development of constructive historical work on the Old and New Testaments will be discussed in the next two chapters, and the literary dimension, anticipated in Strauss's view of myth, in Chapter 7. Even the new social scientific dimensions of biblical study (Chapter 5) have roots in Strauss's account of the unconscious and communal creativity of the first followers of Jesus. The present chapter is concerned only with the destruction of the traditional view of the Bible, most evident in Strauss's arguments against the historicity of the Gospels.

Strauss's Gospel criticism was not entirely new, but his argumentative power and the over-ripeness of the time made 1835 the year in which the rationalist criticisms of the Bible, pioneered in the seventeenth and developed in the eighteenth centuries, finally entered the bloodstream of Christian theology—at least so far as German Protestantism was concerned. English theology in the nineteenth century, and Roman Catholic and Eastern Orthodox theology for most of the twentieth, were less progressive. The English and Irish deists had pioneered these critical investigations and influenced the German 'neologians', or Enlightenment theologians of the eighteenth century. But it was not until the late nineteenth century that historical research took root in the English Church, and later still before Roman Catholicism officially accepted it. The rest of this chapter illustrates the death of the old view of scripture with a Hamburg schoolmaster and a bishop to the Zulus.

Rational criticism of Christianity: H. S. Reimarus

The one predecessor that Strauss himself later singled out for a monograph was also singled out by Albert Schweitzer as the author of 'perhaps the most splendid achievement in the whole course of the historical investigation of the life of Jesus . . .' (*Quest*, p. 23): H. S. Reimarus.

Writing in 1906 under the pressure of a fixed idea, Schweitzer saw the significance of Reimarus (as of Strauss) differently from contemporary New Testament scholars who have a longer perspective. The quotation from the *Quest* continues, 'for he was the first to grasp the fact that the world of thought in which Jesus moved was essentially eschatological'. The interest that Reimarus holds for New Testament scholarship today is better expressed in Schweitzer's final remark (p. 26) about a 'magnificent overture in which are announced all the motifs of the future historical treatment of the life of Jesus'. His achievement lay in writing a non-supernatural, historical account of Christian origins in which he anticipated many of the insights of twentieth-century 'history of traditions' research on the Gospels.

These insights, corrected and refined by Strauss, have also determined the shape of much modern Christology, and this gives Reimarus a special place in the history of any theology that has been deeply influenced by biblical scholarship. But that only became apparent much later. As with Strauss, the significance of Reimarus looked very different in 1774–8 when parts of his work were published anonymously by Lessing. At that point only his attacks upon the biblical history, and therefore on biblical authority, were visible. These were explosive enough, but the secret of their authorship was preserved for many years. Reimarus was in any case beyond reach of persecution. He had died in 1768, leaving behind him two or three forms of a large German manuscript finally called an *Apology or Defence for Rational Worshippers of God*. This was not published until 1972. The historical significance of Reimarus rests on the seven fragments artfully released by Lessing in Wolfenbüttel before the censor caught up with him and the Duke of Brunswick made him stop.

Reimarus was a deist, i.e. he believed in God, but not in revelation, miracles, or other supernatural interventions. The first fragment of his work, published by Lessing in 1774, argued for the toleration of deists on the improbable grounds that Jesus also taught rational religion. Of the five fragments published in 1777, two continued the 'reason versus revelation' debate in general terms, while two others contain close analyses of biblical texts: the passage of the Israelites through the Red Sea, and the Resurrection narratives. Reimarus demonstrated the logistic impossibility of the former, given the numbers supposedly involved, and the irreconcilable contradictions of the latter. These rational attacks upon the historicity of the biblical narrative were part of his attempt to destroy a traditional Christianity based on biblical revelation and miracle, and replace it with the rational, natural religion popular among intellectuals of the Enlightenment or 'age of reason'. They reached their climax in the final, seventh fragment, 'On the Intentions of Jesus and His Disciples' (1778, republished in English, together with the sixth, in 1970). Reimarus here produced his alternative, non-supernatural account of Christian origins.

In the light of twentieth-century Gospel criticism with its clear distinction between the historical reality of Jesus and early Christian evaluations of him, and its attempt to distinguish between these different layers in the Gospels, it is natural to admire both Reimarus and Strauss for doing precisely that. The Gospels are doubly exposed photographs, containing two (or more) pictures superimposed upon one another; critics try to reconstruct each layer, tracing the faint outline of the charismatic teacher, prophet, and healer from Nazareth who was executed by Pontius Pilate. They also try to identify the successive stages of early Christian interpretation of him as the decisive manifestation of God. Modern historians thus seek to explain, without recourse to the super-natural, how the Gospel traditions developed in the course of being handed on by believers. Such a non-supernatural account of Jesus and early Christianity was inevitably in effect an anti-supernatural account. If the historian had no need of that hypothesis (God), why should anyone else adopt it? Modern rationalism held a dagger to the heart of Christianity.

Whereas Strauss thought he was doing Christianity a favour, Reimarus had no such illusions. Not only did Strauss offer an interpretation of the mythic material intended to preserve its essential truth; his explanation of how it developed in the imagination of believers was fairly positive towards religion. Strauss saw the 'mythic' language of religion as a vehicle of truth for children and primitives. Only modern theology and philosophy demanded something more rational. Reimarus was far more hostile to non-rational material, and denied its truth altogether. He was also, writing up to a century earlier, less historically informed about the Gospels. He accepted the traditional view of their apostolic authorship, and accepting that, he was suspicious. Rightly so. Matthew's story of the guard at Jesus' tomb looks as if it was designed to answer Jewish suggestions that the body of Jesus had been stolen by the disciples. Knowing as we do that the Gospel attributed to Matthew was probably written towards the end of the first century, this legend poses no problems for Christian belief. One may see it as an answer to anti-Christian propaganda without concluding that the propaganda itself was historically early or well based. If, however, one thinks like Reimarus and his contemporaries that this Gospel was written by the apostle St Matthew, then this story becomes very suspicious.

Reimarus concluded that the disciples did indeed steal the body, and he suggested a motive. They had enjoyed being in the limelight with Jesus, as religious personages. When Jesus was arrested and executed they had forsaken him and fled, and were faced with the wretched prospect of returning to working for their living, not to mention the mockery and possible persecution in store for them after following a lost leader. Faced with a crisis, they acted as smartly as the unjust steward. They doctored the record of Jesus' teaching to make it appear that Jesus had seen himself as a suffering Messiah who would be raised on the third day. Having stolen the body they then proclaimed that this had indeed happened, as he had foretold. They reinforced their claims by twisting some Old Testament texts into supporting the case, and gave it bite by adding that the world would shortly end and that anyone who had not accepted their message would burn in hell.

This fraud hypothesis is less far-fetched than it initially appears. Apart from the suspicious story of the guard at the tomb, Reimarus had put his finger on certain discrepancies within the Gospels which are indeed best explained in terms of some tension between the historical reality of Jesus and the early Church's memory of him. He also argued that since Jesus did not explain his meaning in using the phrase 'the kingdom of God' he must have meant by it what it meant to his Jewish hearers. This was sound historical reasoning, even though the Jewish background was more complex than Reimarus realized. Similarly he observed that the Gospel phrase 'Son of God' meant at the time much less than Christians have subsequently read into it in the light of Trinitarian discussion. Against its (supposed) Jewish background it represents a human figure, not divinity.

Again, who can deny that many in the early Church expected the end of the world soon, and that they were mistaken?

The two main arguments by which Christian claims were defended by theologians at that time were the so-called proofs from miracle and prophecy. Like David Hume, Reimarus pointed out that the former were plausible only for as long as the historicity of the Gospels was unchallenged, and even then did not prove Jesus' divine status. He also showed that in their original contexts the Old Testament passages cited in the New meant quite different things, and that they therefore carried no evidential weight. None of this was new. Reimarus was familiar with the English deist Anthony Collins's attack on the argument from prophecy (1724), and Thomas Woolston on miracles (1727–9), and several others. Peter Annet had criticized the Resurrection narratives (1744) and Thomas Chubb had claimed that the apostles had falsified the original teaching of Jesus (1738). In *Christianity as Old as Creation* (1730) Matthew Tindal had even discussed the early Christian belief in an imminent Parousia, some time before the German quest began.

The genius of Reimarus lay in synthesizing all these observations and producing a genuinely historical, if profoundly mistaken, account of Christian origins. Once Strauss had removed its weakest link, the fraud hypothesis, it represented an alternative account of Christianity which was very difficult to fault. Its main significance was that it could be answered only by theologians allowing themselves to be drawn on to Reimarus's rational ground, and arguing *historically*, i.e. non-supernaturally. If any apologia for historical criticism in Christian theology is needed, it may be found here. Once a devastating rational hypothesis had been presented it could only be countered by better historical hypotheses. The Bible had become a battleground for rational debate, and some of its students no longer believed the biblical revelation. The question for Christianity was whether to retreat into a ghetto or engage in reasoned argument. The theologian Strauss and his teacher Baur, whom we shall meet in the next chapter, show progressive theology opting for the latter.

These nineteenth-century liberal theologians had already abandoned the older views of scripture. Others had not. Reimarus had thought that belief in revelation was being ground to dust in the mill of the contradictions he found in the Bible. Christian belief did not need the support of the quasi-historical arguments drawn from miracle and prophecy. But it was vulnerable to Reimarus's arguments in other ways. These cut more deeply than many who answered him realized: a new era was slowly dawning.

Just how slow it was in coming may be gauged by returning to England a generation after Strauss and a century after Reimarus. The great advances made by liberal theology in coming to terms with the new intellectual situation were largely restricted to German universities. English free-thinking, which like English political thought had led the Western world in the early eighteenth century, had failed to penetrate the English Church or its universities. In the early 1860s two controversies took place which show how little English church doors had been open to German theology over the previous generation. These controversies also give as good a guide to the original reception of Reimarus and Strauss as any modern appreciation of their works can do.

The English Church: Bishop Colenso

Despite an early translation (1846) by the free-thinker George Eliot, it had not been difficult for English churchmen to dismiss Strauss as only the latest manifestation of 'German rationalism' and 'infidelity'. It was not until 1860 that the dam began to break and the possibility of a more rational approach, at least to the Old Testament, was admitted. In *Essays and Reviews* (1860) a group of seven clergymen of the established Church edged more or less cautiously in the direction of denying the traditional understanding of biblical inspiration and authority. As the most intellectual bishop of the day, Connop Thirlwall (who had himself in 1823, before his ordination, translated Schleiermacher's work on Luke), observed:

It was not either the novelty of the opinions themselves, or the originality of the arguments by which they were maintained, that attracted public attention . . . It was just because the opinions were by no means new, but familiar to persons conversant with such subjects in the works of writers who, as holding such opinions, had deemed themselves and been regarded by others, as hostile to Christianity, that they produced so startling an effect when they were announced by ministers of Christ . . .

Thirlwall saw further than most into the implications of biblical criticism for the whole fabric of traditional Christian belief. If one allows rational enquiry an inch it will take a mile. Yet the point had come when intellectual integrity demanded just such enquiry, whatever the risks for religion. The gulf between the 'official view' of the Bible and the common sense of educated Englishmen was becoming intolerable. As Robert Browning wrote in *Dramatis Personae* (1864):

> The candid incline to surmise of late
>   That the Christian faith proves false, I find;
> For our Essays and Reviews debate
>   Begins to tell on the public mind,
> And Colenso's words have weight.

John William Colenso, the missionary bishop of Natal, had by that time published only two of his seven large volumes (totalling over 3,000 pages) on *The Mosaic Authorship of the Pentateuch* (1862-79). Its detailed arguments are tedious, but the work is instructive in revealing the credibility gap that had by now opened up between the plain words of scripture, which were still officially held to be inerrant, and what educated people in fact believed. As Colenso wrote early in 1861, he was as a bishop required to demand of others a declaration that they 'unfeignedly believe all the Canonical Scriptures of the Old and New Testaments' (p. xii). This was intellectually dishonest and undermined the credibility of the clergy. 'There can be no doubt, however, that a very widespread distrust does exist among the intelligent laity in England, as to the soundness of the ordinary view of Scripture Inspiration' (p. xxiii). Geology had shown that 'a *Universal* Deluge, such as the Bible manifestly speaks of, could not possibly have taken place in the way described in the Book of Genesis' (p. vii). Some had spoken instead of a partial flood. 'But such attempts have ever seemed to me to be made in the very teeth of the Scriptural statements, which are as plain and explicit as words can possibly be . . .' (p. viii). This meant that a most un-Protestant surrender of freedom of thought had become a condition of ordination. 'The Church of England must fall to the ground by its own internal weakness—by losing its hold upon the growing intelligence of all classes,—unless some remedy be very soon applied to this state of things . . .' The conspiracy of silence would finally discredit faith (p. xxiv).

It was plain common sense and honesty which compelled Colenso, when challenged by his Zulu converts, to admit that he did not believe all the Old Testament stories literally. 'I dared not, as a servant of the God of Truth, urge my brother man to believe that which I did not myself believe, which I knew to be untrue, as a matter-of-fact historical narrative' (p. viii).

Here was no eighteenth-century rationalist bent on attacking the Christian Church, but a missionary and apologist who saw when the time had come to ask who was fooling whom. As a Cambridge mathematician he may have lacked imagination, but he did not lack integrity. He recognized, and was prepared to face, the implication that Jesus' knowledge was limited by the conditions of his day. He recognized also that some would say that his 'whole apparatus is drawn bodily from the German Rationalists' (p. xiv). This he denied. He had worked much of it out for himself, and only subsequently read de Wette, Bleek, and Kuenen. What he had read of conservatives such as Kurtz and Hengstenberg had convinced him that they had no satisfactory answers to the questions raised by the critics. In struggling to hold together Christian faith and reason he was engaged in the perennial task of theology.

Within a few years one of the contributors to *Essays and Reviews* (Frederick Temple) had become Archbishop of Canterbury, and a cautious biblical criticism was becoming accepted in English Christianity as compatible with the doctrine of the Incarnation. That, rather than the 'Bible question' as such, is what interested Anglicans. The doctrine of scripture, which seemed so important to Continental Protestants, was not even in the creed. The Bible was used in the liturgy, and that was not the context in which to press awkward questions. When controversy broke out it was usually because the doctrine of the Incarnation seemed threatened, or because clergy were not expected to question doctrine.

Among conservative Christians in Germany and North America the 'Bible question' continued to burn. Where Protestant faith is strong, and reason undervalued, holding fast to the Bible in an uncritical way is a natural response to the threat of modernity. Ordinary Christians were right to be suspicious of the biblical critics. The very word 'criticism' has negative connotations where historical research rather than literary study is the ruling paradigm. Biblical scholars were more successful in destroying than in building up. Their positive restatements of Christianity were often religiously weak.

Where the Bible is no longer venerated, a massive religious resource has been lost. Nietzsche's famous saying in *The Gay Science* (1883) about 'the death of God' suggested a title for this chapter. If not 'God', then perhaps at least Holy Scripture '. . . is dead; we have slain [her]. The holiest and most powerful that the world has ever possessed has ebbed its blood away beneath our knives . . .'

That is reminiscent of our opening quotation from Strauss (p. 44 f.), from half a century earlier. The microscope which modern critical thinking has applied to the biblical texts sometimes looks like a butcher's knife. Historical critics might well feel challenged by Nietzsche's crazy man to 'ponder the enormity of what we have done'. The Bible (Old and New Testaments) remains the scripture of the Christian Church, as the Hebrew Tanak remains the scripture of Judaism. But the holy book has apparently lost much of its ancient power. Modern attacks on Judaism and Christianity, from Reimarus and Voltaire through Marx, Nietzsche, and Freud to the more recent enemies of religion, in politics, education, and the media, have drawn much of their ammunition from rationalist criticism of the Bible.

This has also had an effect on the religions themselves, at the practical and devotional, as well as theoretical, levels. The new methods and results have helped bring about a reorientation in theology and have had some impact upon liturgical practice and Christian life-styles. But the Bible continues to be read, both religiously and non-religiously. The sometimes tense relationship of these different aims has provided biblical interpretation with its hidden agenda ever since rational investigation began to threaten religious beliefs that had looked to the Bible for their justification.

The tension between faith and reason will therefore continue to occupy us in what follows.

Further reading

CHADWICK, O., *The Victorian Church*, ii (London, 1970).

ELLIS, I., *Seven Against Christ: A Study of Essays and Reviews* (Leiden, 1980).

FREI, H. W., *The Eclipse of the Biblical Narrative* (New Haven and London, 1974).

HARRIS, H., *David Friedrich Strauss and his Theology* (Cambridge, 1973).

HINCHLIFF, P. B., *John William Colenso* (London, 1964).

KELLER, E. and M.-L., *Miracles in Dispute: A Continuing Debate* (1968; ET London, 1969).

KNOX, B., *A Layman's Quest* (London and New York, 1969).

KÜMMEL, W. G., *The New Testament: The History of the Investigation of its Problems* (1970; ET Nashville, 1972, and London, 1973).

SCHWEITZER, A., *The Quest of the Historical Jesus* (London and New York, 1910).

SMART, N., *et al.* (eds.), *Nineteenth-century Religious Thought in the West*, i (Cambridge, 1985).

STRAUSS, D. F., *The Life of Jesus Critically Examined* (Philadelphia and London, 1972).

TALBERT, C. H. (ed.), *Reimarus: Fragments* (Philadelphia and London, 1970).

3

History and the Growth of Knowledge

Strauss, Baur, and beyond

In a conversation during 1860 two former student friends were reminiscing: Wilhelm Vatke looked back to 1835 as 'a good year for wine'. 'Yes', replied David Friedrich Strauss, '—and for theology too.' Strauss was thinking of three epoch-making books. First, the source of his own fame and troubles, *The Life of Jesus Critically Examined*; secondly, his friend Vatke's masterpiece, *Biblical Theology: The Religion of the Old Testament*, i (never translated), which Wellhausen called 'the most important contribution to the historical understanding of ancient Israel'; and thirdly, perhaps, his one-time teacher Ferdinand Christian Baur's work on Christian Gnosticism. All three books remain landmarks in the history of theology, and they had one thing in common: they all owed much to Hegel, the philosopher who aimed to overcome the 'big ugly ditch' (above, p. 47) which Lessing and the Enlightenment had posited between the 'accidental truths of history' and the 'necessary truths of reason'.

The decade following Hegel's death in 1831 was the period of his greatest prestige and influence. We have noted (p. 50) Strauss's proposal for developing this system. In his 'concluding dissertation' he translated (i.e. reinterpreted) the mythical elements in the Gospels into a Hegelian 'idea', or concept, of the unity of the human and the divine, and then (unlike Hegel) referred this to the human race, rather than to Jesus. At the beginning of his book he explains how Hegel's philosophy had brought him 'internal liberation of the feelings and intellect from certain religious and dogmatic presuppositions' (ET, p. lii). It had freed him for untrammelled academic work by convincing him that 'the essence of the Christian faith is perfectly independent' of historical criticism (ibid.). Four years earlier he had travelled to Berlin to sit at the great philosopher's feet, and although he had arrived only in time for the cholera epidemic and Hegel's funeral, this had not diminished his enthusiasm.

Vatke had been inspired by Hegel in a quite different way. He applied the Hegelian notion of development in history to the Old Testament, and wrote the first truly historical Old Testament theology. The reason for its great importance was that it reversed the order of the Old Testament writings. Vatke recognized that the writing prophets were historically *prior* to the composition of the Pentateuch.

Hegel's notion of development was becoming decisive for Baur also, but in *Die christliche Gnosis* the Hegelian accent was more upon the philosophical theology than the historical development. Baur here shifted his allegiance from Schleiermacher to Hegel because he saw in this philosophy a way of combining a truly historical reconstruction of Christianity with a (to him) rationally satisfying doctrine of God.

The three authors used Hegel in different ways, but they all used him in their new *theological* interpretations of the Bible and Christian tradition. 1835 was a good (or at least an important) year for *theology*, or talk of God. However, the scholarly significance of all three books turned out to lie elsewhere. Hegelian theologies faded fast, but these books remain important for their influence upon the critical historical study of the Bible and Christianity. Paradoxically, and contrary to his own intentions, the long-term importance of Hegel for biblical interpretation lay in the impulses his thought gave to historical research. The three 'theologians of 1835' who were stimulated by him are generally reckoned important for their contributions to the *historical* study of the Bible. But the fact that they were all theologians before they became critical historians, and that they did their history for the sake of their theology, will prove significant for our later discussions of theological interpretation (below, Chapter 6).

Of the three, Strauss was the least interested in history as such. His criticism of the Gospel narratives was intended to destroy their pseudo-history, but was not designed to replace this with real history. Strauss made no effort to reconstruct the biography of Jesus or the history of the early Church, though he had some important ideas about both. His chief interest lay in his theological interpretation of the Gospels, which involved translating their quasi-historical 'mythical' material—which presented Jesus as God-man—into something different.

But whatever his personal motivations, Strauss's destruction of the Gospels' quasi-history stimulated critical historical reconstruction. Distinguishing between the sources and the events reported is the foundation of critical history, and if the sources are unhistorical, recognizing that is a major advance. Like Socrates, we have to realize that we know less than we thought, before we can progress to genuine knowledge.

The historian investigating Jesus is greatly helped by having four sources rather than one. Comparison of these lies at the heart of critical study of the Gospels. Strauss made the contradictions between the accounts, especially between John and the Synoptics, crystal-clear and drew negative conclusions about their historicity.

This method was totally successful in destroying the traditional view that all four Gospels are historically reliable. The centuries-long practice of Gospel harmonization is now intellectually discredited, though far from dead. But contradictions between the four Gospels do not mean that nothing is historical—only that they cannot *all* be historical. Recognizing the contradictions poses the challenge of deciding which parts are most reliable. Strauss took a great step in this direction by judging that in general the Synoptics are more reliable than the Fourth Gospel. Schleiermacher had preferred the latter, and had constructed his Christology on that basis. Some seventy years later Albert Schweitzer celebrated the reversal of this as one of the major achievements of Strauss's *Life of Jesus*. But true as that is, and important as it was for subsequent research, Strauss was not himself interested in the historian's critical evaluation of sources and did not discriminate further among and within the Synoptic Gospels.

Liberal Christology remained caught in the bind of Strauss's distinction between the Jesus of history and the Christ of faith, but unlike him gave precedence to the former. New Testament scholarship accordingly proceeded to determine which of the sources for historical knowledge of Jesus were earliest, and how far they could be trusted. Strauss had given Gospel criticism a necessary stimulus, but the greatest advances were now made by others. Among them F. C. Baur is so pre-eminent that a survey of his work on Christian origins will provide some indication of the future shape of New Testament scholarship as this criticized, corrected, and continued his methods and conclusions.

The main complaint of conservatives against Baur was that he did what Reimarus and Strauss had done: he replaced the traditional supernaturalist account of Christian origins with a non-supernatural account. Unlike Reimarus, and differently from Strauss, Baur thought he could perceive God in the historical process. But God for him was immanent divine Spirit, moving through history and recognized by the rational historian's own finite spirit or mind. It was not the God of supernatural interventions such as miracles, as presented in the Old and New Testaments. Baur, like other modern historians, saw a straight choice between historical causation and an account of Christianity in which (as he explained at the beginning of his *Church History*) 'the only-begotten Son of God descended from the eternal throne of the Godhead to the earth, and became man in the womb of the virgin'. As Strauss had recognized (though Baur avoided the inflammatory word), that manner of speaking is *myth*, not history.

Baur insisted that there are no absolute beginnings in history, no events outside natural causation. His historical theology is *theology* because he claims to detect God in the history of religion, but it is also critical *history*, using the rational methods pioneered by Ranke and Niebuhr. Perceiving God as infinite Spirit, i.e. Reason, in this history depended for Baur on historians using their own reason and not accepting the records uncritically. Christian theology involves reason, and Christian faith is faith in God revealed in history, not faith in the historical reliability of the Bible.

By the time he summarized his conclusions in the first volume of his *Church History* (1853) Baur had already published his critical analyses of the four Gospels. Strauss's stimulus had marked an epoch in the history of theology, and he had been right about the Fourth Gospel. But Strauss had not taken criticism of the sources far enough and had never attempted to write a history of Christian origins. As Baur wrote in 1846, in his account of the origin and character of Luke's Gospel:

Strauss's criticism of the Gospels had caused the complete dissolution, for everyone who accepts criticism and critical results at all, of the old harmonizing approach that puts the four Gospels together. This has posed a new task for criticism. One cannot stop at the merely negative result that the four Gospels are so historically contradictory that they more or less exclude one another. If they cannot be taken together as a unity in a way that recognizes only a quantitative difference as regards the material they have in common, then each of them can only be considered on its own merits and specific qualities. Taken together they constitute a plurality of accounts in which the same material has been differently shaped and given its own individuality according to the differences of their compilers. Criticism must therefore answer the same question about each of the four Gospels: how is it to be understood in its particular character and its difference from the others? But this question itself is given precision by asking in each case about their specific *tendency* in addition to their general aim to present the Gospel history. (Morgan translation)

This is Baur's famous 'tendency criticism'. It is taken for granted by scholars now, but in the nineteenth century caused widespread horror because it undermined the way the doctrinal unity of the New Testament was generally understood. If the writers held different theologies then the unity of the New Testament could no longer be found in a unified dogmatic structure. Baur himself saw this unity in the historical development, and many twentieth-century theologians have found it in the 'kerygma' or 'apostolic preaching'. But the 'dogmatic textbook' view of scripture was not easily given up.

Strauss's historical perspective anticipated twentieth-century form criticism of the Gospels by focusing upon what had happened to the traditions about Jesus in the early Church between his death and the composition of the earliest Gospel (which Strauss thought was Matthew). Baur, as the quotation above indicates, examined the theological *tendency* of each Gospel, and in this respect anticipated redaction criticism, though without twentieth-century sophistication in distinguishing within each Gospel between the traditions inherited by the evangelist and all the 'redactional', or editorial, modifications of this material. That was only possible later, in the light of a more satisfactory solution of the 'synoptic problem', i.e. the source-critical question of the literary relationships between the Gospels.

Like Strauss, Baur continued to maintain the traditional view that Matthew was the earliest Gospel. Despite recent attempts to revive the 'Griesbach hypothesis' of Matthean priority, it is almost certainly mistaken. But while neither Strauss nor Baur made any significant contribution to the solution of the synoptic problem, *The Life of Jesus* provoked intensive study of the Gospels. Following its demonstration of the contradictions between the Gospel sources, anyone interested in reconstructing the history of Jesus had to determine which one was the most original and hence (presumably) the most reliable.

In their responses to Strauss, both published in 1838, C. H. Weisse and C. G. Wilke argued independently (as Lachmann had done in 1835) for the priority of Mark. Weisse further proposed that Matthew and Luke shared another source, and in 1863 H. J. Holtzmann gave classic expression to this 'two-source theory' that the later Synoptic Gospels, Matthew and Luke, used both Mark (or an earlier form of Mark) and also a collection of Jesus' sayings, a hypothetical second source later labelled 'Q'.

'Source criticism' thus made its most important advances, and these assumed central importance as 'life-of-Jesus research' now began to dominate the liberal theological agenda. Mark and Q, the Markan outline of Jesus' ministry and Passion supplemented by some 215 verses of early, presumed authentic, sayings, provided the scholarly basis for liberal Protestant life of Jesus research, from Holtzmann's sketch in *Die synoptischen Evangelien* in 1863 to his final work on the messianic self-consciousness of Jesus, published in 1907, and beyond.

This era of New Testament scholarship, complete with its theological motivations, was brought to an end in Germany (though not elsewhere) by twentieth-century 'history of traditions research'. The next chapter will relate how William Wrede demonstrated in 1901 that Mark was shaped largely by theological interests and could not be made the basis for a psychologizing history of Jesus' ministry. The Markan outline was then further undermined in 1919 by K. L. Schmidt's recognition that the Synoptic Gospels consist largely of individual units of tradition strung together by link-words, and arranged more by subject-matter than by chronology. This atomizing approach was also characteristic of the form-critical works of Dibelius and Bultmann. Their accounts of how the needs of the early Christian communities influenced the shape of the material during the period of oral transmission of the synoptic tradition between Jesus and the Gospels is in some ways reminiscent of Strauss, and led some to similarly sceptical conclusions about the historicity of the Gospels.

Within this breakdown of the liberal Protestant 'quest for the historical Jesus', the historical investigation of Jesus through the critical study of the Gospels might seem to have regressed three-quarters of a century to Strauss and Baur. In some respects the work of these pioneers is indeed less dated than much of what followed. But the intensive study which followed them was not wasted. Measuring contemporary critical study alongside the founding fathers gives some indication of what has been aimed at and how much achieved.

Historical scholarship and theological interpretation

Strauss, Baur, and Vatke all followed Reimarus in opting for a rational, historical, i.e. non-supernatural, account of Israel and of Christian origins. All three used historical methods to undermine supernaturalist theologies, and all three used Hegel's philosophy in their alternative theological proposals. Strauss's heterodox sugges-tion was logically independent of his historical criticism. Baur and Vatke, on the other hand, used Hegelian metaphysics in more orthodox attempts to relate history and faith. Baur's grand construction proved vulnerable to subsequent historical scrutiny and lost its philosophical and theological attraction as Hegel's influence declined. Vatke's synthesis totally failed to attract support, because he was ahead of his time. Hegel had opened Vatke's eyes to historical development, but the philosophy now proved a handicap, hindering acceptance of his historical construction until Wellhausen espoused and established it, without the philosophical ballast.

The syntheses of our three 'theologians of 1835' were thus abandoned. Under the new leadership of Wellhausen, Holtzmann, and Harnack, late nineteenth-century biblical scholarship congratulated itself on cutting loose from the snares of philosophy in much the same way that it had earlier celebrated its liberation from the dogmatic constraints of the old theology.

The price of this freedom was high. What Vatke and Baur were trying to achieve in their syntheses of historical and philosophical construction was a true rational translation of the Bible's talk of God. When their syntheses broke down, biblical scholarship and theological interpretation drifted apart. Historical scholarship became more positivistic, and normative (i.e. believing) talk of God (as opposed to merely historical description of the biblical writers' beliefs) disappeared from biblical as from other historical scholarship.

If that was a loss, the gains were considerable. By accepting the step taken in biblical studies and historical theology, and adopting the methods of historical research whatever the cost for traditional forms of supernaturalism, Christian theology kept reason as well as faith alive in biblical study, even if it was failing to integrate them satisfactorily. Acceptance, within their proper sphere, of the methods pioneered by Baur became a test of whether a theology is truly rational, and therefore one test of whether it is truly theology. Some late nineteenth-century Protestant theology passed this test with distinction, even if in other respects it was unsatisfactory.

An illustration of how far Baur's historical principles have gained acceptance may be seen by reference to the most sensitive issue in all Christian theological discussion of faith and history, the resurrection of Jesus. Baur's Hegelian theological interpretation of this event may or may not be thought illuminating, but what concerns us here is how clear he is about the bounds of historical sense:

The question as to the nature and the reality of the resurrection lies outside the sphere of historical enquiry. History [*die geschichtliche Betrachtung*] must be content with the simple fact that in the faith of the disciples the resurrection of Jesus came to be regarded as a solid and unquestionable fact. It was in this faith that Christianity acquired a firm basis for its historical development. What history requires as the necessary antecedent of all that is to follow is not so much the fact of the resurrection of Jesus, as the belief that it was a fact. The view we take of the resurrection is of minor importance for the history. We may regard it as an outward objective miracle; since, though we assume that an inward psychological process was possible by which the unbelief of the disciples at the time of the death of Jesus was changed into belief in his resurrection, still no psychological analysis can show what that process was. In any case it is only through the consciousness of the disciples that we have any knowledge of that which was the object of their faith; and thus we cannot go further than to say that by whatever means this result was brought about, the resurrection of Jesus became a fact of their consciousness, and was as real to them as any historical event. (*Church History*, p. 42)

That is not substantially different from G. Bornkamm, *Jesus of Nazareth* (1956; ET 1960, p. 180):

The event of Christ's resurrection from the dead and his life and his eternal reign, are things removed from historical scholarship. History cannot ascertain and establish conclusively the facts about them as it can with other events of the past. The last historical fact available to it is the Easter faith of the first disciples . . .

Neither Baur in 1853 nor Bornkamm over a century later denies the objective reality and truth of the resurrection of Jesus, though both would have doubts about the actual traditions preserved in the Gospels—and for some of the same reasons as Reimarus and Strauss. The contradictions between these accounts are plain, and it is difficult to be sure which are the earliest strata of the tradition. But the point at issue is simply that acts of God cannot be spoken of, let alone established, by historical research. That is a presupposition or axiom: it defines what is meant by historical research. And it means that believers who do wish to speak intelligently of God on the basis of the biblical witness cannot allow biblical interpretation to be restricted to the task of historical research. That is necessary, but never sufficient to fulfil the requirements of Christian belief.

Baur is the best illustration of the uses of history in biblical interpretation, partly because he pioneered the methods and determined the shape of much subsequent New Testament research, and partly because he combined historical research with a clearly articulated theological interest. He forged a theological proposal, which remains instructive for all concerned, with the religious and theological dimensions of biblical study. Anyone who is dissatisfied about the way biblical scholarship and theological interpretation moved apart in the second half of the nineteenth century can learn from the few great historians who were also considerable theologians.

We have stressed Baur's insistence upon a 'purely historical' account of Christian origins. Historical study must be genuinely historical. It is not only the programme itself, but how he carried it out that has been influential. His attempt to place the Gospels in the history of early Christianity by looking for the distinctive 'tendency' or ideological emphasis of each has become a fundamental task of New Testament scholarship. His recognition that this loss of reliable information about Jesus is compensated by gain in historical knowledge about the early Church(es), in which and for which the evangelists were writing, is also now commonplace. But his actual placings and datings of the Gospels have been rejected as his outline of early Christian history has been corrected. Like many pioneers, Baur made mistakes. But his methods have provided the tools by which his results have been revised.

Contrary to a once widely held opinion, Baur did not force his history into a 'Hegelian' pattern of thesis–antithesis–synthesis. He did detect in first-generation Christianity an opposition between Jewish Christians and Gentile Christians, and saw this as being gradually softened until they came together into the early catholic Church of the late second century. But he reached this view of opposing parties in the early Church on the basis of historical and exegetical study of Paul's epistles, starting (in a monograph published in 1831) from 1 Corinthians 1: 12. His theological evaluation of historical development as the self-expression of the divine Spirit (learned from Hegel) no doubt encouraged him as, we are told, he started work at 4 a.m., without central heating, ink in winter freezing in the pot. But this philosophical and theological understanding of Christianity required him to get his history right. True philosophical theology depended upon true history for Baur. He therefore laid great stress upon being as 'objective' as possible.

That does not mean that his reconstruction of early Christianity was satisfactory. Subsequent research, by Reuss, Ritschl, and Weizsäcker in particular, improved on it while remaining deeply indebted to the pioneer. Baur had been right to emphasize the conflict between Paul and some Jewish Christians, but it is not clear what support they had from the Twelve. By making this conflict the key to the whole development, Baur failed to give due weight to other factors. Since different strands coexisted in early Christianity there was no need, either, to string out the development and place the Gospels in the second century.

When the seven Ignatian epistles were later shown by Zahn and Lightfoot to be authentic, Baur's chronology was seen to be wrong. Ignatius, Bishop of Antioch, wrote in the first few years of the second century, and these letters show that he was familiar with monarchical episcopacy. The development of Christian thought and institutions was clearly much faster than Baur had realized; the Gospels must be dated earlier, in the last third of the first century. But that did not guarantee their historicity, as conservatives assumed, any more than the historicity of Acts was rescued by the modifications made to Baur's account of its date and its theological 'tendency'. A comparison of the first part of his monograph on *Paul* (1845; ET 1875), where Acts is analysed, with the corresponding first part of Bornkamm's *Paul* (1969; ET 1971) shows how Baur's principles, methods, and many of his actual results are now more widely taken for granted. Paul's epistles are given priority as the primary sources, and as the historicity of Acts sinks, its value as a source of information about the theology of its author's own period rises.

The monograph on Paul also summed up Baur's literary judgements on the epistles. He had in 1835 demonstrated by a combination of linguistic, literary, and above all historical arguments that the Pastoral Epistles were not written by Paul, but came from a later period. He now cautiously cast doubts on all except the four major epistles (Romans, 1 and 2 Corinthians, Galatians). Subsequent scholarship has judged that there is no good reason to deny the authenticity of Philippians. Baur was misled by the untypical character of the Christ hymn in 2: 6–11, which is probably a quotation. 1 Thessalonians and Philemon are also almost certainly by Paul himself. But on the essential points Baur's methods and many of his judgements stand. Pseudonymity, or at least collaboration, is now generally recognized in the Pauline corpus, and the historical Paul is drawn mainly from the major epistles.

The third part of Baur's monograph on Paul raises questions of a very different order from these purely historical and literary judgements. In his monographs on the history of dogma (1835–43) he had attempted to interpret those developments theologically with the help of Hegelian metaphysical language, and he now borrowed some of the same categories to communicate Paul's meaning. The rationale for such a philosophically articulated piece of New Testament theology is that a theologian has to show that these texts are speaking of God, i.e. the God that he or she acknowledges. A theologian cannot, like a historian, rest content with having described someone else's religion. But in order to fulfil this further, theological, task of speaking of God in tune with the texts being interpreted, it is necesary to use language which is not only appropriate to the texts, but which the modern interpreter also deems appropriate to the subject-matter. Since theologians understand the subject-matter of the Bible as the transcendent God who lays claim to them too, theological interpretation has to use the language in which the modern interpreters themselves speak of God. Conservative theologians, who are happy to express their own faith in purely biblical terms, have no problem here; they can simply repeat Paul's language. But liberals, conscious of the difference in world-view between themselves and Paul, are more acutely aware of the problem of translation or interpretation.

The only question is whether this task of theological interpretation, i.e. a translation intended to communicate what believers acknowledge as the transcendent subject-matter of these texts, should be separated from historical description, or whether the two tasks can be combined. Baur and Vatke in the nineteenth century, and Bultmann in the twentieth, combined their historical description and theological interpretation in modern theological syntheses as imposing as the conservative biblicist syntheses which have continued to be written. The great liberal synthesizers composed *new* theologies, i.e. new interpretations of the Christian tradition in the light of their contemporary experience, through their biblical interpretation. Where this project has succeeded it has proved religiously valuable, helping believers to read and expound their scriptures in ways that combine the claims of faith and of reason.

Most biblical scholars, however, have found such syntheses dangerous. They are successful only if they stand up to historical scrutiny, as well as being theologically attractive. A philosophically articulated piece of New Testament theology is thus open to philosophical, theological, and also *historical* critiques. If its philosophical bases crumble it will fall or be neglected. If it fails to maintain sufficient continuity with the tradition, as in the case of Strauss, it is subject to theological criticism by believers. Above all, if it fails as historical description it can be criticized by rational argument.

Baur's interpretation of Paul, like his somewhat Kantian account of Jesus' teaching in the *Church History*, finally fails as historical description, and therefore fails as theological interpretation. It was above all the growth in historical knowledge of the religious environment of Jesus and Paul which later in the century showed Baur's descriptions to be seriously defective. He had pioneered the history of religions approach to be discussed in the next chapter, but subsequent research improved on his historical conclusions. The history of religions agenda for twentieth-century scholarship was set by Droysen's new understanding of the Hellenistic age, the rediscovery of Jewish eschatology, of Hellenistic and oriental mystery religions, and further research on gnosticism. But most of that came later, helped by the discovery of new documents. A theological interpretation of the New Testament can be judged only in the light of the state of historical knowledge and the religious and philosophical climate of its own day. The question of principle remains, whether the attempts to *combine* historical reconstruction and theological interpretation are justified or whether the tasks are better separated.

Most modern biblical scholars have separated them because they see no way of combining them without endangering the integrity of historical work. The triumph of historical research in biblical scholarship was achieved by cutting loose from doctrinal pre-suppositions, and the price of freedom is eternal vigilance. But that freedom is adequately preserved by allowing further historical research to challenge any proposed synthesis, as Baur's and Bultmann's were more or less successfully challenged. Conservative syntheses combining historical exegesis with theological statements have also been successfully challenged. That is an argument for better syntheses, not for abandoning the project.

The reason why biblical scholars who are also theologians continue to attempt such syntheses of historical knowledge and theological meaning is that without them the religious use of the Bible would be in danger of becoming irrational and irresponsible. It is a theological interest that motivates theological interpretation of scripture. Simple historians and simple believers can manage without it. The problem for the thoughtful believer or believing biblical scholar is how to get from historical conclusions to a theological position. The biblicist 'solution' is to deny the existence of the problem, and claim that one's historical conclusions provide a satisfactory theology for today. The alternative strategy, repre-sented by Baur and Bultmann, is to hold the two sides together from the outset by doing one's history in the light of a rationally defensible religious vision of the world.

Bultmann's theological interpretation will be discussed in the next chapter. It impressed a whole generation before its philosophi-cal and theological bases wore thin and enough of its historical and literary judgements looked vulnerable for the synthesis to begin to lose credibility. Baur's philosophical language faded more quickly and was disowned by his heirs. But the chief reason for Bultmann's greater success was that he could build with the results of a century's radical historical criticism, and build for a Church that had learned to live with these results. Baur, by contrast, like Strauss and Vatke, met instant rejection, not because his synthesis was found defective, but because its historical-critical components were found shocking. His novel proposals for theological interpretation were drowned in the commotion caused by his literary and historical conclusions. These seemed to contemporaries to undermine biblical authority by denying the apostolic authorship of most of the New Testament and also by denying its doctrinal unity. Above all his denial of the historical character of the Fourth Gospel seemed to threaten Christian belief in the divinity of Christ, since this was still widely thought to depend upon the record of Jesus' self-attestation as God incarnate.

Now that many of Baur's literary and historical results have been broadly accepted, it is possible to see the strength of his proposals for the structure of a theologically interested biblical interpretation. These were ignored by his immediate successors, but taken up by Bultmann and his school, and are again widely ignored today. We shall consider them at the end of this chapter. But our first task has been to place in a positive light Baur's purely historical (with its attendant literary) work in order to show how far one man was able to anticipate the shape of the historical-critical movement which has dominated biblical scholarship for 150 years.

In the criticism of the Hebrew Bible, the scholar whose stature invites comparison with that of Baur belongs to a later generation. Julius Wellhausen (1844–1918) was roughly contemporary with H. J. Holtzmann (1832–1910) and the Berlin historian of dogma, Harnack (1851–1930). These three scholars were the pillars which the young Turks of the Göttingen 'history of religions school'— notably Gunkel, J. Weiss, Wrede, and Bousset—criticized when they brought the historical movement within theology to its climax at the beginning of the present century. Since their work set the agenda for twentieth-century biblical scholarship it will be considered in the next chapter. But first the formative period itself must be understood. Our key figure for the first half of the nineteenth century was (among other things) a New Testament scholar. Our representative from the latter part of the century is best known for his work on the Old Testament.

Wellhausen and the Old Testament

To understand the importance of Wellhausen's work it is necessary to go back to the beginnings of the critical study of the Pentateuch in the seventeenth and eighteenth centuries. Unlike Gospel criticism (which anyway began later), criticism of the Pentateuch did not originally flow from either historical or religious interests, but was literary in character. Indeed, it could almost be seen as the product of pure intellectual curiosity. Careful readers of the Pentateuch had always noticed discrepancies and inconsistencies in the narrative. There are places where history seems to repeat itself inconsequentially (compare Genesis 12: 10–20 with 20 and 26: 1–16); characters are introduced more than once, each time as if we had never heard of them before; stories are internally incoherent (e.g. the Flood story, Genesis 6–9). The suggestion that these problems could best be explained by seeing the Pentateuch as a patchwork of disparate pieces, or rather as the result of weaving together several originally separate narrative strands, commended itself in the two centuries before Wellhausen more as a satisfying intellectual solution to a puzzle than as a historically or theologically significant theory. In itself it did not even necessarily represent a challenge to the essential Mosaic authorship of the Pentateuch: Jean Astruc's pioneering work of 1753 was called *Conjectures about the Original Documents which Moses Appears to Have Used in the Composition of the Book of Genesis.*

By the early nineteenth century, however, it was becoming clear that a good deal of the material in the Pentateuch must in fact be later than the time of Moses. But for most scholars it remained almost axiomatic that the latest sources must be those which had least to do with the specifically Jewish religious and ritual system; in other words, that J, E, and D must all be later than (what we now call) P, since P enshrines the essential legislation whose contribution to the overall effect of the Pentateuch makes it reasonable to call it 'the Law' (*torah*). As everyone 'knew', the Law was the original and most characteristic portion of the Hebrew scriptures; subsequent writers and thinkers, such as the prophets, relied on a knowledge of the Law to give their teaching its moral authority, and in New Testament times it was still possible to refer to the whole Old Testament by the shorthand term 'Law' (see e.g. John 10: 34). The Torah is the central pillar of Judaism, and it was therefore assumed that its principal document, the cultic, dietary, and purity laws as recorded in P, must be older than any other parts of the Bible. The laws might not go back to Moses, but for all practical purposes they might as well have done, since even as early as the time of the earliest kings of Israel they were already of undisputed antiquity.

It was this assumption that Wellhausen was to succeed in overturning; but it took seventy years or so for the ground to be prepared for biblical scholars to accept such a radical shift in understanding, seventy years in which Wellhausen's solution to the problem of the Pentateuch was anticipated more than once, but then abandoned again, without its consequences being properly appreciated. A new phase in Pentateuchal studies began in 1806–7 with the work of W. M. L. de Wette (*Contributions to Old Testament Introduction*). De Wette retained the belief that P was the oldest of the Pentateuchal sources, but he succeeded in providing (for the first time) a fixed date for D by identifying it with the 'book of the Law' found in the temple in the reign of Josiah (see 2 Kings 22: 8–20). In itself this was an old idea; St Jerome had suggested it, and a detailed version of the theory can be found in Hobbes's *Leviathan* of 1651. But de Wette argued that D was not just *discovered* but actually *written* in the seventh century, and that its provisions had not been known in earlier times. Thus a large and important portion of the Pentateuch came to be seen not merely as non-Mosaic but actually as later than almost all the kings of Israel and Judah; later, too, than prophets such as Amos, Hosea, and Isaiah, on whose ideas it to a great extent depended. Once this was established, theories about the dating of the Pentateuchal sources ceased to be primarily solutions to a literary puzzle and became a tool for rewriting the history of Israel, and especially its religious institutions and theological ideas, in a way that was not merely a sophisticated or more circumstantial retelling of the biblical story. Since de Wette, Old Testament scholars have had to allow for distortions of the objective history of Israel, resulting from the influence of later sources such as D on the way older accounts were edited and transmitted; so that it can rightly be said that 'de Wette's *Contributions* is the first work of Old Testament scholarship to present a view of the history of Israel that is radically at variance with the view implied in the Old Testament itself' (J. W. Rogerson).

The next and most crucial step was to come with the realization that not only the laws in D but almost all the laws in the Pentateuch in fact post-dated the monarchy and the prophets: in other words, that P was even later than D. This insight dawned on Vatke, and might have become generally accepted when he published it in his *Biblical Theology* in the vintage year 1835. Its implications were seen at once, and rejected, by the conservative Hengstenberg, who neatly summarized it in the phrase *lex post prophetas* ('the law is later than the prophets')—a phrase which in the 1890s would become a classic way of stating Wellhausen's hypothesis. But wine that would be acclaimed in an average year seems unimpressive when it comes from a year as good as 1835; and Vatke's breakthrough, real though it was, was lost to sight in the upheaval resulting from Strauss's *succès de scandale*. Anyway, Vatke was a Hegelian; and though his redating of P did not in reality depend on his adherence to Hegel's philosophy (indeed, Wellhausen was to show that it ultimately led to conclusions irreconcilable with Hegelianism), he did not realize this himself, and his critics thought the two were inextricably connected. Unfortunately for Vatke he had needlessly hitched a perfectly sound historical and literary theory to a philosophical star that was just about to fall. As Hegelianism ceased in the later nineteenth century to be a live option in Germany, so Vatke's theories about P were largely forgotten. Wellhausen was to learn of the hypothesis that P was later than the prophets from K. H. Graf, whose research was inspired directly by his reading of de Wette, unmediated by any familiarity with Vatke; and Wellhausen himself apparently did not read Vatke until after he was already convinced of the late dating of P.

Wellhausen had, in fact, rather little interest in philosophy as such, whether Hegelian or not. In 1908 he wrote: 'The two friends who published their work in 1835 [i.e. Vatke and Strauss] were indeed Hegelians; but what is of value for our discipline in their work does not derive from Hegel.' What was 'of value', in Wellhausen's view, was not Vatke's dubious philosophy of history, but his solution of the essentially *literary* problem of the relative dates of the four Pentateuchal sources. This literary theory, in its turn, mattered to Wellhausen not for its inherent interest but rather because it provided the necessary precondition for writing a properly critical and objective *history* of Israel, free from contamination by *any* particular philosophical theory. In this

Wellhausen is clearly the direct heir of de Wette, undertaking precisely the same task de Wette had set before him, but without (as he saw it) de Wette's mistaken assumption of the antiquity of P in relation to the other Pentateuchal sources.

The detailed evidence for the precise division of the sources and their dates is not to be found in Wellhausen's famous *Prolegomena to the History of Israel* (1878, as *History of Israel*, i; renamed for the 2nd edn. of 1883), but in a series of articles published in the *Jahrbuch für deutsche Theologie* in 1876–7. The *Prolegomena* makes it clear that (as we have said) this complex literary analysis of the Pentateuch had its primary importance in the access it gave to the history of Israel and of its institutions, and that this in turn was of interest because it had abiding importance not just for knowledge but also for faith. Most students of the Bible probably think of Wellhausen's theory as merely the most successful among a number of rival nineteenth-century theories about the literary analysis of the Pentateuch, and would never think of bringing it into a discussion of Old Testament *theology*, let alone religious *faith*. Indeed, one of the commonest reactions to Pentateuchal criticism is to ask how the Bible can continue to have any religious value once it has been torn (as people say) into countless fragments. Yet this reaction amounts to a complete misunderstanding of Wellhausen's aims, as we shall see.

First and foremost, Wellhausen was a historian. Unlike Vatke, he had little concern for a philosophy of history—indeed, he was impatient with large systems and abstract speculation. He was anti-Hegelian in spirit, interested far more in the detailed particularity of contingent historical events than in overarching theories about the 'self-realization of Spirit in the world', or similar grandiose matters—which by the 1870s had long been out of fashion anyway. Wellhausen's affinities are rather with the great nineteenth-century German historians, B. G. Niebuhr, Ranke, and Mommsen. These historians of classical antiquity certainly did not restrict their concern to 'mere' brute facts—they were not positivists; but on the other hand they were concerned that any large-scale reconstruction of the history of nations, still more of 'world history', should rest on a painstaking examination of original sources, with a close attention to detail and an openness to whatever might turn out to be the case that altogether avoided any presuppositions about what 'must have' happened. Mommsen summed up his procedure in these words, which can still stand today as the hallmark of responsible historical scholarship:

Our life-nerve is research free of presuppositions: the kind of research which does not discover what it thinks it desirable to discover, for the sake of some particular aim or interest . . . but discovers what appears to the historian to be logically and historically correct—in a word: the pursuit of truth.

Just as the historian of ancient Greece or Rome must first date, classify, and critically evaluate his sources, so Wellhausen believed that any serious historian of Israel must begin with a rigorous examination of the available source-material. But a century and more of critical literary scholarship had shown that this material was not to be found in the Old Testament writings taken simply as they now stood: such an approach would be simply naïve, as de Wette had convincingly shown seventy years before. There was no alternative to an objective and 'presuppositionless' attempt to date and assess the historical reliability of *all* the strata of tradition in the Old Testament, taking nothing for granted. De Wette had indeed already gone a long way down this road, but in spite of recognizing that D was a work of the late pre-exilic period he had continued to assume that the great bulk of legislation in the Pentateuch, the 'priestly' teaching in Exodus, Leviticus, and Numbers (P), dated from, and had been determinative for, the life of Israel under its kings. This assumption, as Wellhausen saw it, was largely the result of failing to compare the central part of the Pentateuch with the historical evidence for what life under the monarchy had actually been like.

Wellhausen proposes that we abandon altogether speculations about which parts of the Pentateuch are *inherently* likely to be old, and instead try to establish a framework by examining the evidence from other parts of the Old Testament for the practical development of Israel's institutions. There are three great blocks of material in the Old Testament that have to be considered: the work of the 'Chronicler' (1 and 2 Chronicles, Ezra, and Nehemiah), universally agreed to come from well after the Exile; the earlier histories

(Joshua, Judges, Samuel, Kings), which are our main source for the political and social history of the pre-exilic age; and the works of the pre-exilic prophets (Amos, Hosea, Isaiah, Micah, Jeremiah). So Wellhausen combed these books for material about Israelite institutions in the periods with which they deal; and the conclusions he came to—summed up in the formula 'JEDP', which seems innocent to the point of banality to so many students of the Old Testament—changed the face of biblical studies and had immense repercussions for the faith of any reader of the Bible, Jew or Christian. Wellhausen's method is historical and literary, but its implications are deeply theological.

Wellhausen's conclusions are simple to state. The Priestly Document (P), which contains almost all the laws and customs that go to produce the religious system we know as 'Judaism', was unknown until after the Exile. Neither the earlier histories nor the pre-exilic prophets show any awareness of the distinctive P material. It is not until the Chronicler that we find evidence that Jewish institutional life was modelled on the ideals that P sets before its readers. Israel before the Exile knew nothing of complex rites of atonement, nothing of food laws and regulations about ritual purity, and little, indeed, of the transcendent monotheism that Jews and Christians were later to take for granted. All this comes in after the Exile, and the P document cannot therefore be earlier than this. When modern students come to Wellhausen, they tend to see his argument that P is the latest source rather than the earliest as the important point, with the examination of the rest of the Old Testament that led to this conclusion as mere background. But in reality the late dating of P is a consequence of a radical shift in understanding the development of Israel's institutions and hence the development of its religion. It is not merely a minor adjustment to a theory about the Pentateuch; it is a new way of seeing the entire Old Testament.

On Wellhausen's hypothesis, Israel before the Exile did not practise anything that could reasonably be called 'Judaism'; for the religion of that time lacked almost all the distinctive features of the faith and practice of the religion we now call Jewish. The god of the pre-exilic Hebrew kingdoms, 'Jehovah' or Yahweh, was thought of by most people as one among many, and although from the time of

Elijah (ninth century BC) there was an increasing movement towards the worship of Yahweh alone, it was not until after the Exile in the sixth century that this became monotheism properly so called. But the achievement of a theoretical monotheism was not, for Wellhausen, the unmixed blessing that more 'evolutionary' scholars such as the Hegelian Vatke had thought it: in good measure it represented the triumph of abstract speculation over spontaneous feeling for God and his ways. Thus, for example, the sacred festivals of pre-exilic, polytheistic Israel, like those of Israel's neighbours, were joyful and spontaneously lively occasions, altogether lacking the rather dismal and exclusive interest in atonement for sin that came to characterize the worship of the post-exilic Temple and the Synagogue. Early Israel had few regulations about purity, and indeed its religion had in general little connection with the ethics of a rule-book or systematic code: it was the 'natural' religion of a simple agricultural people. If there are any 'presuppositions' here, they are more Romantic than Hegelian; Wellhausen is the heir of Herder (see p. 97) rather than of Hegel. But, in any case, however much such presuppositions may have influenced Wellhausen's *value-judgements* on the religious outlook of Israel before and after the Exile, his *reconstruction* of it appeals exclusively to evidence which is publicly available in the biblical text, and should be tested against that evidence, not judged according to whether or not one happens to share his preference for 'natural' religion.

The profoundest and most individual expression of what was best in pre-exilic religion is to be found, according to Wellhausen, in the prophets. In them the spirit of spontaneous response to the living God of Israel reaches its most perfect form. Other scholars in Wellhausen's day emphasized the creative and innovative achievements of the prophets to an extent that he himself thought rather exaggerated. In the work of B. Duhm (1847–1928) the prophets come to be seen almost as the *founders* of that 'ethical monotheism' which people in the twentieth century have sometimes seen as the Old Testament's chief contribution to religious thought. Though Wellhausen himself did not detach the prophets so sharply from their context as this, he did nevertheless regard them as representing a high point in pre-exilic religion. He approved of them as individual religious 'geniuses'—in this, no doubt, revealing his essentially romantic sympathies; and there is evidence that he saw in them the kind of 'hero' that Carlyle (whom he enjoyed reading) saw as crucial in the development of any great nation. He believed that they had seen, as few others before them ever had, the importance of a personal and freely given response of obedience to a personal and gracious God, untrammelled by ethical 'systems'. The 'Yahwism' of the prophets, in fact, seems not unlike the Christianity of Adolf Harnack.

'Judaism', the religion of the artificial religious community (scarcely any longer a 'nation') that returned from exile or that continued to live dispersed among other peoples, represents a decisively new, and for Wellhausen utterly unattractive, religious outlook. In the proclamation of the prophets there had been no attempt to codify the response to God into any kind of religious 'law'. But after the Exile the Priestly writers took precisely this fateful step. In P, ethical obligation is no longer the spontaneous overflow of devotion to God: it is a system, with minute regulations to govern every aspect of life, in which the prophetic imperative to 'do justice and love kindness, and walk humbly with God' (Micah 6: 8) has been turned into a purely negative and restrictive set of devices for avoiding sin, and there is an enormous superstructure of petty regulations to enable the consequences of such minor sins as will unfortunately remain to be ritually averted. Post-exilic Israel, said Wellhausen, misheard and misunderstood the prophets, and its spiritual leaders devised a religion which was, indeed, marked by a monotheistic faith and a concern for ethics—so far, so good—but also by a leaden legalism and an obsession with the minutiae of meaningless rituals. In short, post-exilic Judaism, the religion of the Priestly document, was enslaved to the deadness of the letter instead of being liberated by the freedom of the Spirit. The 'Pharisaism' which we encounter in the Gospels is just the logical conclusion of the course on which the writer of P had set the nation—a joyless, loveless religion of rules and regulations, from which in reality the living God has been banished, despite the hypocritical pretence that he is being duly honoured.

Modern Jews and Christians alike will recoil in horror from what must now seem a caricature of Judaism, and will not be surprised that Wellhausen has been suspected of anti-Semitism. But seen in historical context he is not at all the monster that such an instinctive reaction would make him. His concern was not to awaken hatred for Judaism; his presentation of it, misleading as it is, was merely a commonly received opinion in the academic world of his day. In concluding that P was the latest of the sources, indeed post-exilic in date, Wellhausen was not seeking to debunk it or the Jewish system that flowed from it, but was clearing it out of the way so far as the reconstruction of *pre*-exilic Yahwism was concerned. 'Judaism' or 'legalism' (in many ways equated more with medieval Catholicism than with the Judaism of his own day) is merely a foil for presenting the religion that had its finest flowering in the preaching of the great prophets, and which for him is the element of lasting value in the Old Testament. Even if Wellhausen's work on the Pentateuch is sometimes rejected, the position of prominence that his theory gave to the prophets lives on, and has been a source of inspiration to both Jews and Christians. It does not take much imagination to see that Jesus, as understood in liberal Protestant circles of Wellhausen's day, is very like one of the pre-exilic prophets as Wellhausen reconstructs them: preaching the sovereignty of God and the superiority of spontaneous ethical conduct over ritual observance, of open-hearted love for God over legalistic piety. Wellhausen's hypothesis about the development of the religious institutions of Israel, far from being an arid or obscurantist dissection of the Pentateuch as an 'academic' exercise, belongs to the world of theology and even of religious preaching. It does not merely provide historical data which biblical interpretation then has to deal with; it is itself an example of biblical interpretation.

It is tempting, of course, to say that Wellhausen's subconscious theological agenda must have determined his conclusions—the apparatus of scholarly study was only a cover for a theological theory arrived at on quite other grounds. Even if he is acquitted of anti-Semitism, we can convict him of liberal Protestantism, or of romanticism. But this would be to miss the point. Wellhausen was, as we have seen, first and foremost a historian. Almost all readers of the Old Testament can feel the plausibility of saying that you do not need to know your way around the ritual laws of the Pentateuch to understand what is going on in the historical and prophetic books, whereas you cannot possibly understand post-exilic or modern

Judaism without a detailed knowedge of them: this is a historical judgement, which commends itself to many readers with no theological axes to grind. It is quite possible to set up alternative theories to account for this fact, but the data that Wellhausen's theory seeks to explain are really there, not figments of the imagination. To say that Wellhausen had religious or theological interests, then, is not to accuse him of a lack of objectivity in applying historical methods. Such an accusation could not possibly rest merely on knowing what his 'presuppositions' were, but only on actually examining his arguments in detail and checking them against the evidence of the text. To say that he had religious interests is, rather, to defend him against any suspicion that he was a mere antiquarian. In reconstrucing the growth of the Pentateuch and the history of Israel's religious institutions, Wellhausen used historical methods: no other methods will do the job. But he did not attempt this task simply because it was inherently interesting (though it is), but because, in the end, it was deeply relevant to questions of religious faith current in his own day.

Wellhausen was as astonished at suggestions that his work had no importance for theology but was 'mere history', as he was at the equal and opposite suspicion that he had smuggled covert theological presuppositions into his historical reconstructions. As a historian, he had no other motive than to write about the history of Israel and its institutions 'as it had really been' (in Ranke's famous phrase). But as a Christian, and a theologian, he saw no reason why he should not express value-judgements on the various historical realities he had discovered. He did not have what would now be called a 'hermeneutic' of the Old Testament, in the sense of seeking to read it from a particular theological standpoint that would render every part of it fruitful for faith, however apparently unpromising. Rather, he tried to read the Old Testament with the greatest possible objectivity, but then to reflect theologically on what he had read. He wrote what may be called the first fully 'secular' or 'non-miraculous' history of Israel, thus bringing the wrath of ecclesiastical authority down on his head; but for him the very fact that a 'profane' (to use his favourite term) history of Israel was possible had rich implications for the character of God and the manner of his involvement with human affairs. It was, surely, of the utmost religious significance that God had chosen to reveal himself by getting involved in the ordinary life of a nation 'like other nations', which was not exempt from the normal pressures of historical forces, and whose history could therefore be written according to the normal canons of historical enquiry, rather than being known only in an unreal or imaginary world of miracle on a supernatural plane.

In trying to turn itself into a 'holy people', an ark of salvation which rejected all the characteristics of 'normal' nations, post-exilic Israel had, in Wellhausen's judgement, erred grievously; for true holiness, he believed, lay in the living of 'profane' life in the presence of God, as in earlier times the Israelites had well understood. It did not lie in an attempt to *abolish* the profane and secular and to escape into a hermetically sealed realm with its own special rules. Wellhausen, in fact, anticipated some of the 'secular theologies' of the 1960s, as well as hinting (more profoundly) at themes which modern sacramental and liturgical theology has rediscovered. Undoubtedly he believed that the Christian Church had erred in many periods in encouraging an unnatural detachment from the secular world—as though God could be contaminated by contact with realities he himself had made! Those who suspect anti-Semitism in Wellhausen's stance should note that his most barbed criticisms are always of forms of *Christianity* that exhibit the tendencies he identified in P.

Lothar Perlitt sums up the theological conclusions to which Wellhausen's historical work on the Old Testament led him, in words which show clearly how far he was from being a 'mere' historian, and how potentially exciting a theology could be erected on the solid base constructed by so much patient and detailed textual study.

For Wellhausen, the witness that history bears to God lies—hidden, yet at the same time clearly revealed—in its givenness and in its natural course, in such a way that the 'earthly nexus' of events resists any attempt to spiritualize or theologize it. Because God's activity in history cannot be grasped with one's hands, but only with faith, Wellhausen writes the history of Israel as a 'profane' history, analogous to any other history, and renounces any attempt to demonstrate special 'revelations' in it with the tools of the historian. But for him this 'profane' character of history does not exclude 'religious' history, but on the contrary includes it. The historian cannot write salvation history [*Heilsgeschichte*]; but this is because 'salvation history' is simply secular history, seen with the eyes of faith.' (Barton translation)

Liberal Protestantism and beyond

Nobody in late nineteenth-century scholarly work on the New Testament can match the stature of Wellhausen on the Old. This is partly because the decisive historical steps had already been taken by Baur, and the main historical tasks remaining were to correct his reconstruction rather than to establish a totally new outline. The point at which a new approach seemed to be necessary was over the question of how the new historical results could be integrated with Christian (in effect, Protestant) theology. Biblical research was being done primarily in German theological faculties whose main responsibility was to train Protestant clergymen. If there was a hidden theological agenda in the historical (including literary) study of the Christian Old Testament, it was inevitably even more apparent in New Testament scholarship. The destruction, so far as academic theology was concerned, of the old biblicist and dogmatic theology had left a theological vacuum, and the Hegelian recipes for filling it had been rejected. Where was the unity of theological study to be found?

It was to the credit of Baur's one-time follower Albrecht Ritschl (1822–89) that he attempted to answer this question, however unsuccessful he may have been at both the historical and the philosophical levels. Despite his efforts, what actually happened was that with the increasing specialization demanded by the new historical disciplines, biblical studies and systematic theology grew apart in a rift which has never been fully healed. Historical study of the prophets, and of the life of Jesus in particular, and also study of the religion of Paul and Luther, provided sufficient religious impulses to allow the theological children of romanticism to pursue their properly academic, i.e. historical and linguistic, tasks without worrying about the truth claims of the doctrinal tradition. Great scholars such as Deissmann and Harnack were religious, moral, and patriotic churchmen, but systematic theology was not their business.

Whereas Baur had wrestled to hold together his critical conclusions in a theological and philosophical interpretation of Christian history that allowed him to speak normatively of God, historical scholarship in the succeeding generations became more positivistic. The implications of this for Christian theology remained more or less concealed for as long as most biblical scholars were themselves personally religious. But however inadequately recognized, the problem of 'the historian and the believer' had in fact arrived: namely, how to combine or integrate biblical (Jewish or Christian) belief in God with a biblical scholarship that was wholly secular in its methods and results, and even in its aims.

The solution outlined in our introductory chapter was dimly perceived, but the hostile philosophical climate of positivism hindered its systematic unfolding, and the political disasters of the twentieth century required stronger medicine. By 1920 in Germany and 1939 in England a liberal theology based on the sympathetic study of religion was out of tune with the times.

The 'eternal covenant', envisaged by Schleiermacher between Christianity and culture, did not fulfil the promise it had held out in the heyday of philosophical idealism. In Germany Hegelianism evaporated, and in Great Britain where it revived, critical biblical scholarship was accepted too late to form a fruitful alliance with it. But the demise by about 1860 of such sophisticated attempts as those of Vatke and Baur to integrate the new historical research within a vision of God and the world did not mean that subsequent biblical scholars allowed the historian and the believer in them to fall apart. The liberals' enthusiasm for the prophets and for Jesus was strongly religious and moral in character. Historical study nourished faith by providing inspiring models, and the religious values of the Bible could be combined with a residual idealism and a new romanticism. This was not quite what Christianity has traditionally expected from its scripture, but it contained elements which need to be included in any account of how the Bible is used in the Synagogue and the Church.

It does not, however, provide much of a foundation for Jewish or Christian belief in God, and it proved religiously satisfactory only to those who already believed in God on other grounds. So long as religion seemed reasonably buoyant, Christian scholars could afford themselves the luxury of a biblical interpretation which sustained religious life at the level of private feelings but failed to integrate their research with a theologically and philosophically responsible Christian talk of God. The collapse of a residually Christian cultural optimism during the First World War precipitated a dissatisfaction with the liberals' 'purely historical', largely untheological, approach to the Bible. This helps explain the eager response in Germany to Karl Barth's extraordinary outbursts, and the later brief enthusiasm for the so-called 'biblical theology movement' in English and American Church circles.

Barth's commentary on *The Epistle to the Romans* (1919, 1921[2]; ET 1933), remains a classic of biblical interpretation, however debatable its value as a contribution to biblical scholarship. His principle (as stated in the prefaces) was to accept the legitimacy and necessity of historical and linguistic scholarship and to preserve their integrity, but to subordinate the application of these methods to the theological aims and interests with which he approached the texts. In opposition to the liberals' tendency to restrict serious academic work to the linguistic and historical tasks, and demote theology to the level of pious afterthoughts, Barth agreed with Strauss, Vatke, and Baur that attaining one's philosophical and theological understanding of God and the world was as intellectually demanding a task as any historical work, and at least as important for biblical interpretation. He differed from these early nineteenth-century idealist theologians in claiming to derive his theological framework more from the Bible itself than from human reason. But his model for the relationship of historical reconstruction and theological interpretation had more in common with Baur's integration of historical research within a philosophical theology, than with most of the later liberals' separation of religiously tinged historical work from theology proper.

This separation of historical scholarship and theological interpretation was challenged and overcome in different ways by Barth and Bultmann, and those influenced by them (e.g. liberation theologians, see p. 157). But it survived, and has remained dominant in the English-speaking world.

There is much to be said for a degree of separation—both from the historical and from the religious side. Where theological interests inform (or infect) historical work the dangers of distortion are high. And from the other side, a Church that wants to be challenged afresh by the biblical witness will welcome a historical research that is not mortgaged to current theological preferences. It also makes sense to settle out of the theological court, and by ordinary rational argument, matters of historical and exegetical concern which have no immediate religious bearing.

But there is then still the problem of the historian and the believer—how to get from historical to theological judgements, if that is one's ultimate aim. The solution proposed in the first chapter was to describe the subject-matter of the Bible as man or religion. Historical and other approaches to the Bible then become part of the scientific study of religion. This may either be an intellectual end in itself, within the humanities, or may provide a new natural theology, by grounding religious talk of God in human experience, and so making intelligible the stance of those who accept the biblical witness and participate in the Jewish or Christian religions. The move from an 'outsider' view of the biblical religion to a Jewish or Christian theological stance, i.e. from description to participation, can be made in private. It need not be visible in one's biblical interpretation.

Our suggestion is that this has been happening in biblical interpretation over the past 150 years. Although most students of the Bible in fact start with religious interests and have these challenged by subsequent historical study, it is also possible to move in the other direction, from reason to faith, however jerky the passage. This involves a jump, and it is not a path taken by many. It is, however, likely to become more common where religious studies are pursued in schools, and the university system continues to cater at a deeper level for interests aroused in this way. Understanding religion is compatible with believing. This convergence of intellectual and religious interests must now be traced beyond the three 'theologians of 1835' and the later leaders of historical theology, to the history of religions school in which the historical movement within Christian theology reached a climax.

Further reading

CHEYNE, T. K., *Founders of Old Testament Criticism* (London, 1893).

CLEMENTS, R., *A Century of Old Testament Study* (London, 1976; Philadelphia, 1984).

GASQUE, WARD W., *A History of the Criticism of the Acts of the Apostles* (Tübingen and Grand Rapids, 1975).

GREENSLADE, S. L. (ed.), *The Cambridge History of the Bible*, iii (Cambridge, 1963).

HARRIS, H., *The Tübingen School* (Oxford, 1975).

HODGSON, P., *The Formation of Historical Theology* (New York, 1966).

JOHNSON, R. A., *The Origins of Demythologizing* (Leiden, 1974).

KNIGHT, D. A. (ed.), *Julius Wellhausen and his Prolegomena to the History of Israel* (Semeia, 25; Chico, 1983).

KRAELING, E., *The Old Testament Since the Reformation* (New York, 1955).

KÜMMEL, W. G., *The New Testament: The History of the Investigation of its Problems* (ET 1970, Nashville, 1972, and London, 1973).

PALS, D. L., *The Victorian 'Lives of Jesus'* (San Antonio, Tex., 1982).

ROGERSON, J., *Old Testament Criticism in the Nineteenth Century: England and Germany* (London, 1984).

SMART, N., *et al.* (eds.), *Nineteenth-century Religious Thought in the West*, iii (Cambridge, 1985).

WELCH, C., *Protestant Thought in the Nineteenth Century*, 2 vols. (New Haven and London, 1972 and 1985).

4

History of Religions and History of Traditions

History and history of religion

The previous chapter focused on the two giants of nineteenth-century historical criticism: Baur, who died in 1860, and Wellhausen, who dominated its later decades. These two men symbolize an astonishing growth in historical knowledge of Israel and early Christianity. Together with such supporting figures as Vatke and Strauss in the earlier period, and Holtzmann and Harnack in the later, they also illustrate another change which took place around the middle of the century: the shift away from synthesizing the new historical knowledge with philosophical and theological convictions to a new historical realism that was hostile to philosophical and theological speculation.

Both Baur and Vatke realized that their understanding of what a text meant to its author could not be entirely separated from what it meant to them. But they were nevertheless as conscious as their successors of the need to see the texts in their original setting; their theological reflection was integrated within conscientious historical research, whatever the flaws in their pioneering work. Subsequent theologically interested biblical interpretation has been historical rather than 'religious' in any pre-critical sense. Only very recently has this fundamentally historical orientation been challenged from within biblical scholarship itself (see Chapters 6 and 7).

The successors of de Wette, Vatke, and Baur fought shy of philosophical terminology and produced historical work that looks much like contemporary biblical scholarship. They were content to describe and reconstruct the past, to understand it from a distance, rather than to penetrate it with their own categories until (as Karl Barth wrote about Calvin's theological interpretation) 'the walls which separate the sixteenth century from the first become transparent. Paul speaks and the man of the sixteenth century hears. The conversation between the original record and the reader moves round the subject-matter . . .' (*The Epistle to the Romans*, p. 7).

The way Barth continues both his preface and his commentary, 'until a distinction between yesterday and today becomes impossible' (ibid.), is intolerable to most historically schooled biblical interpreters. The distinction must be respected. But in his account of the Reformers and conservative nineteenth-century theologians Barth captures something of the way Vatke on Old Testament religion, and Baur and later Bultmann in their theological interpretations of Paul, were 'rethinking the whole material and wrestling with it till the walls . . . become transparent'.

Barth's criticism of the more narrowly historical and linguistic view of interpretation taken by such great historians and textual scholars as Jülicher, Lietzmann, and Harnack continues to pose a challenge to a historically oriented biblical scholarship. It remains an important question for theology whether historical criticism offers it an adequate understanding of the Bible. What is meant by 'genuine understanding and interpretation' in a theological context? Ought it to mean 'that creative energy which Luther exercised with intuitive certainty in his exegesis' (Barth)? If such creative energy is combined with meticulous historical-critical exegesis, as in Bultmann's commentary on John and Käsemann's on Romans (see below, p. 190 f.), are these classics aberrations, or do they highlight an aspect of biblical interpretation which is unduly neglected in contemporary scholarship? If both historical and theological interpretations of the Bible are legitimate, the decisive issue is the aims of the interpreters.

These larger issues will be taken up in Chapter 6. But first it is necessary to trace some significant shifts within the historical paradigm that has guided most modern biblical scholarship.

The late nineteenth-century liberals' stringent historical exegesis did not mean that they were interested in the Bible only as evidence for historical events. Wellhausen was trying to write a political, and to some extent social, history of Israel. Though the route he took led him through questions of literary history and religious practice, he was interested in the *literature* of the Old Testament primarily for what it could tell him about this *history*. But even within his own lifetime the interest in reconstructing the events of Israel's past was being overtaken by a concern to trace the development of its *religion* and its *faith*. And it is again noticeable that the ultimate aim of such enquiries was to find something that would have relevance to the modern believer. But for Wellhausen's successors as for his contemporaries, this relevance was still found in links made between modern concerns and the faith of Israel as reconstructed by normal methods of historical investigation. Theologians were still looking through and behind the texts, not at the literature itself.

This combination of historical scholarship and religious interests both helped and hindered the development of a fully scientific study of biblical religion which could (but need not) be integrated within a modern theology. Religious interests directed attention to biblical religion, but a one-sided emphasis upon religious ideas delayed the development of what W. Robertson Smith (below, p. 140) had begun in *The Religion of the Semites* (1889). The sociological and anthropological study of religious institutions which that work initiated was elsewhere impeded by theological interests in the *ideas* of the Bible. These were considered most important for Christians, and therefore dominated biblical study.

Even when liberal Protestants became more interested in 'religion' than in doctrine, it was ideas and feelings, not rituals or other institutions, that mattered most to them. The prophets' ideas were found more religiously interesting than the law or priesthood; these bore little relation to Protestant practice. New Testament institutions were insufficiently developed to provide much guidance for a later age, but it is striking that controversy about the ministry in the New Testament raged longest in the Anglican Church, which set great store on such matters of Church order and apostolic succession. The recent expansion of sociological interest in both Old and New Testaments has rectified this imbalance. Before considering that, we now trace the development of historical-critical study in its most impressive period.

History of traditions and Old Testament theology

By the last decade of the century the literary questions which had engaged Holtzmann in the New Testament and Wellhausen in the Old, and which continued to exercise Harnack, were no longer at the cutting edge of research. A new generation of scholars felt compelled by their historical interest in the religion of this literature, and their religious interest in the history, to go behind source criticism. They presupposed the results of the older generation, but asked about the prehistory of the traditions, and sought to illuminate this by comparing the biblical material with similar material found elsewhere.

Wellhausen had noted that the great mass of legends and traditions that make up the narrative of the Pentateuch might have a prehistory, rather than having been freely composed by the authors of the four 'sources'; but he saw little point in trying to reconstruct it. Such a task was too hypothetical to be worth while: it would have represented a kind of 'antiquarian' interest, detached from the exegetical study of the actual text before him. Within his lifetime, however, Old Testament studies had shifted its focus, and the 'history of traditions' had become almost the central task of the Old Testament scholar and interpreter. It has remained the characteristic mark of mainstream Old Testament criticism ever since, to such an extent that to some it seems the only scholarly way to read the Old Testament.

Many strands go to make up 'traditio-historical criticism'. Perhaps the chief is the realization that religion in the ancient world was an experience of communities as much as (maybe more than) of individuals, and that significant texts from ancient religions are likely to be the product of lengthy transmission by anonymous groups in the community, rather than the compositions of unusual, gifted individuals. Hermann Gunkel (1862–1932), a younger contemporary of Wellhausen, was the first to develop this insight in relation to Old Testament studies.

In Gunkel's 'history of literary forms', traditionally known in English as 'form criticism', the stories in the Pentateuch (especially the stories of the patriarchs in Genesis) are seen as traditional tales handed down over the years long before any 'author' or 'compiler' fixed them in writing or wove them into a finished document. They do not come to us from individual religious or literary figures, as Wellhausen was felt to have implied; they are an expression of the genius of the Israelite people at large. This sense, that what finds expression in the 'legends' of Genesis is a folk-mentality, fits in with certain trends in the thinking of anthropologists and students of sociology in the early twentieth century, though it also has roots in the eighteenth. The best-known precursor is Herder, with his sense that each 'people' (*Volk*) has its own distinctive character which can be seen in its traditional poetry no less than in the productions of its conscious art. (See the comments on Robert Lowth in Chapter 7.)

But Gunkel went further than this and argued that once we had recognized the proper context in which the individual stories of Genesis had grown up, we could start to reconstruct the various stages through which they had passed. We could press back to the earliest forms of each story; then we could trace the process by which the stories were joined together until they turned into a coherent, connected narrative. The aim of this kind of study was not, it should be noted, to discover 'what really happened'—for many of the stories were legends or myths even in their earliest forms—but to learn about the religious faith which expressed itself in and through such stories. Instead of a monolithic Pentateuch, or even the four independent source-documents postulated by Wellhausen (whose theory he accepted, as far as it went), Gunkel saw the Pentateuch as a *process*. The two-dimensional text contained all the clues we needed to reconstruct the three-dimensional development of Israel's theological traditions, and from it we could discover how the distinctive faith of Israel grew and imposed order on the welter of historical memory, heroic legend, and half-remembered reminiscence which existed dispersed through the folk-consciousness of the nation.

If Wellhausen began to answer the question 'What happened in Israel's history?', Gunkel set the scene for a more obviously theological enquiry into the subtler question, 'How did Israel come by its distinctive faith?' But the full theological implications are scarcely more obvious to the casual reader of Gunkel than they are in Wellhausen. From our perspective, historical questions seem uppermost in his work, even though it is now the history of *traditions* rather than of events or institutions. It is in the generation of scholars that followed Gunkel that the theological agenda in tradition history become apparent; and the great name here is Gerhard von Rad (1901–71).

Significantly, the finished elaboration of von Rad's study of Israel's traditions is enshrined in his *Old Testament Theology*, a title which positively invites the reader to expect some engagement with questions of theological truth as well as with 'merely' historical issues. Nevertheless, von Rad's work is far from tackling the theology that might be found in the Old Testament as it now stands. Theological significance is found, rather, in the basic outline into which the diverse theological and historical traditions of the *community* of the Old Testament ('Israel') have been fitted, and in the meaning which has been given to originally separate stories by their place within this outline. It is possible to state von Rad's theory about the tradition-history of the Old Testament (or more specifically of the Hexateuch, Genesis–Joshua) in theologically neutral terms: possible, but not, he would have thought, profitable. Still, for us it *is* worth attempting this, if only so that the essentially theological interest which the theory serves can be made clearer when the attempt fails.

Von Rad accepts Gunkel's thesis that each of the stories in the Pentateuch had its origin in the life of the early (i.e. pre-tenth-century) Israelite community, or in some particular tribe or local group within the community. Like Gunkel, he sees the context for the transmission of such stories as primarily cultic or liturgical. In other words, any given patriarchal story (e.g. Jacob's dream at Bethel, Genesis 28) was told again and again in the worship of the local sanctuary at Bethel as an explanation of the Israelite cult there. It was a local tradition, unrelated to wider perspectives on the history of the Israelite 'nation'—which at this early period did not yet exist as a unified whole. But even in this early period *some* group or groups within what was later to be 'Israel' did already discern the dim outlines of a larger historical scheme. This scheme, which von Rad believed to be preserved in such texts as Deuteronomy 26: 5–10, spoke of Israel's history as a series of purposive acts controlled by its God, Yahweh. As a minimum, the series included the idea that the Israelite ancestors had come from the east (from Aram, i.e. Syria), had endured bondage in Egypt, and had been miraculously delivered by Yahweh and given the land of Palestine as a permanent home. With later additions, such as details of the covenant made through Moses at Sinai, the story of Joseph, and so on, this basic historical outline had become the ground-plan of the whole Hexateuch. By the end of the long process (lasting some six or seven hundred years) by which the Hexateuch took its present shape, all the old traditions had been loosed from their moorings in the cultic life of individual groups and made to serve the overall purpose of showing how Yahweh's plan for his whole people had come to fulfilment. What von Rad gives us, therefore, is nothing less than a complete history of Israel's historical traditions; a history which plausibly shows how memories originally transmitted orally, and for some entirely local purpose, came eventually to be part of an extremely distinctive faith, the faith of the Israel of 'Old Testament times'.

It is possible to argue that the traditio-historical method is not so rigorous as it looks in the hands of a master such as von Rad, or that the material on which it is practised is actually too vague or fragmentary for these reconstructions to carry conviction. Nevertheless, it is bound to strike most observers as a method that could in principle be applied to any ancient corpus of narrative literature; if it has shortcomings, they do not seem to be related to any particular theological concern that von Rad may have had. It looks like a particular kind of historical method, developed with a rather special kind of historical evidence in mind, namely, literary versions of ancient folklore. It comes as no surprise to find that similar methods have been used in studying the Homeric literature or the sagas of medieval Iceland. Yet von Rad himself clearly thought that to do traditio-historical work on the Hexateuch was in itself to do Old Testament *theology*; and the interesting (perhaps puzzling) feature of his work for our immediate purposes is this sense that, when the history of the traditions has been written, there is no more for the biblical theologian to do. Von Rad was deeply opposed to the positivism of scholars who thought that the biblical specialist's work had been done once he had recovered the 'real history' of Israel—as though brute facts about the past constituted theology. Tradition-history marks a great advance on that view. What mattered theologically for Israel was not *what actually happened* at the Red Sea—a seasonal wind rippling some reeds, or seasonal flooding leaving suitably sticky mud for Pharaoh's chariots to get stuck in; what mattered for Israel's faith was the Exodus *as interpreted by her theological traditions*. Belief in 'the Exodus' is a matter of credal affirmation or of faith-commitment, not an acceptance of some particular historical reconstruction.

Yet this assertion of a peculiarly theological dimension does not seem, on reflection, to go quite far enough. True, it substitutes for a historical reconstruction of events a historical reconstruction of theological beliefs; and it is perhaps better to be interested in 'what Israel believed' than in 'what happened to Israel', if one is looking for something of religious value in the Old Testament. But there is still a logical gap between 'what Israel believed' and 'what we (should) believe'. The fact that what has been reconstructed is faith, rather than event, does not remove the reconstruction from the realm of historical study and bring it into systematic theology or contemporary belief. An interest in the religion rather than the history of Israel still does not bridge the gap between *then* and *now*.

So there is something paradoxical about von Rad's use of traditio-historical criticism to write an *Old Testament Theology*. On the one hand, it makes the theological concern of his study explicit in a way that was not the case for Wellhausen or even for Gunkel. He does not claim to be a 'mere' historian; his work is, and is explicitly acknowledged to be, *theological* interpretation of the Bible. Yet, on the other hand, when we examine his work it seems in reality much more neutral theologically than he himself was willing to recognize. In the last resort his *Theology* is a description, based on historical reconstruction and vulnerable to historical examination, of what ancient Israelites believed; it is historical theology rather than an interpretation of the Old Testament in a modern context. Wellhausen, in a way, seems to have had a much simpler and more satisfactory view of these matters. He wrote a straightforwardly 'secular' history of Israel, conceiving his duty as being to historical truth rather than to religious faith; but, as a believer, he then felt entirely free to comment theologically on the history he had written.

Von Rad's attempt to fuse history with theology looks superficially as if it will be more 'religious', but perhaps in the end is merely more ambiguous and confused, and open to the suspicion that it smuggles religious prejudices into historical reconstruction under cover of darkness.

Is it possible for tradition-history to contribute more than this to biblical interpretation? Old Testament scholarship continues, as we have said, to be primarily traditio-historical in orientation, and so it may be supposed that biblical scholars in general do think that the method is more than merely an aid to writing a history of religious thought in Israel. One possible line of approach might be as follows. Taken at face value, the Old Testament depicts the history of Israel as a history of salvation, in the straightforward sense that God himself was the agent of all the great events which the Old Testament records. Until the rise of critical scholarship, Jews and Christians substantially accepted this account of the matter. Once biblical scholars had cast doubt on the veracity of many Old Testament accounts (including even those of such crucial events as the Exodus), it could superficially have seemed that this whole notion of divine guidance in history was discredited. However, it might be thought that God's purpose in guiding the nation of Israel was not really located in what *happened* to the people, but in the *ideas* they formed of him and the theological *understanding* at which they arrived. The true 'history of salvation' is therefore the history of traditions. In giving an explanation of the route by which Israel came to an understanding of the nature of God and of her relationship to him, tradition critics are in reality telling the true 'saving history'. The process of tradition, rather than the political history of Israel, is the true *locus* of God's self-revelation to Israel; to enter imaginatively into that process *is* therefore to grasp theological truth. Along these lines some later disciples of von Rad have tried to show that historical scholarship is a properly theological pursuit, provided that it takes the form of traditio-historical criticism. As D. F. Knight puts it, 'Our access to Old Testament revelation is through the tradition and the tradition process.'

This is a subtle and persuasive suggestion, and some such rationale probably underlies a great deal of historical-critical work on the Bible. In many ways it amounts to a return to Vatke, and even to Hegel himself, though Old Testament scholars may not relish this suggestion. The flaw in it, however, can be stated very simply. How can we locate 'revelation' in the process that led Israel to develop and eventually to 'canonize' traditions, when the explicit conceptual content of these traditions states that revelation is actually located somewhere else, namely, in certain things that God has said and done? The fundamentalist, who naïvely feels that it is odd to claim that you have deepened your understanding of the religious claim a biblical book makes on you when you have shown it to be full of historical inaccuracies, has a point against this kind of claim for tradition-history. It is quite consistent to claim that divine Providence both directed *events* in a certain way in Israel's history and controlled the *traditions* that grew up to interpret those events in such an unerring way that they were correctly interpreted: one can, that is, consistently locate revelation in both events *and* traditions. It is also quite consistent to say, as von Rad does, that *as evidence for the faith Israel actually held*, the history of traditions is more important than the history of events: it was the Red Sea crossing as remembered and recounted that influenced the faith of the Israelites, not the (perhaps rather trivial) incident that lay at the root of that memory and that tale. This is a purely historical point about what as a matter of fact was important in ancient times. But once we try to make the traditio-historical approach theologically normative *for ourselves*, the fact that many of the traditions falsified the events they recounted needs once again to be on the agenda. There may be ways out of this impasse, but it strongly suggests that the history of traditions alone does not form a broad enough base for integrating biblical study with theology. To interpret the Bible today we cannot bypass tradition-history, but nor can we regard tradition-history as sufficient.

However, though tradition-history is not in itself a theological discipline, there is another, more specific, way in which von Rad's own particular brand of it does make very close contact indeed with one major brand of systematic theology. For him, it is not a shortcoming that in its traditions Israel held by faith to an interpretation of its history so much at odds with what we can reconstruct of the political realities of that history. On the contrary, he thinks this is an advantage from a theological point of view.

'Salvation history' is confessional history *by contrast with* 'mere', 'factual', 'positivistic' history. The Israel of von Rad's *Old Testament Theology* walks by faith, not by sight, believing where she may not prove. The English reader may well suspect here that a rather particular theological axe is being ground, which goes by the name of Justification by Faith. To rest faith (Israel's faith *or* our faith) on the historically provable is nothing more than to rest it on a human 'work', on 'evidence'; Israel (and we) must believe that God is her (and our) saviour as an article of *faith*, not as a matter for historical *proof*. Indeed, Israel did not even have *articles* of faith in any intellectualist sense; the outline of their history, through which they expressed their belief that God was, had been, and would be with them to save, was for use in praise and confession, not in abstract speculation. Now the voice here is von Rad's voice, but the hands are the hands of Luther. One reason, perhaps, why English readers do not find von Rad as obviously attractive as many scholars in Germany or America have done may be that they do not naturally warm to this approach. Points that for von Rad were too obvious to need stating do not seem evident at all in a non-Lutheran context, especially when the indigenous tradition has tended to be definitely historicist. Bultmann has suffered from a similar lack of sympathetic understanding in Britain, and for much the same reason.

But once again we must be on our guard, and not suggest that confessional prejudice has simply *replaced* academic objectivity. As with Wellhausen, so too here: the interpretation of the biblical data may owe much to a particular theological position, but it is an interpretation of data that are really there in the text. The Old Testament very plainly *is* a book of faith, expressing a conscious decision to take history as manifesting a certain divine plan, whatever the odds; and the stories in Genesis, which surely *must* have had an oral prehistory (just as Gunkel thought), do now serve the purpose of endorsing Israel's faith, rather than of providing objective historical information about clan-movements in the second millennium BC. Von Rad did not invent the idea that the first story about an Israelite ancestor has him setting out in faith, not knowing what is to befall him, but trusting in the promises of God: Genesis 12 is there for all to read. And what of the idea of justification by faith? In applying it to the study of the Old

Testament, von Rad may be reading Lutheran notions into the Bible—but where do those notions come from in the first place? Partly, at least, from the Bible itself. The matter is not so simple as it may seem to a critic on the look-out for chinks in the armour of great scholars. 'Objectivity' and 'prejudice' are both quite slippery terms.

From history of traditions to New Testament theology

The natural New Testament parallel to von Rad is Rudolf Bultmann. Just as Baur's achievement in New Testament history and theology matches both Vatke's theological interpretation and Wellhausen's historical reconstruction, so Bultmann's dual achievement parallels both the form criticism of Gunkel, developed further by von Rad, and also the latter's attempt to interpret these traditions and their history in the new theological situation after the First World War.

Bultmann's theological interpretation (and here again he is like Vatke and Baur) involved a more deliberate use of modern philosophy than did that of Wellhausen or von Rad. The determination to combine talk of God with talk of human existence owes as much to Luther as to the 'existentialism' of Kierkegaard, which is most apparent in Bultmann's interpretation of the Fourth Gospel. But his interpretation of Paul in particular borrowed the philosophical conceptuality through which his friend and colleague Heidegger had, in 1927, analysed human existence. The resulting 'existentialist theology' consequently excited more opposition than the theology of his younger contemporary, von Rad.

But despite opposition, Bultmann's synthesis dominated the field for over a generation. His existentialism, like Baur's Hegelianism a century earlier, is now proving less durable than the historical methods with which both were combined. Its individualism and pessimism, which found an echo in mid-twentieth-century Europe, are an inadequate response to the challenges of contemporary society. Furthermore, the Pauline and Lutheran 'kerygmatic theology' (so called on account of its emphasis upon the 'kerygma' or preaching) with which this was associated sounds rather narrow in a socially engaged Church. Bultmann is more central to contemporary scholarship than to contemporary theology. At least, there is nowadays more serious discussion of the history of traditions and history of religions emphases that he inherited from his liberal Protestant teachers than of the philosophical and theological components of his New Testament theology.

Even those historical emphases are now under some pressure from the anti-historical mood of a new generation. But before reaching these latest developments we must consider from the New Testament side the combination of historical research and theological interpretation achieved in the German Protestant context as liberal Protestantism gave way to more Reformation styles of theology. This combination of the liberal Protestant achievements in historical research with a new theological impetus resulted in some of the present century's most creative and characteristic biblical interpretation.

In his classic form-critical work, *The History of the Synoptic Tradition* (1921, 1931[2]; ET 1963), Bultmann followed Gunkel's method of analysing the small units of tradition from which the Synoptic Gospels, like Genesis and the Psalter, were largely composed. He thought that literary analysis of the typical forms in which the traditions were preserved would show how they had been used in the early communities. Recognition of their *Sitz im Leben* or 'setting in the life' of the early Church would throw light on the tunnel period between Jesus and the Gospels.

Bultmann was not much interested in the literary analysis for its own sake, nor in the sociological insights into the early Church which this approach suggested. His analysis of how the various forms of tradition functioned in their original social contexts was undertaken, as the title of his book implies, for the sake of the historical investigation which had already (in 1921) dominated biblical scholarship for almost a century. The literary and sociological questions implicit in form criticism would have to wait a couple of generations for a theological climate more favourable to social-scientific and literary approaches. From the 1920s to the 1960s and beyond history remained the dominant intellectual partner for theology.

But as with von Rad, it was the history of the word proclaimed and traditions transmitted, rather than events and social realities, that interested Bultmann. And this shift of attention away from the events reported and towards their transmission by anonymous preachers, teachers, worshippers, collectors, and editors contributed to a renewed scepticism about the historicity of the Gospels. 'We must recognise', wrote Bultmann in 1926, 'that a literary work or fragment of tradition is a primary source for the historical situation out of which it arose, and is only a secondary source for the historical details concerning which it gives information.' That had negative implications for life-of-Jesus research, and so for the liberal theology based on that, while proving positively suggestive for the new theologies of the Word. This partly explains the impact of form criticism within German Protestantism and the resistance it encountered elsewhere.

But only partly. The other reason why form criticism took instant root in Germany was that its presuppositions were already present in German history of religions and history of traditions research. Bultmann's expectation that the comparative study of folk literature would clarify the laws governing the transmission of such material, and so illuminate the history of the synoptic tradition, was over-optimistic; the time-span between Jesus and the Gospels is too short. Non-Germans were unimpressed by the extravagant claims made for the new method, quite apart from their hostility to its sceptical conclusions. But where history of traditions work was already gaining recognition, form criticism made a decisive impact. Bultmann's analysis of the synoptic tradition was particularly influential because it picked up and significantly advanced the preceding generation of German research, and focused it in a way that carried the new history of traditions approach to its dominating position in biblical scholarship. Its impact was then gradually felt outside Germany as its antecedents became more widely accepted.

One aspect of Bultmann's work which was to develop a long tail was his attention to the alterations to Mark made by the later evangelists. His intention was to derive criteria for judging how the tradition may have developed in the earlier stages, from what can be observed (assuming Markan priority) at these later stages. That was precarious, because oral and written traditions develop differently in the course of transmission; but it does provide some guidance. More importantly, it laid the ground for the later elaboration of history of traditions research in 'redaction criticism', where the individual evangelist's 'redaction' (i.e. editing) of his traditions was subjected to microscopic scrutiny.

In both form and redaction criticism, history of traditions research drew the consequences of William Wrede's pioneering monograph *The Messianic Secret in the Gospels* (1901; ET 1971), which has thus emerged (after strong initial resistance) as the harbinger of twentieth-century Gospel criticism.

Despite some unclarities and some flaws in his explanation of what he observed, Wrede made a strong case for saying that much in Mark's narrative which had been read as accurate historical reporting in fact reflected a theological or doctrinal interest of the early Church and the evangelist. Strauss and Baur had long since persuaded liberal scholars that the traditions of Jesus' supernatural acts, and the legendary stories about him, had a history of their own in the early Church, and that the Johannine discourses were unhistorical. Wrede now expressed a similar scepticism about some of what in the Synoptic Gospels Jesus said on the theologically sensitive topic of his status. He argued that Jesus' instructions to keep his messianic identity and activity secret, and the evangelists' comments about this, are early Christian theology, not historical report.

Neither Wrede nor Bultmann would have wished to be linked with Strauss, but the comparison spotlights the negative consequences of their history of traditions work. Since neither Strauss nor Bultmann was theologically interested in the historical Jesus, the scepticism endemic in their history of traditions accounts of what had happened to the Gospel material between Jesus and the evangelists caused them no embarrassment. Strauss boasted in his Preface of 'the internal liberation of the feelings and intellect' from traditional Christology, which resulted from accepting Hegel; and Bultmann wrote, in 1927,

I have never yet felt uncomfortable with my critical radicalism . . . I calmly let the fire burn, for I see what is consumed is only the fanciful portraits of Life of Jesus theology.

The critical radicalism of Strauss and Bultmann posed no problems for their Christologies, which required little history. But it was deeply at odds with the liberal theology of Wrede's contemporaries whose Christology was supposedly based on the 'historical Jesus' as distinct from the 'Christ of faith' and dogma, i.e. as distinct from the Jesus elaborated in the early Church's memory. That distinction is essential to critical historical study of the Gospels and lay at the base of the liberals' Christology. But Wrede and later Bultmann drew historical consequences which threatened not only the classical dogma, but also the liberals' substitute. If the historical truth about Jesus was too far removed from the Gospel pictures, the liberal appeal to this could no longer provide a credible Christian alternative to orthodoxy. Furthermore, the century-long attempt to answer Reimarus by securing the connection between the historical Jesus and the Christ of faith had apparently failed. A flight from history was perhaps the best theological option for anyone convinced by the new scepticism.

Needless to say, many were not so convinced. It is impossible to say how far theological interests contributed to their hostility to form criticism. But non-Germans who had only recently accepted the liberals' historical Jesus as a substitute for, or modification to, their traditional Christology were hardly likely to welcome these latest critical bombshells from Wrede and Bultmann. Historical scepticism had positive attractions for Germans committed to Karl Barth's theology of the Word, but none for other theologians. Before considering these neo-Reformation theologies there is another point at which the liberals' own further historical research undercut their theological reliance on the historical Jesus.

The history of traditions problem focused by Wrede and developed by Bultmann can be matched by a history of religions problem posed by Bultmann's teacher, Johannes Weiss, and highlighted for English readers by Albert Schweitzer's *Von Reimarus zu Wrede* (1906; ET 1910: *The Quest of the Historical Jesus*, see above, p. 45).

In *Jesus' Proclamation of the Kingdom of God* (1892; ET 1971), Weiss expressed a fundamental principle of the history of religions school (and also of Reimarus, see above, p. 55), that New Testament terms must be understood in the context of their first-century Jewish background. The key phrase in Jesus' message must therefore be given its full eschatological force and not be translated into the ethical idealism of Kant's philosophy and Ritschl's theology. This rediscovery of eschatology, dramatized in Schweitzer's *Quest*, made more headway in England than Wrede's scepticism. Jewish apocalyptic had already been studied by British biblical scholars, and some theologians felt (rather dubiously) that an apocalyptic Jesus was more Christian, because more mysterious and more God-centred, than the liberals' perfect man. Schweitzer himself, by contrast, thought that his historical conclusion that Jesus was a deluded apocalyptic fanatic was religiously worthless. The different historical conclusions of both Schweitzer and Wrede on the Gospels undercut in different ways any theology based on the historical Jesus.

A more directly theological attack on liberal 'life of Jesus theology' was made by Martin Kähler, whose pamphlet *The So-called Historical Jesus and the Historic Biblical Christ* (1892, 1896[2]; ET 1964) in effect adopted the liberals' distinction between the historical Jesus and the Christ of faith, but argued against the liberals that Christianity was interested only in the latter: 'The real Christ is the preached Christ', i.e. the Christ of faith. Kähler's Pauline and Lutheran stress upon the 'preached' Christ of the whole Bible, at the expense of the hypothetical figure reconstructed by modern historians, thus foreshadowed the theological movement of the 1920s initiated by Barth's *Romans* and embraced by Bultmann.

This twentieth-century 'theology of the Word', like parts of Paul and Luther, located the contemporary event of revelation in the proclaimed Word that is heard in faith. Like the Fathers and Reformers, it did 'theology as interpretation of scripture', and so produced a theology closely related to preaching. Bultmann was able to combine the new kerygmatic emphasis with his form-critical interest in the preaching of the early Church reflected in the Gospels because these early Christians had also expressed their faith by interpreting their traditions, and were more concerned to preach than to preserve history or biography. History of traditions work thus supported the new theology in two ways: negatively, by undercutting the liberals' Christology through its historical scepticism ('I calmly let the fire burn', above, p. 107); and positively, by focusing on how the New Testament material was itself shaped by the processes in which the new theology claimed that revelation still occurs today. There is no evidence for a causal connection between Bultmann's historical conclusions and his theological interpretation, but they certainly dovetail neatly.

The positive side of Bultmann's synthesis became clear in his interpretation of Paul (1930, and at length in *The Theology of the New Testament*, i (1948; ET 1952)), and above all in *The Gospel of John* (1941; ET 1971). History of religions and history of traditions hypotheses here form part of an elegant historical reconstruction which meshes with his existential theological interpretation of the New Testament.

A detailed discussion of Bultmann would question the appropriateness of the categories he draws from Heidegger to articulate Paul's anthropology, and from Kierkegaard to interpret John. But in our discussion of Bultmann it is the strategies which he employs in order to do theological interpretation rather than the particular concepts he chooses which are at issue. It is possible in theological interpretation to combine critical historical reconstruction with more traditional categories than those supplied by Hegel or Heidegger (see below, p. 188). But Bultmann's work illustrates what happens in all theological interpretation of the Bible (though in the work of others it often happens less consciously than with Bultmann). It therefore provides a model which will relate our earlier discussions to more recent developments and to the new directions to be discussed in the remaining chapters.

Bultmann and beyond

First, Bultmann's use of modern concepts to express the meaning he finds in ancient texts whose world-view differs from his own can be defended in terms of what happens generally in interpretation. Modern interpreters have to employ terms which make sense to themselves if they are to understand a text, despite the danger of thereby imposing their own views upon it. That danger is partly met by interpreters remaining open to argument and self-correction, but it has to be admitted (as Bultmann repeatedly insisted) that interpretation is always a venture and a risk.

Secondly, this procedure does not commit an interpreter to

agreeing with the text. It is possible to understand without agreeing, even if (see above, p. 16) a person who denies God's existence understands 'God' differently from worshippers. In this complicated case of religious texts, the context in which the words are used is relevant to their meaning. Students of religion attend to the ways participants use their religious language, whereas theologians speaking from within a tradition can often take this for granted. But even theologians sometimes need to use modern concepts in order to clarify their tradition.

Thirdly, theological interpreters in every religious group have found in this use of modern concepts to draw out the meaning of their authoritative texts a way of understanding and expressing their faith in modern terms. They do their own theology through their interpretations of scripture. The necessity, common to all interpretation, of using language which makes sense to them helps theological interpreters to *appropriate* scriptures whose view of the world they themselves no longer share.

This way of doing 'theology as scriptural interpretation' is opposed by those who prefer to keep biblical exegesis and theology separate (above, p. 25, and below, p. 179). Some degree of separation is healthy for both sides. It reduces the danger of history or philology being corrupted to serve religious interests, and it preserves their capacity to surprise and stimulate theological thought. On the other hand, what Gadamer calls a 'fusion of horizons' between text and interpreter allows the Bible to be interpreted theologically, i.e. on the assumption that it speaks of the God whom both acknowledge.

This 'theology through scriptural interpretation' only works smoothly where the interpreters are happy with what they think the text is saying, as Bultmann is with his understanding of Paul and John. But it *can* also work in a negative way where the interpreter disagrees with the text's theology. Thus a Protestant interpreter like Käsemann can express his own theological judgements by disagreeing with the alleged 'early Catholic' theology of Luke or 2 Peter which he is describing. Wellhausen's low opinion of 'law' in the P-source of the Pentateuch functions theologically in a similar way. By drawing from its interpreters a theological judgement, even a negative one ('that's not how it is with God and the world, according to Christianity as I understand it'), the text stimulates contemporary theology.

Such 'theological criticism' has antecedents in Luther's criticism in 1522 of the Epistle of James. It contradicts biblicist versions of the Protestant scripture principle, and strains even Catholic respect for the whole canon of scripture. It involves appealing to one's sense of scripture as a whole, rather than to the totality of its individual witnesses. But it remains just within the bounds of doing theology through interpreting scripture, i.e. reflecting theologically on these scriptural texts.

This procedure, sometimes called 'critical theological interpretation' (in German *Sachkritik*), can be applied even within the work of an author whom the theological interpreter accepts. Thus Bultmann argues that Paul has on occasion failed to maintain his own high theological standards. He thinks (in disagreement with Barth) that 1 Corinthians 15: 1–11 offers a historical argument for the resurrection of Jesus, and criticizes this on the basis of his understanding of the *Sache* (theological subject-matter) gained from the rest of Paul's writing. He is not (as in the previous examples) saying simply '*I* theologically disapprove of this', but 'Paul himself, in his better moments, would not argue like this.' Authors sometimes fail to say what they really mean, and may be corrected by interpreters in the light of what they say elsewhere.

Clearly this kind of almost circular argument increases the risk of reinterpreting scripture according to one's own subjective preferences. But it is reasonable in principle, since human authors are rarely fully consistent with themselves, and this kind of argument can be maintained without reference to the interpreters' own convictions. Whether it is workable in practice is another matter. Most interpreters do it, but find it hard to justify to those who are not willing to be persuaded. Interpreters working for consensus (as theologians always are) therefore argue in this way as rarely as possible.

The procedure is easier to defend as analogous to modern literary judgement than as historical conjecture about an author's intentions. Literary critics often criticize a particular passage on criteria acknowledged by, and even partially derived from, the author. Whether the author would agree with their particular judgement is irrelevant. This point is important, because whereas Bultmann can conceivably claim that Paul would have agreed with him if pressed, Käsemann cannot claim this for Luke, nor Wellhausen for Leviticus. Those who believe in 'critical theological interpretation' (and many historians would say that it has no place in biblical scholarship) might be more comfortable within a literary than a historical paradigm or framework for biblical interpretation. (See below, Chapter 6.)

In a historically conscious age, and within the historical framework of biblical scholarship, this form of 'theology through interpretation' is rationally defensible only when applied to texts whose authors were themselves seeking to express what is still the interpreter's own religion. This raises interesting questions, because in some respects many Christians find it easier to identify with Isaiah than with Jude. But generally this style of theology has been more persuasive in the interpretation of the New Testament than the Old, because in the New the biblical text and the theological interpreter more clearly share the same religion. Christian theological interpretation of the Old Testament is always in danger of imposing theological criteria upon it that are historically inappropriate. Historical integrity here yields theological insufficiency.

We have noted von Rad's failure to overcome the hiatus between his history of traditions study and his contemporary Christian theology, and it is no coincidence that neither Baur nor Bultmann was able to draw much theological capital from the Old Testament, and that modern liberal theology from Schleiermacher through Harnack to the present day has tended to devalue it. A different approach is called for in that area at least, if the Old Testament is to be given its due theological weight as Christian (as well as Jewish) scripture, and not relegated to the historical presuppositions of Christian faith and theology. Literary study, which is less tied to the author's original intentions, may prove more important than historical exegesis in the theological interpretation of the Old Testament.

How believers evaluate any modern theological interpretation of the Bible will depend first on how satisfactorily it is able to do justice to the linguistic, literary, and historical reality of the text itself, and secondly on whether it is thought to provide an authentic expression of their own religion. Bultmann's synthesis found far more support than Strauss's, not only because it was better history (and people had meanwhile become more used to radical historical questioning of the Gospels), but also because some of his interpretative categories, and certainly his overall theology, were recognizably Christian. Bultmann could appeal to Paul and Luther in defence of his understanding of revelation, and his existentialist language also has strong roots in the Augustinian tradition. Even his sceptical Gospel criticism dovetailed with his theological emphases, and was therefore found inoffensive where these were shared.

Strauss's negative Gospel criticism, by contrast, was combined with a novel Hegelian theology which, for all its Christian ingredients, could not at the decisive point claim continuity with the Christian tradition. His novel theological proposal (above, p. 50) was attached quite loosely and extrinsically to his interpretation of the New Testament. It was dependent on this, but did not follow so directly from it as Baur's and Bultmann's theology followed from theirs. The destruction by Strauss of the Gospels' historical credibility made room for his understanding of their true metaphysical meaning, but did not suggest this. The classification of many of their narratives as 'myth' was a precondition, but not a support, for their interpretation into the Hegelian 'idea' of the unity of the human and the divine.

Baur's theology, by contrast, required no such raw material as its precondition. Neither did Bultmann's. Both could sit lightly to the results of their historical research. Their theological interpretations also followed more directly from their readings of other New Testament texts. Neither needed to impose a new metaphysical claim which actually contradicted the Gospel texts, as Strauss had done with his dictum (learned from Schelling) that 'the idea . . . is not wont to lavish all its fulness on one exemplar', namely Jesus (p. 779). If Baur believed the same, he never said so.

Bultmann's Gospel criticism could be said to perform a theological function analogous to that of Strauss's. It helped destroy his predecessors' theology (the liberal 'life-of-Jesus theology') and so made room for his new kerygmatic alternative, based on the

Church's proclamation of Christ crucified and risen. But sceptical historical judgements about the Gospels are not intrinsic or necessary to that type of theology, as the examples of Martin Kähler and Luther himself make plain. And kerygmatic theology flows quite naturally from at least one interpretation of Paul and John. It does not require the imposition of a Hegelian philosophical system clearly at odds with the text. Heidegger's analysis of human existence may not do justice to the New Testament, either, but it is close enough to be worth trying out.

These differences between Strauss and Bultmann help clarify what is and what is not acceptable in theological interpretation. Its ground rules can also be illuminated by summarizing what the two controversial figures have in common. That will in turn suggest how far the project of 'theology done as historically responsible New Testament interpretation' can be rescued from the particular weaknesses of these exponents.

First, both Strauss and Bultmann employed a sceptical historical criticism which destroyed current theologies (whether conservative supernaturalism or liberal life of Jesus theology), and combined this with a new theological interpretation. Historical criticism has continued to undermine theological interpretations, including those of Baur and Bultmann—and even Käsemann, whose Lutheran interpretation of Paul has recently been thrown on the defensive by the historical work of K. Stendahl and E. P. Sanders among others.

Secondly, neither Strauss nor Bultmann offered a satisfactory Christology, though Bultmann's is not so seriously at variance with traditional Christianity as Strauss's is. Bultmann does not quite abolish the connection with Jesus of Nazareth, and the 'Christ event' remains central for him. But it lacks content, and seems hardly to speak of a person. This is a point at which some of Bultmann's followers introduced modifications (below, p. 119).

Thirdly, both Strauss and Bultmann shared modern theories about the emergence of myth. The religious consciousness of the earliest believers found expression in such language, as happens generally in such communities.

Fourthly, neither considered myth acceptable for 'modern man'. That is another point which has been disputed. It seems likely that modern people can no more live without myths than their predecessors, however clearly these must now be distinguished from other kinds of knowledge and belief.

Fifthly, both interpreted the myth, rather than simply eliminating it, as some liberals did. Bultmann's interpretation of myth does at least partial justice to the New Testament authors themselves. These have an existential interest even if they also have cosmological beliefs which Bultmann ignored or repudiated.

Sixthly, the theologies of Strauss and Bultmann spurn historical events and prefer ideas or 'revelation events'. Despite the fruitfulness of Bultmann's synthesis for Lutherans, with their emphasis on 'the Word', this tendency towards isolation from social realities and depreciation of historical events has failed to satisfy most Christians on account of their religiously motivated engagement with the real world. Contemporary developments of 'theology through the interpretation of scripture', such as some liberation theology, now emphasize the necessity of praxis or discipleship. The social and political structures of the ancient world are discussed with an eye to contemporary realities.

Bultmann's synthesis of kerygmatic theology and history of traditions research has been losing ground since the late 1960s. But it has not yet been replaced by any biblical interpretation of comparable stature. For several years after the period of his major publications (1921–52) his synthesis was maintained throughout the next generation's Gospel criticism even as it was being challenged in some New Testament theology.

Gospel criticism in Germany since the Second World War, and elsewhere since the 1960s, has been dominated by 'redaction criticism'. Like form criticism, this new twist to history of traditions research was foreshadowed by Wrede's monograph on Mark's redaction of the secrecy material available to him in the tradition. Bultmann also had in 1921 included some redaction-critical notes at the end of his form-critical classic. But neither Wrede nor Bultmann nor Dibelius was specially interested in 'Mark the evangelist or theologian'. When the theologies of the synoptic evangelists were studied systematically a generation later, this therefore took place as reaction and correction to the typical form-critical view of them as 'only to the smallest extent authors' and 'principally collectors, vehicles of tradition, editors' (Dibelius). But, like the form criticism to which it was closely related, redaction criticism began as history of traditions work, and therefore dovetailed as well as form criticism did with the kerygmatic theology of its earliest exponents, Bornkamm on Matthew, Marxsen on Mark, and Conzelmann on Luke. The evangelists were seen as interpreting the tradition for their own day in much the same way as modern preachers interpret the biblical traditions for theirs.

Both form and redaction criticism provide possible bridges from history of traditions research to the new directions in biblical interpretation considered in the next three chapters. But the major exponents of these methods did not take either of these routes to sociological or to literary analyses. One explanation for this is that as long as kerygmatic theology remained in the ascendant, history of traditions research on the Bible remained theologically fruitful and in consequence multiplied. Reason and faith had found a happy partnership, or at least a working relationship. It was only when kerygmatic theology lost much of its plausibility in the late 1960s that history of traditions research lost much of its theological potential and significance.

Of course, the wheels of research have continued to turn, and have churned out more and more monographs, as Roman Catholic and English-language research have joined forces with German Protestantism in a largely united front of technical biblical scholarship. But the original theological impetus for this research was weakening, leaving a European butter mountain of research out of all proportion to its religious usefulness. It retains its value in training newcomers in a method which remains important for biblical scholarship, but the most theologically interesting biblical research is no longer to be found in history of traditions research.

In its heyday, history of traditions work was done in partnership with, if not for the sake of, kerygmatic theology. This happy relationship was not, however, free from strain. Theologians could not for ever acquiesce in its historical scepticism and 'let the fires burn' (above, p. 107), as Bultmann had done in 1927. In the 1950s and 1960s this tension between the history of traditions methods, which yielded very little secure knowledge about the historical Jesus, and the common-sense Christian interest in such knowledge surfaced. Ernst Käsemann, Günther Bornkamm, and others saw the need for some self-correction within their Bultmannian kerygmatic theology. They were sufficiently influenced by Barth (and Kähler) to be uneasy with the way Christology had almost disappeared into soteriology in their teacher's existential or anthropologically oriented theology. The most natural way for these New Testament theologians to recover the theological priority of Christology was to reopen the question of the historical Jesus posed by the Synoptic Gospels. They therefore abandoned the over-reaction against the old liberal theology which had led Barth and Bultmann to profess theological indifference to the 'historical Jesus', and tried to combine this renewed interest with their still kerygmatic theology.

For and against the 'new quest'

This development among Bultmann's former pupils was a symptom of theological more than historical discontent with the master's synthesis. Behind Bultmann's theological hostility to the liberals' quest for the historical Jesus stood a variety of Lutheran and existentialist emphases and phobias. First, faith must not be bolstered by rational argument, lest this undercut its sole sufficiency for salvation. Secondly, faith must not be exposed to the risk of rational investigation, and is therefore best severed from historical claims. Thirdly, faith is directed to God, who cannot be 'objectified' or identified with a bit of worldly reality—a view which contradicts some understandings of the Incarnation. Fourthly, and supporting other understandings of the Incarnation against liberal Protestantism, Christian evaluation of Jesus must speak of God at this point, as historical research does not.

For all the theological differences among the 'new questers' they were in broad agreement with Bultmann on these points. But they rightly sensed that a religion which centres on the crucified and risen Jesus as the decisive revelation of God must be at least interested in anything that can be known about him by rational enquiry. If true, this may provide a criterion for Christian faith, whether or not it provides a supporting argument. What is known about Jesus by historical enquiry may not be much, and will always remain a matter of probabilities. But the question of certainty is irrelevant here, because neither side is wanting to substitute historical knowledge for faith. Even probabilities, including historical probabilities about Jesus, could in principle alter, erode, or undermine Christian belief. That is one reason why theologians have to remain historians. There is an apologetic imperative laid upon Christians to answer Reimarus and his successors, quite apart from their natural interest in what Jesus was like.

By denying the resurrection of Jesus and substituting an anti-theological explanation of this claim, Reimarus had cut the thread of legitimacy which joins the faith of the early Church to the historical figure of Jesus. If he was right, Christianity as generally understood, hinging on the claim that 'Jesus is Lord', was false. In speaking of their risen Lord (John 20: 28), Christians are referring to Jesus of Nazareth. This involves (in principle at least) the risk of discovering that Jesus was not after all a person who could responsibly be venerated and followed as the decisive revelation of God.

The Bultmannian tendency to evade this (theoretical) risk by professing no interest in the historical reality of Jesus is unsatisfactory for two reasons. First, although Christian interpreta-tions of Jesus cannot be validated by historical argument, they need to be shown to be reasonable, and arguments against them countered. Since Christianity is open to historical attack and may conceivably be false, it is bound to engage in this counter-argument. That requires some account of the historical and theological continuities that exist (alongside discontinuities) between the historical reality of Jesus and his followers' faith in him.

Secondly, the Christian community has always asserted that this piece of history is where God is decisively present, and that its response to God is inseparable from its response to Jesus. To abandon that incarnational claim—as some of Schleiermacher's 'enlightened' predecessors had done (above, p. 31), as some of his liberal successors did, and as Bultmann came close to doing—is to part company with what has hitherto been called Christianity.

It is in accord with this incarnational claim that Christian faith and theology are, like at least some, and perhaps all the New Testament authors, interested in the earthly ministry of Jesus. A theology which ignores the witness of the Synoptic Gospels is likely to be distorted. However, this interest is best satisfied by the inclusion of sections on the theologies of these evangelists in a New Testament theology, not by imaginatively elaborating upon the meagre results of historical research on Jesus himself. The legitimate theological interest in historical research on Jesus falls short of justifying the attempt to reconstruct a 'historical Jesus', i.e. an interpretation deliberately contrasted with, and often hostile to, the theological judgements of his earliest followers. That was considered neither convincing nor desirable by the 'new questers', Käsemann, Bornkamm, and Conzelmann. This distinguishes their work from the old liberal 'life of Jesus' research. They thought such reconstructions unconvincing because they shared Bultmann's form-critical scepticism about the historical reliability of the Gospel tradition, and like him they thought it theologically undesirable to make such a 'historical Jesus' into a substitute for the crucified and risen Lord Jesus of Christian faith.

However, while agreeing with Bultmann on these essential points, they introduced some correctives. It is possible to say more as a historian than Bultmann at times seemed willing to concede, and there are good apologetic reasons for drawing historical pictures of Jesus which illustrate the continuity between pre- and post-Easter faith. The results would not provide a sufficient basis for Christology, much less a substitute for it, but that is not what the better new questers wanted. Their ambitions were more limited. They were also less clear-cut. As a theological movement (as opposed to an ongoing historical enterprise) the old quest ended in Germany with a series of bangs; the new simply petered out.

The history of traditions research which buried both the old quest and Albert Schweitzer's alternative reconstruction of Jesus has lost none of its destructive potential. Christian theology has had to find other ways of satisfying its interest in the earthly ministry of Jesus. Instead of hoping to reconstruct this historically it has had to relearn its dependence upon the Gospels as narratives. It needs enough historical information to identify the Lord of faith as the man from Nazareth, but does not need to establish the historicity of the Gospels in any detail.

The apologetic task of answering such anti-Christian polemic as that of Reimarus and his successors at the historical level cannot, however, be neglected. But making this the foundation and framework for Christology was, from the standpoint of orthodox Christianity (Protestant as well as Roman Catholic), a theological mistake. It provided too narrow a base for the kind of claims that Christians have always made about Jesus. A theology which restricts its statements about Jesus to what historians can say is no longer Christian in any traditional sense.

Christian theology is reflection on a faith in God, which centres on the incarnate, crucified, and risen Lord Jesus. This faith is nourished by the Gospel story and stories. Such a faith does not need the historical reality of Jesus to be laid bare or fully disclosed. But it does need to know that it is based on that historical reality, and that it has nothing to fear from historical research. If the historical root of Christianity could be fully exposed its power might even be reduced, since the religious picture gains from symbolic heightening and this might well be eroded by detailed historical knowledge. For Christians the element of mystery is perhaps better preserved by the partial inaccessibility of Jesus to historical reason (Wrede) than by the unsubtle apocalyptic mentality attributed to him by Schweitzer or even Sanders.

The historical seed of the Christian gospel fell to the ground, died, and was buried. It became (Christians claim) not only the now-hidden root, but also the risen shoot—the true vine through which the creative goodness of God nourishes the branches. It was some of the earliest of these branches that in due course flowered and developed the Gospel stories through which subsequent believers have learned to know Jesus as their Lord and their God.

Christian faith and theology do not depend on reconstructing the history of Jesus. It does not matter theologically if the roots are lost to sight. Faith's interest in the ministry of Jesus can be satisfied by studying the Gospels even if the question of their historical accuracy remains incompletely answered, and even where it remains unasked. On the other hand, a critical intelligence is bound to raise historical questions, and theologians seek to integrate into their Christologies whatever firm conclusions are reached at the historical level. If these conclusions are fragmentary, that does not matter; the framework of Christology is not drawn from historical research— or should not be. Christology expresses God's concern with the world today by pointing to Jesus of Nazareth, in whom (with the help of the New Testament witness) Christians recognize that concern.

Strictly speaking, the Bultmannian 'new quest' of the 1950s and 1960s limited itself to correcting Bultmann's kerygmatic theology. It did not pursue an alternative (narrative) theological approach to the Gospels. There are pointers towards a more literary approach to the Bible inherent in form criticism, and also in redaction criticism's concern with the final form of the text. But the step to literary criticism (in the usual secular sense of the phrase) was not taken by these history of traditions researchers. The reason is not simply that they were *historians* of literature and religion rather than literary specialists. The step (to be discussed in Chapters 6 and 7) was resisted by some of these scholars in part because as *theologians* they saw the importance of history for Christian faith.

Where biblical interpretation follows literary approaches at the expense of history, and so claims no interest in the historical reality of Jesus, that implies a different kind of break with traditional Christianity from the liberal preoccupation with the historical Jesus just noted. For all the theological reservations that have been expressed about an anti-theological 'historical Jesus', this at least retains one point of contact with traditional Christianity. 'Jesus myths', on the other hand, ideas, stories, etc. which set no store at all by the historical reality, may be religiously moving, but they fail to express a necessary part of the central Christian claim: that it is in *Jesus* that God is known. Continuing historical research does at least bear witness to that, however meagre, uncertain, and religiously uninteresting some of its results may be. The quest itself is perhaps theologically more important than its results.

It is no coincidence that in the 1950s, precisely when the history of traditions approach to the Gospels was pressing through redaction criticism in the direction of a more literary approach, its theologically most sensitive pioneers moved simultaneously in the opposite direction by reopening the question of the historical Jesus. Redaction criticism of the Gospels took scholars even further away from the historical reality of Jesus than form criticism had done. It therefore made theological compensation, in the form of a new quest for the historical Jesus, necessary. Redaction criticism of the Old Testament needed no such counterbalance because that history was not so theologically important for Christians.

Outside the Bultmannian camp theologians had continued to insist that Christians were interested in what could be historically known about Jesus. Some still thought that faith would be threatened if not much could be known. In Germany, Joachim Jeremias used history of traditions methods to peel off the layers of Gospel tradition in pursuit of the historical Jesus behind them. His books on *The Parables of Jesus* (1947; ET 1954) and *The Eucharistic Words of Jesus* (1936, 1960; ET 1955, rev. 1966) consequently contributed significantly to the acceptance of the history of traditions approach outside Germany.

Jeremias's continuation of the old quest was criticized by Käsemann, who is usually credited with starting the new one. Käsemann argued, surely rightly, that to opt for the historical Jesus against the kerygmatic Christ is more unorthodox than the Bultmannian opposite error. It looks more shocking to Lutheran eyes than to English ones, since English religion is more influenced by the Gospels than by Paul. Käsemann and the other 'new questers' succeeded in maintaining the importance for Christianity of both the Jesus of history and the Christ of faith. They were rather less successful in fusing these two abstractions into a satisfactory expression of traditional Christian faith in the one Lord Jesus Christ. It seems that Christologies 'from below', which proceed from a historical approach to the Gospels, cannot say what Christians have to say about Jesus. A reading of the Gospels fully satisfactory both to historical reason and to religious faith needs to *start* somewhere else, not with the historical quest. Christian theology cannot neglect historical study, but requires other approaches to the Gospels also.

To abandon the historical quest would be to break with something that has always been important for Christianity. This 'something' is not the so-called 'historical Jesus', i.e. modern historians' critical reconstructions of Jesus, but the largely inaccessible earthly historical reality of Jesus himself. Keeping alive the question of the historical Jesus by continuing attempts at historical reconstruction is the most natural way for modern

Western thinkers to keep alive their sense of that reality. This, rather than the meagre and uncertain conclusions of even a Jeremias or a Sanders, is the main theological importance of both old and new quests.

It is also the value of the late Bishop John Robinson's 'new look' for historical information in the Fourth Gospel. The 'question of history in John' is a healthy theological warning against the dangers of Docetism (i.e. denial of Jesus' true humanity) posed by that Gospel. Neither the 'new quest' nor the new historical interest in John achieved significant new knowledge (as opposed to a few further suggestions) about Jesus. The history of traditions research which is necessary in the historical study of the Gospels yields only fragmentary information about the history of Jesus.

The historical information which this approach to the Gospels provides about the early Church is also rather limited. The most interesting and promising developments of form and redaction criticism have been in the sociological, linguistic, and literary directions, to be considered in subsequent chapters. There are limits to the unintended historical information about the authors, their sources, their readers, their communities, their sources' communities, etc. that can be squeezed out of a text that, at least on the surface, is reporting something quite different.

It was the alliance with kerygmatic theology which gave the history of traditions approach much of its vitality in biblical interpretation. The best way to recover some bearings after the demise of this theology is therefore to return to the pioneer who was untouched by kerygmatic theology, but who had religious and theological interests of his own in the application of history of traditions method: Hermann Gunkel.

History of religions research

Gunkel's research on the prehistory of the biblical literature, launched in the first edition of his commentary on Genesis (1901), grew out of his history of religions research, notably his work on *Creation and Chaos* (1895; partly trans. 1984). It became clear to Gunkel that one could not trace the history of biblical religion without studying the history of the traditions contained in this literature. Form criticism was thus a child or necessary adjunct of history of religions research. Though it gained a new significance within biblical interpretation through its alliance with kerygmatic theology, it was first developed as a historical method independent of this, and was associated with a totally different theology, namely, one which centred on the notion of 'religion'.

The same combination of history of religions and history of traditions research, and the same Christian theological interest in 'religion' as a middle term for connecting faith and reason, is found in the biblical scholarship of other members of the Göttingen group (or 'mini-faculty', as they were then called), who, though not really a 'school', later became known as the 'history of religions school'. Their original number included Bousset (and, through close friendship with him, the systematic theologian Troeltsch), Wrede and A. Eichhorn (also student friends), and (peripherally) Ritschl's son-in-law, Johannes Weiss. All had been originally attracted to Göttingen by the reputation of Ritschl, but were dissatisfied with his failure to draw the full implications of historical research for theology.

The first book to come from this group was Gunkel's pioneering work, *The Influence of the Holy Spirit: The Popular View of the Apostolic Age and the Teaching of the Apostle Paul* (1888; ET 1979). In an age of increasing (and, within the humanities, unfortunate) specialization it is refreshing to recall that two of the most creative contributors to New Testament scholarship in the golden age of historical criticism were Wellhausen at the end of his career, and Gunkel at the beginning of his. As the old Wellhausen provides a link from Old Testament scholarship by his history of traditions work on the Gospels, so the young Gunkel bridges both disciplines with his history of religions research.

The main thesis of Gunkel's book, implicitly directed against Ritschl, was that the New Testament must be understood in its contemporary religious and cultural context, rather than directly from the Old Testament: 'We must therefore designate Judaism as the real matrix of the gospel' (p. 13); though on this topic it made little difference, because the Old Testament view of the Spirit had survived with little change into the first century.

Like Weiss's account of Jesus' eschatology four years later in *Jesus' Proclamation of the Kingdom of God* (1892, 1900²; ET of 1st edn. 1971) this historical approach was damaging to modern spiritualizing interpretations of the New Testament influenced by German idealism. Just as 'the kingdom of God' meant something very different for Kant and Ritschl from what it had meant for Jesus, so *pneuma* (spirit) meant something different for Hegel and Baur, with their roots in classical Greek philosophy, from what it had meant for the biblical writers. Paul was distinctive in his ethical evaluation of spiritual gifts and, even more significantly, saw the whole of Christian life as directed by the spirit. But he too presupposed not Greek (and German) philosophy, but the usual Hellenistic religious view of the spirit as a miraculous and empirically manifest divine power.

The public impact of this 'history of religions' approach to the Bible stemmed from its use of extra-canonical sources to illuminate the Bible. It was this, rather than particular results, which gave rise to the 'Babel–Bible' controversy of 1902. Friedrich Delitzsch told the Kaiser and the German public what every Assyriologist had known for years: that there were interesting parallels between biblical and early Mesopotamian literature. This caused a shock. Historians had long examined the Bible by the same methods that they applied to other documents, illuminating it by similar materials recovered from the ancient world. But believers thought of it in terms which set it apart as unique.

Christians and Jews still do consider their scriptures a unique source for their knowledge of God. But many more have now learned to think of revelation in terms which allow them to study the Bible as human traditions also. When historical criticism was still new and strange, believers rightly sensed that its methods were undermining their dogmatic view of the Bible, and most of them lacked a view of revelation compatible with the new approaches. They saw that traditional views of scripture were being denied by being ignored. As Wrede put it drily in 1897: 'No New Testament writing was born with the predicate "canonical" attached.' Later ecclesiastical evaluations were irrelevant to historical study.

Like Strauss before them and Bultmann later, these liberal theologians at the turn of the century were not themselves worried by what their historical work did to popular views of Christianity, because they had an alternative theology. They were interested not in doctrines which might be obtained from an infallible Bible, but in religion which was best understood by studying its history, and which was a matter of personal experience for themselves too. The preference is clear in Gunkel's title and subject-matter: the early Christians were not interested in a 'doctrine' of the Spirit; it was a living experience. Even Paul, whom Gunkel recognized as 'a man by nature given to reflection' and obliged to curb the excesses of the Corinthians, presupposes supernatural views of spirit possession.

Some of the judgements made by these pioneers have been revised in the light of subsequent research, and some of their theses were valuable only in provoking thought. Gunkel's remark that Christianity is a syncretistic religion, Wellhausen's that Jesus was not a Christian but a Jew (both echoed by Bultmann), and Heitmüller's that Paul's sacramentalism makes him the father of Catholicism rather than of the Reformation, all contain provocative half-truths. But neither the more serious history nor the theology of the original history of religions school has dated as much as was thought during the Barthian reaction which followed. For all the advances made by subsequent research, especially in the light of newly discovered documents, both historical and theological pendulums have swung back in their favour.

First the historical: whatever the Old Testament tradition owed to Babylon, it was clear to Gunkel, as it was to J. Weiss, Bousset, and Wrede, that the New Testament must be understood in the context of first-century Judaism. Any influence of more distant cultures on the New Testament was mediated through contemporary Judaism. Shortly afterwards, in the early years of the present century, history of religions research on the New Testament spread out from Judaism to the Hellenistic world and the Orient, partly on account of the influence of the classicist R. Reitzenstein on Bousset, and on account of the stimulus of newly discovered Manichaean and Mandaean documents. Despite their late date the latter were deemed important by Bultmann when in the 1920s he began his great work on John. Though Bultmann's prestige gave these sources and Reitzenstein's hypothesis of a pre-Christian gnostic redeemer myth more prominence in German research than they

deserved; the emphasis returned decisively to the Jewish matrix of
early Christianity with the discovery of the Dead Sea Scrolls at
Qumran in 1947. These converted some quite conservative scholars
to the value of history of religions research for understanding the
New Testament.

In recent years history of religions research has often been
pursued without the strong theological interest in religion and
religions characteristic of the original history of religions school. By
the time their historical methods were generally accepted among
biblical scholars the historical study of the Bible was no longer
clearly bound up with any particular theological direction. Therein
lie both a strength of contemporary biblical scholarship and the
problem discussed in our opening chapter. Christians and Jews of
various persuasions work together in the study of these texts, but
their resulting interpretations are felt by many believers to have
little religious interest. That partly accounts for some of the new
directions in biblical interpretation being explored today.

Another way in which the discoveries at Qumran vindicated the
pioneers of the history of religions school was in the types of
Judaism they revealed. Scholars as different as Schürer, Dalman,
Schlatter, and later Moore and Kittel, emphasized the importance
of first-century Judaism for understanding the New Testament.
But they all concentrated on what subsequently became the
'normative' Judaism of the rabbis, at the expense of what came to be
considered heterodox strands, visible especially in the apocalyptic
literature. The importance of the rabbis is indisputable. The study
of their scriptural interpretation, styles of argument, and theology,
by G. Vermes, W. D. Davies, and E. P. Sanders among others, has
continued to yield fresh insights into the New Testament. These
scholars have concentrated on the rabbinic material without
neglecting other strands in first-century Judaism. But Qumran, and
indirectly also the gnostic literature found at Nag Hammadi in
Upper Egypt in 1945, placed sectarian Judaism (first studied with
the help of late nineteenth-century discoveries by scholars such as
Hilgenfeld in Germany and R. H. Charles and his associates in
England) nearer the centre of the history of religions investigation
of Christian origins.

Rabbinic Judaism still provides the most helpful material for understanding Paul the ex-Pharisee and 'Matthew', presumably a 'scribe discipled' to Jesus. The history of religions background to the Johannine community, by contrast, is more esoteric, sectarian, and uncertain. The historical Jesus himself remains an enigma, different from his closest analogues, including Qumran sectaries, apocalyptic visionaries, charismatic prophets, and even John the Baptist. But all these analogies remain important for the historical investigation of this 'Jesus who became the Christ'. The balance between history of traditions sifting of the Gospels and the history of religions study of the actual context in which the material was transmitted is now being restored in favour of the latter.

The study of apocalyptic has made steady progress over the past century and has recently been enriched by the newer social-scientific and literary approaches to be considered below (see pp. 161 and 246). This progress contrasts with history of traditions research, which is in constant danger of sterility, because fewer advances are possible there. Competing scholarly hypotheses do battle in ever-lengthening footnotes, but nobody knows who is right, and finally few people care. History of religions work, by contrast, has been kept relatively fresh by the discoveries of new source-material. Even without any alliance with theology it continues to excite intellectual curiosity, but it has also lent itself to a revival of that alliance.

The scientific study of religion has flourished outside theology and biblical studies during the present century, and has enriched history of religions research. The importance of the new social sciences for Christian theology, as well as for biblical studies and Church history, was at once recognized by the systematic theologian of the history of religions school, Ernst Troeltsch. It is now recognized by many more theologians. The social sciences can contribute both to the rational historical study of the Bible, and to its religious appropriation. Both these aspects will be explored in the following chapter.

Further reading

ANDERSON, B. W. (ed.), *The Old Testament and Christian Faith* (London and New York, 1963).
—— *Creation in the Old Testament* (London and Philadelphia, 1984).

ANDERSON, H., *Jesus and Christian Origins* (Oxford, 1964).

BARR, J., *Old and New in Interpretation* (London, 1966).

—— 'Biblical Theology', in *Interpreter's Dictionary of the Bible: Supplementary Volume* (Nashville, 1976).

BARTSCH, H.-W. (ed.), *Kerygma and Myth* (London, 1962).

BORNKAMM, G., *Jesus of Nazareth* (1956; ET London and New York, 1960).

BRAATEN, C. AND HARRISVILLE, R. (eds.), *Kerygma and History* (Nashville, 1962).

—— *The Historical Jesus and the Kerygmatic Christ* (Nashville, 1964).

BULTMANN, R., *Faith and Understanding* (1933; ET London, 1969).

—— *Primitive Christianity in its Contemporary Setting* (1949; ET London, 1956, and New York, 1959).

CHILDS, B. S., *Biblical Theology in Crisis* (Philadelphia, 1970).

CHILTON, B. (ed.), *The Kingdom of God* (London and Philadelphia, 1984).

CLEMENTS, R., *A Century of Old Testament Study* (London, 1976; Philadelphia, 1984).

COLLINS, R. F., *Introduction to the New Testament* (London, 1983).

CRENSHAW, J. L. *Gerhard von Rad* (Waco, Tex., 1978).

EBELING, G., *Word and Faith* (1960; ET London and Philadelphia, 1963).

—— *Theology and Proclamation* (1962; ET London and Philadelphia, 1966).

EISSFELDT, O., *The Old Testament: An Introduction* (London and New York, 1965).

GUNKEL, H., *What Remains of the Old Testament* (London, 1928).

HARRINGTON, W., *The Path of Biblical Theology* (Dublin, 1973).

HARVEY, VAN A., *The Historian and the Believer* (New York, 1966; London, 1967).

HENGEL, M., *Judaism and Hellenism* (1970, 1973²; ET London, 1974).

HENRY, P., *New Directions in New Testament Study* (Philadelphia, 1979; London, 1980).

KÄSEMANN, E., *Essays on New Testament Themes* (London and Philadelphia, 1964).

KELBER, W., *The Oral and the Written Gospel* (Philadelphia, 1983).

KNIGHT, D. A. (ed.), *Tradition and Authority in the Old Testament* (Philadelphia, 1977).

KOCH, K., *The Growth of the Biblical Tradition* (1964; ET New York, 1969).

KOESTER, H., *Introduction to the New Testament*, 2 vols. (Philadelphia, 1980).

KÜMMEL, W. G., *The New Testament: The History of the Investigation of its Problems* (1970; ET Nashville, 1972, and London, 1973).

MCARTHUR, H., *In Search of the Historical Jesus* (New York, 1969; London, 1970).

MACQUARRIE, J., *An Existentialist Theology* (London, 1955, 1973).

MEEKS, W. A., *The Prophet-King: Moses Traditions and the Johannine Christology* (Leiden, 1967).

MORGAN, R., *The Nature of New Testament Theology* (London, 1973).

PERRIN, N., *The Kingdom of God in the Teaching of Jesus* (London, 1963).

RAD, G. VON, *The Problem of the Hexateuch and Other Essays* (London and New York, 1966).

RAST, W. E., *Tradition History and the Old Testament* (Philadelphia, 1972).

REVENTLOW, H. GRAF, *Problems of Old Testament Theology in the Twentieth Century* (1982; ET London, 1985).

ROBINSON, J. M., *A New Quest of the Historical Jesus* (London, 1959).

—— (ed.), *The Nag Hammadi Library* (Leiden and New York, 1977).

—— and COBB, J. B. (eds.), *The New Hermeneutic* (New York, 1964).

ROHDE, J., *Rediscovering the Teaching of the Evangelists* (1966; ET London, 1968).

ROWLAND, C., *Christian Origins* (London and Atlanta, 1985).

SANDERS, E. P., *Paul and Palestinian Judaism* (London and Philadelphia, 1977).

—— *Jesus and Judaism* (London and Philadelphia, 1985).

SCHMITHALS, W., *An Introduction to the Theology of Rudolf Bultmann* (1967²; ET London, 1968).

SMART, J. D., *The Interpretation of Scripture* (London, 1961).

—— *The Past, Present, and Future of Biblical Theology* (Philadelphia, 1979).

SPRIGGS, D. G., *Two Old Testament Theologies* (London, 1974).

THISELTON, A. C., *The Two Horizons* (Exeter, 1980).

TUCKER, G. M., *Form Criticism of the Old Testament* (Philadelphia, 1971).

TUCKETT, C. M. (ed.), *The Messianic Secret* (London and Philadelphia, 1983).

—— *Reading the New Testament* (London, 1987).

VERMES, G., *The Dead Sea Scrolls: Qumran in Perspective* (London and Philadelphia, 1977).

WESTERMANN, C. (ed.), *Essays on Old Testament Interpretation* (London, 1963). American title: *Essays on Old Testament Hermeneutics* (Atlanta, 1979[7]).

5

Theology and the Social Sciences

Faith and Reason

The preceding chapters have surveyed some of the most influential biblical study of the past 150 years. During this period the critical study of the Bible, which in the previous century had transformed a few European intellectuals' understanding of religion, was gradually assimilated by a larger constituency within Christianity and Judaism. Most of the pioneering historical work of this later period was done in the Protestant theological faculties of the research-oriented universities of Germany. The tense relationship between critical historical scholarship and the religious orthodoxies dependent on the Bible was therefore always a sensitive issue.

Contrary to the charges and countercharges of undermining the faith or perverting the course of historical reason, both liberal and conservative theologians were engaged in modifying inherited positions and reformulating Christian belief to take account of the new knowledge. The liberals were more consistent in applying the new methods, and less cautious in their treatment of the tradition. But they could refuse to compromise their historical integrity only because they saw no ultimate contradiction between the claims of reason and those of true religion and morality. Like the more enlightened of their conservative contemporaries, they sought an accommodation between them.

Nineteenth-century theology thus learned to combine the rational methods of modern scholarship with a religious belief based on the Bible. But these methods *can* be pursued without reference to contemporary religious belief, without interest in either sustaining or discrediting it. Historical research on the Bible may be motivated quite simply by an interest in the past. This particular past is still religiously significant for some, and culturally important for others, but for many the awareness of it is fading or already faded. Historical interest in retrieving it may or may not be religiously motivated.

Personal motivations are generally invisible, but scholars are naturally influenced by the context in which they work and the expectations of those who hear and read, pay and promote them. German theological faculties shared the university ethos and valued academic freedom. But they were also oriented to training clergy to preach on the biblical text. This dual allegiance made them seed-beds for modern Old and New Testament theologies which reconciled the competing claims of Christian faith and rational, especially historical, study of the Bible.

This academic location of rationalist biblical scholarship within strongly theological contexts helped to ensure that an approach that was initially hostile to religion was soon serving religious purposes. Neither the methods used nor even the content of the Bible would have achieved this without external institutional support, as the long history of 'independent' (i.e. non-theological) biblical research makes clear. The methods have an implicitly anti-religious bias, because they operate without reference to God, and the content studied in this way is simply human religion of the past. It becomes present, living religion only when a reader takes a further step and shares some of the authors' intentions by accepting their view of the subject-matter (see Chapter 1).

Historical respect for the authors' intentions does not on its own make what was living religion for them religiously effective for the historian. It is more likely to have the opposite effect by highlighting the distance that separates the texts from their modern interpreters. That is why the further step of theological appropriation has always been necessary. Where the gulf of historical distance between biblical writer and modern reader or interpreter is recognized, this act of identification or appropriation has to be deliberate and self-conscious. Because it is not obvious how the historical distance is to be overcome, theological appropriation constitutes a problem. It is often called '*the* hermeneutical problem', because it dwarfs all other problems of biblical interpretation (see above, p. 16).

'Hermeneutics' is a word we have until now avoided, respecting the traditional English distrust of German and German-American jargon. But in recent years the word has become widely used in literary criticism and the social sciences, and its theological ancestry acknowledged. Insularity is therefore no longer appropriate. One of the tasks of theology is to do business with other disciplines, and the word is useful currency, despite some problems about its meaning.

The word itself does not in fact have a very long ancestry, even in theology. The first book entitled (in Latin) *Sacred Hermeneutics, or the Method of Expounding Holy Writ* was written in Lutheran Strasburg in 1654, and the word is not found in English before 1678 (*OED Suppl.*). A little later the new philological methods were applied to the Bible, and the old distinction between sacred and profane hermeneutics began to disappear, to be buried finally by Schleiermacher.

This general acceptance of normal rational methods, which has roots in the Reformers' hostility to allegorical interpretation, has meant, ironically, that from the 1920s to the 1970s the word usually referred to the specifically theological interests present in some biblical interpretation, rather than to theory about the methods used. That was because the modern rational methods soon ceased to be controversial in university theology and therefore needed no theoretical justification. The problems in modern biblical interpretation have arisen mainly from its theological dimensions. That is therefore what hermeneutics has been about. The very recent swing to controversial non-theological styles of interpretation means that the word is now used in these contexts too. Since theory and practice cannot be wholly separated, it is often used with an adjective to describe actual proposals, not simply theoretical discussions (see below, pp. 157–60, for Freudian, Girardian, feminist, liberation, etc., hermeneutics).

Some biblical theologians or theological interpreters of the Bible try to solve the hermeneutical problem, i.e. bridge the gulf between ancient and modern beliefs, in one jump. They make rational criticism serve religious ends directly, by developing Old and New Testament theologies which are simultaneously rational-historical in method and theological in aim. That is a bold move, but typical of how theology relates to other disciplines, using them where possible in the service of its own all-embracing claim to truth.

But the theological grand span, which covers everything, is too ambitious for many. Historical methods of interpreting the Bible encourage historical aims, which are not those of religion, and some systematic theologians are content with that. They use the historical conclusions of biblical scholars in constructing their own theologies but accept that biblical scholarship is a thoroughly secular discipline. They seem willing to dispense with Old and New Testament theologies that mediate between secular scholarship and religious belief, but they then produce (usually piecemeal) their own theological interpretations of the Bible. So the argument is not about the necessity of theological interpretation, but about who should do it. Since the efforts of systematic theologians in this field are generally less persuasive than those of theologians who are themselves biblical specialists, such demarcation disputes are pointless. Theological interpretation should be done by whoever wishes to do it, and judged on its merits.

The underlying question here is the relationship between theology and secular biblical scholarship. The solution that dispenses with a genuinely theological Old and New Testament theology implies that theologians should follow the fluctuations of biblical scholarship, but not seek to influence their direction.

That is a dangerous policy for theologians to pursue in a culture where the subject-matter of the Bible is contested. Historians and believers may read it very differently. The real justification for letting biblical scholarship set the agenda for theological interpretation of the Bible is that the scholars' questions are those of the contemporary culture which theology seeks to address. But that is only part of the truth. The world may have more to learn from the Bible than what the scholars are experts in unravelling. A theology (and so a theological interpretation of the Bible) which allowed itself to be directed by the discoveries of biblical scholarship alone would be starved of fresh air and suffocate. Believers have other interests in the Bible, and there is no reason why these too should not guide and motivate (though not compel) their biblical interpretation. These other interests may also draw upon the resources of scholarship.

Believers use the ordinary rational methods taken for granted in a secular culture, and secular methods encourage secular aims. This implies that unless theological counter-forces prevail upon biblical scholars to engage in a specifically theological interpretation, the discipline (if not all its practitioners) will tend to drift away from the interests of religious faith, and will cease to serve religious aims, except by handing over its secular historical conclusions to systematic theologians. Historical scholarship has its own agenda and its own secular university base, even if its numerical strength remains parasitic upon people's religious interests in these texts.

The counter-force that has until recently continued to prevail, even where the institutional encouragements to engage theologically with these texts are no longer present, is the religious motivation and denominational loyalty of individual scholars, often sustained by ministerial responsibilities. Where this is absent, theologically useful forms of Old and New Testament study, which serve the religious community by nourishing its preaching and teaching, are liable to decline.

Confronting this secularization of biblical scholarship with forms of Old and New Testament theology that integrate the new methods within a wider theological intention and framework is not guaranteed success. It is possible that biblical scholarship and the religious use of the Bible will go their separate ways. But the 'mediating' approach, which in the nineteenth century found an accommodation between faith and historical reason, has found considerable acceptance within Christian theology and is now being developed in response to the challenges posed to religious faith by the social sciences. In both cases, as with the challenges to patristic and medieval faith from Platonic and Aristotelian philosophy, theology integrates the new rational methods and insights into its own reflection on its tradition, while rejecting what is deemed incompatible with its faith. Opinion differs about what is incompatible, and the perennial argument between liberals and conservatives continues on any particular issue until a consensus is reached or the issue itself recedes.

The integration of social-scientific methods and insights within Christian theology has been facilitated by the extent to which modern theology had already abandoned what clearly conflicted with modern knowledge during its earlier confrontations with the natural sciences and critical history. It is also helped by the social sciences having themselves partly outgrown their earlier positivistic hostility to religion. Theology will no doubt be influenced by observations made by other disciplines, but it is now possible to understand a religion in ways that combine rational and empirical or descriptive investigation with belief in its transcendent referent.

How far these new understandings of faith imply doctrinal development is not our concern here. The nineteenth-century experience suggests that the need for restatements will become clear to the religious community partly through the use of the new methods in the theologically sensitive area of biblical scholarship. This provides a starting-point for discussing 'theology and the social sciences' in biblical interpretation.

A new era

The recent developments in biblical scholarship with which the remaining chapters are concerned have produced new leaders in the field. The emergence of the United States as trend-setter in place of Germany reflects its economic strength and its large market for religious ideas of all kinds. Departments of Religion were established in secular universities in the 1960s and, unlike the Germany theological faculties, these had no institutional relationship to the Churches. Biblical scholars' closest colleagues here were not systematic and practical theologians but secular university professors of literature, ancient history, and the social sciences. New possibilities of academic collaboration brought new kinds of writing. These will be described in a chapter on literature and in this one on the social sciences, taking the latter first because they stand closer to the historical scholarship discussed so far, and because it is here that the changing climate is most clearly visible.

The new cultural mood of the 1960s was anticipated shortly before his early death by C. Wright Mills in *The Sociological Imagination* (1959). What this phrase represented, he claimed, was becoming 'the major common denominator of our cultural life and its signal feature'. It was once Newtonian physics and later Darwinian biology that provided styles of reflection and popular metaphysics in terms of which scholars and cultural commentators came to refocus their observations and reformulate their concerns. But now it is the 'sociological imagination' which is required 'in factual and moral concerns, in literary work and in political analysis'. This is the 'quality of mind that seems most dramatically to promise an understanding of the intimate realities of ourselves in connexion with larger social realities'. For 'social science deals with problems of biography, of history, and of their intersections within social structures' which are the 'co-ordinate points of the proper study of man'.

According to Mills, the natural sciences no longer provide cultural orientation or solve the human problems they raise. But neither art nor literature is adequate to interpret historical and political realities in terms which command general assent. People want facts, and only a discipline which combines these with reflection on meanings and values will provide an empirical age with a view of the world in which it can believe. 'They want orienting values too, and suitable ways of feeling and styles of emotion and vocabularies of motive', and should look to the social sciences to articulate their self-understanding.

Mills's great expectations of the 'sociological imagination' were partially vindicated in the 1960s and 1970s when many academic disciplines, notably history, literature, and philosophy, as well as theology, absorbed insights and perspectives from the social sciences. This relationship with the humanities, already present in the work of Marx, Weber, Freud, and Evans-Pritchard, indicates how far some have moved from earlier attempts to model the social on the natural sciences. The search for laws on which societies operate (laws which would make predictions possible) has been largely abandoned. There are still disputes about the scope and methods of the social sciences and the character of their explanations, as there are in every academic discipline. But it is now evident that sociology and anthropology have close affinities with history. These are proving significant for biblical scholarship.

The main differences between history and sociology are that history attends to the individual and particular, sociology to what is general or typical; and that whereas history describes (and occasionally explains) the past in terms of its extension and change through time (diachrony), sociology looks at past and present societies as systems or structures frozen at a particular moment (synchrony). This implies that the disciplines are complementary. Anyone wanting to understand past or present societies will use both. Whether or not either can 'explain' a society, both offer partial explanations of particular features.

The difference of focus on the unique and on the typical implies that history rather than sociology should provide the framework for studying the biblical past. But within this framework sociological theory based on empirically grounded generalizations may improve the picture. On the basis of observing many societies it offers theories about the way they work; for example, about the ways religion functions in society, how groups within society come into conflict and resolve their conflicts, the typical roles that individuals perform, and how authority is exercised and status recognized. These kinds of questions, and suggestions obtained from looking at many societies 'in the round' or holistically, taking account of everything that is going on at a given moment, can place old data in new contexts and so contribute to historical knowledge.

One technique which has proved its worth is the construction of 'ideal types' or models of social roles and institutions such as the prophet, charismatic leader, or sect. The 'type' which is constructed by generalizing from a large number of cases will not correspond exactly to any actual historical instance, but sharpens observation of particular cases and throws light from comparative data on their character and social functions. This enrichment of social history by sociological theory can help illuminate biblical religion.

Since religion is a social phenomenon, the history of religion must be social history. The theologically motivated emphasis upon the history of ideas was rightly corrected by Baur's liberal successors in their attention to the non-doctrinal dimensions of religion. Some of their historical work provided data for the great sociological theorists. Durkheim acknowledged his debt to Robertson Smith's classic, *The Religion of the Semites* (1889), and Max Weber drew deeply on both Old and New Testament scholarship. The New Testament furnishes less material about religious institutions than the Old, but many scholars had some training in ancient history and could relate the texts to their wider social and cultural settings. Thus, in his 1880 Bampton Lectures at Oxford on *The Organization of the Christian Churches*, Edwin Hatch discussed briefly 'the circumstances of the society in which those communities existed'. Later on, the New Testament research of the 'Chicago school', represented by S. J. Case's *The Social Origins of Christianity* (1923) and *The Social Triumph of the Early Church* (1933), was explicitly social-historical.

However, these and other probes at social history such as Johannes Pedersen's *Israel: Its Life and Culture* (1926 and 1940) and collections of social data such as Roland de Vaux's *Ancient Israel: Its Life and Institutions* (1961) achieve and even attempt less than some more recent work. One reason for the great advances of recent years is the increase in our knowledge of the Ancient Near East and the Greco-Roman world through the availability of further archaeological, epigraphic (inscriptional), and literary material. Another is the use of sociological theory to help interpret the biblical data within this wider context. The applicability to the ancient world of models based on modern anthropological data cannot be taken for granted, but some have proved illuminating. An example is the use of Leon Festinger's social-psychological theory of 'cognitive dissonance' to interpret responses to the failure of Old Testament prophetic predictions and the non-arrival of the Parousia in early Christianity.

In *When Prophecy Fails: A Social and Psychological Study of a Modern Group that Predicted the Destruction of the World* (New York, 1956), Festinger and others reported on the effect that disconfirmation of eschatological expectations had among some millenarian sects. Instead of disbanding, the groups engaged in intense missionary work to compensate for the 'dissonance' or discrepancy between their belief and empirical reality. The authors discuss early Christianity as a possible case, but are cautious about the applicability of their model here on account of the gaps in our historical knowledge. In *Kingdom and Community* (New Jersey, 1975) John Gager tries to reduce these gaps and suggests that both the unexpected death of Jesus and the non-arrival of the Parousia may have given rise to a sense of 'cognitive dissonance' which galvanized the disciples.

Despite Gager's repudiation of any suggestion that cognitive dissonance was the single explanation of missionary activity or early Christian polemic against Judaism, he treats it as a causal explanation. A more cautious use of the theory is made by Robert P. Carroll in *When Prophecy Failed* (London, 1979), which claims rather to 'add a new dimension to our understanding of the prophets'. Both Carroll and Gager are able to provide examples of 'rationalization' following disconfirmation, but the explanatory power of the theory is not clear. What the sociologists provide here is some support for what historians usually draw from their imagination and experience: hypotheses to be tested by the available evidence.

The temptation to use theory as if it were itself evidence has to be resisted. But historians often have to risk a construction where evidence is in short supply, and guesses informed by analogies from a variety of other cultures may be more persuasive than others. At the very least, sociological theory offers new hypotheses and suggests connections which enable us to see old material in new ways. Beyond this, provided the models derived from other cultures are appropriate to the material being interpreted, such new hypotheses may well provide the best historical guesses. In the absence of secure knowledge, ancient historians often have to be satisfied with plausible suggestions. Anything which increases the plausibility of a hypothesis is to be welcomed.

These methods are no longer new, but were slow to gain acceptance in biblical scholarship. Many scholars have correctly emphasized the limitations of such methods in the field of ancient history where the data are sparse. Clearly, statistical work, important in some sociology and economics, is impossible here. It is also obvious that psychological approaches have only a very limited viability. Such psycho-history as E. Erikson's *Young Man Luther* (1958) fails to impress sceptical historians—and we know far more about Luther than about any biblical character. It is rather in the interpretation of particular texts (such as an Eriksonian interpretation of the parable of the Prodigal Son), not in their contributions to biography or history, that these perspectives are beginning to prove fruitful for biblical interpretation. If this impression is correct, then 'psychological hermeneutics' and psychoanalytic interpretation of the Old and New Testament belong in our chapters which move from the dominant historical paradigm, or framework of research, to the more literary orientation actually suggested by the words interpretation and hermeneutics.

The general preference of biblical scholars for historical research partly explains the hesitations about using social-scientific models. Within the historical paradigm for research their usefulness is limited. Suggestions drawn from psychology (for example) are unlikely to persuade biblical historians, because the supporting evidence is never strong enough to sustain a historical case. Psychologizing explanations of Paul's conversion, based on an interpretation of Romans 7 as autobiography, are largely discredited now. In contrast to these, Gerd Theissen's explorations of *Psychological Aspects of Pauline Theology* (1983; ET Philadelphia, 1987) rightly focus on texts, not on the person Paul. This turn (or rather, return) to a more literary framework, which takes over what historical exegesis offers but does not aim to write history or biography, provides more opportunities for introducing psychological insights into biblical interpretation.

Psychology is an extreme case because it requires so much historical and biographical information. But anthropology reinforces from another angle our suggestion that much depends upon whether the biblical interpreter is still working within the historical paradigm or has shifted to a more literary interest in the texts as such. There are different schools of thought in social or cultural anthropology, as in all the social sciences. Some thinkers, such as E. E. Evans-Pritchard, see a close relationship between anthropology and history. Others, especially those influenced by the structuralist anthropology of Lévi-Strauss, are more conscious of the differences.

It was to be expected that some biblical scholars would find in the more historical anthropology, introduced into biblical research a century ago by W. Robertson Smith, a natural development of their own work, but that they would be uncertain how to react to a more structuralist approach. To the uninitiated, structuralism at first appears perverse. Its jargon is horrific and it seems to be asking the wrong questions and ignoring the obvious ones. But that could simply show how far we are imprisoned by our familiar categories and questions. Even had it not proved fruitful in some other disciplines, especially linguistics and social anthropology, a new approach which challenged what was previously taken for granted would seem worthy of attention.

Structuralism has made its mark in biblical scholarship more upon literary than social-scientific kinds of analysis. Like psycho-analytic interpretation (with which it is sometimes combined) it is better considered in our 'literary' Chapter 7. But it has probably been more successful in the social sciences than in literary criticism. Societies and cultures clearly have a structure that can be analysed, and for this purpose there is some obvious sense in temporarily setting aside questions about historical development. The analogy with the structure of language provides models by which to analyse systems of kinship and religious rituals. The Old Testament, especially the Pentateuch, provides some material which lends itself to such approaches. Sometimes they make some sense of obscure texts which other approaches left obscure (see below, p. 253). But the evidence is too uncertain to encourage the expectation that ancient Israelite society can be greatly illuminated in this way. Even this structuralist analysis of particular texts needs to be co-ordinated with the insights gained by more traditional methods. The discussions of biblical material by Sir Edmund Leach have received short shrift on account of their sometimes arbitrary exegesis. But even when this is corrected, structuralism remains less attractive to historians than to those biblical scholars who are more sympathetic to literary approaches.

Another difference among social scientists is found in their attitudes to religion. Evans-Pritchard at Oxford was a Roman Catholic and ended his classic work on *Nuer Religion* (1956) by gracefully handing over to the theologians. For all his advances in other respects, the anti-religious positivism of Leach at Cambridge is more reminiscent of Sir James Frazer.

In *The Golden Bough* (1890–1915), which eventually contained a whole volume on The Day of Atonement, and in *Folk-Lore in the Old Testament* (1918), Frazer applied comparative ethnography to the Bible on a grand scale, and in the process brought the whole approach into disrepute. But Frazer's positivism is no objection to the discipline itself and no longer dominates it. Corrections have also been made at the historical and exegetical levels. Recent anthropological research on the Bible, by Rogerson, Lang, Carroll, and Malina among others (see Further Reading, and p. 142 above), is the work of professional biblical scholars who are neither careless of exegesis nor prejudiced against religion.

Mention of Frazer spotlights the suspicion about the social sciences on the part of theologians and earlier biblical scholars. The threat to religion posed by historical criticism in the eighteenth and nineteenth centuries had been countered by the liberals. By the mid twentieth century even conservative theologians found they could accept it. The social sciences looked far more dangerous. In the early twentieth century their interpretations of religion were generally reductionist, i.e. eliminating what believers consider important. Any theologian hoping to use them (such as Ernst Troeltsch) had first to engage in the massive philosophical task of combating that. But this was not recognized as a high-priority task by German theologians after the First World War. The new social-scientific approaches to the Bible did not have to be taken up, because unlike early historical research their competing accounts of the biblical data were not obviously more persuasive than what the historically schooled theologians were themselves now offering. The new methods could safely be ignored, as least until they were justified by their results, or the cultural climate made them inescapable.

Today, sociologically informed descriptions are more persuasive than they were at the beginning of the century. That is partly because they are more sophisticated, both at the historical and the theoretical levels. But changes in the cultural and theological climate are also significant factors in their wider acceptance. The first factor has been noted in the words of C. Wright Mills. The second, the theological climate, can be illustrated by the example of form criticism.

This approach raised sociological questions from the outset. It directed attention to the communities in which the biblical material took shape, and to the locations and social functions of the material within them. Its characteristic phrase *Sitz im Leben* refers to the 'setting in the life' of the religious community. But the form critics concentrated on cultic practice, and scarcely related this to the wider social and political realities of Israel and the early Church. The cultural influences on Gunkel's view of religion were romanticism and idealism, not sociology, and his comparative material was drawn mainly from folklore studies. The next generation could have learned from Weber and Durkheim, or even from Troeltsch. But the sociological potential of form criticism was not developed. Gunkel had at least been interested in 'religion', if not in a sociologically informed way. Those mesmerized by Karl Barth were hostile to the concept.

The theological revival of the 1920s pointed kerygmatic theologians such as Bultmann and von Rad to the transmission and interpretation of traditions (through which the Word of God was heard) rather than to social description. Discussion then fastened on the historicity of the material which form criticism seemed to undermine. Neither progressives nor conservatives between the 1920s and the 1970s were theologically interested in the sociological questions suggested by the Bible.

Both the arguments over historicity, and the kerygmatic theology of the Word, were partly eclipsed in the later 1960s by more socially engaged styles of theology. In Europe the student revolutionary excitement was soon deflated by economic pressures and by social and ecclesiastical conservatism. It was in the more open atmosphere of the United States that the new developments flourished.

The social sciences had long had a place in American pastoral and ethical courses. These have usually been oriented to the practice of ministry, and without significant impact on biblical research. But they offer a reminder that biblical interpretation is in principle open to infiltration from the social sciences at two different points: through the methods of historical scholarship, enriched by these new perspectives, and also through the theological interests of the biblical interpreters themselves, whose own theologies (in the world described by C. Wright Mills) are increasingly likely to have been partly shaped by the social sciences.

These two points are doubtless linked. Biblical scholars, like anyone else, may be attracted by the theological opportunities offered by the social sciences to broaden their historical questioning in these directions. But there is some advantage in distinguishing between the way historical methods have been properly enlarged by social-scientific methods on the one hand, and the hermeneutical or theological dimensions of this approach on the other. To clarify this distinction our set of three examples begins with a book which until the last chapter is largely social-historical, though as theoretically sophisticated as anything in the field; and ends with an author who is explicitly developing a sociological hermeneutics, though still working within the historical paradigm. The perspective is too short for the contemporary scene to be easily epitomized by identifying towering figures such as Baur, Wellhausen, Gunkel, Bultmann, and von Rad. The Further Reading sections will hint at increased fragmentation, but symmetry with previous chapters may be preserved here by giving three outstanding examples.

Three examples

Wayne A. Meeks's account of 'the social world of the apostle Paul' in *The First Urban Christians* (1982) is able to draw on ten years of recent sociological approaches to this material, especially the research of Theissen, Schütz, and Holmberg (see Further Reading), in addition to the advances made in the study of the social history of the Hellenistic (including Hellenistic-Jewish) world. His book will unquestionably stand as a classic presentation of the possibilities and limitations of a social-historical approach within New Testament studies, partly on account of Meeks's learning and judgement, and partly because the Pauline mission provides by far the fullest material for an approach which is generally handicapped by the paucity of evidence. Not only do we possess in the authentic Pauline epistles considerable evidence of the beliefs, rituals, and moral norms of these congregations, but we also know their locations and (within a very few years) the date of writing of each. It is therefore possible to correlate the internal evidence to be gleaned from the epistles with what is known from archaeology, inscriptions, and classical authors about life in a first-century Eastern Mediterranean city. The deutero-Pauline literature also throws indirect light here, by showing something of how the beliefs and social organization of these Pauline communities developed. Nowhere else in the New Testament is there so much material for the social historian. The temptation to fill in gaps from guesswork based on allegedly analogous sectarian movements is therefore less serious here than elsewhere.

Unlike some who have engaged in the sociological investigation of early Christianity, from the Marxist Kautsky (1908) onwards, Meeks suffers from no anti-theological animus. He is as clear about the theological potential of this approach as are Theissen, Schütz, and Elliott. Although he does not develop this, a reference to *The Nature of Doctrine* (1984) by his Yale colleague George Lindbeck indicates how Meeks might see his work dovetailing with what Lindbeck calls a 'post-liberal' theology.

Lindbeck takes from the social anthropologist Clifford Geertz ('Religion as a Cultural System', in *The Interpretation of Cultures*, see Further Reading) a 'cultural linguistic' theory of religion as a system of symbols, i.e. a 'system of meanings embodied in the symbols which make up the religion proper' (p. 27). But as a Christian theologian Lindbeck also lives within a particular (Lutheran) religious system. It is evidently possible to describe a religion in social-scientific terms and at the same time to practise it.

Meeks's social description of early Christianity is similarly compatible with belief in it, as discussed above (p. 32 f.). But he does not pursue these hermeneutical issues explicitly. He simply tries to illuminate the epistles historically and finds sociological categories more helpful than the Christian theological ones usually found in New Testament scholarship. Just as Deissmann at the beginning of the century found it liberating to present Paul in his social and historical context, cut loose from the older dogmatic categories still common then in New Testament theology, so have many contemporary New Testament scholars found it necessary to break out of the sometimes stifling atmosphere of the past two generations' existentialist and related New Testament theologies.

Asking new questions, even more than the use of new data, is proving illuminating in this as in other fields of historical research. As J. G. Gager observed in his attempt to use explanatory models from the social sciences, 'Progress, or more modestly change, in the study of early Christianity will come about not through the discovery of new historical information, which can always be assimilated within old paradigms, but through new questions and new perspectives' (1975, p. 13). Again, the aims of the interpreters are decisive. In *The First Urban Christians* Meeks is a social historian who wants to know what it was like to be an ordinary Christian in this segment of the early Christian movement. That is not the question that guides New Testament theology, but answering it could both stimulate and contribute to future developments there too.

The greatest advance of Meeks's work over the social history of the old Chicago school of S. J. Case and others lies in its use of sociological theory. This is not allowed to pressurize the data, but by drawing on various theorists who ask what social functions are fulfilled by social institutions, Meeks achieves the kind of 'new questions and new perspectives' that Gager called for. One can ask of the texts what they *do*, not merely what they say. They do it by saying something, but that is only part of the transaction, and conveying information is not always what is most important.

After meticulous accounts of the urban environment and 'social level' of Pauline Christians, Meeks describes the formation of these communities with the help of models from the environment (household, voluntary association, synagogue, philosophic or rhetorical school), all of which offer significant analogies, though no more than that. The language of belonging and separation, by which these groups preserve boundaries while remaining open to outsiders, is analysed, and new definitions of purity considered. Chapters on leadership and ritual analyse their organization and worship, again in sociological terms which place familiar texts in a fresh light.

Only when these visible dimensions of the new community life have been considered does Meeks go on to discuss 'patterns of belief and patterns of life'. Theological and ethical statements depend for their meaning partly on the context in which they are uttered. Paul's symbolic language is here investigated with an eye to its social implications, and while Meeks avoids crude Marxist ideas about these 'superstructures' being *caused* by material (i.e. economic) factors, he is prepared to look for significant correlations and tentatively to suggest why certain beliefs may have been attractive to certain types of people.

Clearly this is the most speculative part of the enterprise, but whatever one makes of specific suggestions, the general claim that these people were engaged in constructing a new social reality and symbolic world is convincing, and viewing the New Testament in that light is both rationally satisfying and theologically suggestive. The interconnections between doctrine, ethics, and spirituality, for example, become much clearer in this frame of reference, and the challenge to make explicit (and so open to criticism) the theory of religion with which they are working cannot be ignored by theologians.

Meeks's book is taken first because while our three representative authors are all deeply rooted in critical historical research, this social history stands closest to the traditional concerns of modern biblical scholarship. The theory it contains is subordinated to a clearly defined historical goal.

Our second example is perhaps the most creative and fertile mind in biblical scholarship and interpretation today. Gerd Theissen is now a Heidelberg professor, but he was an assistant and schoolmaster in Bonn during the mid-1970s when he published a series of outstanding articles on the sociology of early Palestinian Christianity and of Paul's mission. Responding to the mood described by C. Wright Mills (above, p. 138), Theissen began a methodological essay on 'The Sociological Interpretation of Religious Traditions' (1975) as follows: 'Every age has its preferred intellectual procedures for grappling with the irritating and fascinating phenomenon of religion . . . By all indications, questions from the sociology of religion are in the forefront today' (ET 1982, p. 175).

In Theissen's work the sociological theory is closer to the surface than in Meeks's, though he too is eclectic, taking his theory piecemeal and using it where it fits. His essays likewise could be called social description or social history. But he is evidently also interested in developing a 'theory of early Christian religion' including psychological perspectives and drawing upon linguistics as well as the sociological dimensions illustrated by these probes. His subsequent monograph on *Psychological Aspects of Pauline Theology* (1983; ET 1987) and his earlier article on 'Paul's Soteriological Symbolism' (1974; ET in press) give some hint of both his wider programme and his versatility. They also show how a theological framework can simultaneously serve both historical research and the practical use of the Bible by religious communities or anyone else interested in the human issues the Bible raises.

Like Meeks, Theissen explains clearly what he is doing and why. He faces possible objections and lets the results speak for themselves. Each article in *The Social Setting of Pauline Christianity* (ET 1982) focuses on a quite narrow topic, in four cases taken from the Corinthian situation. Paul's pastoral skill in the realistic and practical management of conflict is illuminated with the help of conflict theory. New questions lead to new connections, such as that between Paul's legitimacy as an apostle and his subsistence as a (controversially) non-stipendiary missionary. They also lead to fresh theological reflections on such questions as the social contexts of ministry, the adequacy of certain ethical stances, and the dynamics at work in a local Church. Finally, the new questions yield new information, for example concerning the social stratification of the Corinthian Church.

Theissen does not doubt that there were theological reasons for the dispute between 'the strong and the weak' at Corinth, but he insists that where social relationships are at issue, a sociological analysis is also possible, and need not involve reducing the controversy to social factors. Again, sociological analysis can make surprisingly constructive use of such knowledge of ancient society as eating habits, which hardly seem directly relevant to a theological reading of the Bible, but which may, in the context of a rational theory of religion, become theologically significant. Theissen's essentially integrative theory of religion may require qualification, but he has already made seminal contributions to our understanding of the New Testament.

The aims of the present chapter are best served by taking as our Old Testament example one which deliberately, creatively, and provocatively goes beyond the normal concerns of biblical scholarship. Enlarging the historical perspective and sharpening historical observation with help from the social sciences is by now accepted in principle, whatever scepticism remains about its successful application. But to assess this approach by its historical results alone would be to ignore other dimensions present in modern interpretation of religiously significant texts. Two hundred years of critical historical study have not merely provided a new account of the material; they have also changed the interpreters' relationship to these texts. That was no accident. Some of the pioneers saw their new methods as potentially liberating: human reason would free mankind from the shackles of religious authority and tradition.

This emancipatory thrust of the new rational methods has been even plainer in some social-scientific research. Marxism is not alone in its intention of changing the world, as opposed to merely understanding it. This 'committed' stance of some social science (psychoanalysis as well as Marxism) invites comparison with some religious interpretation of the Bible (see above, p. 23 f.). Biblical scholarship might recoil at such threats to its objectivity, but social-scientific methods offer a resource to those interested in practical religious forms of biblical interpretation. In order to illustrate these dimensions of our topic it seems best to pass over with appreciation such a sound and relatively uncontroversial book as R. R. Wilson's *Prophecy and Society in Ancient Israel* (1980), and to take as our Old Testament example one which shares but also goes well beyond the historical aims of most biblical scholarship.

Norman Gottwald's *The Tribes of Yahweh* (1979) uses social-scientific models and methods to illuminate a stretch of history. But this 'sociology of the religion of liberated Israel, 1250–1050 B.C.E.' (subtitle) goes further, and also calls for a new style of theology and biblical interpretation to replace the liberals' concordat between faith and historical reason. That gentlemen's agreement has allowed biblical scholarship to pursue its academic interests undisturbed by practical religious concerns and left these practical concerns undisturbed by biblical scholarship. Gottwald senses that the late twentieth-century world needs a more fruitful engagement between scholarship and the wider world, and he has become the most disturbing figure in contemporary biblical studies. It is hardly surprising that many prefer to ignore the implications of his work.

Like earlier syntheses of history, exegesis, philosophy, and theology, such as those of Baur and Bultmann, *The Tribes of Yahweh* can be challenged on any of these four fronts. But the most generally convincing criticisms will be those which undermine its historical (and related linguistic) proposals. Unlike much philosophy, theology, and literary criticism, these are directly testable.

Gottwald seeks to illuminate two centuries of history, for which some (though not many) literary and non-literary sources of information are available. Some direct appeal to these is possible. Even if this evidence is too fragmentary to settle most disputes definitively, it is possible for the scholarly community over an extended period to balance the probabilities and evaluate controversial judgements.

Most sociological enrichment of historical study, including that of Meeks and Theissen, and Gottwald himself on occasion, draws on structural-functional models stemming especially from Max Weber. By contrast, Gottwald generally prefers the 'historical material' approach of Karl Marx, with its emphasis upon such basic economic factors as how societies feed themselves, and the social effects of changes at that material level. This offers a better model for explaining social change than structural models which observe a society at a particular moment. However, since the Marxist model can incorporate Weberian typologies these alternative strategies can both be used. They suggest hypotheses to be tested by all the relevant data.

Gottwald adopts and expands G. Mendenhall's historical thesis that the Israelite 'conquest' was not an invasion from without, but rather a peasants' revolt within Canaanite society. This 'class-struggle' theory, in Gottwald's case inspired by the Marxist model, is only a hypothesis, and the question for biblical scholarship is whether Gottwald has rendered it plausible. But even if the thesis is rejected, historical study of early Israel will have benefited from this challenge to build more social and economic data into its historical theories.

However, the implications of Gottwald's work for theology and biblical interpretation extend far beyond this historical argument. They do not depend on the author's historical hypotheses, but upon his theory of religion, which embraces his own Christianity as well as influencing his perception of early Israel. He writes of a 'socio-economic demythologization of Israelite Yahwism', and sees the religious symbol 'Yahweh' as a function of an egalitarian movement. Whether the symbol points to a reality independent of particular social systems is a philosophical and theological question which he does not discuss. Most Christians and Jews believe that

God, the focus of their religion, has an independent reality, however dependent the symbols are on social conditions. Gottwald does not deny this, as those who pioneered the sociological analysis of religion did, but his descriptions and explanations leave no necessary place for it. Much the same could be said of critical historical research. The most that belief and theology can expect from either approach to religion is their compatibility with some forms of religious belief.

The resolution of this tension between social and historical description on the one hand, and religious faith on the other, will be found (if at all) in the experience of practising one's religion. Gottwald's sociological hermeneutics imply an invitation to participate. But to participate in what? In a this-worldly struggle for freedom, and engagement on behalf of the poor and oppressed? Something is surely missing here, but what is presented is arguably more Christian than religious escapism or the comfortable acceptance of an unjust status quo. Gottwald recognized that a sociology of religion drawn from Durkheim can have very conservative social implications. His choice of the Marxist alternative is certainly a value-judgement and arguably a theological decision based on his Christian understanding of what Jesus was about. Many other Christians will welcome this choice, while insisting that a theological interpretation of the Bible must involve more than what Gottwald in this book has discussed.

Gottwald's 'sociology of the religion of liberated Israel', like earlier forms of biblical theology, has a normative thrust concealed (or barely concealed) under its historical descriptive cloak. Whether this and other liberation theologies are right to place such emphasis on freedom and justice in this world, and other questions about the limits of Christian fellow-travelling with Marxist programmes, do not concern us here. The choice of Gottwald's book as our third example was intended only to hint at one way in which this development within biblical scholarship could have wider theological implications. When and if the full impact of such analyses is felt, and scholars learn to ask what interests their 'objective' research is serving, the scholarly guild will be a less comfortable society. The pursuit of truth has a personal dimension, as theologians, Marxists, and others have always insisted.

Within and beyond the historical pale

The three authors considered above stand firmly within the tradition of critical historical study of the Bible. Their bold proposals seek to extend and expand its scope, but at the same time ask to be evaluated according to its well-established norms. All three write history; they seek to increase our understanding of the Israelite and early Christian history which lies behind the biblical texts. That is what distinguishes their approach from those to be considered in Chapter 7.

However, it is evident that these new dimensions recently introduced into historical scholarship not only enlarge our understanding of the past, but also offer historians a new consciousness about their own locations and interests. This 'turn to the subject' is apparent in recent theoretical discussion of historiography, even where no direct influence of the social sciences is visible. New emphases upon the narrative character of history, and the element of construction involved in writing it, have 'softened' both history and some social science (especially cultural anthropology), and brought them closer to literary theory than the older positivists would have countenanced.

In this intellectual climate the ways in which much of the best biblical scholarship has been guided by theological interests no longer seem either surprising or disreputable. Distortions arising from these interests still require correction, but the mutual correction of differing perspectives, and consequent enlargement of vision, is normal practice within the humanities. Religion elicits a higher degree of personal interest than most research areas. But this need not be a handicap. This subject-matter is elusive and requires some empathy if it is to be understood.

The admission of interests in historical research, the acknowledgement of similarities between historical and literary narrative, the centrality of methods which attend to the modern student's own interests, are all contributing to what Clifford Geertz has recently called a 'blurring of genres' within the humanities and social sciences. This makes mapping contemporary biblical interpretation difficult. Recent developments suggest that it should be divided by reference to the dominance and, in some circles, eclipse of the historical paradigm or framework of research. But this places social-scientific approaches in an ambiguous position. Most of the biblical scholarship which uses these methods remains firmly within the historical paradigm, as our three examples have illustrated. By contrast, the structuralism touched on briefly above, p. 143, is a deliberately non- and sometimes anti-historical method which has proved fruitful within the social sciences, especially anthropology. Its failure to make much impact upon biblical scholarship through anthropology (where it is strong)—as opposed to through literary criticism (where it is weak)—shows that the historical paradigm still controls biblical scholarship. Only where this had been abandoned on other grounds was structuralism able to make a significant mark.

One exception to the failure of non-literary structuralism to make an impact deserves attention in this chapter. This lies in its association with Marxism. Whereas Gottwald and others have introduced Marxist sociology into the historical paradigm, Fernando Belo has combined it with a structuralist exegesis of Mark. Biblical scholars have found the result hard to digest, but it falls within the purview of 'theology and the social sciences', not 'the literary study of the Bible'.

In *A Materialist Reading of the Gospel of Mark* (1974; ET 1981) Belo discusses the economic realities of first-century Palestine, and refers on occasion to normal biblical scholarship. His book cannot be simply contrasted with this. But it is quite unlike most other biblical interpretation, and not even its introductory section on 'The Mode of Production in Biblical Palestine' is guided by a historical interest. The actual 'reading of Mark' which Belo offers is almost unreadable for anyone unfamiliar with structuralist terminology. But that is effective in shaking readers out of their usual questions and forcing them to attend to a new agenda arising not from the history, but from the narrative—or rather, not arising from the narrative, but imposed upon it. To historically conscious scholarship this sounds like a damaging criticism, but history is not everything, and even historical scholarship may be serving contemporary interests. Theologians, at any rate, are in no position to cast the first stone at anyone for having interests, however strongly they may dispute this untheological reading of Mark.

One test of this interpretation of Mark's narrative account of

Jesus' messianic practice, generated by Belo with the help of structuralist analysis, is whether it persuades anyone else. It makes no claim to be judged by reference to authorial intention, and yet does claim to be humanly significant. The success it has had among French Marxists who want to claim the Gospel heritage as their own is a challenge to theology. Whether it can be called Christian is a matter for theological dispute. Whether it can be called scholarship is more a matter of convention. But it is certainly biblical interpretation; and such a powerful, if unorthodox, witness to Jesus stimulated by Mark's Gospel must interest theologians, if not historians.

Belo's is an isolated case of structuralist tools drawing a sociological interest in the text away from the historical paradigm but not into the literary paradigm. It is unlikely to be widely imitated outside the coterie of Marxists impressed by structuralism. But two other developments on the overlapping borders of theology, social sciences, history, and literature deserve mention here.

The points at which Marxism has made its greatest incursions into biblical interpretation are neither the impressive scholarship of Gottwald nor the arcane mysteries of Belo, but the clarion-calls of Latin-American liberation theology. It is impossible to do justice here to the importance of this, and it is better omitted than surveyed superficially. Western biblical scholarship has not yet engaged satisfactorily with it, any more than Western culture has adequately faced the challenges posed by the Third World. Christian theology still has much to learn from the Latin-American Churches about the relationship of biblical interpretation and the religious, social, even political commitment with which this confronts us.

The second large issue to be merely skirted here is the branch of liberation theology that has made the greatest impact among North American and European theologians and biblical scholars, namely feminist theology. The most impressive contributions to New Testament scholarship from this perspective have been those of Elizabeth Schüssler Fiorenza. Her book *In Memory of Her* (1983) illustrates both the strengths and the limitations of addressing this challenge of a new Christian consciousness in terms of the historical paradigm that still dominates biblical scholarship.

A 'feminist theological reconstruction of Christian origins' is both a historical and a theological enterprise. Historical methods serve theological or ideological as well as historical interests. The author not only wants to know how significant a role women played in the Jesus and early Christian movements; she also wants to argue a case in support of her beliefs. Sociological insights sharpen both her historical vision and her critical eye for the interests which have partly erased early Christian women from the record and rapidly reversed the liberating trend begun by Jesus himself and generally supported by Paul. The same 'hermeneutics of suspicion' sharpens her eye for the unconscious bias present in a still largely male scholarly guild. She does not, however, 'want to advocate a value-free exegesis but only to clarify the values at stake' (p. 207).

The more that women have been erased from the record, the more difficult it becomes to argue that they once had a more significant role than now appears. But historians in general, and New Testament historians in particular, are skilled in recognizing stray hints and building far-reaching hypotheses upon them. Despite some historical improbabilities, *In Memory of Her* makes out a strong case for both the startling freedom of Jesus and the earliest missionary movement, and the increasing patriarchalism of the second and third generations.

Historical arguments such as this do not lead most theologians directly to theological judgements that are timelessly valid, though the appeal to a historical reconstruction of Jesus' ministry in order to criticize the canonical record is an interesting move. Since the New Testament records aim to interpret *Jesus* theologically, such a claim to the historical truth about him has to be taken seriously. It would be very bad theology to allow a purely historical interpretation of Jesus to *replace* the evangelists' theological interpretations, but within a Christian theological frame of reference new historical insights can find a valuable role. The critical power of historical appeals to Jesus against aspects of the religious tradition have played an important part in the history of modern theology and in the popular religious and cultural consciousness.

Apart from providing tools for theological criticism, such new historical reconstructions may offer specific theological suggestions and proposals, in this case concerning the ministry of women. More generally, our understanding of the whole development of our tradition, together with some understanding of contemporary experience, provides the basis of most theological reflection. It is therefore important to make our historical understanding of Christian origins as accurate and truthful as possible. Clearly the evidence is in certain respects one-sided, and most readings of it biased. Corrections and correctives are therefore welcome.

Rewriting history as 'herstory' is one intellectual task to be undertaken by those who realize how far our identity is shaped by our perception of the past. Nevertheless, it leaves one uneasy. Usually when we unmask history as ideology it is to argue for *less* ideology, not for an alternative one. Of course the plea for less ideology can also be a self-interested move to preserve the status quo and resist revolutionary attempts to change society; but that is a reason for being clear about one's interests and values and about the appropriate means of achieving one's goals. The more we wish to change our own society in order to embody human values in it, the less we should wish to do so by destroying other human values. Historical truthfulness is a value worth preserving. That sets limits to ideological rewriting of history—limits which are respected by responsible historians such as Fiorenza. She can press her case only within the limits of what she can show to be historically plausible.

That rather strict limitation leads some biblical scholars who wish to press a theological or an ideological case to choose other, more literary styles of interpretation over historical reconstruction, as the next two chapters will explain. Especially in Old Testament scholarship, Jewish and Christian feminist interests are best articulated through a literary criticism which explores the feminine imagery which is present in the tradition but insufficiently appreciated. Phyllis Trible's *God and the Rhetoric of Sexuality* (Philadelphia, 1978) is an excellent example. This alternative framework can equally well be informed by sociological insights, as Marxist literary criticism demonstrates. But this frontier between the social sciences and literary criticism is only slowly being occupied by biblical interpreters.

The one part of this frontier already mentioned is psychoanalytic interpretation. It did not get far when attached to historical study of the Bible but has much better prospects within the new literary-critical paradigm. The task of interpreting the symbolic language of the Bible is the most immediately obvious theological task awaiting biblical scholars. Any system of thought and practice that is largely concerned with the interpretation of symbols, as is psychoanalysis, is bound to be suggestive in respect of method, and to interact with theology in content. The human sciences are near neighbours to theology. Good relations are desirable.

It remains to be seen how far liberation and feminist theology follow psychoanalytic interpretation by taking a more literary direction. At present, what they have in common is their sometimes subtle combinations of historical and hermeneutical interests. The claim to be illuminating the biblical history acts as a control against arbitrary exegesis. On the other hand, the evidence is sufficiently thin and the history sufficiently ambiguous for this not to be a tight control, and to allow some experimentation with 'how things might have been'. These experiments will often fail to persuade anyone who does not want to be persuaded that the historical past actually was as the revisionists claim. But so long as their suggestions are worth discussing they will be discussed, and by being discussed will generate some reflection on how things ought to be today. And that is partly how the Bible functions as scripture: not by providing historically demonstrated normative propositions and injunctions, but by providing a foundation narrative, and provoking reflection about it within the religious community.

This double interest in illuminating both past and present is normal in the study of both history and literature, though the emphasis falls differently. History is primarily interested in the past, literary study in the present. The social sciences can combine with either of these disciplines and illuminate both past and present. They can also strengthen the links between past and present, which both history and literature tend to weaken by their emphasis upon one or the other. Finally, and most importantly for religious interpretations of the Bible, they can help integrate theory and practice, belief and life (both moral and spiritual), by analysing the component parts of religious systems and exposing the hidden connections.

An example of this is provided by the new theological

appreciation as well as historical understanding of apocalyptic literature, made possible through the enrichment of historical research by sociological perspectives. One may doubt whether this strange imagery has been explained by speculation about its social locations. The imagery originates mostly in the creative interpretation of earlier traditions, especially scripture, not in superstructures sprouting from social and economic conditions. It is therefore impossible to deduce social locations from the surviving literature with any confidence or precision. But where these are known (as in the case of the Qumran community and Paul's congregations) significant correlations between apocalyptic imagery and socio-historical situations can be identified, and this makes possible a more sympathetic understanding of the literature, and enlivens its application to the contemporary world. Marx's 'cry of the oppressed creature' can be heard in the Book of Revelation; it can today motivate Christian and Jewish responsibility for those who are oppressed, and can do this in ways that earlier biblical scholarship did not envisage.

No chapter in this book has attempted to give a complete account of even the main trends in biblical scholarship. This one also has stood back from the rising swell of books and articles which have used social-scientific methods, and has taken examples only to expose some of the underlying issues. The very select Further Reading list adds a few pointers to indicate that here is a growing field of biblical research. Its theological impact is beginning to be felt as believers seek to understand their faith with the help of categories and perspectives drawn from the social sciences.

Before turning finally to the other main developments in biblical scholarship and their importance for the wider aims of biblical interpretation, it is necessary to let the theological and hermeneutical reflections introduced in Chapter 1 catch up on the scholarly achievements surveyed in Chapters 3, 4, and 5. By offering a theory about the relationship between faith and reason in this central area of theological study, the transitional chapter which follows will also offer a perspective from which to view the new literary framework adopted by some biblical interpreters. As biblical scholarship takes a new secular turn in secular institutions, it is necessary for theology to consider how it can best engage with these promising developments.

Further reading

In addition to the works discussed or mentioned in the course of the chapter the following selection indicates some of the directions currently being pursued. It cannot indicate how far a more sociological consciousness has affected historical work on the Bible generally. More elementary books are asterisked.

General

ABELSON, R. P., *Theories of Cognitive Consistency: A Sourcebook* (Chicago, 1968).

BANTON, M. (ed.), *Anthropological Approaches to the Study of Religion* (London, 1966).

BAUM, G., *Religion and Alienation: A Theological Reading of Sociology* (New York and Toronto, 1975).

BELLAH, R., *Beyond Belief: Essays on Religion in a Post-traditional World* (New York, 1970).

*BERGER, P. L., *The Sacred Canopy* (New York, 1967). English title: *The Social Reality of Religion* (London, 1969).

—— and LUCKMANN, T., *The Social Construction of Reality: A Treatise in the Sociology of Knowledge* (New York and London, 1966).

BOURDILLON, M. F. C., *et al.* (eds.), *Sacrifice* (London, 1980).

BURKERT, W., *Greek Religion* (1977; ET Oxford, 1985).

—— *Homo Necans: The Anthropology of Ancient Greek Sacrificial Ritual and Myth* (1979; ET Berkeley, 1983).

BURRIDGE, K. O. L., *New Heaven: New Earth* (Oxford, 1969).

CAPPS, D., *et al.*, *Psychology of Religion: A Guide to Information Sources* (Detroit, 1976).

COSER, L., *The Function of Social Conflict* (Glencoe, 1956).

DOUGLAS, M. *Purity and Danger: An Analysis of the Concepts of Pollution and Taboo* (London, 1966).

DURKHEIM, E., *The Elementary Forms of the Religious Life* (1912; ET London, 1915).

EVANS-PRITCHARD, E. E., *Theories of Primitive Religion* (Oxford, 1965).

FINNEGAN, R. and HORTON, R. (eds.), *Modes of Thought: Essays on Thinking in Western and Non-Western Societies* (London, 1973).

FROMM, E., *The Dogma of Christ* (1930; ET New York, 1963).

GEERTZ, C., *The Interpretation of Cultures* (New York, 1973).

GERTH, H. H. and MILLS, C. WRIGHT, *From Max Weber* (Oxford and New York, 1958).

GIRARD, R., *Violence and the Sacred* (1972; ET Baltimore and London, 1977).

HABERMAS, J., *Knowledge and Human Interests* (1968; ET Boston, 1971).

HOLLIS, M. and LUKES, S., *Rationality and Relativism* (Oxford, 1982).

LEACH, E., *The Structural Study of Myth and Totemism* (London, 1967).

LÉVI-STRAUSS, C., *Structural Anthropology* (1958; ET New York, 1963 and London, 1968).

LUCKMANN, T., *The Invisible Religion: The Transformation of Symbols in Industrial Society* (1963; ET New York, 1967).

MOL, H. J., *Identity and the Sacred: A Sketch for a New Social Scientific Theory of Religion* (Oxford, 1976; New York, 1977).

MOORE, R. L. *Anthropology and the Study of Religion* (Chicago, 1984).

NEUSNER, J. (ed.), *Religions in Antiquity: Essays in Memory of Erwin Ramsdell Goodenough* (Leiden, 1968).

PICKERING, W. S. F. (ed.), *Durkheim on Religion* (London and Boston, 1975).

—— *Durkheim's Sociology of Religion: Themes and Theories* (London, 1984).

PITT-RIVERS, J., *The Fate of Shechem, or the Politics of Sex* (Cambridge, 1977).

RIDDLE, D. W., *The Martyrs. A Study in Social Control* (Chicago, 1931).

*ROBERTSON, R., *The Sociological Interpretation of Religion* (Oxford, 1970).

SADLER, W. A. (ed.), *Personality and Religion* (Philadelphia and London, 1970).

STURROCK, J., *Structuralism and Since: From Lévi-Strauss to Derrida* (Oxford and New York, 1979).

THEISSEN, G., *On Having a Critical Faith* (1978; ET London and Philadelphia, 1979).

TROELTSCH, E., *The Social Teachings of the Christian Churches and Groups*, 2 vols. (1912; ET London, 1931 and New York, 1960).

TURNER, V., *The Ritual Process: Structure and Anti-Structure* (Chicago, 1969).

VERNANT, J.-P., *Myth and Society in Ancient Greece* (1974; ET Brighton, 1980 and London, 1982).

WEBER, M., *The Sociology of Religion* (1920–1; ET New York, 1963 and London, 1965).

WILSON, B., *Sects and Society* (London and Berkeley, 1961).

—— *Magic and the Millennium: A Sociological Study of Religious Movements of Protest Among Tribal and Third World Peoples* (London and New York, 1973).

—— (ed.), *Rationality* (Oxford, 1974).

WORSLEY, P., *The Trumpet Shall Sound* (London and New York, 1968).

Old Testament

CULLEY, R. C., *et al.* (eds.), *Anthropological Perspectives on Old Testament Prophecy* (Semeia, 21; Chico, 1982).

GASTER, T. H., *Myth, Legend and Custom in the Old Testament* (New York, 1969).

GOTTWALD, N. K. (ed.), *The Bible and Liberation: Political and Social Hermeneutics* (Maryknoll, 1983).

—— *The Hebrew Bible: A Socio-literary Introduction* (Philadelphia and London, 1985).

HANSON, P. D., *The Dawn of Apocalyptic* (Philadelphia, 1975).

LANG, B., *Monotheism and the Prophetic Minority* (Sheffield, 1983).

*—— (ed.), *Anthropological Approaches to the Old Testament* (London and Philadelphia, 1985).

LEACH, E., *Genesis as Myth and Other Essays* (London, 1969).

—— and AYCOCK, D. A., *Structuralist Interpretation of Biblical Myth* (Cambridge, 1983).

LEMCHE, N. P., *Early Israel: Anthropological and Historical Studies on the Israelite Society before the Monarchy* (Leiden, 1985).

ROGERSON, J. W., *Myth in Old Testament Interpretation* (Berlin, 1974; Sheffield, 1983).

—— *Anthropology and the Old Testament* (Oxford, 1978; Sheffield, 1984).

ROHRBAUGH, R. L., *The Biblical Interpreter: An Agrarian Bible in an Industrial Age* (Philadelphia, 1978).

SCHOTTROFF, W. and STEGEMANN, W., *The God of the Small People* (1979; ET Philadelphia, 1986).

WALLIS, L., *A Sociological Study of the Bible* (Chicago, 1912, 1927⁵).

New Testament

BANKS, R., *Paul's Idea of Community: The Early House Churches in their Historical Setting* (Grand Rapids and Exeter, 1980).

ELLIOTT, J. H., *A Home for the Homeless: A Sociological Exegesis of 1 Peter, its Situation and Strategy* (Philadelphia and London, 1981).

—— (ed.), *Social Scientific Criticism of the New Testament and its Social World* (Semeia, 32; Decatur, 1986).

ESLER, P. F., *Community and Gospel in Luke–Acts* (Cambridge, 1987).

GAGER, J. G., *Kingdom and Community: The Social World of Early Christianity* (Englewood Cliffs, 1975).

*GOTTWALD, N. K. (ed.), *The Bible and Liberation: Political and Social Hermeneutics* (Maryknoll, 1983).

HAMERTON KELLY, R., *God as Father* (Philadelphia, 1979).

HARRINGTON, D. J., *The Light of all Nations: Essays on the Church in New Testament Research* (Delaware, 1982).

HOCK, R. F., *The Social Context of Paul's Ministry: Tentmaking and Apostleship* (Philadelphia, 1980).

HOLMBERG, B., *Paul and Power: The Structure of Authority in the Primitive Church as Reflected in the Pauline Epistles* (Philadelphia, 1980).

HYNES, W. J., *Shirley Jackson Case and the Chicago School* (Chicago, 1981).

JUDGE, E. A., *The Social Pattern of Christian Groups in the First Century* (London, 1960).

KECK, L. E., 'On the Ethos of Early Christianity', *Journal of the American Academy of Religion*, 42 (1974).

*KEE, H. C., *Christian Origins in Sociological Perspective* (Atlanta and London, 1980).

—— *Miracle in the Early Christian World: A Study in Sociohistorical Method* (New Haven and London, 1983).

MACDONALD, M. Y., *Institutionalization in Pauline Communities* (Cambridge, 1988).

MALHERBE, A., *Social Aspects of Early Christianity* (Philadelphia, 1983).

MALINA, B., *The New Testament World: Insights from Cultural Anthropology* (Atlanta, 1981 and London, 1983).

—— *Christian Origins and Cultural Anthropology: Practical Models for Biblical Interpretation* (Atlanta, 1986).

MEEKS, W. A., 'The Man from Heaven in Johannine Sectarianism',

Journal of Biblical Literature, 91 (1972); repr. in J. Ashton (ed.), *The Interpretation of John* (London and Philadelphia, 1986).

—— and WILKEN, R. L., *Jews and Christians in Antioch* (Cambridge, Mass., 1982).

MURPHY-O'CONNOR, J., *St Paul's Corinth: Texts and Archaeology* (Delaware, 1983).

OSIEK, C., *What are they Saying about the Social Setting of the New Testament?* (New York, 1984).

*PIXLEY, G., *God's Kingdom: A Guide for Biblical Study* (Maryknoll and London, 1977).

RICHES, J. K., *Jesus and the Transformation of Judaism* (London 1980 and New York, 1982).

RUBENSTEIN R. L., *My Brother Paul* (New York, 1972).

SCHOTTROFF, L. and STEGEMANN, W., *Jesus and the Hope of the Poor* (1978; ET Maryknoll, 1986).

SCHÜTZ, J. H., *Paul and the Anatomy of Apostolic Authority* (Cambridge, 1975).

SCROGGS, R., 'The Earliest Christian Communities as a Sectarian Movement', in J. Neusner (ed.), *Christianity, Judaism, and other Greco-Roman Cults* (Leiden, 1975).

*—— *Paul for a New Day* (Philadelphia, 1977).

—— 'The Sociological Interpretation of the New Testament: The Present State of Research', *New Testament Studies*, 26 (1979–80); repr. in Gottwald, 1983.

*STAMBAUGH, J. and BALCH, D., *The Social World of the First Christians* (Philadelphia and London, 1986).

THEISSEN, G., *The First Followers of Jesus* (1977; ET London, 1978); American title: *Sociology of Early Palestinian Christianity* (Philadelphia, 1977).

*TIDBALL, D., *An Introduction to the Sociology of the New Testament* (Exeter, 1983).

VERNER, D. C., *The Household of God: The Social World of the Pastoral Epistles* (Chico, 1983).

WAETJEN, H. (ed.), *The Gospel of John in Sociolinguistic Perspective* (Berkeley, 1985).

WINK, W., *Transforming Bible Study* (Nashville, 1980; London, 1981).

6

Theology, History, and Literature

Biblical scholarship and theology

The strength of Old and New Testament studies in university departments that are not oriented to religious interests is evident from some of the best recent work in these disciplines. Neither historical nor social scientific research on the Bible actually requires theological interests. These are often present, but are to be found in the aims of some interpreters, not in the methods used. The Bible is a religious object and contains religious material, but there is a difference between studying other people's religion (including their theology) by historical, sociological, or philosophical methods and actually doing theology, i.e. developing one's own theology.

The distinction is obscured by the phrase 'studying theology', which can mean either studying other people's theologies or doing one's own. The ambiguity runs deep, because doing theology today includes describing and analysing, as well as developing, a tradition, and also because in universities most people learn to do theology, i.e. reflect critically on religious faith, by studying other people doing it. It is therefore not easy to detect the transition from studying religion to doing theology, though for some it is like being in an aircraft taking off—the change from grinding along the runway to a still sense of the reality of what it is all about.

In other contexts the experience of God, or wonder, or being religious, precedes rational reflection. It is hard from the perspective of such an experiential theology to see much point in the biblical scholars' concern for minutiae, and it is easy to resent the kind of exercises that a formal theological education imposes upon candidates for ministry in the Church. There is nothing more boring than learning answers to questions one is not asking.

Some knowledge of the development of the Church and its theology in the modern world is a cure for this frustration. It is not difficult to see that many questions discussed by biblical scholars are those which might occur to any thoughtful reader of the Bible. But what our preceding survey of biblical study in the modern world has confirmed is how much what readers or interpreters find in the Bible depends upon their own aims and interests.

The underlying theme of all these discussions has been the relationship between the rational methods used to understand the biblical writings and the religious interests which not only made them a subject of enquiry in the first place, but also drove some seekers after truth to press questions that threatened the fabric of traditional belief.

The final section of this survey (Chapter 7) will report on a recent challenge to the dominance of theologically interested historical research in biblical scholarship. Literary-critical approaches may also be theologically motivated and will be seen to antedate the critical historical work of the past 150 years. But recent attempts to understand 'the Bible as literature' coincide with some loss of confidence in theological reflection on the Bible, and so appear to have accelerated the secularization of biblical scholarship.

Neither historical nor literary research requires any alliance with theological reflection. But over the past 150 years a strong tradition has grown up combining theology with historical scholarship. The new trends of sociological and literary study inherit no such tradition. It remains possible for theologians to forge new connections with these disciplines, as is in fact beginning to happen. But both new trends are notable for their distance from familiar theological commitments. It would be possible to report on the shift in some biblical scholarship to sociological and literary questions without mentioning the religious and theological interests which until recently have dominated scholarly as well as most other interpretation of the Bible.

However, to describe the changing scene in biblical scholarship without reference to the theological undercurrents which are still powerfully present would be to miss the point of most biblical interpretation. Despite the secular methods used by modern scholars in such secular contexts as modern universities, most people's interest in the Bible remains primarily religious. The relationship between the various rational procedures applied to these texts and the religious and theological interests of most interpreters therefore remains the focus of our enquiry.

Earlier chapters have suggested that theological interests have not merely been residually present in modern historical scholarship, but have fuelled it. That is no longer so plainly the case today. A secular culture has finally produced a genuinely non-theological biblical scholarship. But this does not exclude the majority interest in the Bible. It simply sharpens our question of the relationship between historical or literary studies on the one hand, and theological reflection on the biblical witness on the other.

The present chapter seeks to throw light on that issue by drawing from the earlier discussions an account of the relationship of faith and reason in Christians' use of the Bible. What emerges will provide some theological justification for the recent turn to literary approaches. Not that these need any such justification beyond the wishes of some to read the Bible as literature. But for those who still read it as their scripture, some theoretical underpinning is necessary before the religious value of these literary approaches can be understood.

This necessity for theoretical underpinning can be illustrated by the instinctive reservations felt by many Christians a generation ago concerning *The Bible Designed to be Read as Literature*. This elegant volume reproduced large parts of the Bible, mostly from the Authorized Version, without the distraction of chapters and verses. It might almost have been called 'the Bible designed to lie on coffee-tables', and that was the problem. Reading the Bible purely for its literary merit is understandably felt to trivialize it and to neutralize its religious impact.

The point can be reinforced by contrasting the frosty reception given to *The Bible Designed to be Read as Literature* with the religious reassurance communicated by the title *The Bible as History*. Modern understandings of history are on the whole more hostile to religious claims than literature is. The reason that this title nevertheless sounds positive and encouraging (the German title is explicit and could be translated 'the Bible is true, after all') rather than reductive ('the Bible is merely the history of some early

Semites and Christian groups') is that it echoes a long line of Christian defence of traditional claims in the face of modern criticism. That particular form of apologetic was defeated at the scholarly level by Strauss and his successors, but the memory of its orthodox motivation persists. Many Christians *want* to believe the Bible is historically reliable because that is taken to guarantee the truth of its witness to real events. Whether divine events are accessible to the historian is barely considered by an apologetic that wants facts, not problems. In other words, the innocent phrase 'the Bible as history' trails clouds of theological theory. This chapter will uncover some good, as well as some bad, theory.

Our reason for drawing some provisional conclusions at the penultimate stage of this book is to provide a theological bridge from the still dominant historical scholarship, lately enriched by social-scientific perspectives, to the alternative 'literary paradigm' now available. By setting *both* these scholarly approaches within a wider theological context we hope to show how such thoroughly secular disciplines can be integrated within the theological type of perspective on the Bible still shared by the great majority of its readers. Nobody *has* to combine the rational methods of biblical study with a religious interest, but anybody *may* do so, and many *want* to, without knowing how this is best achieved.

As our survey moves from historical to literary approaches there is no need to choose between the different methods. Linguistic study remains foundational, and literary, historical, and sociological questions are all posed by these texts. The question for biblical scholarship is simply whether they are best organized within a historical or a literary frame of reference.

The answer is simple. It depends on each particular interpreter's aims or priorities. Historians will continue to organize all the necessary scholarly tasks to serve their historical goals, and literary critics will order them differently to serve their different ends. Theologians' choices are more complicated because their aims are less clearly defined and more varied. But they should follow the same principle and ask which approach serves their aims, which include but are finally different from those of both historians and literary critics.

One advantage of seeing the literary approaches as a challenge to the dominance of the historical paradigm is that this highlights the difference of aims possible in biblical interpretation. Because scholarship consists largely in linguistic and historical tasks and these call for methods now free from theological constraints, it is easy to lose sight of, or lose altogether, the aims and interests which led to biblical scholarship in the first place. 'Aims' and 'methods' are clearly different, but the word 'tasks' (*Aufgaben*), which was prominent in German theoretical discussions, stands close to both. It led such brilliant scholars as Wrede and Wellhausen to slide from using historical methods in fulfilling historical tasks to the more questionable assumption that these are the only proper aims and goals of biblical scholarship.

Historical study of the Bible thus gained a life of its own. On the one hand it has been domesticated by Christian theology, and integrated within the perennial task of theology to articulate the faith in a new intellectual environment. On the other hand it has moved from defending the freedom of its rational methods from theological constraints to defining biblical scholarship itself in terms of these non-theological aims. The new literary approaches provide a valuable reminder that historical aims, though legitimate and even important, are not the only possibility. Literary methods can serve historical aims, and historical methods can serve literary aims, or both may serve religious and theological aims. The step from using historical *methods* to defining the *aims* of biblical scholarship in exclusively historical terms set it at odds with the interests of most other readers and students of the Bible, for whom both historical and literary approaches are important only because they subserve religious (including theological) aims.

One purpose of this book, and this chapter in particular, is to clarify the relationship between academic research and the religious use of the Bible. That is not to deny the legitimacy of non-religious interests in these texts. It is simply to recognize the character of biblical interpretation in the past, which has been to a large extent religiously motivated, and to draw from this some suggestions for the future. It is likely that most interest in the Bible will continue to be religiously motivated, though religion may come to be more broadly defined. Denominational commitments apart, anyone concerned about the future of humanity has reason to be interested in the religious interpretation of these texts, if only because they motivate and inform or misinform a politically powerful majority in a nation with the military capacity to destroy the world. The apocalyptic imagery of the Bible, for example, may yet contribute to the self-destruction of the human race. These cultural resources may equally contribute to its survival. That is how much depends upon biblical interpretation.

The present chapter will draw upon the material already considered, and offer a general account of theological interpretation of the Bible. The suggestion that 'rational methods combined with religious interests yield theological interpretation' has been tested over a period in which the rational methods have been mainly historical. But it should also clarify the theological potential of the new literary approaches, which at first sight seem more remote from theological concerns. The first step is to see why in the modern world a theologically interested biblical scholarship had to become so historical in orientation.

Historical criticism and theological interpretation

An account of the theological connections of biblical scholarship must touch on religious motivations which are rarely explicit in modern research. If challenged to explain the overwhelmingly historical and exegetical bias of their work, biblical scholars could point out (a) that the meaning of texts is usually understood by reference to the semantic conventions of the original writers; (b) that historical questions are raised by the biblical texts themselves; and (c) that historical information is important for the religions that use the Bible as their scripture.

The first two points have been discussed at length in our first chapter. Several qualifications were found necessary. Most of these concerned the interpreters' own aims or interests. That suggests that the reasons which at least until recently have led biblical scholars in a historical direction have usually related to the third point: the importance of history for religion, especially for Christianity. The debates sparked by Strauss, and more recently by Bultmann, have shown that there is room for theological disagreement about how important historical information is for Christianity. But in view of the central position of Jesus, there has been a fairly general recognition that these questions cannot be evaded.

The dominance of historical research in biblical scholarship is best explained by recalling the 'Reimarus factor'. In Chapter 2 Reimarus represented the collision between traditional supernaturalist belief and modern rational historical methods. The new scientific and historical knowledge was rendering many of the biblical traditions implausible. For Christianity to survive this rationalist onslaught it had to sift the new knowledge, accept what was evidently true, and hold the line against unwarranted and damaging suggestions.

Reimarus's criticism of traditional religion by means of a non-supernatural account of Israelite history and Christian origins could be convincingly met only on its own terms. His damaging explanation of belief in the resurrection of Jesus as fraudulent could not be discredited by dogmatic assertions to the contrary. The only convincing answer was rational argument exposing the historical weaknesses of the fraud theory. But that was to concede Reimarus's main point. His daring hypothesis was almost certainly mistaken, but his new approach was vindicated. Once drawn on to Reimarus's own ground, Christian theology was committed to the enterprise of a non-supernatural, historical account of Christian origins.

This in turn posed the theological task of showing that the new historical picture, which was evidently at odds with traditional assumptions, was compatible with at least the heart of Christian belief. Liberal theologians have been insisting on this for over a century, but what constitutes the heart or essence of Christianity is itself a disputed question and religious majorities have often been impatient and suspicious of their theologians.

However, the new rational methods of biblical study were by the end of the nineteenth century quite widely accepted among thoughtful Christians in the West. They had subverted the old views of biblical authority and changed the way many Christians read their scriptures. But these changes have not fundamentally altered the general pattern of Christians' theological study of their scriptures. This has always used the available rational methods, but used them on the assumption that the Bible speaks of God whom the community worships. In a secular culture these methods can go their own scholarly way, independent of, or opposed to, religious belief. As the culture's literary property, the Bible can be read according to the culture's norms. But it is primarily the scripture of those who acknowledge its claims, and these secular methods can also be harnessed to serve the religious interests represented by theologians.

Theologians are expected to explore their tradition in the light of contemporary experience, including modern knowledge and methods of research. Introducing such modifications and new formulations as seem necessary, they articulate and defend the truth of their religion. This involves explaining what its scriptures mean in terms which express and so sustain their particular religious faith, without transgressing the literary and historical claims of the texts. The most appropriate name for this theological task of interpreting scripture in accordance with both faith and reason is *theological interpretation* of the Old and New Testaments. That is a clearer description than the more common phrases: biblical theology, Old Testament theology, and New Testament theology. It avoids the ambiguities which have arisen through those phrases being sometimes improperly applied to purely historical, non-theological clarifications of biblical ideas.

The problem which has haunted our whole discussion, and which remains the fundamental problem of biblical interpretation today, is that in a secular culture the rational methods used to interpret texts are not competent to speak of God in the way that religious believers do. A rift has therefore developed between the rational methods and conclusions of biblical scholarship and the way that believers use their scriptures to inform and nourish religious faith. The task of theological interpretation is to heal that rift, and hold together faith and reason.

Modern biblical scholarship has been remarkably successful in providing rational solutions to problems posed by the texts. It has been less obviously successful in expressing Christian faith through its interpretations. This is because the rational tasks have provided its declared agenda, whereas much of the theological appropriation has been an undeclared by-product. Theology proper has sometimes been a kind of black economy in biblical scholarship, not much advertised but important to all concerned. Only a small proportion of biblical scholarship outside Germany tries to make theological claims directly. All biblical scholars invite assessment by the rational methods which they share with other academic disciplines, but not all aim to express a religious position or invite *theological* assessment of their work.

The one sector of biblical studies in which the name itself invites the latter sort of assessment is 'biblical theology', an originally German occupation, which since the early nineteenth century has been divided by disciplinary specialization into Old and New Testament sections.

Old Testament theology could not be expected to express Christian faith directly, but it could try to show that the Old Testament or Israelite religion pointed in this direction. New Testament theology could aim to express a recognizably Christian position in and through its historical reconstructions. In this theological perspective the other textual, literary, and historical tasks of biblical scholarship could be seen as leading 'up' (from 'lower' through 'higher' criticism) towards this theological crown of biblical studies. Biblical scholars worked historically on the title-deeds of the faith, but their students, training to be German Protestant clergymen, soon to preach at length from the Bible, would be taught something usable in that context before being passed on to colleagues in dogmatic theology.

As the nineteenth century progressed, and historical research on the Bible became more confidently independent of dogmatics, the connections creaked. The clearest sign of this was in the decline of Old and New Testament theology as disciplines mediating between a largely historical scholarship, and contemporary theology. The name was still used, but it came to refer more to the history of the ideas contained in the Bible, and less to a theological reflection on the Bible which combined rational study of the text with contemporary religious faith.

Despite this late nineteenth-century decline in biblical theology, historical research continued to fulfil theological tasks. By continuing and correcting the work of Reimarus in Germany and his deist predecessors in England, liberal theology's historical investigation of Israel, Jesus, and early Christianity confronted and overcame the most dangerous intellectual attack ever faced by Christianity. The historical study of the Bible became a flashpoint in the long conflict between traditional religion and modern critical thought, and marked out a priority area for theological reappraisal.

The greatest achievement of nineteenth-century Protestant theology lay in integrating these new historical methods and conclusions within its reflection on Christian faith. In the process it proposed some restatements of Christianity which the religious community has refused to endorse. Religions require continuities as well as developments, and to see Jesus of Nazareth as anything less than the final and decisive manifestation of God was felt to surrender what historic Christianity had rightly deemed essential. But some change was inescapable, and when Christians change their understanding of the Bible to accommodate modern historical consciousness of its fallible authors' intentions, they open a door to doctrinal revision. The new view of the Bible is the visible part of an iceberg whose underwater dimensions are still not altogether clear. The future shape of Christianity, like everything else, remains an open question.

Liberal Protestantism, and more recently liberal Catholicism and evangelicalism, have investigated the Bible and Christian tradition by the best available rational methods. But this combination of rational methods and religious interests noted in earlier chapters is threatened on both sides. Like other religions, Christianity is capable of massive resistance to modern thought, especially where this touches holy scripture. On the other side, the scholarly study in a secular society's educational institutions of this monument of Western culture may detach itself from the religious community's reading of it as scripture. Christian and Jewish theological interpretations of the Bible, which seek to combine rational approaches with religious appropriations of its witness, are flanked, and may eventually be outflanked, by irrational religion on the one side and irreligious rationalism on the other.

Theological interpretation is not guaranteed success against either of these distortions of the biblical witness and the human spirit, but up to now Christianity has strongly maintained a theology that combines faith and reason. That is how it came to house modern biblical scholarship despite the risks involved, and why, at least until recently, this historical scholarship has generally retained a theological flavour not required by the methods themselves.

As both a cause and an effect of modernity, historical study of the Bible has been deeply implicated in the reorientation of Christians' self-understanding in a changing world. In using Reimarus's historical methods to defend themselves against his results they inevitably altered their own positions.

Another point at which historical study changed Christianity was less dramatic. In addition to the apologetic necessity for a true account of the history behind the biblical texts, there were benefits to be obtained at the exegetical level from applying the new rational methods to scripture.

The demise of traditional religious authority in the eighteenth-century Enlightenment emboldened scholars to apply more consistently to the Bible the philological methods used to interpret other ancient texts. In rejecting the competence of an ecclesiastical hierarchy to decree which interpretations of scripture were Christian, Protestantism had already depended on rational study to secure the necessary agreement. Since rational argument is possible only where the rules of interpretation are shared, hermeneutics became a central theological discipline in German Protestant faculties. This provided an entrée for the new philology into biblical interpretation.

The methods applied to scripture since the Enlightenment have not on their own produced agreement about its meaning. The possibilities for interpreting the Bible remain countless even when historical and linguistic study have excluded irrational suggestions. Some exegetical problems cannot be definitively resolved, and the meaning of the Bible as a whole depends on what is considered central and what peripheral—something which these methods cannot decide. But used within an agreed theological framework they have helped limit disagreement and have provided a grammar for believers' conversation about the meaning of their authoritative texts.

This theological importance of historical *exegesis* helps explain the resistance to any new directions in biblical study which seem to threaten it. But it was what Reimarus represents that revolutionized biblical interpretation and explains the central position given to historical *reconstruction* of events and traditions over the past 150 years. An orthodoxy stuck in its dogmatic rigidities could have been battered to death by modern rationalism. But theologians, whether reluctantly or with alacrity, followed the new light of reason and have gradually persuaded their Churches to make some adjustments to traditional systems of belief.

All religious traditions both change and struggle to retain their identity. Disagreements about which adjustments are appropriate give modern theology the appearance of a battleground, but are not unusual. Tension between conservatives and liberals is character-istic of any living tradition. For the dead theologies to be buried, and living believers turned from party battle to sane theological argument, what is most needed today is some agreement about the rules for conducting these disputes. That includes rules for Christian understanding of the Bible. Theological hermeneutics, or guidance for interpreting texts theologically, is always a priority in times of deep theological division. Christian theological interpreta-tion of the Bible has generally sought to maintain the respective claims of faith and reason. Since the eighteenth century that has involved reconciling Christian faith with the claims of historical reason.

History and hermeneutics

Some of the best nineteenth-century German biblical scholarship described itself as 'purely historical'. This was a declaration of independence from the doctrinal constraints which obscure the historian's vision. It was necessary to set theological considerations firmly aside, and to allow historical research to advance on its own terms. Most biblical scholars had theological interests, but one way of limiting the distorting effect of these was to keep them out of historical work altogether.

Some division of labour is clearly defensible. Biblical scholars clarify what the Bible meant for its original authors, not (if that is different) what it might mean for anyone today. They would not deny the importance of the latter hermeneutical question, but some would say that it is not for them to answer it. Their particular specialism is exegetical and historical; the hermeneutical question raises wider issues. Biblical scholars fulfil a negative role in theology by saying what the Bible cannot mean today, protesting when theologians or others do violence to the original meaning of the text. But the positive theological and hermeneutical task of relating the Bible to contemporary belief and practice is not one that they are particularly equipped to perform.

A further argument for separating the historical from the hermeneutical task has been adduced by Krister Stendahl: the Church needs on occasion to hear the biblical message in all its . strangeness, its cutting edge not blunted by the familiarity of hallowed religious expectations. A historical scholarship that stands at one remove from the Church's daily converse with its scripture fulfils a valuable function.

But this religious requirement is plainly subordinate to the primary need of religious groups for some kind of 'normal' theological interpretation of their scriptures, informing and sustaining the community's life by speaking to it of the God it worships. If 'purely historical' scholarship were ever to become a substitute for theological reflection on the Bible, Christianity and Judaism would cease to exist as living faiths. Stendahl's religious argument for separating the two tasks underlines the value of an independent historical research, but does not undermine the case for also combining this with an ongoing tradition of theological interpretation in which the Church identifies the subject of its scripture with the God it worships. The value of a purely historical study of ancient Israel and early Christianity is not in dispute, but that does not preclude a different style of interpretation in which historical and theological interests are fused. This is the life-blood of the religious communities that use the Bible as scripture, carrying religious messages to believers' hearts and heads. The other is a secular scholarly activity, deeply entwined with modern theology, but also able to exist on its own non-theological terms.

It has sometimes been thought that only the linguistic, literary, and historical tasks can be done in a secular university, theology proper being the special concern of particular religious groups. It is true that theology is a function of actual religions, and that the university cannot impose religious tests on its students or teachers.

But it is possible to see what a text means for believers without joining their community. There is therefore no reason why biblical scholars employed by the secular state should restrict themselves to historical and exegetical work and not reflect in a disciplined and truth-seeking way upon the whole range of possible contemporary meanings of these texts. The interconnected literary, historical, philosophical, and theological questions posed by the Bible may not find such generally agreed answers as do the simpler historical questions, but they are no less worthy of serious study.

It is possible for individual scholars to focus their research more narrowly and restrict themselves to historical and exegetical work. Their concentration on the narrow range of questions which their intensive study of related material from the ancient world equips them to answer with some authority has made important contributions to the larger task of biblical interpretation. But theologians are bound to ensure that these necessary historical disciplines do not relegate the hermeneutical tasks, which are important for the religions concerned, to the periphery of biblical studies. One attraction of the new literary approaches for theologians is that they are loosening the stranglehold of historical scholarship and so giving wider hermeneutical issues the chance to breathe.

The religious and theological value of both historical research and the secular literary approaches now flourishing in Old and New Testament studies has to be assessed by believers. Unless these rational approaches are understood in relation to the wider aims of theological interpretation, that will be eclipsed and the religious institutions which depend on it weakened. Some biblical scholarship will in any case move from a historical to a literary paradigm, bypassing theology altogether. But that is not a necessary development. Literary study can also help reconnect specialist academic work with believers' use of the Bible. It is particularly suited to restating the subject-matter of the Bible in terms which illuminate contemporary human existence. It also places the Bible back in the hands of the common reader. The great attraction of modern literary study is that it enables even beginners to engage with significant texts.

The value of historical research is not necessarily denied when this reorientation takes place. Specialists make their contributions, and the historians' call to respect the integrity of the past commands a double respect: their charge that we do not force the texts to say what suits our immediate interests is a call for truthfulness which demands unqualified assent; and their suggestion that we are more likely to learn from the past if we respect its integrity is also an appeal to our long-term investment in knowing the human past, over the quick buck to be made by turning its monuments to our immediate advantage.

In an age that will make anything into a vehicle for its own ideological commitments, that case for historical study deserves all the support it can get, especially from theologians who have a stake in the past as well as the present and future. But it leaves unanswered all the important questions about the value of historical knowledge relative to other legitimate and often more pressing human concerns. It also ignores the way that historical research itself can serve ideological interests, both wittingly and unwittingly. Respect for the past can be a powerful tool for resisting sometimes desirable change, not least in religion. It is commonly found amongst those who are well satisfied with, and benefit most from, the status quo.

Historical research is valuable in itself, but can hinder as well as support the life of a community, as Nietzsche insisted in 'On the Uses and Disadvantages of History for Life'. To be culturally effective it needs to engage with other interests. On its own it can prop up a fruitless conservatism and make the Bible marginal to contemporary concerns. This is why some liberals today, taught to interpret it in an exclusively historical way, argue for relativizing its authority, lest it impede Christian life and thought. The more they respect historical truth, the less use they can find for the Bible today.

But that response cuts across the grain of every religion's use of its scriptures. It does not make religious sense to reduce the religious authority of scripture, except where this has been confused with revelation itself. The distinction between revelation and scriptural traditions must be preserved, but the necessity and centrality of scripture is crucial. Where scripture is neglected, believers' hold on their founding revelation is weakened and the dissolution of a religious tradition is in sight. When the Bible becomes marginal to the life and thought of the educated believers on whom the transmission of the tradition in a pluralist culture significantly depends, Christianity and Judaism will be endangered. Both religions need ways of reading their scriptures which maintain the necessary continuity without stifling new insights or preventing growth. Living with, and learning from, an authoritative canon of scripture requires a flexible response.

To provide this has always been the task of theological hermeneutics. That ancient discipline has enabled religious communities to draw new meaning from their scriptures in agreed, controlled, non-arbitrary ways. It has combined the community's religious interest in these texts with a sense of what is true and what requires correction.

In a historically conscious age some of the older methods of theological interpretation are irrational and unconvincing. But the task of sifting possible meanings, and looking for those which support the admitted religious interests of the community, remains unchanged. Much modern theology has therefore engaged in biblical interpretation by combining a strong rational input from the side of historical research with some remarkably flexible hermeneutics.

This balance between history and hermeneutics is essential in theology. Without history, exegesis, and other rational controls, interpretation can become arbitrary, as allegory did where it was not controlled by the literal meaning of other biblical texts. But without the possibility of finding new meaning in a text, an authoritative scripture stifles development. Historical exegesis is opposed to the multiplication of meanings and this makes it a valuable control. But if biblical scholarship is restricted to this, then theologically motivated scholars are likely to become either biblicist conservatives opposed to any development or ultra-liberals who have little use in their own theologies for what they learn from the Bible. The only way to maintain some theological flexibility while retaining the benefits of an authoritative and well-used scripture is to combine hermeneutical creativity with historical controls.

That argument suggests that historical judgement has a secondary, corrective role within theological interpretation, but that there is something else requiring 'hermeneutical creativity' which precedes it. This recalls what Karl Popper claims is characteristic of scientific research: conjecture and refutation. An imaginative leap is followed by rational testing of the hypothesis. By analogy, as theological interpreters we make an intuitive jump to what we think the text is getting at, and then see if it will stand up to the cool rational scrutiny of our historical judgement. It is only by some such imaginative leap, based on our own whole experience of reality as much as our attention to the text, that we can sense what a religious text might mean. Subjectivity is a necessity for grasping religious truth. Some measure of objectivity and critical distance follows.

If this is the shape of theological interpretation it is more like literary than historical criticism, though there too imagination arguably comes first and calculating reason, weighing the evidence, second. It also corresponds to the way we normally get to know people, an initial hunch preceding observational confirmation.

We should expect theological interpretation of texts to conform to our experience of persons and literature rather than to more calculating disciplines, because its focus is on the text and the reader, rather than on the author or what the text refers to, in the first instance. Information about the author and original context is useful to the student of this literature because it may throw light on the text, whereas historians are more likely to value the text as a source for information about what lies behind it.

Theologians initially look more like historians than literary critics because the subject-matter of the text is more important to them than the text itself. But this theological subject-matter is elusive. It is not dug out from behind the text, like historical information, even though some such information is an indispensable feature of the biblical witness. But the theological subject-matter of the Bible 'happens', as some believers claim, from time to time, in and through the reader's engagement with the text. The appreciation of art or literature provides the closest analogies.

The qualification 'as *some* believers claim' is significant and points back to Chapter 1. For how theologians understand the elusive subject-matter of the Bible depends in part on their own theology, especially how they understand revelation. The theologians who developed historical research on the Bible held views of revelation that dovetailed with their historical conclusions. This partnership between theology and history survived the German theological revolution of the 1920s that ousted the liberal Protestant coalition of theology and history. Kerygmatic theology could have entered into a new coalition with the literary aspects of form criticism, but instead remained in partnership with the history of traditions.

If today a partnership with literary study proves more promising to theologians, this too will imply a corresponding view of revelation and religion. Theological interpretation must always harness the rational methods of studying texts with some theory of what these texts are about.

It is commonly assumed that this theory and the resulting theological interpretation should *follow* historical and exegetical research: first see what the text meant, then (perhaps) what it means. But this model of objective scholarship, taking the Bible-reader to the end of its line and then handing over to 'application' or the religious appropriation of scripture, is unsatisfactory. Historical conclusions are uncertain, and historical work is never complete. More seriously, disinterested historical research is quite likely to lead away from contemporary religious use of the Bible. Biblical interpretation once seemed to move *from* historical research *to* theological interpretation—but only because religious viewpoints were being smuggled into the historical research. Now that biblical scholarship has been more thoroughly secularized, such religious smuggling has become refreshingly difficult. A more accurate account of how believers read their scriptures religiously while still benefiting from historical scholarship is therefore necessary. What in fact has been going on needs to be made explicit and rationally justified.

The key is to recognize that historical research and theological interpretation are in principle different tasks, done by two different interpretative communities. Modern theological interpreters belong to both the rational community of historians and the religious community of God-worshippers. They often seem to tack their theological judgements on to their historical conclusions, because the latter are cognitively 'harder' and must not be contradicted. But the more sophisticated theologians have always had their provisional theological frameworks prepared before doing their historical research. This is justifiable, because it is impossible to present even the history of religion intelligibly without first having some idea of what religion is. There is no reason why believing historians and social scientists should not select a theory of religion which is compatible with its truth, i.e. open to the possibility that the transcendent to which it refers actually exists. Provided this prior understanding of the religious subject-matter of the Bible is sufficiently flexible to be modified in the light of new evidence, it is appropriate to clarify it first. That is what the theologians discussed in earlier chapters generally did.

The alternative and still popular account of the division of theological labour, in which biblical historians leave theology to the systematic theologians, gives no account of how to move from historical conclusions to theological judgements. Theological reflection on the biblical witness cannot begin where historical research stops. It begins with the texts themselves, and reads them with all the help that historians and linguists can provide. The 'two-stage' model of theological interpretation *following* historical scholarship should therefore be abandoned in favour of an account of what actually happens.

The necessity of theory

The theological value of historical exegesis, and the apologetic necessity of historical reconstruction, have been emphasized throughout this discussion. But what made Christianity vulnerable to historical criticism (Chapter 2 above), namely, that it locates the revelation of God in a patch of contingent history, was also a positive reason for trying to reconstruct that history with the best available methods. The resulting scholarship (Chapter 3) was impressive, but it exposed the deep tensions between religion and modern rationalism. The best rational methods for uncovering the past are not competent to reveal what believers find in this history. Historical research uncovers the human past but does not of itself speak of God. It is relevant to the Christian religion because it can describe and perhaps even falsify it. But it cannot on its own express it.

The same problem arises with textual exegesis as with historical reconstruction. This can clarify what the texts say, but does not enable the modern exegete to affirm their theological truth. Historical understanding of the texts does not provide contemporary religious guidance unless one is already convinced of their authority, and this authority has been eroded by studying them as fallible human documents. The context within which the Bible is assumed to yield religious truth no longer coincides with the culture itself. There is a new hiatus between the meaning of the Bible, established by exegesis, and its truth, which is the concern of theology. The self-limitations of modern historical and exegetical study, whose rational methods do not authorize normative talk of God, have distanced it from believers' reading of these texts as speaking of the God they worship. Rational methods are indispensable, but they read the texts as human utterances, and cannot themselves speak normatively of transcendence. The theologians' problem is how to connect those methods with the presupposition of their religious communities that the Bible speaks normatively of that transcendent reality which they worship.

In an age whose rational methods do not speak of God in the way that believers do (i.e. in worship and theology), theological interpreters of the Bible have had to bridge the gap between what these methods can achieve and their own understanding of God. Understanding any text theologically involves the latter as one's pre-understanding. It must therefore be somehow combined with the rational methods to be used.

One way of bridging the gap is by stretching historical methods to make them speak of God. That is a common-sense response of any believer who does not acknowledge the limits set on historical method by the intellectual community of historians. It is a common shorthand for affirming the reality, truth, and objectivity of the divine event confessed in faith. When some Christians speak of the divine mystery of the Incarnation or Resurrection as a 'historical' event or fact that is what they are affirming, however imprecisely.

But this 'stretching the method' approach is less defensible when found among professional theologians. It brings theology into disrepute by attracting suspicion to its use of rational methods. There is some justification for the protest that the conventions of historical method mean that it cannot handle unique events, such as the resurrection of Jesus. But that is a reason for denying that this method is the sole arbiter of truth, not for stretching and destroying the method itself.

Redefining historical method to allow it to speak of God would put theology back into the ghetto from which its use of rational methods is intended to rescue it. If believers want the benefits of using public discourse in communicating the message of their scriptures they must keep its rules. Historical methods may need refining to interpret religion, but their integrity has to be respected. They do not on their own yield theological interpretations of the Bible.

The alternative strategy, present in the biblical study discussed in earlier chapters, is to use the rational methods on their own terms, but set them in a wider context that embraces both the witness of the texts and the modern theological interpreter's own understanding of their subject-matter—which alone makes possible a theological understanding of the texts.

This suggestion that a theological understanding of the Bible requires a theological pre-understanding on the part of the reader or interpreter does not mean that only a Christian or a Jew can understand the Bible. But understanding it in a Jewish or a Christian way clearly requires some understanding of Judaism and Christianity respectively.

The wider context in which historical and literary study must be set for theological interpretation to be possible is a theory of religion and human existence, including history, language, and literature. This combination of method and theory makes possible an understanding of the biblical texts (whether of the statements they contain or of the events behind them) which synthesizes in a contemporary interpretation all that can be established by history and exegesis.

The middle term which here links reason (rational methods) and faith (religious understanding of the Bible) is a theory of religion which can make sense of the historian's empirical data without denying the truth of a religion's own claims. Ancient and modern believers alike acknowledge God through religious systems which can be described by non-participants. Anyone may have a theory about what is thus described, and believers choose a theory which is compatible with their experience that their religion points them to the divine reality beyond the system of symbols. Schleiermacher and Hegel proposed different theories of religion and reality, but both theories elicited critical historical study of the Bible and Christianity, and related this to Christians' sense of God. Strauss destroyed history to make room for his kind of theology; his proposal, too, involved a theory of religion and reality. Those who later kept his history but ignored his theory and repudiated his theology had alternative theories of religion and reality as well as new theologies of their own.

The main kinds of theory of religion and human existence implicit in earlier chapters have been those involving the Hegelian distinction between religious and philosophical language (Strauss), Hegelian metaphysics of history (Vatke and Baur), romantic theories of religion (liberal Protestantism), and a Heideggerian form of existentialism, influenced by Herrmann, Luther and Kierkegaard (Bultmann). Each of these theories has been brought by the theological interpreter to the biblical text being interpreted, and each has made possible a rational theological interpretation of the Bible, whether satisfactory or not.

Not every theory of religion is compatible with the truth of Christianity. Marxist or Freudian theories of religion would not yield traditional interpretations unless modified. But theologians can attack reductive theories of religion and reality, and choose one which is both rationally defensible and compatible with the truth of their religion.

Where this element of theory is present, it does not entirely determine the interpretation, however. The biblical text itself also contributes to the interpretation, and the partly determinate quality of the text makes possible genuine argument between interpreters whose theory differs. In the course of such arguments a theologian may be persuaded to read the text differently or to find a better theory.

What earlier chapters have shown happening in the case of interpreters with novel and clearly articulated theories of religion and reality is also present in other theological interpretations, though not always recognized. Many interpreters have been content with an orthodox Christian view of the world, articulated in traditional doctrinal language. They have not agreed with the leading liberals that this framework has been shattered by natural science and historical research, and have continued to work with it while in effect modifying it and reducing its brittleness. But while their theology has been less novel, the structure of their theological interpretations has been the same as that of the liberals. They too have brought their (orthodox) pre-understandings into their interpretations and so understood the biblical texts as speaking of the God they know in their own belief and experience. Here too the reader's contribution is crucial.

What has been asserted about liberal and conservative theological interpretation of the Bible is a variant of what happens in all interpretation—at least, according to the account of interpretation given in our opening chapter. Interpreters always bring their own view of the world to the text they are reading. The special feature of theological interpretation is that a theological belief and theory of religion is brought into the act of interpretation. In a secular culture some theory of religion is always necessary, whether or not it is made explicit, in order to connect believers' talk of God with the generally acknowledged reality that can be investigated by anyone. Theologians choose a theory of religion and reality which does not deny the reality of their religion's transcendent referent. This general theory of religion is then joined by a theological judgement, specific to the religion concerned, about where revelation is located—which in the Christian case includes a view of how it is related to the Bible. This judgement is a consequence of the interpreter's own theology and will decide whether the interpretation focuses on the text itself (as with Strauss, Kähler, Bultmann, Frei) or on the history behind the texts (as with Baur, Wellhausen, Harnack, Jeremias), or whether it tries to combine both.

The advantages of this 'theory of religion' approach to the problem of theological interpretation in a culture whose rational methods do not speak of God are, first, that it fits a general theory of interpretation and is therefore rationally defensible (theological interpretation is simply an instance of what happens in all interpretation); secondly, it respects the integrity of the rational methods used.

Historical supports for theological proposals

Stretching rational methods to achieve an interpretation of the Bible that speaks normatively of God (above, p.186), and the better alternative of supplementing them with a theory of religion for the same reason, have important features in common. They both presuppose the authority of the Bible for their religious community, and seek to express its theological meaning for that community today. Both approaches have strong theological interests and are (often silently) making theological proposals *through* their biblical interpretation.

Both sides are also seeking support for their theological proposals from the prestige of rational methods. This is common theological practice. Theologians have to give reasons for their beliefs, even if they hold them on quite different grounds. They may not be able to prove the truth of a religious faith which is tested only in experience, but they generally try to minimize the tension between faith and reason. It is therefore no surprise to find theologians looking for rational support for their beliefs.

The conservative's use of historical arguments in support of religious beliefs may not have convinced many sceptics, but this defective apologetic has reassured some believers. Only when it makes God into an object of historical enquiry is this preoccupation with 'evidences' religiously offensive as well as historically suspect. The alternative and better strategy for gaining rational historical support for theological proposals can be illustrated by two examples.

If (*a*) the Fourth Gospel is somehow normative for Christianity, and (*b*) Bultmann's theological interpretation of it is a historically plausible account of John's theology, and is also (*c*) an expression of Bultmann's own modern theology, then Bultmann's own theology is partly vindicated.

It is not thereby shown to be the only possible modern theology, because even if Bultmann understands John aright (which can only ever be a matter of informed opinion), John is still only one biblical witness among many. Since John is perhaps one-sided, Bultmann's Kierkegaardian interpretation may be an unsatisfactory modern theology, even if true to John. This example is further complicated in that Bultmann, like many other scholars, sees the Fourth Gospel as the work of the evangelist (using sources) and a later 'ecclesiastical redactor' or editor. One might reasonably argue that the Fourth Gospel is orthodox only in its canonical form, but anyone who accepts the Bible as scripture and is persuaded by Bultmann's historical and exegetical arguments could admit that Bultmann's hypothetical reconstructed evangelist adds credibility to his own theology.

A less fragile example is provided by another classic of theological interpretation: since (*a*) Romans is somehow normative for Christianity, and especially for Lutheranism, and Käsemann's commentary is both (*b*) an expression of his own theology and (*c*) a historically and exegetically plausible account of much of the text, then Käsemann's theology finds some support from rational exegetical arguments. Again there is the question of one-sidedness, and room for debate over whether some of what may be judged historically implausible in Käsemann's commentary can be vindicated as deeper penetration into the implications of Paul's argument, rather than dismissed as Lutheran misreading. Nothing is ever finally settled in these arguments; they are part of the Church's ongoing listening to its scripture. But on any showing, Käsemann has strengthened his own modern Lutheran theology by interpreting Romans through that prism.

This style of theology as biblical interpretation is important for our argument because it helps explain the great attraction of historical reconstruction and exegesis as the main rational component in modern theological interpretation, both progressive and conservative. Historical and philological results are in principle, if not always in fact, relatively 'hard'. Not so hard as scientific results, but harder and more 'objective' than literary interpretation or philosophical theory. They are also cognitively much harder than theological affirmations, based as these partly are on non-universal religious experiences. Theological interpretations are therefore destroyed when they clash with hard historical facts, and threatened by even tentative historical reconstructions. Conversely, the more historically 'hard' struts that can be built into a theological edifice the stronger this will be.

Most of the biblical scholarship discussed so far can be seen from the perspective of theological interpretation as the necessary replacement of faulty planks in the historical foundations and rational supports of Christianity. New accounts of Christian belief have been developed which take account of modern knowledge and gain some support from it. But the modern theological constructions achieved by combining historical research with theories of religion and reality have always been fragile. Either subsequent historical research has invalidated them, or the theory invoked has failed to satisfy the next generation—or both. The great syntheses of theological interpretation have collapsed with depressing regularity.

When the classic syntheses of historical reconstruction, philosophical theory, and theological interpretation achieved by Baur in the nineteenth century and Bultmann in the twentieth lost credibility, some biblical scholarship retreated to more tractable, less directly theological goals. Some systematic theologians (notably Schillebeeckx, Ebeling, and Jüngel) have helped fill the gap left by the retreat of some biblical scholars from Old and New Testament theology. There is much to be said for biblical theology as a cooperative enterprise involving systematicians and ethicists too. But there are also good reasons for recalling biblical specialists themselves, especially those teaching in theological or religious studies environments, to this task. Scholars are free to pursue any interest they like, but they are also answerable, and the main reason why even a secular culture wants the Bible studied has to do with its religious and cultural significance. Interest in the religious content of the Bible is not restricted to believers.

The alliance weakens

The capacity of historical scholarship, now reinforced by sociological perspectives, to perform its historical tasks is not in question. The necessity of taking account of this in modern theology is also widely accepted. When in recent years a few theologians have spoken unguardedly of 'the bankruptcy of historical criticism' they are not disputing its legitimacy, but expressing unease about its failure to lead to satisfactory theological interpretations of the Bible today.

Academic theology has been rightly wary about these protests because they could easily cover a retreat to irrationalism. Modern biblical scholarship is vulnerable to conservative reactions, especially since their protest against admitting modern thought uncritically into the theological enterprise has some validity. But the best guard against losing what has been gained is to take due account of the protest and find ways of remedying any deficiencies. If theological interpretation of the Bible is in short supply, those who want it must first reconsider its character and the conditions under which it thrives.

We have suggested that a satisfactory modern theological interpretation combines rational methods with a theory of religion and reality, whether this is worked out philosophically, as by some liberals and radicals, or taken over from systematic theology, as more traditional Christians have preferred. These two ways of supplementing rational methods with a religious pre-understanding can take many and overlapping forms, but they represent one type of solution to the problem of biblical interpretation in a secular culture, and are superior to the alternative strategy of stretching rational methods to do what they are not intended to do.

For over 150 years historical research has orchestrated the rational-methods side of this combination. A succession of theories of religion and reality has provided the often invisible partner enabling this biblical scholarship to generate theological interpretations. The value of this partnership for theology was that it gained some hard rational support for its theological interpretations and established an interface between faith and modern rationality.

But it was always a precarious alliance, at least in its liberal form of historical scholarship dovetailing into a theory of religion and reality to produce theological interpretations directly, without the help of systematic theology. This is not much in evidence today because such syntheses are easier to destroy than to construct.

The more traditional form of the 'supplementing' approach, i.e. supplementing rational methods with a pre-understanding shaped by doctrinal belief, is not in such a poor state. But that is because it aims less high. The liberal version attempts to forge new theological understandings of *Christianity* in the course of its interpretations of scripture. This is what made it the pace-maker of modern theology.

The traditionalist version leaves others to set the theological pace in forging new understandings of God and the world, and simply adopts what it finds helpful. This is less ambitious, but entirely legitimate, and it allows the Bible to function religiously, if not in a revolutionary way, in the life of the Church.

When integrated within a confident doctrinal framework, as in some Roman Catholicism and evangelicalism, historical study of the Bible thus continues to contribute to theological interpretations. The results have sometimes been original, as for example in the work of Schürmann and Schillebeeckx, the latter modifying the doctrinal framework more than the authorities happily tolerate. Liberal evangelical scholars have similar problems, as they try to enlarge the boundaries of their constituency's tolerance. More commonly, integration between doctrine and historical research is achieved in this conservative camp by avoiding or rejecting unproven historical hypotheses which would embarrass Christian theology.

Although theology seeks truth, its truth is not drawn directly, like historical truth, from the biblical sources. It emerges from a religious community's critical (i.e. taking due account of other relevant knowledge) reflection on its faith. The aim of theological interpretation is to contribute to that critical reflection by promoting a religious appropriation of the Bible which takes account of, and benefits from, rational enquiry. It stirs up the conversation between the Church and its scripture, rather than stopping this with definitive rulings. The Bible is authoritative for Christians; they are committed to hearing it again and again. Theological interpretations have no such authority or permanence. They contribute to contemporary theology indirectly by informing, sustaining, and structuring the contemporary faith on which this reflects.

The circularity of this traditional form of theological interpretation, which presupposes the religious truth of both the documents being interpreted and the theological presupposition on which they are read, is not a problem for those inside the community to whom it is addressed. They turn to it more for effective religious sustenance than for new knowledge. Any progressive theological interpretations of the Bible here stem from a bold systematic theology being introduced into the interpretation, as in Schürmann's use of Karl Rahner.

But Protestants have usually expected more from their scriptures than this. Breaking with the Church's authority they had to justify their religious positions more directly from the Bible. Whether or not it is finally possible to play off the Bible against the Church, or even against the hierarchy, this background indicates that the more liberal or radical form of theological interpretation is Protestant in inspiration. It does not in fact play off the Bible against the Church, because it presupposes the faith of the Christian community, though not the reliability of popes or general synods. Any theological interpreter forging new Christian readings of the Bible must start from the community whose faith is what enables the Bible to be read as the revelation of God. Since this faith can always be expressed in a systematic theology, the main differences between Catholic and Protestant, traditionalist and liberal, lie in the actual theological pre-understandings with which the Bible is read, and the relative weight accorded to them in the process of interpretation.

Theological interpretations of the 'liberal' type are sometimes less bold than traditionalist ones that use a progressive systematic theology. 'Liberal' in this context does not indicate theological radicalism, but merely an impatience with the doctrinal tradition. Recognizing that modernity had severely damaged it, such theologians as Harnack saw no point in major salvage operations, and adopted non-dogmatic interpretations of Christianity by combining their historical study with their (usually unstated) theory of religion and reality. Other Christians value continuity with the doctrinal tradition more highly, and have salvaged far more of it than Harnack did. But even liberals need theological interpretations of the Bible, to give form and content to their Christianity. They need them more than the traditionalists do, because they discard more of the other elements which constitute the Christian religious system.

That is why it has been liberal Christians who have pioneered some of the best modern theological interpretations of the Bible since the Enlightenment. But it is precisely these which are not working well today. The close 'fit' between the conclusions of historical research and a philosophical theory, found in the theological interpretations of Baur and Bultmann, is apparently not available today. Liberal biblical scholarship and liberal theology have therefore drifted apart, weakening both.

The reasons for the near collapse of this alliance are clear. In a pluralist culture no theory of religion and reality can command wide assent. Even the great syntheses were no more than attractive options persuading a minority of educated believers. Historical research on the Bible is also a tangle of competing hypotheses. Few command sufficiently general assent to bear the weight of the theological constructions once placed upon them. One synthesis after another has been destroyed by further historical study. It is hard to feel confident about such precarious combinations. If a theological interpretation had to dovetail with the results of historical exegesis and reconstruction it would be confined within quite narrow limits.

The exclusion of interpretations which actually conflict with the historical intentions of the text is reasonable. But it is possible to retain this negative control while remaining open to a much wider variety of possible interpretations. The 'history supplemented by theory' approach leaves theologians far less room for manœuvre than they had when the texts themselves, with their multiple possible meanings, were their raw material.

Neither the liberal nor the traditionalist versions of this approach have fitted the historians' conclusions very easily. They only ever fitted some of the conclusions of some of the historians, and often left much of the Bible out of theological account. It is not surprising that over the past decade or two a secular historical scholarship seems to have left the older theological interpretation behind. Many biblical scholars have reservations about biblical theology, and many systematic theologians have ceased expecting it from their biblical colleagues. Because believers need to read their scriptures theologically, and the vacuum is otherwise filled with trivia, some systematic theologians do their own theological interpretation of the Bible. Our question is how biblical specialists also may best recover the theological orientation that some of them still want.

Alternative forms of theological interpretation

The difficulties noticed in the liberal version of supplementing rational methods with theory suggest other ways forward. Since no theory of religion and reality has ever commanded general assent in the modern world, and since historical conclusions are always open to correction, the combination of history and theory has never yielded rational theological certainties. Rather, it offers rationally and sometimes religiously satisfying interpretations, and a language for contesting and defending them. It has thus enriched theological discussion of these texts within the community which depends on that for both vitality and identity or self-definition.

But if that is what theological interpretations provide—a plurality of more or less rationally and religiously satisfying 'readings' of these texts, rather than clear-cut theological certainties based on a single correct interpretation of biblical passages—then the historical emphasis which aims at that loses both its urgency and much of its appeal. The ideal of a biblical scholarship progressing towards that goal seems both unrealistic and sterile. Were it possible to state definitively and for all time 'what the Bible means', or even part of the Bible, Christianity would no longer live from ongoing reflection on its scripture.

The notion of a single correct interpretation, identifiable with the intention of authors who succeed in saying what they mean or with the meaning of the semantic conventions actually used by the authors, is sometimes within reach and remains a useful ideal norm for arguing about, and distinguishing between, valid and invalid interpretations. But when clearly invalid interpretations have been excluded there often remains a range of better or worse, more or less satisfying, interpretations. Historical and exegetical discussion still offers the clearest common ground for supporting and disputing all interpretations, but it is the aims of the interpreter or reader that determine which ones satisfy.

Theological interpretations aim to clarify, communicate, and sustain religious faith, criticizing it from within in order to purify it, not destroy it. This means that historical exegesis alone, while providing theology with necessary controls, is unlikely to fulfil its interpretative task. An additional element is needed, involving the interpreter's own religious interests and (potentially) those of the reader or hearer. What the text says has to be respected and communicated, but this must also be set in a modern framework designed to clarify its religious import.

Because biblical scholars today are sometimes ill-equipped to design such philosophical and theological frameworks, and have even learned to distrust them, some deny that the Bible can function as it once did, and say that Christian faith must learn to live without an authoritative scripture. But obituaries for scripture are premature. A great variety of theories of religion and culture are available to help articulate the theological significance of religious texts. Process theology, neo-Marxist, neo-Freudian, Jungian, Girardian, and other interpretative proposals are currently seeking to attract support by claiming that they make sense of both the Bible (or parts of it) and some people's contemporary experience.

But it is hard to demonstrate a close 'fit' between these theories and the historical meaning of the texts. At best the correspondence is a loose one, intuitively sensed by imaginative interpreters, and unlikely to persuade sceptics. This problem is eased by the switch to a literary paradigm for biblical interpretation. Modern literary interpretation tolerates and even encourages a greater variety of valid 'readings' than an exegesis more tightly bound to the authorial norm. Making this a control in adjudicating between conflicting interpretations, rather than the ideal norm for all interpretation, gives biblical interpretation greater freedom to connect with the modern theologian's preferred theory of religion.

This pluralism of possible interpretations allows scripture to illuminate the great diversity of human experience. The price to be paid is that it then becomes more difficult for rational argument to exclude unacceptable interpretations. The community that wishes to preserve its boundaries must therefore introduce other doctrinal, moral, or liturgical tests. But this is not a new situation. Theological arguments have never been settled by establishing the single correct meaning of scripture, though they have often been conducted by discussing individual texts. At a particular moment, a particular text and interpretation may be decisive for an individual, as Matthew 19: 21 was for St Antony, and Romans 1: 17 for Luther.

But in practice all Christians depend on a large configuration of many passages, some wrongly interpreted, others whose meaning is uncertain. Believers thus live with a wide range of possible readings of their scriptures.

There are other reasons why Christians who find a bridge between the biblical witness and their own modern theology in a theory of religion may choose to interpret the Bible as religious literature, rather than as sources for the history of religion. The strong rationalist bent of critical historiography, with its interest in setting the human record straight and exposing illusions, is quite unsympathetic to religion. Historical study of the Bible has often enjoyed debunking it.

By contrast, the religious subject-matter of the Bible is sufficiently closely related to those aspects of human existence explored in art and literature for methods attuned to understanding these to be better placed than most for understanding religion. Not every kind of literary criticism will illuminate the religious dimensions of the Bible. Some kinds are as positivistic as any historical criticism. Theologians and students of religion will choose their tools with care. But it is potentially useful, on account of the close affinity between literature and religion.

Theology is equally interested in the critical power of historical study, as an instrument for performing its own critical task of attacking untrue expressions of religion. But theological interpretation of the Bible aims to sustain as well as correct religion. Its theological insights stem from the combination of the interpreter's religious insight and his understanding of these texts. Its most natural ally is therefore the kind of literary criticism that enhances the appropriation and enjoyment of literature. This can help the Bible function as a catalyst of Christian faith and life. Without this there is nothing for theology to reflect on and criticize.

If historical research is not at present yielding theological interpretations which sustain liberal Christianity, and if a literary criticism that welcomes a pluralism of interpretations offers better prospects, that is a reason for theologians to welcome the new trend. The health of even conservative theology depends on opponents to its left, and a religious community without tension between those who overvalue the tradition at the expense of what is good in modern thought and those whose tendency is the reverse, would stagnate. If liberal theology lacks theological interpretations of scripture, it will simply use the Bible less. Its own Christian identity will then be jeopardized.

Whether a change of focus will rejuvenate Christian theological interpretation remains to be seen. The conclusion to be reached is simply that it *can*. But quite apart from this, the biblical material itself supports a more literary approach. The Bible is literature, and some of it (especially parts of the Hebrew Bible) great literature. The literary weight of the Bible has also been increased by some classic translations, notably the Luther Bible and the Authorized Version, perhaps even by some modern translations. Theological preferences have long favoured historical research and hindered the development of a secular literary criticism of the Bible. It was the recent relaxation of these theological pressures that encouraged the change, but theologians have begun to recognize that it also has considerable potential for their own purposes.

Further reading

The bibliography to Chapter 1 is germane to this chapter. Those to Chapters 5 and 7 are also relevant. In addition, the following books are recommended:

BARR, J., *Holy Scripture: Canon, Authority, Criticism* (Oxford and New York, 1983).

BARTLETT, D. L., *The Shape of Scriptural Authority* (Philadelphia, 1983).

BOERS, H., *What is New Testament Theology?* (Philadelphia, 1979).

COLLINS, A. Y., *Crisis and Catharsis: The Power of the Apocalypse* (Philadelphia, 1984).

FIORENZA, E. S., *Bread Not Stone: The Challenge of Feminist Biblical Interpretation* (Boston, 1984).

FREI, H. W., *The Identity of Jesus Christ: The Hermeneutical Basis of Dogmatic Theology* (Philadelphia, 1975).

GRANT, R. M. with TRACY, D., *A Short History of the Interpretation of the Bible* (Philadelphia and London, 1984).

GUNKEL, H., *The Folktale in the Old Testament* (1917; ET Decatur and Sheffield, 1987).

HANSON, P. D., *Dynamic Transcendence: The Correlation of a Confessional Heritage and Contemporary Experience in a Biblical Model of Divine Activity* (Philadelphia, 1978).

—— *The Diversity of Scripture: A Theological Interpretation* (Philadelphia, 1982).

HENRY, P., *New Directions in New Testament Study* (Philadelphia, 1979; London, 1980).

HOULDEN, J. L., *Patterns of Faith* (London, 1977).

—— *Connections: The Integration of Theology and Faith* (London, 1986).

JOHNSON, L. T., *The Writings of the New Testament: An Interpretation* (London and Philadelphia, 1986).

KAUFMAN, G. D., *An Essay on Theological Method* (Missoula, 1975).

KLEMM, D. E., *Hermeneutical Inquiry*, 2 vols. (Atlanta, 1986).

KRENTZ, E., *The Historical Critical Method* (Philadelphia, 1975).

LASH, N., *Theology on the Way to Emmaus* (London, 1986).

MARSHALL, I. H. (ed.), *New Testament Interpretation. Essays on Principles and Methods* (Exeter and Grand Rapids, 1977).

MUDDIMAN, J., *The Bible: Fount and Well of Truth* (Oxford, 1983).

NIEBUHR, H. R., *The Meaning of Revelation* (New York and London, 1941).

RAJCHMAN, J. and WEST, C., *Post-analytic Philosophy* (New York, 1985).

REVENTLOW, H. GRAF, *Problems of Old Testament Theology in the Twentieth Century* (1982; ET London, 1985).

RICŒUR, P., *History and Truth* (1955, 1964²; ET Evanston, 1965).

—— *Interpretation Theory* (Fort Worth, Tex., 1976).

—— *Essays on Biblical Interpretation* (Philadelphia, 1980; London, 1981).

RORTY, R., *Consequences of Pragmatism* (Minnesota and Brighton, 1982).

SYKES, S. W., *The Identity of Christianity* (London and Philadelphia, 1984).

TERRIEN, S., *The Elusive Presence: Toward a New Biblical Theology* (New York, 1978).

TRACY, D., *The Analogical Imagination* (New York and London, 1981).

WHITE, H., *Metahistory: The Historical Imagination in Nineteenth-century Europe* (Baltimore and London, 1973).

WOOD, C. M., *Theory and Religious Understanding: A Critique of the Hermeneutics of Joachim Wach* (Missoula, 1975).

7

Literary Study of the Bible

Different aims and methods

The previous chapter elaborated on the theological dimension present in most nineteenth- and twentieth-century biblical scholarship and made a case for reconsidering the partnership between religious interests and rational methods that is characteristic of theological interpretation. Historical reconstruction of biblical persons, events, and traditions is an entirely legitimate activity, but possibly less fruitful for theology than the newly emerging literary approaches. These offer more points of connection for the theories of religion and reality which seem to be necessary if secular methods are to yield theological interpretations.

That suggestion does not detract from the traditional disciplines of biblical scholarship. The student of ancient literature can never have enough factual information about the languages, history, literary conventions and genres of the culture concerned. But this indispensable spadework can lay a base for several modes of interpretation, and some of the different ways that interpreters read a work of art today may prove more suggestive for theological interpretation than a historical scholarship which is less interested in the aesthetic and moral significance of great literature.

Whether or not this diagnosis is accepted, and whether or not theological interests are still strong enough to carry through a partial reorientation of biblical teaching, the suggestion itself serves the purpose of an introduction to biblical interpretation by providing a perspective on its different dimensions. It is simpler to describe the task of biblical interpretation than to survey all the contemporary theology, hermeneutics, and biblical scholarship that it involves. So much detail could obscure as much as it revealed. A theory about theological interpretation offers a route through the history of interpretation; one which highlights the different aims and methods open to biblical interpreters.

The thesis introduced in Chapter 1, illustrated in the subsequent chapters and elaborated in Chapter 6, is that all interpretation of texts is guided by certain interests, and that the theological interpretation of its scriptures by a religious group aims to sustain and correct that community's faith. But because religious faith makes claims to truth, it can be arraigned before the bar of reason. Christian theological interpretation of the Bible depends as much on reason as on the religious imagination. It is answerable both to historical scholarship and to the faith of its religious community.

In a culture whose rational norms are no longer grounded in religious belief, this dual responsibility of all theology to religion and to reason makes for tensions. Western Christianity has faced challenges from modern philosophy, sciences, and history. It has resisted what seemed incompatible with its own best insights while absorbing what seems true in these disciplines.

Biblical scholars have participated in both the rational challenges and the constructive restatements of Christianity. Their rationalistic criticisms of traditional beliefs have sometimes overshadowed their more constructive aims. But most of those who forced the theological pace by their rational study of the Bible were themselves theologians, accommodating the ever-developing tradition to new knowledge, and aiming at a synthesis between their faith and their reason.

If increased disciplinary specialization and further secularization have made some contemporary biblical scholarship less interested in the *theological* task, then the religious communities who use the Bible as scripture will have to train others to rebuild these bridges between their corporate faith and contemporary knowledge. If neglected, these bridges fall into disrepair and the religion's lines of communication are weakened. But there need be no conflict between a biblical scholarship independent of religious interests and a theological bridge-building type of interpretation which shares the same rational methods as the other but whose ultimate aims differ. There is room in the world of biblical interpretation for historical curiosity, literary taste, religious hunger, and theological cooking, and the occasional conflict of interests provides mutual stimulus.

Any attempt to illuminate the interplay between scholarship and religious interests must make explicit those matters which usually and rightly remain unstated. Biblical scholarship discusses the texts themselves, not the motives of the interpreters. It sometimes reflects on its methods, but motives are private, and identifying them (or impugning them) is no substitute for the rational discussion of public results. However, what follows is concerned with neither results nor motives. The argument is that it is essential to be clear about one's own and others' objectives. The variety of possible aims authorizes some variety in the methods used.

Religious aims remain the underlying concern in most biblical interpretation, and the 'literary turn' in some recent biblical scholarship is rich in its potential for sustaining religious faith. But a post-Christian culture can also find here a source and resource worth studying without bringing to it specifically religious interests. The Bible contains some reliable information about those parts of the ancient world which have most influenced subsequent history, and also some literature which is central to the Western tradition. Neither the historical nor the literary aspects can be separated from the institutions which have used the Bible as scripture, but where that ecclesiastical dimension recedes it is the impact and influence of the Bible as literature which commands most attention.

The recent renewal of this interest is in part religiously and in part non-religiously motivated. That is itself confirmation of how biblical scholarship helps constitute the interface which theology cultivates between the religious tradition and contemporary sensibility. This underlines the theological value of a biblical scholarship that is not under pressure to produce instantly relevant theological interpretations. It also invites some reassessment of the earlier history of research.

Earlier literary interests

The problems raised for orthodox Christianity by rationalist historical criticism of the Gospels and the Pentateuch, and the theological benefits drawn from the new historical research, have during the past two hundred years sometimes eclipsed the essentially *literary* character of most normal study of these literary texts. All literary study of ancient texts has a historical dimension because exegesis clarifies what the words meant at the time they were written. Languages develop, and until quite recently the great advances in modern classical and Semitic scholarship came from studying languages historically. But the primary aim has been to elucidate these texts, not to reconstruct what they refer to. Meaning and reference have usually been distinct.

The changing relationships between literary and historical tastes, and the interrelationships of both with religious aims, cannot be reduced to a simple formula. But it is clear that the historical task of reconstructing persons, events, and traditions did not gain independence, channelling literary insights to serve its own quite different aims, until it became a weapon of the modern rationalist assault on traditional Christianity. Before that, and even subsequently in more orthodox circles, historical questions were raised and answered in order to resolve difficulties in the *texts*. They were guided by the *literary* interest that is inseparable from any intelligent reading of the Bible, not by a specifically historical interest. That did not develop until Richard Simon (1638–1712), and then the deists, saw its anti-Protestant potential. When St Augustine devoted a whole treatise to the disagreements between the evangelists, he was not engaged in the quest for the historical Jesus.

Less dramatic inconsistencies than those between the Gospels had also been observed in the Hebrew Bible by Jewish commentators in the Middle Ages. The rabbis were puzzled by the books of Moses recording Moses' own death, and began to ask how the biblical books cohered. But if Deuteronomy 34 made it irrational to treat the Pentateuch as a single whole written by Moses, the difficulty could be removed without losing the coherence of the whole, simply by suggesting that Joshua had added the final chapter.

Neither historical nor stylistic observations about the biblical literature led at that stage to far-reaching historical or theological conclusions. This only happened when other factors—especially the rise of modern rationalism—made these attractive to critics of traditional religion, and in consequence a challenge to its more adventurous defenders. But medieval rabbis had noticed variations in style between different prophetic books, and back in the third century Clement of Alexandria and Origen had seen the stylistic differences between the Epistle to the Hebrews and the Pauline epistles. Origen's pupil Dionysius of Alexandria had similarly contrasted the Book of Revelation with the Gospel and First Epistle of John, and had denied the apostolic authorship of Revelation. But all these matters were discussed piecemeal, usually when the text presented a difficulty. Clement suggested that the Greek text of Hebrews was a translation of what Paul had written in Hebrew, and Origen also assumed some connection with the Apostle. There was no impulse to use such doubts about the apostolic authorship of a New Testament book as a weapon against the canon. These theological consequences were not drawn, even where on occasion modern literary insights about style and genre were anticipated.

Some anticipation of later discussion of genre was natural, because it is impossible to understand a text at all without some idea of what kind of a text it is. But these matters of both genre and literary style were finally raised far more sharply during the eighteenth century, as the canons of literary taste and scholarship which had been applied to classical literature since the Renaissance were gradually applied to the Bible.

To modern ears, accustomed to Benjamin Jowett's instruction in *Essays and Reviews* (1860, p. 338; cf. p. 404. See above, p. 57 f.) to read the Bible 'like any other book', i.e. disregarding 'all the after-thoughts of theology', the eighteenth-century move to treat the Bible as the literary deposit of ancient Israel and the early Church, as the classics are the deposit of Greek and Roman antiquity, sounds like a secularizing move. Some of its consequences later threatened the whole fabric of Christian belief. But this new view of the Bible as literature was not originally conceived in such hostile terms. The great pioneering work in modern literary criticism of the Bible was admittedly published in Latin, as some thought Strauss's *Life of Jesus* should have been. But far from suffering a similar fate, Robert Lowth became Bishop of London. It was not thought that his earlier work as professor of poetry at Oxford would endanger his flock.

Lowth's lectures *On the Sacred Poetry of the Hebrews* (1753; ET

1815) could be described negatively as an attempt to analyse the conventions and distinctive forms of classical Hebrew verse without paying attention directly to the divine inspiration which was supposed to have produced it. God might be the author of sacred psalmody, but he had used the verse-forms native to Hebrew culture, and these could be described without raising religious questions.

That account of the task Lowth set himself is true as far as it goes, and indicates its affinity with subsequent study of Hebrew and early Christian literature. This proceeded without invoking divine inspiration, and led eventually to the 'non-miraculous' histories of Baur and Wellhausen. But that knowledge of hindsight was not available to Lowth. The intellectual assumptions prevailing in Oxford were inhospitable to any idea of the Bible as a special case among the literatures of the world. In this mildly rationalist environment Lowth was confronted with critics who might concede for the sake of conventional piety that the Bible was divinely inspired, but who for all practical purposes thought of it as a collection of fairly barbaric and primitive literature which lacked the grandeur of Homer or Virgil. If today some would discount the Bible's religious claim but allow it to remain as a great literary monument, the English intelligentsia of the 1750s was far more likely to think that religious value was all it had. Since it was obviously inferior to the classics as literature, only its traditional religious standing could preserve it in modern culture. More bluntly, Christians had it as their scripture and must simply accept its poverty when judged by other criteria. There are still a few classicists who react in this way to the poor Greek (by classical standards) of some parts of the New Testament.

Against this background, Lowth saw his task as being to vindicate scripture by showing that ancient Hebrew literature was different from the classics but not inferior to them, because it had its own rules and conventions which were no less rigorous than those of Greek and Latin literature. He was influenced by the idea, soon to be developed by Herder, that each culture in the world had its own characteristic genius, and formed a distinct note in the divine symphony. By the early twentieth century this historicism had issued in a somewhat nihilistic cultural relativism, but in the eighteenth and early nineteenth century it liberated European culture from its self-obsession and opened people's minds to the possibility of finding value in alien cultures. Lowth 'discovered' Hebrew poetry rather as the Romantics were to discover 'folk-culture': an alien system but a mature and serious one, not to be called 'primitive' by contrast with some later classical ideal. It was no accident that the divine revelation had come in Hebrew rather than in Latin, and the Christian interpreter must attend to the form as well as to the content of the revelation, trying to understand the internal system of genres which held Hebrew poetry together.

The practical effect of this openness to alien forms of expression was that Lowth discovered the principle which is still the key to reading the poetic third of the Hebrew Bible: parallelism. He showed that the basic criterion distinguishing verse from prose here is not stress or rhyme (though both occur) but the use of synonyms and antonyms to create balanced pairs of lines. Synonymous parallelism can be seen in Psalm 91:

> He who dwells in the shelter of the Most High,
> who abides in the shadow of the Almighty . . .

Antithetical parallelism is found further on in the psalm:

> You will not fear the terror of the night,
> nor the arrow that flies by day;
> nor the pestilence that stalks in darkness,
> nor the destruction that wastes at noonday.

Lowth's work represents a vital breakthrough in understanding the literary forms of Hebrew literature. While much historical criticism rests on such insights into the forms of the literature, his most obvious descendants are the form critics. Gunkel shared the same concern for the characteristic forms in which the ideas of the Old Testament find expression, and the same belief that this provides insight into the culture in which, for all its subsequent developments, Christian faith is still rooted. The Hebrew Bible is seen here as the product of the distinctive genius of the Hebrew people, which God chose as the vehicle for his own self-disclosure, and the critic's task as getting inside the mentality of that people to hear their songs and psalms with their original harmonies unmuffled by the intervening, and quite different, classical tradition. There is an important historical dimension to such a task, but it is essentially a matter of understanding the literature (some of it oral or 'pre-literary') of the Bible.

Lowth and Gunkel are separated by a century and a half, and belong to different worlds. The line of descent is far from direct, whatever the family resemblances. Whereas Lowth could keep his literary insights separate from his traditional theological beliefs, it was Gunkel's theology, based on a romantic theory of religion, which made him so interested in the literary dimensions of the texts. Lowth was scarcely a biblical critic in the later sense, for all the importance of his scholarship in the development of the discipline. Gunkel's literary work, by contrast, was closely integrated with his historical research as the leading figure of the 'history of religions school'.

If Gunkel's brand of liberalism kept the literary dimensions of the Bible prominent, this was not true of his most influential predecessors and successors. From the 1830s to the present day *history* has been the biblical scholar's stock in trade, and much of it has been sharply rationalistic.

The uses made of the pre-eminently literary category of 'form' have already been noticed (p. 105). The equally literary category of 'myth' provides further examples. For Strauss the literary judgement involved in applying this label was merely the means to a historical judgement and a theological conclusion. Gospel material designated 'myth' was not historical, and establishing that would undercut his supernaturalist and rationalist theological opponents. This material could then also be translated (granted Hegelian premises) into a philosophical truth. The literary qualities of the Gospels had no intrinsic interest for Strauss. His successors also saw 'myth' as something to be rid of, whether by elimination or by existential interpretation, and whether because it was not history or because it was unsatisfactory theology. It is only since the 1960s that the more positive evaluation of myth in literary study and social anthropology has been influential in religious studies, and so has affected both biblical scholarship and Christian theology.

Back to literature

The eighteenth- and nineteenth-century shift in biblical scholarship from a literary to a more historical frame of reference has been
brilliantly illuminated by Hans Frei in *The Eclipse of Biblical
Narrative* (1974). Further research on the more specialist work of
the biblical scholars would be valuable. In eighteenth-century
Germany, Lowth's literary studies of the Hebrew Bible were
annotated by J. D. Michaelis and drawn into a more pointedly
historical-critical research. In the nineteenth century the literary
insights of the classicist C. G. Heyne (1729–1812) into the
relationship of poetry and myth were similarly given a more radical
twist by Strauss. Finally, in the twentieth century the literary
dimensions of form criticism, still important for the pioneering
Gunkel, were not pursued by his successors. As the kerygmatic
theology of the 1920s was dovetailed with the history of traditions
aspect of form criticism, this part was developed, whereas the
literary and sociological dimensions of form criticism were not
pursued until the 1960s (see below, p. 253).

The initial failure of form criticism to unfold its literary potential
is significant in view of its importance in twentieth-century
scholarship. Another important development within history of
traditions study was also unsuccessful in carrying biblical scholarship into the more literary study towards which it pointed:
redaction criticism. The phrase refers to a literary activity—editors
or composers pasting together and commenting on sources to
produce new works. The activity was thus implicitly present in
nineteenth-century source criticism and even earlier. But the phrase
is used only of the explicit attention given much later to these
editors or composers or authors.

Those alternatives (editors, composers, authors) reveal some
uncertainty and ambiguity about the writers' status. The evangelists and the Chronicler have been increasingly appreciated as
authors, whereas the editors responsible for the final form of the
Pentateuch are more shadowy figures. But either way, redaction
criticism investigates a literary activity, and even though it
concentrates on the 'seams' where the editors' work can be detected
and tradition distinguished from redaction, it has to look at each

writing as a literary whole, as Baur did in his 'tendency criticism' (Chapter 3). Its failure to develop in a properly literary-critical direction is therefore striking.

The reason is clear enough. Redaction criticism of the Gospels, if not of the Pentateuch, has been oriented to the *historical* task of clarifying the emphases of the authors and the development of the tradition. This has remained the case whether or not the aim was to assess their historical reliability. Even when the interest was focused on neither the subject-matter nor the earlier sources *behind* the existing sources, the interest of Gospel critics remained primarily historical. Interpreters were interested in what those first-century evangelists were doing, not what these literary texts might be saying to contemporary readers. There were two reasons for this stubbornly historical orientation: first, the theological importance of history in the Gospels; and secondly, the modern preacher's need to identify with the way the evangelists handled their tradition in order to preach the Gospel.

This contrast between a historical and a literary orientation is much less sharp in the Old Testament, where the theological reasons for it do not apply. Redaction criticism of the Pentateuch is more obviously a literary-critical than a historical activity, though its historical flavour is reminiscent of literary criticism prior to the New Criticism of the 1920s (see below, p. 217).

Both historical and literary questions about the Bible have to be asked. The emphasis given to each will depend on what kind of knowledge or insight or enjoyment a particular interpreter wants. A historical aim or interest is naturally met by historical methods, and a literary one by methods of literary analysis. Religious and theological interests are met by theological interpretations which draw on various rational methods. Which methods are today most appropriate for that, is one question raised in the previous chapter. Different answers may be given, but clarifying one's aims is in any case the first step.

The aims of the interpreters constitute one pole in biblical interpretation, the nature of the given material constitutes the other, and more stable, one. Both form- and redaction-critical methods are tools designed to fit the biblical material and also to yield what the interpreters want from this. But the first pole has been more powerful than the second. The historical aims of the Gospel critics have proved decisive. Had the material itself been the decisive factor in determining the methods used, a more literary approach would presumably have prevailed, since the Gospels are religious literature. This natural slant towards the literary paradigm is still apparent in form and redaction criticism, despite their being reoriented to satisfy interpreters' historical interests in the Gospels.

One other phenomenon in contemporary biblical scholarship can be adduced, again contrary to its own intentions, in support of the shift back from a historical to a more literary frame of reference. Brevard Childs's 'canonical criticism' is motivated by his conviction 'that the relation between the historical critical study of the Bible and its theological use as religious literature within a community of faith and practice needs to be completely rethought' (*Introduction to the Old Testament as Scripture* (1979), 15). Many would be sympathetic to Childs's theological motive while rejecting his actual proposal.

Instead of relativizing historical scholarship by opening up literary and social-scientific perspectives on these texts, Childs engages in a wholesale and sometimes ill-judged attack on it. His suggestion that a theologically interested biblical scholarship should attend only to the final form of the text, and be guided by the 'canonical shape' of the whole Bible, is not carried through consistently (because the Old Testament is separated by Childs from the New) and remains a curious mixture of good and bad suggestions set in a framework which is damaging to theology. The reason for adding a negative judgement from the theological side to the predictable hostility of biblical historians is that this 'canonical' approach introduces a series of conflicts between faith and (historical) reason which it is the responsibility of theologians to resolve, not multiply.

The phrase 'canonical criticism' would have been better reserved for J. A. Sanders's quite different project in *Torah and Canon* (1972²). The sub-discipline of Bible study which Sanders introduces still belongs within the historical frame of reference, not as part of the history of Israel, but as part of the history of biblical literature. It has literary and theological dimensions, because 'it is the nature of canon to be contemporized' (p. xv), but its focus remains on the origins and function of canon. Though later generations also use scripture as a mirror for their identity as a believing community, nevertheless 'canonical criticism starts by defining the hermeneutics of that generation which gave the canon its basic shape' (p. 120).

This essentially historical scholarly task is not open to the criticisms of Childs's more directly theological project. But both forms of canonical criticism agree on the importance of taking the Bible in its final state more seriously, and this brings them closer to a literary criticism which appreciates the Bible in its present form. What then follows varies, according to the different aims of interpreters or (where all have theological aims) the different judgements about how theological aims can best harness the rational insights of historical and literary criticism. Throughout the history of the Church and Synagogue the most impressive theological interpretations of their Bibles have taken up the best rational insights available, not declared war on them. Childs cannot be followed by theologians committed to historical truth, but he can point them towards alternative ways of attending, as they must, to the form in which their scriptures are used by their religious communities. Contrary to his own intentions he is thus a witness to the theological necessity of a more literary approach to the Bible.

The literary frame of reference

In the context of this whole discussion, the phrases 'literary frame of reference' or 'paradigm' imply that the Bible is read and analysed as literature, albeit of a special kind. The qualification 'of a special, i.e. religious kind' hints at complications without resolving them. It is not easy to say what should count as religious literature and how this differs from other literature. Content provides an inadequate criterion, because any content is potentially religious. Our two 'poles' in interpretation are once again involved. All scriptures are by definition religious literature, whether or not they speak of God or the gods, on account of their use (and so interpretation) by a religious community. But their content is usually the major reason for their canonical status. Again, as that community dimension implies, most people read their own scriptures differently from other people's. Even that distinction fails to capture either the great variety of practice within Christianity, or the peculiar positions of the Bible in a largely post-Christian culture.

Such complications apart, the phrase 'literary frame of reference' means here that the Bible is approached with questions, expectations, and techniques appropriate to the modern study of literature, rather than as a historical or theological source. This in turn implies an answer to the question, Who is thought of here as approaching it as literature? The original readers (and authors), or the modern readers? The phrase could refer to either, and very often there is no appreciable difference. Partly because our literary categories derive largely from the ancient world, there are strong continuities in how a work of art is 'received'. The expectations with which literature is read today have much in common with those of the past, despite ancient Jewish rules of exegesis and the change in perspective built into our reading of ancient literature by our historical consciousness.

In what follows, the 'literary frame of reference' will generally refer to the modern reader's perceptions, contrary to the tendency of most biblical scholarship to concentrate on the author's intention. The more historical aspects of literary study are not thereby underrated. They have a special usefulness in bridging historical scholarship and modern literary and religious appropriation of the Bible. Hans Windisch, an early advocate of a more literary interest within historical biblical scholarship, recognized how Gunkel's investigation of the authors' literary style and conventions could nourish a modern sense of the permanent value of the Bible. He saw that historical criticism alone could conceal rather than account for its impact on its readers through the centuries, and needed supplementing (not replacing) by a more literary study. But Windisch's own work on the 'Narrative Style of the Fourth Gospel' (*Gunkel Festschrift*, 1923) and similar studies of its dramatic qualities fit easily into the historical paradigm of normal biblical scholarship, as history of literature.

The same is true of some impressive recent developments in the 'rhetorical criticism' of biblical books. Their genres and conventions are being analysed in the light of other ancient literature and its literary categories. The value of this 'literary-historical' approach is evident in H.-D. Betz's major commentary on Galatians. Betz analyses the epistle according to Graeco-Roman rhetoric and epistolography, seeing it as an example of the 'apologetic letter' genre that perhaps originated with Socrates (Plato, *Ep.* 7). The response by George A. Kennedy in *New Testament Interpretation through Rhetorical Criticism* (1984) shows what differences of opinion are possible within this specialism also.

Where it has not proved possible to find close analogies for whole books, as for example with the Gospels, parts of books may nevertheless be illuminated in this way. What form criticism did in classifying small units has been taken further, and similar attempts made to improve the identification and classification of larger units within literary wholes. Thus Vernon Robbins, *Jesus the Teacher* (1984), draws on Xenophon's account of Socrates, and other Greek and Jewish literature, to illuminate aspects of Mark's complete Gospel—not simply Mark's material. John Van Seters, *In Search of History* (1983), has clarified Old Testament historiography by comparing it with Greek and Ancient Near Eastern material. The study of biblical apocalyptic has also been advanced by setting it in the context of 'Apocalypticism in the Mediterranean World and the Near East'—the volume-title (ed. D. Hellholm) of a major international colloquium held at Uppsala in 1979.

Clearly the traditional collaboration with classical scholars and the newer partnership with Jewish studies are helping biblical scholars to clarify the genres of the literature they study by comparing it with similar material from the wider cultural context. This is a literary activity. But it was developed within the traditional historical paradigm by scholars whose aims and interests remained predominantly historical. It is thus peripheral to this chapter on modern literary interests in the Bible. But it provides both a warning against too sharp a division between historical and literary study of this ancient literature and another pointer to the possibility of reordering priorities to concentrate on its aesthetic qualities and their present-day impact.

This change of emphasis in some recent biblical scholarship corresponds to the change which took place some forty years earlier within English and American literary criticism. The new literary study of the Bible can thus be represented as its getting back into step with the wider study of literature. That is only part of a complicated story, but it provides another warning against drawing too sharp a contrast between historical and literary modes of studying the Bible.

The modern study of literature in Britain and North America may be divided into three periods, with boundaries around 1930 and 1960. Before the New Criticism, which originated with I. A. Richards and T. S. Eliot in the 1920s, English literature had been taught in universities since the late nineteenth century with a strongly historical and philological emphasis inherited from the educational model provided by the study of classical literature. The New Criticism won independence from that model, and integrity for the new curricula, by insisting on the autonomy of the individual work of art, which was to be judged by aesthetic norms. This successful struggle for the discipline's identity involved a reaction against the historical emphasis which lasted until the period beginning around 1960, when the new diversity of approaches included structuralism's more radical hostility to history and also a renewal of literary history.

The recovery in the 1920s of the aesthetic dimension in the academic study of literature was good for modern literary criticism. But it was not obviously so important for the teaching of ancient literature, where language study remained a prerequisite. Classical scholarship was not impressed by the reaction against history and philology, and neither was biblical scholarship. Despite the impact in Germany of Karl Barth's theological modernism, with its relegation of historical and philological work to the status of prolegomena (above, p. 94), biblical scholarship remained firmly within the historical paradigm, even where the 'form' and 'style' criticism of Gunkel, K. L. Schmidt, Dibelius, and Windisch was throwing new light on the literature.

Before reporting on the recent move within some biblical scholarship from a historical approach to the more aesthetic emphasis of the New Criticism, some warning must be given of the turbulence ahead for those who embrace a literary frame of reference. The third period in the recent history of secular literary criticism is a hurricane of conflicting tendencies.

The popular phrase 'after the New Criticism' should not be allowed to obscure the extent to which class-room practice is still dominated by that close reading of individual texts. But Northrop Frye's *Anatomy of Criticism* (1957) marks the start of a renewed interest in literary history and theory in North America. This was subsequently fuelled by European philosophy and especially French literary criticism. Structuralism (above, p. 144) was important in linguistics (Saussure), in Prague formalism (R. Jakobson), and in social anthropology (Lévi-Strauss), before it infected French literary criticism (R. Barthes), replacing existentialism as the Paris intellectual fashion, and itself falling prey to its sceptical stepchild, deconstructionism (Derrida). Structuralist techniques have been (and still are) combined with Marxist, psychoanalytic, black, and feminist ideology. Reader-response theory has taken several forms, and phenomenology continues to influence hermeneutics. Surveys such as those of Lentricchia (1980) or Jefferson and Robey (1982) provide further details of these movements.

The importance of all this theory for literary study of the Bible is twofold. First, it is necessary to be aware that a radically pluralist society has spawned a variety of understandings of literature, and opinions about how it should be read. The humanistic values and assumptions which dominated both the older literary criticism and the New Criticism have been challenged by structuralism, its ideological allies, and its post-structuralist offshoots. We are being blinkered if we ignore these challenges and choices when engaging in a literary study of the Bible. Whereas much historical scholarship has remained impervious to theoretical questions, informed literary study in a pluralist society poses them quite sharply. Using structuralist methods does not commit anyone to structuralist ideology, but the existence of this and its hostility to most forms of religion needs to be recognized. When theologians and biblical scholars today adopt a literary frame of reference, they enter a minefield which looks harmless enough and even attractive, on the surface. But it is no less dangerous for religion than the sociological imagination is (Chapter 5), or critical history in the nineteenth century, or Aristotelian philosophy in the thirteenth, or Platonism in the patristic era.

However—and this is the *second* point about the importance of literary theory for theology and a theologically interested biblical scholarship—entering this minefield is one way of making religious talk of God intelligible in a secular culture.

The modern discussion about 'theory', which embraces philosophy and the social sciences as much as literary criticism, takes place on territory that theology has traditionally regarded as its own: the meaning of human life. Far from avoiding it, therefore, a theologically interested biblical interpretation will welcome the literary study of the Bible as a way into the major contemporary debate about human existence and culture.

This suggests that our account of literary study of the Bible should fall into two parts. The first is concerned with what most people still think of as literary criticism, the second with the recent, specialist, and more philosophical debates labelled 'theory'.

Most literary study of the Bible simply opts for humanistic literary criticism. It asks aesthetic questions about its literary forms and rhetorical devices without pursuing more theoretical questions about the meaning of meaning. Some, however, were in the 1970s led by the vogue for literary structuralism away from this broad humanistic path and into less well-mapped territory. This was admittedly experimental, and in some cases undertaken more as a reaction to the dominance of historical methods than out of a genuine literary interest. It has contributed very little to understanding the Bible (see above, p. 144, and below, p. 254 f.) and in its hostility to both history and interpretation is far removed from the concerns of this book. It has on occasion been used as a further tool in the hands of biblical scholars (below, p. 253), but it is far from clear that the exegetical tasks in which it has been applied could not have been done without it.

The wider significance of structuralism for biblical interpretation is that through its more general connections with philosophy and the social sciences, biblical interpreters who enter this foreign territory may be drawn into an encounter with literary theory. Subsequent developments in this area hold out a better hope of sustaining theological interpretations than structuralism itself ever did.

If the account of theological interpretation given in the previous chapter was correct, then this further engagement with literary theory is necessary before aesthetic criticism of the Bible can effectively nourish religious faith. Work at this second level is still at an early stage and there is little to report. But its importance for our thesis about theological interpretation is out of all proportion to its present achievement. Its place in this chapter is justified by the extent to which any delineation and definition of a contemporary movement of thought involves some projection of its future.

But biblical scholars are free to remain at the first level of aesthetic criticism, just as they are free to restrict themselves to historical study. Even the majority who have theological interests usually allow the links between these and their biblical criticism to remain unstated. They make an indirect contribution to the theological task by using the rational methods available in their culture and so working on the interface between faith and reason, not by explicating in a theoretical way the links between religious faith and literary or historical criticism. They leave that philosophical task to fundamental theology and are rarely conscious of choosing a 'theory' about history or literature. They seldom discuss why they pursue some questions raised by the texts, and not others. Like good soldiers they get on with the job and do not reason why.

Only a strong sense of not getting where they want to go drives some people into the second level of theory. Such theological anxieties have recently gained some recruits for the literary criticism of the Bible. But most of this work remains at the first level of formal and aesthetic analysis, justified by the literary character of the texts being studied. The Bible, especially the Hebrew Bible, contains some great literature. Even those parts which have less literary distinction have become important literature through inclusion in the scriptural canons of major religions. It is therefore reasonable to investigate them by literary as well as linguistic and historical methods. Theological interpretation is an optional extra course, whether silently contributed by the religious readers themselves, or cooked and served by philosophically inclined biblical theologians for those who read the Bible from a religious interest.

The breakthrough

The literary frame of reference can be characterized as a shift in the focus of interest from past persons, events, traditions, literary forms, and conventions, to the now available texts and their impact upon present-day hearers and readers. The same texts are analysed, classified, and understood, but now with a view to the enjoyment and instruction readers derive from literature, rather than knowledge of the past. Historical knowledge often contributes to literary appreciation, and the reaction against it by the New Criticism (above, p. 213) has been tempered with time. But within a literary approach to the Bible historical information and understanding are subordinated to literary interests and are not valued as providing more solid knowledge than literature or religion.

Aesthetic concerns have been far from absent in the two centuries of biblical scholarship between Lowth and the 1960s. But they have remained undeveloped, marginal, and exceptional. An interesting, if isolated, example is provided by R. G. Moulton in *The Literary Study of the Bible* (1899), a lengthy 'account of the leading forms of literature represented in the sacred writings'. Moulton included both Testaments in his survey of lyric poetry, biblical history and epic, rhetoric, wisdom literature, and prophecy—though naturally the Old Testament provided most of his material. But more important than the achievement is the promise of a new dawn. He remarks that 'the Study of Literature, properly so called, is only just beginning', and 'when literature was linked with language and history in one common study, it was inevitable that the historical element in literature should become prominent. In the broader field of independent literary study the historical side of literature falls into the background' (p. v).

Moulton also notes that the historical orientation of the 'Higher Criticism' has been bound up with the question of biblical authority, on the false assumption that this is dependent upon how the texts came to be written. He was both more modern and more in tune with the whole history of Judaism and Christianity in judging that such questions are actually less important than the analysis of the texts as they stand, and in seeing that this must be in the first place a literary analysis. He did not argue that literary study was more important than history, only that it was the prior task, and that ignoring it could lead to historical and exegetical mistakes. Few would now disagree.

The extent to which even a properly literary study could be primarily a contribution to *historical* research is exemplified by C. F. Burney, who saw his work on *The Poetry of Our Lord* (1925) as contributing an argument in favour of the substantial authenticity of much Gospel material. Jeremias followed in his wake and gave theological satisfaction for a further half-century. Theological interests were best served by history, whether real history or the existentialist historiography favoured by kerygmatic theology. The time was not yet ripe for the seed of a literary criticism of the Bible to produce its own literary flowers.

The most striking harbinger of spring was neither a theologian nor a biblical scholar, but one whose business was secular literature. Erich Auerbach later became professor of Romance languages at Yale, but his classic description of the 'representation of reality in western literature', entitled *Mimesis*, was first published in German in 1946 (ET 1953). It starts by comparing a scene from Homer's *Odyssey* with the realism of the Abraham and Isaac stories in Genesis 22. Auerbach shows how the biblical narrative is 'fraught with background' and how the human beings in the biblical stories 'have greater depth of time, fate and consciousness than do the human beings in Homer' (p. 12). Taking other examples, he claims that Saul and David are characters with psychological depth, and that the relationships between David and Absalom, and between David and Joab, are 'entangled and stratified' (ibid.).

This is not the place to consider whether the comparison is fair to Homer, or whether such different kinds of writing can properly be compared. Granted that Homer is made a foil, one must at least admit that the literary critic enriches our reading of these biblical narratives.

Auerbach's second chapter contrasts passages from Petronius and Tacitus which 'reveal the limits of antique realism and thus of antique historical consciousness' (p. 40) with Mark's entirely realistic account of Peter's denial. His analysis of Mark, like his analysis of Genesis, insists that the literary effect owes much to the religious seriousness of the narratives. They 'produce lively sensory effects only because the moral, religious, and psychological phenomena which are their sole concern are made concrete in the sensible matter of life' (p. 14). What distinguishes the Gospels from the poetry and history of antiquity is their aim to portray 'the birth of a spiritual movement in the depths of the common people, from within the everyday occurrences of contemporary life, which thus assumes an importance it could never have assumed in the literature of antiquity' (p. 43).

Whether or not Auerbach is right about that is worth discussing, and discussions of this nature stand closer to theology than much biblical scholarship. This is not to devalue the major critical achievements. The source criticism of the Pentateuch resolved certain problems in the narrative, and by making possible a history of biblical religion has had revolutionary consequences for liberal Christianity and Judaism. But discussing the human and moral significance of these stories which help shape the religious identity of millions contributes more directly to the use of the Bible in the Church, the Synagogue, and the wider culture. It clearly has a place in both theological and humanities syllabuses.

Similar observations apply to one of the earliest signs of the change to a more literary approach from within recent biblical scholarship itself. Edwin M. Good's *Irony in the Old Testament* (1965) investigates a topic which takes literary investigation close to some of the religious dimensions in the stories of Jonah, Saul, parts of Genesis, and the Books of Isaiah, Ecclesiastes, and Job. An epilogue on 'Faith and the ironic vision', and also the titles of chapters on Isaiah ('Faith on the brink') and Job ('The irony of reconciliation'), are indications that Good, like Auerbach before him and most of those who have engaged in a humanistic literary criticism of the Bible subsequently, is himself strongly interested in the religious aspects of his topic. The human experience explored in literature and illuminated by criticism includes the religious life expressed in the Bible. Literary-critical approaches to the Bible may therefore be expected to help illuminate this. How they do so remains a question. The best parts of Good's book are those in which his literary observations clarify the *text*, not where his own religious interests are most explicit. That is itself suggestive.

Both the size and the literary quality of the Hebrew Bible provide a greater potential than the New Testament does for literary approaches. The historical questions about the authorship and date of Old Testament writings are in addition often quite uncertain and unimportant for making sense of them or appreciating them. The New Criticism's injunction to treat a poem as an autonomous literary work has an immediate appeal when interpreting a psalm. The question of historical reference is not posed by the Old Testament with the urgency that Christian doctrine and general interest alike demand when reading the Gospels. Finally, the cultural as well as religious significance of the Hebrew Bible for Jews, the revival of Hebrew in the present century as a living language, and the recent expansion of Jewish studies in North America and Israel, all promise rapid developments here, quite apart from progress made in Christian biblical scholarship.

Despite so much promise the results have so far been limited, partly because the training of biblical scholars has done little to develop the literary skills which can no longer be taken for granted as standards of literary culture decline. Old Testament scholars' professional expertise is in Ancient Near Eastern studies, and their most natural entrée into the wider issues raised by their work is through modern theory of language rather than through a modern literary theory stemming from practical literary criticism. Both the best poetics of the Hebrew Bible, *The Art of Biblical Poetry* (New York, 1985), and the most attractive literary study of some of its prose sections have come from a professor of comparative literature who specializes in modern Hebrew literature: Robert Alter. Since literary approaches will not be familiar to all students of the Bible, the flavour of Alter's earlier book, *The Art of Biblical Narrative* (1981), is here communicated by some more extensive quotations.

Alter combines a close study of the Hebrew text with the techniques and sensitivities developed in the study of modern novels. He classifies the narratives he analyses, especially parts of the Joseph and David stories, as '(historicized) prose fiction', with the emphasis on the 'fiction'. This involves no denial of the importance of history for the Hebrew sense of God, but 'fiction was the principal means which the biblical authors had at their disposal for realizing history' (p. 32). Some biblical narratives are fiction, claiming the causation and moral consequences found in history; others are 'history given the imaginative definition of fiction' (ibid.). With the exceptions of the philosophic fable of Job and Jonah's parabolic illustration of the prophetic calling and God's universality, the Bible's uneven mix of factual historical detail with purely legendary 'history', its vestiges of myth, aetiologies, archetypal fictions, folk-tales, fictional personages, and fictional versions of known historical figures, are all 'presented as history, that is, as things that really happened and that have some significant consequence for human or Israelite destiny' (p. 33). But the history-like quality of these narratives is the product of a conscious literary art which deserves investigation.

The analysis of these narratives as fiction does not neglect the Bible's religious character, but

focuses attention on it in a more nuanced way. The implicit theology of the Hebrew Bible dictates a complex moral and psychological realism in biblical narrative because God's purposes are always entrammeled in history, dependent on the acts of individual men and women for their continuing realization. To scrutinize biblical personages as fictional characters is to see them more sharply in the multifaceted, contradictory aspects of their human individuality, which is the biblical God's chosen medium for His experiment with Israel and history. (p. 12)

But the operation of the literary imagination develops a momentum of its own, and the biblical writers are 'endlessly discovering how the permutations of narrative conventions, linguistic properties, and imaginatively constructed personages and circumstances can crystalize subtle and abiding truths of experience in amusing or arresting or gratifying ways' (p. 46). They are telling a story to reveal the truth of God's dealings with Israel and 'close attention to the literary strategies through which that truth was expressed may actually help us to understand it better' (ibid.). Small details such as word-play, and larger features like the psychology of individual characters, contribute to realizing the writers' religious aim of instructing their hearers in ways that less imaginative literature would not. And what worked for the original hearer can be made to work for modern readers. A 'literary perspective on the operations of narrative may help us more than any other to see how this perception was translated into stories that have had such a powerful, enduring hold on the imagination' (p. 22).

Whether one agrees with Alter that 'the depth with which human nature is imagined in the Bible is a function of its being conceived as caught in the powerful interplay of the double dialectic between design and disorder, providence and freedom' (p. 33) is less important than that the matter is worth discussing. Alter succeeds both in illuminating the narrative with minute observations that have escaped eyes not trained to analyse fiction, and in communicating a sense of the human importance of what emerges. The interest of this to 'readers trying to make sense of the Bible as a momentous document of religious history' (p. x) is recognized in the preface but not pressed. However, Alter's insistence on moving from the analysis of formal structures 'to a deeper understanding of the values, the moral vision embodied in a particular kind of narrative' (ibid.) places him firmly within humanistic literary criticism, and at odds with some contemporary narratology. He finds 'the deployment of bristling neologisms like *analepsis*, *intradiegetic*, *actantial*' unhelpful, and 'clings to the belief that it is possible to discuss complex literary matters in a language understandable to all educated people' (ibid.).

As that polemical note in the preface reminds us, there are potentially as many different literary approaches to the Bible as there are different approaches to literature. Interpreters' choices are guided in part by the nature of the literature being studied, but also in part by their own beliefs, aims, and interests. These have usually included religious beliefs, but whereas for Lowth and most believers religion has provided the overarching framework within which biblical scholars once plied their craft, it is now normal for religious questions to be raised within a framework provided by modern knowledge and secular assumptions.

It remains possible, and instructive, to analyse the biblical literature in formal terms without raising the larger questions of its ultimate meaning, but where these are on the agenda it is impossible to avoid the step from methods to theory. Until recently the 'humanistic' frame of reference provided a stable undergirding for both the older literary scholarship and the formalist analyses of the New Criticism. But these have been so fiercely challenged since the

1960s that literary study of the Bible must now take a deliberate stand on the larger question of what literature is, and its relationship to the goals and values of human life on earth. But before commenting on what, for theology, are congenial questions, the more limited ambitions of most biblical scholarship deserve fuller illustration.

The examples of Auerbach, Good, and Alter have suggested that the application of literary categories enlivens readers' appreciation of the Old Testament stories. It sharpens our sense of their moral significance, and much of their religious value has always rested on that. Further examples of this approach may be found in the way that the literary genres of tragedy and comedy have been applied to biblical stories with greater or lesser success. Cheryl Exum has illuminated the story of Saul in terms of the tragic vision and seen Jacob as a comic rogue (Semeia, vol. 32).

What such discussions have done is to draw in other resources of reflection upon human existence to illuminate and deepen appreciation of the biblical stories. This can be done by comparing a portion of the Bible with a particular literary work, as when David Robertson compares Exodus 1–15 with *The Bacchae* of Euripides, or Psalm 90 with Shelley's 'Hymn to Intellectual Beauty', in *The Old Testament and the Literary Critic* (1977). All such attempts have to be judged by what illumination they yield. The dangers of side-tracking or distorting the biblical narratives by inappropriate comparisons are clear. But in principle it is both legitimate and potentially fruitful to draw the Bible into the field of comparative literature. Analogies will sometimes clarify the biblical material by setting it in a wider generic context. At other times the distinctive character of the Bible is thrown into sharper relief by contrasts such as those drawn by Auerbach.

The Gospels as literature and history

If we turn to the New Testament, the remarks of Alter on history and fiction may lead us to suppose that the strong historical dimension of the Gospels and Acts is no barrier to a more literary analysis. Nevertheless, it is striking that this has been most successful where the historical dimensions are most clearly secondary, as in the parables and apocalyptic language, and (arguably) in the Fourth Gospel. Elsewhere, the stronger historical reference of the Synoptic Gospels and the clearer historical context and aim of the epistles have set limits to both the appeal and the yield of literary approaches.

A strong interest in the 'dramatic' character of the Fourth Gospel in the early years of the present century coincided with the growing recognition that it was not a historical record of the ministry, Passion, and Resurrection of Jesus. Strauss had recognized this, and Baur had strengthened the negative argument while drawing other historical information from this Gospel and seeing it historically and theologically as the climax of New Testament theology. Liberal Protestant scholarship agreed with Strauss and Baur about this Gospel's lack of value for historical knowledge of Jesus, but apart from Windisch (above, p. 215) did not much pursue the alternative to historical approaches. It was mainly in the English-speaking world, which thought more highly of this Gospel, that its dramatic character was discussed. An example mentioned by Windisch is F. R. Montgomery Hitchcock's *A Fresh Study of the Fourth Gospel* (1911) with its chapters on 'The dramatic development of the Gospel' and 'The artistic structure of the Gospel'.

Raymond Brown's more recent account of the trial and execution of Jesus in his standard Anchor Bible Commentary *The Gospel according to John*, ii (1970), 843–960, shows that appreciation of the evangelist's art is perfectly possible within the historical paradigm of biblical scholarship, and even compatible with great caution on questions of historicity. But it is instructive to contrast this with even an outstanding older commentary, such as Westcott's, where defending the evangelist's historical accuracy largely blinds the scholar to his literary skills.

Another literary direction (again often guided by theological interest) to spring from a recognition that the Fourth Gospel is not straightforward history is discussion of its symbolism. Everyone agrees on the importance of this and has something to say about it, but the shortage of solid and convincing treatments is another indication that a historically oriented scholarship has had difficulty in adjusting to even the most urgent literary questions, and those with the strongest claim to theological significance.

A literary device of the evangelist, closely related to the dramatic quality of this Gospel, is the series of 'misunderstandings' by which the drama is advanced and its deeper meaning revealed. It requires no great literary sensitivity to recognize these, because they are explicit or virtually explicit at John 2: 19–21; 3: 3–5; 4: 10–15, 31–4; 6: 32–5, 51–3; 7: 33–6; 8: 21–2, 31–5, 51–3, 56–8; 11: 11–15, 23–5; 12: 32–4; 13: 36–8; 14:4–6, 7–9; 16: 16–19. They have been well discussed in commentaries and monographs.

A closely related but more subtle literary device, equally part of the evangelist's dramatic art, and again serving his theological purpose, is his use of *double entendre* in several of the above passages. This in turn is closely connected with the most famous of the evangelist's literary devices, his pervasive irony, found in so many passages that merely listing examples, such as 1: 46; 4: 12; 5: 7; 6: 42, 52; 7: 4, 20, 26, 35, 42, 48; 8: 53; 9 *passim*; 11: 50; 12: 19; 18: 38; 19: 14, 19–22, does scant justice to the topic. This deeply human matter of irony has already been noted as likely to impinge on the religious sensibility of the modern interpreter. It is one of the points at which a modern literary approach to the Bible, informed by recent studies in general literary study of 'the rhetoric of irony' (e.g. Wayne Booth's), has been able to fill an acknowledged gap in the scholarly literature and at the same time open up the Bible further to religious reflection.

The dissertation of Paul Duke, *Irony in the Fourth Gospel* (1985), is equally classifiable within the historical or the literary paradigm of biblical scholarship. It focuses on the first-century writing (and therefore implicitly on its unknown author) and on its attempt to *do* something with its original readers. From there it is equally legitimate *either* to speculate about their historical situation, *or* to ask how the text may similarly affect subsequent readers. Duke, in this respect like non-specialist readers of the Gospel, is more interested in the latter question. The former enterprise is more speculative. Intellectual curiosity keeps such historical research alive, and this sometimes leads to new knowledge, but its limitations are becoming increasingly clear.

The turn to a literary paradigm is more visible in wider-ranging works. A fine example is provided by Duke's teacher, R. Alan Culpepper, in his second book on this Gospel (the first was a valuable contribution to traditional historical scholarship): *Anatomy of the Fourth Gospel* (1983). Here too the focus is on the literary design of the text (and therefore on the author's intention) and on the original readers; contemporary readers are discussed only in 'a churchman's postscript'. While setting aside the question of historicity which has often dominated the study of the Gospel, this investigation of a first-century text and its intended impact remains a historical study, and shows how easily the new literary study of the Bible can mesh with older historical study without replacing it. But this monograph also shows how easy the transition from ancient to modern reader becomes when the historical design and its presumed effects are analysed in terms of modern literary study.

Culpepper draws on resources provided by contemporary literary criticism to analyse the Gospel's narrator and point of view, its narrative time, plot, characters, implicit commentary (including misunderstanding, irony, and symbolism), and its implied reader. The decisive question to pose is how much light this new kind of analysis throws on the Gospel, and whether it enriches our understanding of it—or whether it deflects attention from more important issues. That latter possibility has to be taken seriously because the Gospels are referential texts, and a total interpretation in literary terms (as opposed to illuminating partial aspects) is in danger of obscuring this. Different biblical books invite different kinds of interpretation. Much of the Old Testament, prose as well as poetry, can be read straightforwardly as literature. For the evangelists and most of their readers, on the other hand, the historical reference of the Gospels is an important part of their religious and theological thrust.

There is no necessary contradiction here. Auerbach insisted on how important for the biblical narrators was their conviction that it actually happened thus. Whether or not that is right, there is certainly a danger that a modern literary critic less interested than the author in the presumed historical factuality of the events may, by engaging in a purely literary analysis, be drawn seriously out of step with the author's and most other readers' interests. The literary critic can respond that it is the text that counts, not the author or other readers. But many would be uneasy about any gulf between the text and the author's intentions, and most interpreters (especially theologians) are keen to find agreement in shared interpretations. It is necessary to be alert to this danger inherent in overall literary interpretations of the Gospels when evaluating any attempts at this.

Opinions about Culpepper's new approach will vary. No interpretation of such contentious documents in which so many prior commitments are invested is likely to gain universal approval. A work of biblical interpretation is justified if at least some readers respond to it positively. Perspective may be enlarged and judgement assisted by comparing Culpepper's book with another, much simpler but apparently similar, attempt to analyse a Gospel from a modern literary perspective.

In *Mark as Story* (1982) David Rhoads and Donald Michie discuss this Gospel's rhetoric (the narrator, points of view and standards of judgement, style, narrative patterns, etc.), its setting, plot, and characters. A conclusion deals briefly with its implied reader, actual (first-century) reader, and the twentieth-century reader. Again opinions will vary, but some who are impressed and illuminated by Culpepper may well feel a sense of unease in reading Rhoads and Michie. It is as though the wrong questions are being asked, or at any rate not the usual questions. But that is of course the point. New questions force us to ask which questions are appropriate. The answer may be a larger range than we had assumed.

Granted that possibility, instinctive reservations are worth pursuing. Unpacking them will show whether or not they are justified. Rhoads and Michie certainly provoke thought. Even their title, *Mark as Story*, raises suspicions that a more anodyne title, such as 'a literary analysis of Mark', would not. Literary analyses of literary texts are a natural procedure and make no strident claims prejudging their character. Certainly Mark has written a narrative which can be analysed in literary terms. That is also true for some great works of history, as Hayden White has shown in *Metahistory* (1973). The boundary between history and fiction is more fluid than was once thought. Nevertheless, just as Michelet, Ranke, Tocqueville, and Burckhardt (discussed by White) are writing more than romance, comedy, tragedy, and satire respectively, so Mark is writing more than story. The title chosen by Rhoads and Michie implies a reductive approach.

The overwhelming sense of what is missing when Mark is read merely 'as story' must not be allowed to detract from what is valuable in this approach. That formulation at once raises the questions: 'valuable to whom—and why?' Many will find the view of Mark as narrator or story-teller an improvement upon, or at least a complement to, viewing him as an editor of traditions (redactor) or as the kind of 'theologian' which that label sometimes suggests. Attention to the (ideal) 'reader', corresponding to the study of the narrator, should be interesting to modern theologians because they are concerned with the impact of the biblical witness.

But the most theologically interesting challenge of this book is implicit in its first clause: 'When we enter the story world of the Gospel of Mark . . .'. The import of this metaphorical phrase 'entering the story world' or 'narrative world' will be clear enough to readers of novels. The phrase is also reminiscent of talk about 'social worlds' or 'symbolic worlds' in the social sciences. The theological challenge it poses is whether Christians can understand their religion in these terms.

An apparent difficulty is that the 'story world' of a novel is partial, optional, admittedly unreal, a fiction or figment of the artist's imagination. By contrast, believers find in their 'religious world' a way to that which is (they believe) *most* real, *most* true—namely, God. They interpret the whole of reality in the light of that, and commend it to others as decisive for their well-being too.

According to the argument of our previous chapter, a theory of religion and reality has to be added before the theory of literature implicit in talk of the 'narrative world of Mark' can be related to Christian faith in a theological interpretation. Only so can the secular discipline be related to belief in God. Rhoads and Michie themselves finally propose a much looser connection between their literary criticism and a mildly religious appropriation of the text: 'Having experienced this story world, the readers may be able to see and struggle with the real world in new ways and perhaps be better prepared to live more courageous and humane lives' (p. 142). These are noble sentiments, but not specifically Christian, because they do not speak of God in connection with the historical figure of Jesus.

But it would not be difficult to translate Rhoads and Michie into a more orthodox Christian framework with the help of a theory of religion and reality. Much modern Christian theology is prepared to express Christian doctrine and morality in social-scientific categories, understanding all religions as systems of symbols, and the whole structure of doctrine, patterns of life, and rituals as constituting a 'symbolic world'. Living within this system of belief and behaviour, religious people find meaning and claim to be relating to the mystery they call God. Christians who understand their faith in such terms will have no difficulty with the 'story world of Mark' which they inhabit already and accept as the most truly real. This story world is their own social world and their way to God, the meaning and goal of their own life and the hidden meaning of the world. How they relate this to the other 'worlds' in which they live is a further question.

The question of what theological construction is needed before believers can feel comfortable with a literary approach to the Gospels is barely addressed by Rhoads and Michie, and it would be unfair to say more about the human or religious possibilities they see in their approach. It invites evaluation at theologically less fundamental levels.

Their literary account of the narrator's influence over the reader's responses is genuinely illuminating, not least because it clarifies the way the scriptures are actually heard in liturgical and devotional contexts. Beyond that, their discussion of the settings, plot, and characters adds little to our understanding of this text. They throw no new light on the problems which have perplexed interpreters of Mark since 1901, when Wrede succeeded (where Bruno Bauer had failed) in persuading scholars to ask what the evangelist was doing in this extraordinary narrative. But that is a comment on one very short book, not on the potential of the whole approach. There may simply be little of importance (important to whom?) to say about the Gospel's settings, plot, or characters. In that case, describing them in detail becomes a pointless exercise.

Describing what is *there* in a work of art is the basic task of literary criticism, because what is there is worth admiring for its own sake.

But the Gospels are not primarily aesthetic objects; describing them is only worth doing if it illuminates their content. This cannot be separated from the literary form, but formal literary categories—setting, plot, characters—do not come to grips with the essential subject-matter of Mark. The analysis of Rhoads and Michie contributes something to the understanding of Mark's narrative, but seems tangential to the main point.

Even if this rather negative judgement on one book is justified, a literary analysis may nevertheless work better elsewhere, or be carried out with a sharper eye to the evangelist's readers' theological questions. If Rhoads and Michie cause frustration, Culpepper's achievement is the more remarkable, and raises the question why his *Anatomy of the Fourth Gospel* is more satisfying.

The explanation does not lie simply in the greater detail, which gives it a more 'scholarly' appearance, though the popular style of *Mark as Story* gives it less chance of changing specialists' perceptions than a monograph which engages with other scholarly literature and explains its selection of literary-critical categories. But the main reason why Culpepper has been found more convincing relates to assumptions about John's superiority as a literary artist and to the proximity of Mark's account to the history.

That is not necessarily to say that John is the better theologian, nor to claim for Mark the kind of historical reliability assumed by older life of Jesus research. John may well provide more isolated bits of reliable information than Mark, especially in the Passion narrative, but the teaching, the healings, the suffering of Mark's Jesus come far closer than John's to the historical reality of Jesus himself, and this constrains us to read the Synoptic Gospels as historical narratives, even though they are far more than this. The more obviously mythic elements in the Fourth Gospel free critical readers from this constraint to read it as history, even if they attach some theological importance to its historical framework, and think that the evangelist did too.

The underlying question, when due regard has been paid to both poles in interpretation (the aims of the interpreter and the character of the text), is: What readings of a particular text are appropriate? The art of interpretation involves aligning these two poles. The aims of interpreters take priority, but the character of the text exercises a control. Where agreement about the meaning of a text is important, i.e. where shared interpretations are necessary (as most clearly in law (above, p. 14 f.), but also to some extent in religion), the presumed intention of the author is sometimes invoked as a check upon the interpreters. It is not a very strong check because it is impossible to be certain about that. But it is usually possible to reach agreement about what is *plausible* here, and that narrows the range of acceptable interpretations. In areas where agreement about interpretations is less important, such as literary criticism, appeal to the author's presumed intention is less important also.

The interpretation of the Bible cannot be encapsulated in a set of rules because agreement about some parts of it is more urgent than agreement about other parts, and more important to some interpreters than to others (Chapter 1). Agreement about the Gospels is more important to Christians, and Leviticus to Jews, than is agreement about the details of the Joseph stories to either, or agreement about any of these passages to non-religious readers. The historical character of some texts is one factor determining what is an appropriate interpretation, and their conscious literary artistry is another. The Hebrew narratives discussed by Alter (above, p. 224 f.) vary more than the Gospels in their proximity to historical reality, but like John they lend themselves to the analysis of their authors' deliberate literary art.

How far Mark can be evaluated in such terms is disputed, and the dispute is itself instructive. Here is a puzzling document which can plausibly be read in many different ways. This great variety of conflicting possibilities makes it impossible to believe that many of the subtleties perceived by interpreters were intended by the evangelist. That is not necessarily a problem for literary critics. They can disregard the author's intention and enjoy the variety. But Christian interpreters have good reasons for maintaining their hope that what they say about Mark is what Mark intended, however mistaken the great majority of them must be.

Without this claim that their interpretations represent the author's intention, theologians cannot usually persuade others in the religious community to listen. What the latest professors say about God on their own authority has less claim upon the community's attention than what they say (with whatever authority their scholarship bestows) that Mark or Jesus were saying about God. No one knows what the biblical author intended. We are therefore satisfied with plausible claims. This criterion of plausibility allows us to exclude interpretations deemed 'arbitrary' by the prevailing consensus.

For example, Austin Farrer is a pioneer of literary study of the New Testament, whose claims to have grasped the intentions of Mark, Matthew, and John of Patmos have been generally found implausible. It is arguable that they are nevertheless worth reading for their own sake. But as a theologian Farrer in fact repudiated any such defence. He insisted that if his scholarly conclusions about the New Testament are historically mistaken, we had better not read him. Contrary to appearances, he did not believe in 'free play' with the text.

This argument is not necessarily in conflict with our earlier claim that an interpretation might be religiously fruitful, and so contribute to a valid theology, even if it does not correspond to the author's intention. Interpretations have to be plausible enough to be taken seriously, and the ideal norm against which they are measured is usually the author's presumed intention. But since this is unknown, the 'soft' criterion of plausibility is invoked. It is 'soft' because what seems plausible may be affected by further debate. The earlier argument aimed to open the door to a plurality of plausible but unverified interpretations, not to the interpretative chaos which might follow the failure to exclude palpably false ones.

The discussion of Rhoads and Michie (and the contrast with Farrer) has once again shown how important it is for interpreters to be clear about their aims. Behind the argument about what is appropriate to the particular document stands a difference of aims among modern interpreters. Those who feel that the book by Rhoads and Michie lacks seriousness are probably saying more about their own different aims than about the book itself. As with *The Bible Designed to be Read as Literature* (above, p. 169), the conflicting types of interpretations can be traced back to conflicting aims. All are legitimate, though not all are equally appropriate for readers of Mark who are primarily interested in the theological dimensions of this text. Rhoads and Michie chose not to explore these issues. They simply launched their own interpretation.

Culpepper's book is more sensitive to the theological aspects of biblical interpretation.

Reservations about Rhoads and Michie on Mark do not diminish the possible theological value of literary approaches to this Gospel. Literary strategies do illuminate particular aspects of Mark, as Robert Tannehill's essay on 'The Disciples in Mark: The Function of a Narrative Role' (1977; repr. in Telford, 1985) demonstrates. It is perhaps because Rhoads and Michie appear to be giving an *overall* interpretation of Mark that one feels something essential is missing. That is not a problem when *partial* aspects of the Gospel are illuminated in this way. This would also explain how a stimulating book about interpretation, Frank Kermode's *The Genesis of Secrecy* (1979), can occasionally illuminate Mark, yet be quite unsatisfying if read as a straightforward interpretation of the Gospel.

A final example in this section suggests that on particular topics a literary approach may even be more persuasive at the *historical* level than the older directly historical arguments.

One 'literary' problem (in the older sense) which has long haunted critical historical scholarship on Mark is its abrupt ending at 16:8. Whether the author intended this we shall never know. But once we are satisfied (despite W. R. Farmer, *The Last Twelve Verses of Mark* (1974)) that 16:9–20 is secondary, and that such an abrupt ending is not inconceivable, it is plainly appropriate to try first to make sense of the Gospel on the supposition that the evangelist intended to end it there. Any good suggestion about this will be more satisfying than historical speculations about missing pages, heart attacks, or Nero's soldiers bursting into Mark's study at such an inconvenient moment.

Once it is agreed to proceed on the assumption that Mark intended to end at verse 8, what are the most fruitful questions? Historical or psychological suggestions about the author's motivation cannot be tested. It is therefore better to ask with Via (*The Ethics of Mark's Gospel: In the Middle of Time* (1985), p. 50): 'What kind of closure does the resurrection story in 16:1–8 confer on the narrative? In what way does it satisfy expectations generated by the text and thereby give the reader a sense that the narrative has reached a goal and been completed?' Via attempts to see how 'the absence of resurrection appearances in Mark is congruent with his theology as a whole' (ibid.), and suggests that the women's fearful silence provides a bridge between the time of the plot (the ministry of Jesus) and the time of the Church. Both are times of concealed revelation, though the emphasis changes from concealment to disclosure after the Resurrection. The Gospel is now proclaimed. But fear, misunderstanding, and ambiguity still diminish its effect. Jesus is not present, and the paradox of concealed revelation is not resolved. The kingdom is both present and future; full revelation is reserved for the future.

The applicability of this reading of Mark to contemporary Christianity is not our present concern. Even as a historical hypothesis about the author's barely formulated intention, this literary discussion is more convincing than most of what has been written about Mark's ending.

A whole series of literary explanations of Mark's ending have been offered by Petersen (1980), Boomershine (1981), Via (1985) (below, pp. 258, 267 f.), and J. Lee Magness (1986). They cannot all be right, and some are better than others. But they are all discussable because they argue from the text and invite us to reflect on the text, as purely historical speculations do not. We shall never know either the precise historical situation of Mark or what exactly he had in mind that led him to tell his historically based story in this way. The relevant question is therefore: Which sort of conversation about this text is the more fruitful? Both have their place, but historical speculations take us away from the text, whereas literary analyses make us look at it more closely.

Several of the major critical issues raised by Mark have lately been looked at from historical, sociological, and literary perspectives. Most of the problems remain unsolved, but are still worth discussing. The commands to silence, the role of the disciples' obtuseness, the theory of parables, the significance of Galilee, the relationship of the emphasis on the Passion to the apocalyptic material—these can all be explained hypothetically in terms of the evangelist's historical situation and/or in terms of his literary aims. Both approaches can be linked to suggestions about his theological aims, and these are suggestive for contemporary believers. The literary approaches offer easier transitions to modern theological interests, but that does not make modern historical interests any less legitimate. The conclusion is that interpreters ought to clarify and declare their aims, not that some aims are superior to others.

The teaching of Jesus

The partly historical character of the Gospels, coupled with the theological importance of this history for most readers, raises doubts about any purely literary approach to the Bible. Nevertheless, the small step from a redaction criticism which appreciated the literary and theological skills of the evangelists to a more properly literary analysis of their narrative techniques has been taken, and it implies some change of objectives in Gospel criticism. Instead of merely clarifying the theology of each evangelist historically, sometimes with a view to accepting it or criticizing it theologically, the new approach clarifies how each evangelist aimed to interact with his original readers.

The new literary approach also allows the evangelist's literary web to catch readers who, because they stand at a greater distance from the author, may need some commentary before they can hear that witness clearly. The contrast between historical reconstruction and literary inspiration should not be overdrawn, but the latter is evidently the kind of help that a Church which uses the Bible as its scripture most needs from its biblical scholars. At the same time, this approach fails to do justice to other dimensions of the biblical narrative which are important for believers. Literary appreciation of the Gospels needs to be complemented by attention to historical questions concerning Jesus.

This theological necessity for the historical dimension does not have to be met by writing a modern account of Jesus that can be played off against Christian belief (above, p. 120). Those reconstructions have long been recognized to consist largely in guesswork, like all historical research where the evidence is sparse. The necessary historical reflection about Jesus must consist more in contemplating the surviving fragments of tradition, than in speculating on the missing connections between them.

It is here (paradoxically), in historical Jesus research, that literary approaches to the New Testament have achieved most. The reservations expressed above about a one-sidedly literary approach to the Gospels as wholes do not apply in the same way to the study of the materials they contain. The priority of literary approaches over the equally legitimate historical and sociological study of the forms of traditions behind many biblical writings has already been noted. More surprisingly, literary approaches have proved fruitful in studying the reconstructed oral teaching of Jesus.

Several historical-critical operations are necessary before one can claim to have more or less authentic teaching from the historical Jesus, and some degree of scepticism about the whole enterprise is salutary. But granted that the interest is legitimate and the project possible, if precarious, then a literary analysis of such critically reconstructed teachings of Jesus as seem to be available is justified by the material itself. The prophet Jesus was evidently a poet (cf. C. F. Burney above, p. 222), as were several of Israel's prophets. He was also an aphorist (J. D. Crossan), like other teachers of wisdom. His parables are works of art, though not spoken for art's sake, and eschatological imagery invites literary analysis too.

These last two related and overlapping topics, both focusing on Jesus' preaching the kingdom of God, mark the areas where most progress has been made. The necessity of a literary approach to the parables has long been recognized, as scholars have tried to say what a parable is. C. H. Dodd's often quoted definition in *The Parables of the Kingdom* (1935) remains valuable for its inclusion of their impact upon hearers (or readers): 'At its simplest the parable is a metaphor or simile drawn from nature or common life, arresting the hearer by its vividness and strangeness, and leaving the mind in sufficient doubt about its precise application to tease it into active thought' (p. 16).

Thus, at the heart of the historical quest for Jesus is a literary task. In most historical scholarship, 'literary' judgements belong to the preliminary task of critical evaluation of sources. In this area, by contrast, a properly literary sensitivity is necessary and remains central if the historian is to approach the religious heart of the matter. Historical knowledge and linguistic competence are necessary, but preliminary. Understanding Jesus' teaching requires in addition the skills to make sense of his metaphors and symbols.

This claim may be tested by considering an idea which is widely agreed to have been central for Jesus and the (often unstated) subject of his parables, embracing both his eschatology and (related to that) his 'ethics': the kingdom of God.

It is natural to ask what Jesus meant by the phrase, and to answer on a basis of its background in Jewish tradition, and Jesus' linguistic usage. Both point us to the context of first-century Jewish eschatological expectations and lead us to ask about its imminence and/or possible presence. But have we then really understood what 'it' is? The assurance of Reimarus, Schweitzer, and their successors in 'reading off' the meaning of 'God's kingly rule' by correlating a few possibly relevant fragments from Jesus' Jewish milieu with a few probably authentic sayings, and the subsequent enthusiasms of some of his followers, is too bold.

Certainly guesswork is necessary when the evidence is so sparse, and the better schooled historians are in first-century Judaism, the better informed their guesses should be. But correlations which ignore the nature of Jesus' language are neglecting aspects of the evidence. Both the nature of talk of God and the metaphorical character of the phrase need to be considered.

First, how Jesus thought of God presumably permeated all his activity and teaching. As much material as possible must therefore be drawn into the discussion, not merely passages where the phrase occurs. Secondly, both its metaphorical character and the way Jesus taught in parables imply indirectness. Attempts to say what 'it' means, fostered by the habit of looking to the Bible for revelational content, may well be as misplaced as asking what a difficult phrase in a poem 'means'. Thirdly, an important dimension of both religious teaching about God, and metaphorical language, is what it *does* to the hearer, not simply what information it communicates.

These dimensions of Jesus' language have been insufficiently considered by most historical study of the Gospels, and that explains a feeling, not uncommon among students, that their historical-critical operations have not addressed the most important issues posed by individual sayings of Jesus. Neither arguments about authenticity, nor arguments about stages in the development of the tradition, nor analogies from the history of religion, do justice to the text itself. What was missing has now been partly supplied in a book which grew out of the recent debate about the parables, and provides a convenient introduction to that more extensive discussion.

Robert C. Tannehill's *The Sword of his Mouth* (1975) is a brilliant study of 'forceful and imaginative language' in the synoptic sayings of Jesus, showing how their formal characteristics contribute to their impact upon the hearer or reader. Whereas most scholarship has concentrated on their content, Tannehill aims to 'understand the text as a meaningful whole, in which form and content unite in significant human utterance' (p. 1). Some biblical texts aim to convey information, but these were shaped for a different function, and a literary-critical study of their form illuminates the text–hearer dimension which has been neglected. The story-teller 'invites the hearer to interact' with the story, and this 'may, on occasion, affect the hearer's perspective on self and world, the deep meanings by which he lives' (p. 202). This kind of study can support the modern reader's appropriation of these texts, which (as scripture) continue to invite appropriation. But by showing us how the story is shaping our vision it also leaves us free to accept or reject its challenge, even as it bridges critical study and religious appropriation.

Through his stories and sayings, the Jesus of the Gospels is (as no doubt the Jesus of history was) 'able to involve the reader imaginatively, challenge the assumptions of our ordinary world, and enable us to trust in a kingdom which authorizes us to see and act in new ways' (p. 203).

This is so far from the picture of Jesus as an apocalyptic fanatic, by which Weiss and Schweitzer challenged the liberal Protestant modernizations of Jesus, that we must ask whether Jesus is not again being translated into modern dress. When the phrase 'the kingdom of God' is seen as 'the symbolic name for the reality beyond ourselves which is the cause and justification' of the tension in Jesus' language (p. 56), and as 'the (often uncited) basis for the challenge to the old perspective and the reality which grants us a right to the new vision to which the sayings point' (ibid.), interpretation is certainly taking place.

But even Schweitzer's and E. P. Sanders's more straightforward accounts of Jesus' understanding of the kingdom are interpretations. The difference between Tannehill's sympathetic interpretation and the apocalyptic alternative associated with Schweitzer is not that one is an interpretation. Neither is it to be found at the historical or exegetical level. Tannehill's sensitive literary interpretation is based on a far closer textual study than either Schweitzer's archaicizing or Harnack's modernizing interpretations—but so also is E. P. Sanders's splendidly argued historical hypothesis. The difference is rather between an ordinary historical type of interpretation, which may be right or may be wrong (we shall never know), and one which more disputably seeks to do fuller justice to the extraordinary and elusive theological subject-matter, yet without distorting the historical evidence.

It is not obvious here which interpretation is 'better', because one's prior judgements about the subject-matter are likely to affect one's judgement about which is more true to the reality of Jesus, and therefore more satisfying. This is a point where the very peculiar and perhaps self-involving nature of the topic (Jesus' view of God) means that one's prior evaluation of Jesus may rightly affect even one's historical judgement about him.

Tannehill's literary and theological interpretation of the phrase 'the kingdom of God' is as existentially serious as Bultmann's, while avoiding the gulf which Bultmann allows between the historical Jesus and his own existential interpretation of Jesus' message. It appeals to the nature of religious language and suggests appropriate ways of understanding this, rather than to parallels from the history of religion which may or may not be appropriate. To quote Tannehill once more:

We must not suppose that we know what the kingdom of God is apart from the indirect and tensive language of the sayings, parables and stories in the Gospels. Apart from them the Kingdom of God becomes a cipher in an ideology; it becomes a disguised version of the old kingdom of the world. However, through the forceful and imaginative language of the Gospels this symbol may show its transforming power and become the bearer of a reality by which we can live. Thus God's Kingdom is the basis for the new vision of the sayings, but these sayings themselves, along with the parables and stories of the Gospels, are the gate through which we must pass if we are to discover the reality which is their basis. (pp. 56–7)

Students of the Gospels must choose whether this style of

interpretation comes closer to the reality of Jesus' activity and teaching than one which seeks to do justice to his historical distance by constructing a hypothetical context for him in an 'apocalyptic world of thought', which is itself open to question. Any interpretation of Jesus must, of course, be historically credible (as Tannehill's is, and Ritschl's was not) within the context of first-century Judaism. The apocalyptic view involves picking out and highlighting certain very particular aspects of that context and making them the key to Jesus' mission. That is one correct way of framing historical hypotheses, and it resulted in a great historical improvement on the Kantian Jesus of Baur and Ritschl. But the precariousness of the hypothesis may be underlined by an alternative suggestion about the Gospel evidence to which it must appeal for confirmation. Perhaps Jesus said what he said about the kingdom in response to questions about ideas and aspirations that were in the air (e.g. Luke 17: 20), turning them in unexpected directions by his parables and enigmatic responses. His own elusive position is probably harder to pin down than some historians recognize.

Again, any interpretation of Jesus depends on decisions about which material is most likely to be original. Many of his parables have a better claim to authenticity than the apocalyptic discourse of Mark 13, or Matthew 10: 23, on which Schweitzer's main argument depends, or Mark 9: 1, which is crucial for W. G. Kümmel. So even the evidence on which *any* hypothesis about Jesus' use of this phrase is based is contested. This led Sanders to attempt an alternative (even bolder) approach, less dependent upon the sayings of Jesus.

On this issue, at least, a degree of agnosticism is appropriate among historians. Jesus' understanding of God and the future was probably more elusive than that of his questioners or his followers, and even the latter can only be fragmentarily known. The argument back to Jesus from Paul's eschatology (itself not wholly clear), through the first followers, who have left no records and were perhaps slow to understand, and so to Jesus' grasp of what can never be adequately expressed, is highly precarious. The best historical approach to Jesus is still by pondering his elusive sayings and parables, while being informed by a knowledge of first-century

Judaism and the outlines of his ministry, and also by some understanding of religious language. But in this area it would be rash to claim too much for the historical approach.

The literary qualities of the most probably authentic Jesus material, and the notorious perils of literalizing either poetic speech or the utopian contents of prophecy, speak in favour of the literary approach of Tannehill to the teaching of Jesus, and against the more wooden reconstructions of historians great and small from the *Quest* of Schweitzer to R. H. Hiers's *The Historical Jesus and the Kingdom of God* (1973) or G. R. Beasley-Murray's *Jesus and the Kingdom of God* (1986). Tannehill's approach offers a better way of reflecting on Jesus' teaching than the endless arguments about whether the kingdom is here or near. These fail to clarify what 'it' is. Religious symbols are said to mediate a relationship to God. They are not to be analysed as information about the end of the world. The study of literature probably offers the closest analogies to how religious language works.

Before rounding off this section by returning to the study of the parables, where literary approaches to the teaching of Jesus have been most successful and provide in addition a lead into the more theoretical issues, the wider scope of literary criticism for interpreting biblical eschatology may be noted.

The father of North American literary study of the New Testament is Amos Wilder, who as early as his dissertation (1933) was insisting that 'Jewish and Christian eschatology were essentially symbolic and can best be understood by the analogy of myth'. In 1956, as the demythologizing controversy sparked by Bultmann continued, he called attention to the 'basic semantic question' about New Testament mythology, in contrast to the theological corollaries which most concerned Bultmann. He asked about the nature of imaginative symbol, and suggested that while biblical scholars must still be first of all philologists and historians, their 'tools for dealing with the symbolic elements in our texts are not altogether adequate' (cited by Crossan, *A Fragile Craft* (1981), p. 23).

Jesus' eschatology is still not well understood, and the fragmentary character of the evidence means that much will remain uncertain. But biblical eschatology generally is being interpreted better today than before, and the discovery by historians of further comparative material is only one factor in this advance. The application of new methods is also helping us to understand this material. Amongst the disciplines which New Testament scholars can bring to bear on it, literary criticism takes its place alongside philology, history, sociology, social anthropology, and social psychology. Appeals to the imagination through vision, symbol, and myth are surely best approached with the tools forged for analysing literature, and biblical scholars can learn from a literary study of eschatological fictions such as Frank Kermode's *The Sense of an Ending* (1966)—which itself owes much to biblical scholarship.

The Book of Revelation: Justice and Judgment by Elizabeth Schüssler Fiorenza (1985) offers a good example of how a literary analysis of the symbols used by the prophet can be combined with historical and sociological analysis of the author's situation and of the social functions of this strange language. Another illuminating combination of literary and social-scientific perspectives is N. R. Petersen's *Rediscovering Paul* (1985), a study of 'Philemon and the sociology of Paul's narrative world'. This drawing as necessary upon the different disciplines available is becoming a striking characteristic of contemporary biblical scholarship. That is what one would expect in an intellectual climate in which the boundaries between history, literature, and the social sciences have become blurred. It is also appropriate to the interpretation of texts which claim to speak of the all-embracing reality they call God.

If biblical eschatology in general, and the eschatological teaching of Jesus in particular, offer the new methods areas of still unfulfilled promise, the situation is different with the parables. This is where the recent literary study of the Bible had its earliest successes, and has had the maturity to recognize its failures.

When Dan O. Via published *The Parables: Their Literary and Existential Dimension* in 1967, the prevailing consensus, following Dodd and Jeremias, was that Jesus' parables should be interpreted by reference to the historically reconstructed setting of his ministry. They then provided a most important plank of historical Jesus research, for old and new quest alike. But some change of direction was already under way. In the 'new hermeneutic' of Fuchs and his pupils Jüngel and Linnemann, the linguistic and (more marginally) the literary dimensions of Jesus' teaching were explored. In North America Amos Wilder had published *Early Christian Rhetoric: The Language of the Gospel*, including a chapter on parable, in 1964. Finally, R. W. Funk in *Language, Hermeneutic, and the Word of God* (1964) had tried to combine both those German and North American approaches.

Funk's chapter on 'The Parable as metaphor' took further Dodd's famous definition of parable quoted above (p. 240) and his recognition that 'the parables have . . . an imaginative and poetical quality. They are works of art, and any serious work of art has significance beyond its original occasion' (Dodd, p. 195; cited by Funk, p.151). But Dodd had not developed this literary dimension of the parables with its possibilities for their existential appropriation. That step was taken independently by Funk and Via, both of whom were in different ways deeply influenced by Bultmann's existential interpretation of the New Testament.

Via's study of the parables as aesthetic objects is theologically motivated and philosophically informed, and builds historical research into the undertaking. This distinguishes it from John Drury's more recent and equally legitimate project in *The Parables in the Gospels* (1985), which sets the question of the historical Jesus on one side and simply interprets the texts as they stand in the Gospels. Both Via and J. D. Crossan, whose *In Parables* (1973) remains among the best recent works, combine their literary analyses with history of traditions research on the historical Jesus. There is no conflict between historical and literary approaches, but aims determine priorities. For students of the historical Jesus' actual teaching, history of traditions analysis still has the first word. But it does not reveal what the reconstructed sayings and parables *mean*. By attending to the aesthetic character and function of these works of art, borrowing categories from philosophy and literary criticism where necessary, and not evading theological issues, these two creative interpreters have (arguably) come closer to the historical heart of the matter than historical approaches which depend on hypothetical and quite unverifiable reconstructions of the parables' historical context, or which treat them as illustrations of something else.

These approaches have also provided better bridges to present-day readers. Via insists that 'biblical theology should at least concern itself with what it is in the texts that can be related to later situations' (p. 22). The Bultmannian existential interpretation which he attaches to his aesthetic analyses is now less fresh than it was twenty years ago, but Via's integration of a literary dimension into some sophisticated theological interpretation represents one of the more significant theoretical advances in recent biblical interpretation.

The philosophical and theological dimensions present in this work of Wilder, Funk, Via, and Crossan have taken us beyond our first level of aesthetic criticism, and on to the second, theoretical, level. They cannot be separated, because even practical criticism presupposes theoretical decisions about the nature of literature and reality, when it goes beyond purely formal analysis. Wilder has always gone beyond discussing the figurative mode and imaginative resonances of biblical language, and has asked about the truth or correspondence with reality of these evocations of cosmic transformation. He has insisted that a non-referential literary criticism is finally inadequate in theological interpretation. His successors have not been so sure. They have experimented with the new fashions which overtook humanistic literary criticism in the 1960s. It is to these we must now turn.

Literary theory and theology

Biblical scholarship has always been primarily a form of literary scholarship, as its preoccupation with commentaries indicates. But both the word 'scholarship' and the nature of commentaries imply a literary criticism that elucidates its texts by providing linguistic and historical information rather than educating its readers' literary sensibility. Recent work on the properly literary qualities of the Bible thus represents a genuinely new departure.

The aesthetic aspects of the biblical literature had been neglected while the study of its historical dimensions took on a life of its own, especially in New Testament studies. Without denying that the historical investigation of Jesus is important, we have seen modern literary approaches penetrating even this, and making significant contributions to biblical study generally. But the new interest of biblical scholars in literary form and impact has grown at a time when the New Criticism which introduced this aesthetic orientation into literary study has itself been partially eclipsed by the various new developments from around 1960. This poses the question how a biblical scholarship which has only recently rediscovered the full scope of its literary character is responding to the turmoil of the new literary theory which has followed in the wake of structuralism. Old and new ideologies are now being combined with new techniques of literary analysis in ways that are of interest to theological interpreters of the Bible.

It is important to distinguish the methods of analysis from the aims with which they are applied, and the theory of literature and human life with which they are often accompanied. One welcome feature of contemporary literary study is that its great variety challenges biblical interpreters to clarify their own aims and to say what *kind* of understanding or use of these texts they want to encourage. Are our aims historical knowledge, aesthetic enjoyment, moral instruction, religious experience or inspiration (related to aesthetic enjoyment), religious information (including historical knowledge), religious instruction (related to ethics), or the expression of religious life in confession, prayer, and rituals? Our choice of methods and styles of analysis should surely be determined by the aims with which we read and study the Bible.

Biblical scholars *can* simply do with these texts whatever anyone else is doing—historical, linguistic, and literary research, using whatever methods are used elsewhere, and tuning them finely to fit this ancient material, but without giving any clear definition of their aims, or reasons for doing what they do. Some students are prepared to say, 'This is what biblical scholarship *is*; ours not to reason why.'

Biblical scholarship has indeed borrowed and developed available methods. But most scholars have been quite clear why. If they have not always justified their historical aims against alternatives, that is because at certain times and in certain circles these aims have not been seriously challenged. Some have done historical research out of a purely historical interest, whereas others have used these rational methods and achieved historical results with an eye to larger horizons and different goals. They have hoped to gain a clearer understanding of their own life, and even support in living it, through listening to these texts with the help of all relevant rational methods.

Despite complicating factors, such as the religious community within which people usually read the Bible this way, and the voluntary character of religious association today, the contrast between scholars who view their work strictly in its own terms as a specialist academic discipline and those who take a wider view, relating their small operations to their understanding of reality as a whole, is a feature of all academic disciplines. The balance between narrowly specialist concentration and the wider vision varies between disciplines and also within each discipline, with some social scientists and literary critics more prone to philosophy and cultural criticism than most historians, and far more than most natural scientists, and some biblical scholars more prone to theology than others. One effect of the new interest in theory across several disciplines has been to provide new analogies for theological interests in the Bible, and to make nonsense of the old prejudice that such wider concerns are somehow 'unscholarly'.

The distinction within the study of literature—between formal, aesthetic analysis on the one hand and literary theory on the other—corresponds in part to the distinction also made in this book between biblical scholarship and theological interpretation. Neither distinction provides a good way of classifying the work done, because most of this involves both levels, at least implicitly. The distinction is simply intended to clarify the shape of our subject. It shows how the rational methods of biblical scholarship sometimes mesh with interests of a different and much wider kind which concern interpreters' whole understandings of themselves and their world. Some literary critics and social scientists similarly oscillate between minute analysis and the larger human questions informing their work.

The larger questions about human existence which lie behind the study of literature, history, society, and (more remotely) the natural sciences are those which theologians address from the perspective of their own religious tradition and experience. The natural route for a biblical scholarship which is interested in theology is therefore the route from the rational methods it uses (historical, sociological, or literary) to the questions of theory raised by these disciplines. That is why theological interpreters of the Bible do not stop at aesthetic analysis of their texts, but are interested in questions of literary theory.

Our distinction between these two levels also corresponds to the change of emphasis in secular literary criticism around 1960, marked by a greater concern with theory. Theoretical interests were always present in the earlier period, and the theory of literature was much discussed. But the values and goals of humanistic literary criticism could still be taken for granted. Conversely, long after 1960, New Critical kinds of analysis continue to dominate class-room practice. But the importation into the study of literature, by Roland Barthes in the 1960s, of the structuralist style of thinking by which Ferdinand de Saussure had revolutionized the study of language, and by which Lévi-Strauss had popularized social anthropology in the 1950s, marks a watershed in the modern discussion of 'theory'.

It is not within the scope of this book to summarize the large and diverse portion of twentieth-century intellectual history indicated by the umbrella term 'structuralism'. Its main significance for literary criticism and for theology lies in its challenge to the humanistic values underlying both the older literary scholarship and the New Criticism. Its revolutionary ideas forced renewed attention to theoretical questions about the definition, scope, and value of literature, even though its own apparent hostility to 'works' of literature, history, and religion has appalled many literary scholars and most theologians.

Biblical scholars who have used structuralist methods of analysis have not always been interested in the ideological dimensions of structuralist literary criticism. They have sometimes seen it as merely a technique for analysing texts, and used it to illuminate a few dark corners. That is a reasonable, if limited, aim. But it scarcely does justice to structuralism. It is the combination of these methods with anti-religious ideologies which represents the real challenge to the humanistic biblical interpretation preferred by most literary scholars and theologians alike.

The method itself proved epoch-making in linguistics and fruitful in social anthropology. Languages and social systems are best looked at as systems or structures, though ignoring their historical dimensions is only a methodological step. The usefulness of this approach to literature is far less obvious, and its application to biblical texts has seemed to many biblical scholars entirely without value.

The main reason for this could be said to put structuralist methods outside the bounds of a book on biblical interpretation. Structuralists are not interested in producing new interpretations of literary texts. That is why their exercises on biblical texts strike non-players as tedious, pointless, and trivial. They only gain a recognizable 'point' when combined with some ideology, such as Marxism, as in Fernando Belo's Marxist reading of Mark (above, p. 156 f.). But this example provides two reasons for not dismissing the whole enterprise.

First, structuralism provides a tool for breaking the tyranny of historical interests in biblical scholarship. Theologians have some interest in seeing history cut down to its indispensable but subordinate place. Secondly, if structuralism unites so readily with Marxism, psychoanalysis, and feminism, it may well combine with liberation (black, feminist, etc.) theologies. These ideologies appear at first sight implacably hostile to traditional Christianity, but it is typical of Christianity (and other great religions) to relate positively as well as critically to major cultural movements which evidently contain much that is true and valuable. A biblical scholarship that functions as one of theology's interfaces with contemporary thought was therefore bound to experiment with structuralism.

The experimentation with structuralist methods has not in fact thrown much new light on the biblical literature; nor has it yet proved very interesting for theology. Like the linguistics out of which it developed, its exaggerated promises found most credence amid the 1960s enthusiasm for technology, which infected even literature and theology. So long as anyone shared Saussure's hopes for a general science of signs (semiology) that would provide the basic method for all research in the humanities, or believed Lévi-Strauss's claims to have exposed the deep structures of the human mind, theologians were bound to be interested. But this confident rationalism has been overtaken now by its sceptical stepchild deconstructionism, at least so far as literary criticism is concerned. Derrida's 'grammatology' undercuts the scientific pretensions of structuralist literary theory by uncovering the contradictions present in texts. Far from revealing structures, it subverts the texts.

Despite this gloomy outlook for structuralist literary criticism, both its methods and its theory have some importance for biblical interpretation. Broadly structuralist ways of looking at things are now so much a part of our culture that it would be curious if they had made no significant impression. The impressive results of structuralist methods in social anthropology have some applicability to Old Testament texts such as Genesis 32: 22–32 where an ancient, pre-literary stage of the tradition is still visible. The structuralist analysis of myth has some bearing on biblical myth: it can give students of any literature which contains such earlier, strange material some clues about how they should read it.

More generally, one would expect the structuralist habit of mind to see old texts in new ways and so solve exegetical problems, or present them in a new light. It is hard to find examples, but two books which cautiously combine structuralist methods with more traditional approaches may be mentioned to present the possibilities in a favourable light.

In *The Miracle-stories of the Gospels* (1974; ET 1984), Gerd Theissen uses perspectives drawn from structural linguistics to advance the form criticism of the Synoptic Gospels. This had made surprisingly little progress in the fifty-odd years since the classical works of Bultmann and Dibelius, and had recently been subjected to some severe criticism from a linguistic standpoint by E. Güttgemanns in *Candid Questions to Form Criticism* (1971; ET 1979). Theissen had learned from Güttgemanns, but used these perspectives to enlarge his view without substituting a new tunnel vision for the old. He did not neglect the diachronic, i.e. history of traditions, dimension of Gospel criticism, but considered first the synchronic dimension, or relationships existing within a text. He also attended more closely than others had done to the social functions of the miracle-stories. Both here and in a seminal essay on Pauline soteriology (1974; ET forthcoming) Theissen combines a structuralist approach with historical, exegetical, and social-scientific perspectives to illuminate the biblical texts. Traditional methods can be enriched without being decried.

A more ambitious experiment, using structuralism to illuminate three Pauline texts and a complete Gospel (Mark), is found in Dan O. Via's *Kerygma and Comedy in the New Testament* (1975). This represents 'some modification and reorientation of, but not abandonment' of his literary-existential interpretation of the parables. It engages with a purely historical scholarship, and points out the irony of redaction criticism becoming a historical rather than a literary method. But here, too, structuralist perspectives are taken up only in an exploratory way and combined with traditional methods to serve a literary and theological purpose. The result is a difficult and inconclusive book which has not been so influential as Via's earlier work. But it challenges biblical interpreters to ask what kind of understanding they are looking for. Historical information about Jesus, the tradition, the evangelists, their Churches and their audiences, are not the only kind of understanding that most readers want from the Gospels. Via's literary studies seek from the Bible a better understanding of human reality.

But one may wonder whether structuralism contributes anything substantive to this. It offers a kind of systematization, but this is unlikely to impress those not already attracted to structural analysis. Via synthesizes structuralist, phenomenological, and existentialist modes of interpretation with historical and literary perspectives. Perhaps the main contribution of structuralism is to redirect the attention of those for whom the habit of asking only historical questions has become a kind of tyranny, so that they may learn to attend more closely to the text itself.

Understanding a text need not depend on answering our legitimate historical questions correctly. We ask about the purpose of each biblical writing, and we can rarely be sure how close we have come to the author's motivations. But we do not usually ask out of a biographical interest in the psychical processes of the mostly anonymous or pseudonymous writers. A critical judgement about a writing's purpose is based partly on identifying its genre, and our answers may in turn illuminate the whole internal organization of the writing. This judgement may be made as part of the critical evaluation of sources, which is the historian's first task, or it may equally be made in the interests of understanding a text in its own terms. The historical and the literary goals are different, but involve asking some of the same questions. Again, the prime task for biblical interpreters is to be clear about their aims.

Interpreters who, like Via, are interested in the moral, existential, and theological dimensions of the biblical texts, have been rightly dissatisfied with the one-sided historical orientation of biblical scholarship, and ready to explore alternatives. The introduction of structuralist approaches into literary criticism in the 1960s made that kind of experimentation appropriate for biblical scholars working with literary methods. At its best this was not feeding on scraps from the richer discipline's table. When motivated by a theological interest it was encouraged by the suggestion that our sense of life's meaning nowadays depends more upon our place in social systems than our place in a historical tradition. If that is so, then the structuralist method has some affinity with the existential concerns of theology.

Subsequent developments suggest that this possible attraction of structuralism for theology is better met through its relationship with social anthropology than with literary criticism. The larger, quasi-metaphysical claims of exposing the deep structures of the human mind have been subverted by post-structuralist literary criticism. English critics such as Frank Kermode and David Lodge work with structuralist 'tools', and that is the way Via also uses structuralism, subordinating it to his phenomenological hermeneutics. He rejects the move of structuralist interpretation away from the texts themselves towards those deep structures supposedly underlying them, preferring the move of existential interpretation from the text to the real world where interpreters seek to understand themselves in the light of the possibility that the text projects.

In biblical studies generally the yield from using more strictly structuralist methods, for example in the study of the parables, has proved disappointing. Structuralist analyses of Old Testament narratives were most convincing when they were most tentative and undertaken by scholars, such as David Jobling, who were also skilled in the traditional methods (see Further Reading).

However meagre the results of 'structuralist exegesis' to date, the movement has potential importance for theological interpretation in encouraging literary theory. This form of structuralism was recommended to the English-speaking world by Jonathan Culler as elaborating a poetics, or theory of literature, which explains how literary works mean what they mean. Such a poetics might contribute to the theological task of reaching some agreement about the interpretation of texts deemed authoritative by the religious community. In Culler's view a structuralist poetics does not exclude the first-level task of interpreting particular works, but identifies a further task, that of speaking of literature as a whole. How literature 'works' is of particular interest to theologians because they too are concerned with 'hearing the word'. This points towards the aspect of literary theory to be singled out as perhaps the most important for theological interpretation: reader response. But one less obvious candidate for theological attention must be mentioned first: deconstructionism.

Structuralism itself was rather short-lived in literary criticism, but it was the necessary prelude to post-structuralism, which has made a greater impact upon North American literary criticism than either structuralism or Marxism. The question of its possible value for literary criticism of the Bible is therefore worth asking.

At first sight, a Christian theology heavily committed to a humanistic view of literature seems bound to oppose it. But matters are rarely so simple in a complex religious tradition. Even if most liberal theology rejects it, there will always be radicals (such as J. D. Crossan) who see in the free play of deconstruction a way of using religious texts creatively, and a way of asserting that God is more elusive than we thought. Whether this style will flourish in biblical interpretation, or help unite and build up a religious community, is doubtful. Christian theology has certain metaphysical commitments which cannot easily be reconciled with these latest intellectual fashions. But its subject-matter compels it to sup with philosophers, social scientists, literary and cultural critics, in the interdisciplinary discussion of 'theory'. The responsibility of theologians to interpret their scriptures and help educate the human community is an invitation to that table. When biblical interpreters are no longer present where the theory and practice of interpretation are responsibly discussed, their marginalization will be complete.

The radical indeterminacy of deconstructive criticism, which denies to any text a fixed and stable meaning, is scarcely compatible with the ways religious communities use their scriptures as a norm. But an element of indeterminacy seems inseparable from modern literary approaches. The Bible has meant and can mean somewhat different things to different people, and that is a condition of its capacity to speak of God to different ages and cultures.

No doubt part of the attraction of historical exegesis is its promise (more often broken than kept) of providing a single, rationally established meaning, not for the whole Bible (not even historical exegesis ever expected that), but at least for particular texts. That is valuable in a norm or rule. The alternative advantages of a plurality of plausible interpretations have to be balanced against the loss of the single meaning. They will only outweigh it if a barrier can be set to the interpretative anarchy which would follow were it totally impossible to specify any firm and fixed meaning.

The balance between determinate meaning and the necessary element of indeterminacy can be achieved by respecting the two poles in interpretation. The written text is fixed, and sets limits to how it can rationally be read. It cannot mean anything the interpreter likes. On the other hand, in any act of interpretation the reader brings some pre-understanding, some aims, some interests—and these affect the way the text is read.

The importance of pre-understandings for all understanding was stressed by Bultmann and has long been recognized in theological interpretation. It has now become a major concern of literary theory, through the reader-response criticism of W. Iser, R. Jauss, and others. The more radical indeterminacy of Stanley Fish might undercut some of the ways the Bible functions for Christians, but his attempt to avoid interpretative anarchy by drawing attention to 'interpretative communities' is equally suggestive for theological interpretation. The Christian Church is (among other things) a community which agrees to read certain writings on the assumption that the God of whom these speak is that same reality that it knows in the experience of its members.

If that were all that could be said, the Bible would make sense only to believers, and they would be without the necessary means of communicating their message. But Christians belong also to other interpretative communities, sharing many of the assumptions of a secular society. They can read the Bible as history, literature, and religion, without making any specifically Christian assumptions. The Bible is common ground between the religious community and the wider culture, as well as holy ground to believers. The most fundamental differences within biblical interpretation have to do with the different possible reader responses and the different interpretative communities.

Reader-response theory is still at an early stage. But it is already clear that it goes against the grain of most biblical scholarship, since this excludes consideration of the readers or interpreters. It offers, however, a significant resource for a theological interpretation which takes the aims and pre-understandings of interpreters seriously. Since theology is bound to be at least partly guided by the text of scripture, a theory which takes both text and reader into account, and finds the meaning in their interaction, is preferable to any radical textual indeterminacy.

Thus Dan Via, agreeing with Barthes that no neutral system of reading exists, declares in *The Ethics of Mark's Gospel—in the Middle of Time* (1985) his intention to use the system of W. Iser's *The Act of Reading* (1976; ET 1978):

A text does not contain a formulated meaning but is a potential for meaning; the act of interpretation therefore is the production, performance, or assembling of this potential by the reader. The text itself has various qualities which summon the reader's participation in the constitution of its meaning ... (p. 4)

Via continues his summary of how the text elicits a response from its readers as follows:

What is missing—the gaps in the text—stimulates the reader to fill in the blanks with projections from the imagination. The text then brings the reader to the standpoint from which he or she constructs its meaning. Therefore the text exercises some control, and the reader is not free to have it mean arbitrarily anything he or she wants it to mean. At the same time, the reader's subjectivity—experiences, decisions, and attitudes—comes to expression in the meaning he or she projects. One must expect, then, a multiplicity of possible meanings ... (pp. 4–5)

Via's use of Iser is only one element in his sophisticated theoretical account of his approach to New Testament ethics and narrative. It could alarm religious conservatives who look to the Bible for ready-made doctrinal and ethical answers, and infuriate their scholarly allies, who undertake to dig those meanings out by historical study. But Via's account of the act of reading is surely not far from what happens when the Bible is heard in church or read by Christians or Jews to sustain and correct their faith. It also offers a theoretical framework for relating the biblical witness to contemporary knowledge and insights in a disciplined and responsible way. Some such method is necessary if biblical interpretation is to be of use in the world today.

The recent 'turn to the reader' in modern literary theory, and the recognition of different 'interpretative communities', are both reflections of a modern pluralism in which neither the author nor the text can control meaning, and where social authority is hard to locate. Neither the Christian vision nor the liberal humanist values which have enshrined much of that heritage in a secular society command general assent today. Competing ideologies struggle for social power, and each group has its theorists promoting its beliefs, attitudes, and interests by producing appropriate interpretations of shared texts.

The participation of Christian theologians in this struggle is paradoxical. They have something distinctive to say, but they find it at best difficult to articulate, and find themselves suspected of sound and fury signifying nothing. Their commitment embraces whatsoever things are true, holy, right, pure, lovely, of good report; and their criterion is a symbol of powerlessness. Their claims are more far-reaching than those of their competitors, and yet their methods are subject to stricter internal constraints. The religious community can only offer, never impose. What it offers can be made visible only in the lives of its members. This community life is sustained in part by constructive theological interpretations of its scriptures. These are designed in the first place for those who share a set of assumptions which are no longer self-evident, but they also aim to persuade, and their assumptions are open to correction or development in the light of new knowledge or moral insight.

The responsibility of the interpreters has been frequently

emphasized as a corrective to most discussions of biblical interpretation, which emphasize the other pole, i.e. the texts being interpreted, and imply that the interpreter's task is a self-effacing 'ministry of the divine word'. There is an important grain of truth in that. Theological interpreters are subject to some control by the texts, and by the interpretative communities they represent. But their loyalty to the truth as they see it, which is always to be followed, may lead to conflict with their communities and criticism of particular texts in the light of what these are supposed to be struggling to articulate. Both the necessary respect for the text *and* the necessary freedom with regard to it are arguably best preserved when literary criticism provides the basic model and overarching framework for biblical interpretation.

A parallel case

This long chapter has implied that biblical interpretation will succeed in being more effectively theological only if it can recover the position (not the scale) it once occupied at the heart of Western culture. It does not need to dominate (that would be inappropriate), but it does need to participate in the intellectual debates of the day. This participation can be achieved in a secular and pluralist society only by theological interpreters learning from other disciplines and joining in interdisciplinary discussions of 'theory'. Theologians will bring to this whatever insights have accrued from their own long tradition, which reflects a rich diversity of religious, moral, and intellectual experience.

This plea for wider horizons may be reinforced by the discussion being concluded with a sideways look at the neighbouring discipline least likely to be suspected of selling out on the linguistic and historical skills that are fundamental to the interpretation of all ancient texts.

In his essays *Interpreting Greek Tragedy* (1986), Charles Segal strikes a fine balance between the historical and philological spadework always required of the student of ancient texts and the literary approaches which the study of literature also naturally invites. He notes that 'the paradigm for teaching and criticizing literature is probably shifting from the notion of conveying "solid" nuggets of information, in the tradition of a positivistic historicism, to that of performing a score and teaching an art' (p. 371). Without yielding an inch on the necessity of traditional scholarship he looks for 'the standards of competence which make for a good performance, rather than the existence of objective, scientifically verifiable knowledge' (ibid.).

But it is not simply the step from philological and historical literary scholarship to modern literary criticism that Segal and other classicists have taken. There is also a further step to a more theoretical level: from the New Criticism's aesthetic response to the newer critical theory. With a reference to Roland Barthes, he goes on:

We probably have to admit that we are dealing with texts rather than closed, sealed off 'works'—that is, with complex structures that can be viewed in a very large number of ways, with many shifting perspectives. We have to abandon a final, definitive interpretation for a process of endless interpreting. More important, we need to recognize that we are always interpreting . . . (ibid.)

However, as Segal holds on to historical scholarship when he moves on to aesthetic criticism, so he maintains both of these as he becomes more theoretical. Not only does every work of art require 'reinterpretation in the contempoary idiom and against the contemporary concern of each generation' (ibid.). Each also 'has a meaning—or rather a complex of meanings' in its original historical context, and it is desirable to recover these and so illuminate the gaps and the differences as well as the similarities between ourselves and our predecessors. Classicists, he writes (and the same is true of biblical scholars),

are so imbued with the historical approach that they often have to make a special effort to see literature in more general, more universalizing and synchronic terms. Yet this grounding in the historical dimension of literature is a very important part of all literary study, and classicists here have a major contribution to make. To flatten out the past into a great synchronic mush is like a perpetual diet of hamburger or noodle casserole—nourishing, but we should at least know that tournedos

Rossini exist. Without the historical dimension, our sense of ourselves runs the risk of being thin and superficial. (p. 372)

Segal's collection of essays recommends his 'fascination with the theoretical issues involved in the representation of reality by art, and with the methodologies of structuralism, deconstruction, psychoanalysis, and affective stylistics, which problematize in different ways the nature of literary discourse and the nature of our response to that discourse' (p. 373). But he adds that 'we should not lose sight of the quality of pleasure which literature gives us, and we should not forget the naïve delight in the experience of a text as it enlarges our sensibilities, widens our horizons, broadens the range of our emotions, and teaches us or reminds us of what human life, for good or ill, is like' (ibid.).

These remarks of Segal on 'the peculiar and mysterious co-involvement of both heart and head, feelings and thoughts, in the experience of literature and of every other art' (ibid.) sum up many of our concerns in this book.

First, the Bible is literature, though for some it is also more than that. Secondly, as ancient literature it requires for its interpretation both the resources of linguistic and historical scholarship and the aesthetic analysis which has dominated secular literary criticism since the 1920s. Thirdly, literary critics' concern for theory since the 1960s is particularly important for theological interpreters of the Bible. Anyone who makes a universal claim for the message of the Bible must go beyond historical and aesthetic categories and restore biblical interpretation to the larger debate about the true meanings and goals of human life. This has been classically conducted by philosophy and theology, and most recently in their partnership with literary criticism and the social sciences. Biblical interpretation is thus wider in its scope than most biblical scholarship. The deliberate self-limitation of the latter is characteristic of all scientific work. Its narrow focus has made possible its advances, and is not a vice—except where it makes exclusive claims of a positivistic sort by denying that what is done elsewhere can provide a genuine knowledge or truth.

Then, finally, Segal writes of the pleasure which literature gives us. The formal similarity between this impact of literature in general and parts of the Bible in particular is striking, even though there is more to be said. The specifically religious or gracious character of the Bible does not destroy its natural impact as great literature. The Bible, as interpreted by a particular religious community, embodies a quite particular claim about human life which differs in certain respects from the vision of the Greek tragedians. The religious community calls for a different kind of response, too. But both are speaking of the human condition, and the manner in which they do so is sufficiently close to make comparisons meaningful.

'Pleasure' is not the most obvious category for the impact of religious literature. Nevertheless, the late Rabbi Samuel Sandmel wrote a book on *The Enjoyment of Scripture* (1970), and many religious readers of the Bible would accept the phrase. But distinctions have to be made. The pleasure to be derived from reading such narratives as the stories of Joseph, or David, or Jonah, or Ruth, is quite different from most Christians' experience when reading the New Testament. The limitations of the category 'literature' become clear when believers reflect on how they read their scripture. The category is not inaccurate, simply inadequate. Its inadequacy is more obvious in respect of some parts of the Bible than others, and it varies between believers. The matter turns on how closely their reading of each part of the Bible is related to their apprehension of God.

Further reading

Some of the most important resources on this topic are found in the volumes of the Semeia series (published variously in Philadelphia, Chico, and Decatur, beginning in 1974). In addition to the works discussed in the course of the chapter the following titles are indicative of a trend. More elementary books are asterisked.

Literary theory
CULLER, J., *Structuralist Poetics* (Ithaca and London, 1975).
—— *The Pursuit of Signs: Semiotics, Literature, Deconstruction* (Ithaca and London, 1981).

—— *On Deconstruction* (Ithaca and London, 1982).

Eco, U., *The Role of the Reader: Explorations in the Semiotics of Texts* (Bloomington, 1979).

Felperin, H., *Beyond Deconstruction: The Uses and Abuses of Literary Theory* (Oxford, 1985).

Fish, S., *Is There a Text in this Class? The Authority of Interpretive Communities* (Cambridge, Mass., and London, 1980).

Frye, H. N., *Anatomy of Criticism* (Princeton, 1957).

—— *The Secular Scripture: A Study of the Structure of Romance* (Cambridge, Mass., and London, 1976).

Hartman, G., *Saving the Text: Literature/Derrida/Philosophy* (Baltimore and London, 1981).

Holland, N. N., *The Dynamics of Literary Response* (New York and Oxford, 1968).

Holub, R. C., *Reception Theory* (New York and London, 1984).

Iser, W., *The Act of Reading: A Theory of Aesthetic Response* (1976; ET Baltimore and London, 1978).

Jauss, H. R., *Aesthetic Experience and Literary Hermeneutics* (1977; ET Minneapolis, 1982).

—— *Toward an Aesthetic of Reception* (Minneapolis, 1982: ET in book form of articles written 1969–80).

*Jefferson, A. and Robey, D. (eds.), *Modern Literary Theory* (London, 1982, 1986²).

Krieger, M. and Dembo, L. S., *Directions for Criticism: Structuralism and its Alternative* (Madison, 1977).

*Lentricchia, F., *After the New Criticism* (London and Chicago, 1980).

MacCannell, J. E., *Figuring Lacan: Criticism and the Cultural Unconscious* (London and Sydney, 1986).

McGann, J., *The Beauty of Inflections* (Oxford and New York, 1985).

Martin, W., *Recent Theories of Narrative* (Ithaca and London, 1986).

New Literary History: A Journal of Theory and Interpretation (Baltimore and London, 1969–).

*Norris, C., *Deconstruction: Theory and Practice* (London and New York, 1982).

Ricœur, P., *The Rule of Metaphor* (1975; ET Toronto, 1977).

Robey, D. (ed.), *Structuralism: An Introduction* (Oxford, 1973).

Scholes, R., *Structuralism in Literature: An Introduction* (New Haven, 1974).

—— and KELLOGG, R., *The Nature of Narrative* (New York, 1966).

SONTAG, S., *Against Interpretation* (New York, 1969).

STRICKLAND, G., *Structuralism or Criticism? Thoughts on How we Read* (Cambridge, 1981).

TOMKINS, J. P., *Reader-response Criticism: From Formalism to Post-structuralism* (Baltimore, 1980).

WELLEK, R. and WARREN, A., *A Theory of Literature* (New York and London, 1949).

WRIGHT, E., *Psychoanalytic Criticism: Theory in Practice* (London and New York, 1984).

YOUNG, R., *Untying the Text: A Post-structuralist Reader* (London and Boston, 1981).

Religion and literature, theology and theory

AICHELE, G., *The Limits of Story* (Chico, 1985).

DETWEILER, R., *Story, Sign, and Self: Phenomenology and Structuralism as Literary Critical Methods* (Philadelphia, 1978).

FRYE, H. N., *The Great Code: The Bible and Literature* (Toronto, 1981; London, 1982).

GUNN, G., *The Interpretation of Otherness: Literature, Religion, and the American Imagination* (New York, 1979).

HAUERWAS, S., *Truthfulness and Tragedy: Further Investigations into Christian Ethics* (Notre Dame, 1977).

KORT, W. A., *Narrative Elements and Religious Meaning* (Philadelphia, 1975).

McCONNELL, F. (ed.), *The Bible and the Narrative Tradition* (New York and Oxford, 1986).

McFAGUE, S., *Metaphorical Theology: Models of God in Religious Language* (Philadelphia and London, 1982).

McKNIGHT, E., *Meaning in Texts: The Historical Shaping of a Narrative Hermeneutics* (Philadelphia, 1978).

—— The Bible and the Reader: An Introduction to Literary Criticism (Philadelphia, 1985).

POLAND, L. M., *Literary Criticism and Biblical Hermeneutics: A Critique of Formalist Approaches* (Chico, 1985).

RICŒUR, P., *The Conflict of Interpretations* (Evanston, 1974).

SEWELL, R. B., *The Vision of Tragedy* (New Haven and London, 1959, 1980²).

SIMON, U., *Story and Faith in Biblical Narrative* (London, 1975).

*STROUP, G., *The Promise of Narrative Theology* (Atlanta, 1981; London, 1984).

TESELLE, S., *Speaking in Parables* (Philadelphia and London, 1975).

THIEMANN, R. F., *Revelation and Theology: The Gospel as Narrated Promise* (Indiana, 1985).

WILDER, A., *The New Voice: Religion, Literature, Hermeneutics* (New York, 1969).

—— *Theopoetic: Theology and the Religious Imagination* (Philadelphia, 1976).

—— *Jesus' Parables and the War of Myths: Essays on Imagination in the Scriptures* (Philadelphia, 1982).

General biblical

ALONSO-SCHÖKEL, L., *The Inspired Word: Scripture and Tradition in the Light of Language and Literature* (New York, 1965).

ALTER, R. and KERMODE, F (eds.) *The Literary Guide to the Bible* (Cambridge, Mass. and London, 1987).

CAIRD, G. B., *The Language and Imagery of the Bible* (London and Philadelphia, 1980).

CROATTO, S., *Biblical Hermeneutics* (New York, 1987).

GREENWOOD, D. C., *Structuralism and the Biblical Text* (New York and London, 1985).

GROS LUIS, K. R. R., *Literary Interpretation of Biblical Narratives* (Nashville, 1974).

*PATTE, D., *What is Structuralist Exegesis?* (Philadelphia, 1976).

POLZIN, R. M., *Biblical Structuralism: Method and Subjectivity in the Study of Ancient Texts* (Philadelphia, 1977).

—— and ROTHMAN, E., *The Biblical Mosaic: Changing Perspectives* (Philadelphia and Chico, 1982).

SPENCER, R. A. (ed.), *Orientation by Disorientation: Studies in Literary Criticism and Biblical Literary Criticism* (Pittsburgh, 1980).

WILLIAMS, J. G., *Those who Ponder Proverbs: Aphoristic Thinking and Biblical Literature* (Sheffield, 1982).

—— *Women Recounted* (Decatur and Sheffield, 1982).

Old Testament

ALTER, R., *The Art of Biblical Poetry* (New York, 1985).

*BARTON, J., *Reading the Old Testament: Method in Biblical Study* (London and Philadelphia, 1984).

BERLIN, A., *Poetics and Interpretation of Biblical Narrative* (Decatur and Sheffield, 1983).

CALLOUD, J., *Structural Analysis of Narrative* (Philadelphia, 1976).

CULLEY, R. C., *Studies in the Structure of Hebrew Narrative* (Philadelphia, 1976).

ESLINGER, L. M., *Kingship of God in Crisis: A Close Reading of 1 Samuel 1–12* (Decatur and Sheffield, 1985).

GEVIRTZ, S., *Patterns in the Early Poetry of Israel* (Chicago, 1963).

GITAY, Y., *Prophecy and Persuasion: A Study of Isaiah 40–48* (Bonn, 1981).

JOBLING, D., *The Sense of Biblical Narrative*, i–ii (Sheffield, 1978–86).

KUGEL, J. L., *The Idea of Biblical Poetry: Parallelism and its History* (New Haven, 1981).

LONG, B. O., *Images of Man and God: Old Testament Short Stories in Literary Focus* (Decatur and Sheffield, 1981).

MISCALL, P. D., *The Workings of Old Testament Narrative* (Philadelphia, 1983).

POLZIN, R. M., *Moses and the Deuteronomist: A Literary Study of the Deuteronomic History* (New York, 1980).

*ROBERTSON, D., *The Old Testament and the Literary Critic* (Philadelphia, 1977).

STERNBERG, M. *The Poetics of Biblical Narrative* (Bloomington, 1987).

TRIBLE, P., *Texts of Terror: Literary-feminist Readings of Biblical Narratives* (Philadelphia, 1984).

New Testament

*BEARDSLEE, W. A., *Literary Criticism of the New Testament* (Philadelphia, 1970).

BOOMERSHINE, T. E., 'Mark the Storyteller: A Rhetorical-critical Investigation of Mark's Passion and Resurrection Narrative' (diss., Union Theological Seminary, New York, 1974).

—— 'Mark 16: 8 and the Apostolic Commission', *Journal of Biblical Literature*, 100 (1981), 225–39.

CROSSAN, J. D., *Finding is the First Act: Trove Folktales and Jesus' Treasure Parable* (Philadelphia, 1979).

—— *Cliffs of Fall: Paradox and Polyvalence in the Parables of Jesus* (New York, 1980).

—— *A Fragile Craft: The Work of Amos Niven Wilder* (Chico, 1981).

—— *In Fragments: The Aphorisms of Jesus* (New York, 1983).

DEWEY, J., *Markan Public Debate* (Chico, 1980).

*DOTY, W. G., *Letters in Primitive Christianity* (Philadelphia, 1973).

FOWLER, R. M., *Loaves and Fishes: The Function of the Feeding Stories in the Gospel of Mark* (Chico, 1981).

FUNK, R. W., *Jesus as Precursor* (Missoula, 1975).

JOHNSON, A. M. (ed.), *The New Testament and Structuralism* (Pittsburgh, 1976).

KARRIS, R. J., *Luke, Artist and Theologian: Luke's Passion Account as Literature* (New York, 1985).

KELBER, W., *The Kingdom in Mark: A New Place and a New Time* (Philadelphia, 1974).

—— (ed.), *The Passion in Mark: Studies on Mark 14–16* (Philadelphia, 1976).

—— *The Oral and the Written Gospel* (Philadelphia, 1983).

KINGSBURY, J. D., *The Christology of Mark's Gospel* (Philadelphia, 1983).

MAGNESS, J. L., *Sense and Absence: Structure and Suspension in the Ending of Mark's Gospel* (Atlanta, 1986).

PATTE, D., *Paul's Faith and the Power of the Gospel: A Structural Introduction to the Pauline Letters* (Philadelphia, 1983).

—— and PATTE, A., *Structural Exegesis: From Theory to Practice* (Philadelphia, 1978).

—— *The Gospel According to Matthew: A Structural Commentary on Matthew's Faith* (Philadelphia, 1987).

*PERRIN, N., *Jesus and the Language of the Kingdom: Symbol and Metaphor in New Testament Interpretation* (London and Philadelphia, 1976).

PETERSEN, N. R., *Literary Criticism for New Testament Critics* (Philadelphia, 1978).

—— 'When is the End not the End? Literary Reflections on the Ending of Mark's Narrative', *Interpretation*, 34 (1980), 151–66.

SEGOVIA, F. F. (ed.), *Discipleship in the New Testament* (Philadelphia, 1985).

TALBERT, C. H., *Luke: A Literary and Theological Commentary on the Third Gospel* (New York, 1982).

TANNEHILL, R. C., *The Narrative Unity of Luke—Acts: A Literary Interpretation* (Philadelphia, 1987).

TELFORD, W. R. (ed.), *The Interpretation of Mark* (London and Philadelphia, 1985).

TOLBERT, M. A., *Perspectives on the Parables* (Philadelphia, 1979).

WILLIAMS, J. G., *Gospel Against Parable: Mark's Language of Mystery* (Decatur and Sheffield, 1985).

8

Conclusion: Interpretation and the Life of Scripture

Texts, authors, and readers

A text has no life of its own. It 'lives' only as an electric wire is alive. Its power originates elsewhere: in a human author. There is another point of comparison: however powerful the author's act of creation, the text lies impotent until it also comes into contact with a human reader. Only then can the human power, imagination, and intellect carried by the marks on a page strike a light, communicate warmth, or give a nasty shock.

The medium itself is important, and determines how much of the source's power is communicated. Old wires can give unreliable service and cause accidents. But it is the source that gives the wire its potential for illumination or destruction. Without this, there is no live wire. Once this is present, however, those at the receiving end are in control. It is they who decide what to do with the powerful resource they possess—whether and how to use it. They have all power in their hands.

They may turn off the source and play games or make models with the inert wire. That is how structuralist literary criticism appears to those more concerned to interpret the *meaning* of works of art or other communications. Post-structuralist deconstruction seems to many equally perverse, if more dramatic. It seems to show the wire short-circuiting and blowing a fuse.

In contrast to such subversion of the text, most interpreters assume that they are looking for a message which can be at least partly expressed in other words, and is independent of their own personal needs or preferences. For all the emphasis which literary criticism now places on the reader, common sense continues to look for the grammatical meaning of the text, on the assumption that this usually corresponds to the intention of the writer. Even after two generations of emphasizing the text at the expense of the author, the natural instinct is to ask what the speaker or writer intended.

The electric wire analogy respects both that natural instinct to connect the text with the (sometimes unknown) author, and also our claim that interpreters have greater freedom and power than is often recognized. Not many texts are available for such different uses as electricity. But Chapter 1 argued that the living interpreters have a kind of sovereignty. In the last resort this may shrink to the empty freedom to stop using a text, or to give up sharing its meaning with those who refuse to read it as we do. But before that extremity is reached, interpreters have considerable freedom. If they show respect for grammatical meaning and presumed authorial intention, that is not because the text itself has a right to be understood in this way, but because respect for this suits the interpreters' own purposes. They want to know what the author intends. Or they find in that some basis for shared interpretations. In either case the interpreters' interests are decisive. The texts themselves have no rights.

Speakers and writers have some short-term moral right to be understood as they intended, provided they succeed in saying what they mean. But that right dies with them or with the occasions for which the utterance was intended. Hopes and promises make a long-term claim to be understood as intended, but most private communications can only represent their speaker or writer briefly. In contrast to this longer or shorter connection with their authors, some texts in the public domain are from the start more independent. Not even the author has rights over the interpretation of a work of art. Without the source or author there would be no power, but once it is released all this power resides in the hands or minds of the interpreters, i.e. readers who determine the meaning of what they are reading.

This first point has been laboured because it contradicts some views of biblical interpretation and authority. That is not to deny the power of the text or the inspiration of the authors. But it locates certain key decisions on the side of the users. The interests of the readers or interpreters affect how texts are used and understood. In many cases, especially legal codes and religious scriptures, these interests are those of a community, not simply of individual readers. But it is still the aims or interests of the readers, rather than the intentions of the authors, which are decisive.

Religious and non-religious aims

After emphasizing, first, the importance of *aims* in all interpretation, this book has stressed secondly that in biblical interpretation several *different* aims are legitimate. It is these, not the different *methods,* which provide the best guide through the contemporary maze, because they focus attention on the central problem of biblical interpretation in the West today: the tension between uses of the Bible as scripture in religious contexts and the frequently non-religious aims of modern biblical scholarship.

The rational methods by which texts are understood are the common property of a culture. In a secular society, where the generally accepted norms of rationality no longer correspond to the beliefs of the religious community, some tension with believers' expectations is inevitable when these methods are applied to scripture. Scholarship is bound to respect the rational norms of the day. If these do not speak of God, the result is a biblical scholarship which does not speak directly of God in a believing way either. This is bound to seem alien to those who use the Bible religiously. But the methods themselves are only a symptom of the conflict between religious assumptions and much modern thought. The conflict cannot be resolved by changing the methods. It can, however, be eased by distinguishing between the different aims, and allowing the choice of methods and the style of interpretation to follow from this.

The inevitable tension between believers' interpretations of the Bible, speaking directly of God, and a biblical scholarship which restricts itself to the languages of modern historical research or literary criticism has not always been resolved at the theoretical level. Many simply learn to live with it in a practical way. They accept critical scholarship because it is evidently true as far as it goes, and equally clearly beneficial, but without integrating it with their religious convictions.

Despite this unease in many Christians' use of the Bible, the tension has nevertheless proved creative, contributing both to biblical scholarship and to the life of the religious communities concerned. Religious interests have motivated many to study the Bible, and have contributed to its funding. The resulting scholarship has not only provided new knowledge and insights, but also proved helpful to the religious communities in other ways. It has produced a new measure of agreement within and between denominations that had previously disagreed over their understandings of the shared scriptures. It has also clarified and deepened the relationship between Christianity and Judaism. But above all it has made an enormous contribution to the basic task of theology, by helping the religious communities which accepted its methods and results to come intellectually to terms with the modern world.

Biblical criticism and Christian theology

Readjusting to a rapidly changing world is always painful for communities which are naturally conservative and rightly dependent upon tradition. It is particularly difficult for those which have made exalted claims for their tradition. Religions in the modern world are learning again to distinguish between their foundational revelation and the scriptures (and other traditions) which bear witness to this. They have always in principle distinguished between God and their scriptures, but have sometimes spoken of both revelation and the Bible or Koran in terms which risk identifying them.

If we call the Bible the Word of God, or a liturgical reading of it 'the Word of the Lord', we may be speaking the truth. But we are not speaking literally, and the statement requires careful unpacking. That is an argument for care, not for abandoning a powerful phrase which expresses what believers consider an all-important truth. If there is a case for abandoning this phrase, it is that it can perpetuate misunderstandings and encourage bibliolatry.

The theological error of identifying the Bible and revelation has been widely corrected by the light of rational investigation. But this has brought other dangers upon the religious communities which depend upon the witness of their scriptures to sustain their life. When scripture is rationally challenged, its authority is eroded. The spectre of a 'death of Holy Scripture' raised in Chapter 2 poses a double threat. Not only is a powerful resource weakened, but this in turn provokes a backlash as some believers rightly sense that a diluted view of scripture fails to meet the needs of their community. In reacting against this danger they may lose the commitment to truth expressed in the rational investigation of their scripture.

The solution for a religious community needing both an effective scriptural resource and the freedom to read it truthfully in a hostile intellectual climate must lie in the ways it is read or interpreted. Our argument is that this directs attention not to the methods used, which are the common property of the culture and equally available for all, but to the aims of the interpreters.

Theological interpretation

Earlier chapters have used the phrase 'theological interpretation' to distinguish religious from non-religious aims. The phrase points to a master-code which encompasses the whole operation. It organizes the methods used and determines how, ultimately, the text is to be understood. The code itself stems not from the text, but from the religion whose theology is guiding the interpretations.

Any interpretative system or master-code which imposes meaning on human life and history, whether Christian, Jewish, Marxist, or psychoanalytic, looks suspiciously like allegorical interpretation. Unless subject to strict controls it can easily become arbitrary, and runs the risk of impoverishing literary narratives by rewriting them in terms of something else. It is hardly surprising that some scholars reacted against all theological interpretation as they uncovered meanings which had been overlaid by now-dated interpretations. Some even abandoned the search for usable contemporary meanings in the Bible. But most found religious meaning in it by imposing their own, even more alien, modern historical codes upon the biblical narratives. Our point has been that neither historical research nor historical interpretations are illegitimate, but that theological interpretations of the Bible are also legitimate, and that they are necessary for the life of the religious communities that use it as scripture.

Theology is a rational activity that is parasitic on religious life, i.e. on human traditions and experience. In a secular and pluralist culture, it is typically the reflection of a particular religious group. The phrase 'theological interpretation of the Bible' thus signals participants' attempts to say what it means in a rational way and at the same time express their conviction that they share something of the authors' and editors' sense of 'God whom we worship'.

The moral and metaphysical, liturgical and ascetical, personal and social dimensions which the word 'God' includes when used in religious contexts have to be unfolded in the actual process of interpreting the Bible theologically. The aim of this book is to clarify the task, not actually to perform it. Such theological interpretation actually takes place as often as believers read their scriptures with understanding. The Ethiopian eunuch being taught to read Isaiah through the Christian master-code in Acts 8: 30–5 is a classic case. But not all are apostles or evangelists. The weak word 'participant' has been preferred to the stronger word 'believer', in order to indicate that different degrees and kinds of commitment to the tradition and community are possible even among theological interpreters of the Bible.

The necessity of theological interpretation

The main conclusion, or rather thesis, of this book is that anyone who uses the Bible as scripture engages (whether knowingly or not) in theological interpretation. Since most biblical scholars have been religious as well as rational it is likely that much of their work has included an element of theological interpretation, no matter how honestly they have also plied their trade as historians and exegetes. They have tried to determine what the texts are saying, and what the authors meant, without bending this to fit their own religious systems. But with all due respect to the integrity of the text, many of them have also reflected on the relationship between its several possible meanings and the wider religious contexts within which it is read. These include the religious document that houses an earlier tradition, the biblical canon that contains the religious document, the living community that uses the canonical collection as its scripture, and (sometimes) the interpreters' own theological convictions.

Our survey of the main lines of modern Western biblical scholarship has attempted to make this element of theological interpretation more visible. The intention was to uncover its structures and so clarify the task of interpreting the Bible theologically today. Not all biblical scholars want to engage in theological interpretation, or at least not to do so in and through their biblical scholarship. Good reasons for their separation of the historical and theological tasks have been noted, and the legitimacy of that option defended. But the necessity of combining these tasks has also been defended. A religion gains something from their temporary separation and can therefore even welcome a secular biblical scholarship which lacks theological interests. But without a theological interpretation of its scriptures which continues to express afresh the talk of God that is shared by the biblical writers and centuries of religious readers, the contemporary community would go hungry. Fasting is religiously useful, but it cannot be the norm. Religions have benefited from a non-theological biblical scholarship, but for them to interpret their scriptures only or even primarily in those terms would be suicidal.

The character of theological interpretation

Granted the necessity that religions have for theological interpretations of their scripture, i.e. interpretations which speak directly of 'God whom we worship', the vital question is how these can be responsibly produced in a culture whose rational methods do not speak that religious language. This problem is not peculiar to theological interpretations of the Bible. It is part of the general problem of Christian (or any other) theology today: how to speak meaningfully of 'God whom we worship' in a culture whose rational methods do not use such religious language.

Since this is a problem for theology, it can be ignored by biblical scholars who prefer to restrict themselves to the non-theological tasks posed by the Bible. There is nothing wrong with that, though it is in practice hard for thoughtful believers who study the Bible *not* to engage in theology, even if they choose not to publish their thoughts on religious matters. Some reticence is appropriate here, however important the subject, because the communication of religious truth exposes the whole person. But one way of combining this necessary reserve with the urgent need to elucidate and so encourage an activity of such importance for the life of religious communities is to report on others' attempts, and to draw from them some suggestions about the shape and future of theological interpretation.

What emerged from the survey (in Chapters 3 and 4) of the rather narrow band of biblical interpretation represented by modern Western scholarship was the conclusion that religious aims *have* been satisfied in and through the use of the ordinary rational methods of biblical scholarship, but that this only happened because one way or another the rational knowledge achieved by biblical scholarship was being related to believers' knowledge of God. When in the modern world rational knowledge and religious knowledge fell out of step, the integrity of one or the other was at risk in biblical interpretation. Many preserved one side at the expense of the other.

Chapter 6 argued that the best way of preserving the integrity of both sides was to include within biblical interpretation a theory of religion and reality which (like a two-way adaptor plug) fits both the rational methods used and the religious faith of the theological interpreter. This was consciously developed by our three 'theologians of 1835', and was implicit in much biblical scholarship after the Hegelian bubble had burst. Historical research alone was perceived to be insufficient for theology, because 'history without philosophy [metaphysics] is dumb' (F. C. Baur). Literary analysis of the Bible is, on its own, also theologically mute. Religion and theology are interested in the *meaning* of both history and literature. This leads them into philosophical discussions of 'theory'.

Theory and theology

The importance of religiously interested biblical interpreters bringing to their work some theory about religion and reality, or some theological perspective on God and the world, is the most far-reaching proposal to emerge from all that has preceded. If accepted, it has implications for the character and shape of theological education. The conclusion is that neither history nor literature without theory provides the kind of interpretations that believers need from their scriptures. The reasons for this lie in the nature of modernity.

In a religious culture the Bible (including its historical portions) was read as sacred literature, without this in any way diminishing its religious force. On the contrary, Luther could insist that the study of rhetoric and poetics would enhance this. All forms of reading it served a religious purpose because all modes of thought were subject to an overarching framework which defined reality in religious terms. So long as there was general agreement about the reality of what scripture communicated, literary study, which included a historical dimension, reinforced and did not undermine its religious impact.

But when the cultural grip of Christianity on Western society weakened, the religious frame of reference which guided all reading of the Bible was first supplemented and then at times supplanted by a secular alternative which allowed the Bible to be read as history or literature in new ways that were in principle unrelated to the reader's own religious beliefs. As secularization and pluralism began to drive a wedge between Christianity and the wider culture, the literary appreciation of the Bible was no longer always tied to its religious uses. As art and literature became for some a kind of substitute religion, the aesthetic appreciation of the Bible could even acquire anti-Christian overtones. In a secular culture, to ignore the religious dimensions when handling religious texts implies acceptance of an alternative view of reality.

When a religious context is no longer presupposed, reading the Bible simply as history, or simply as literature, means reading it non-religiously, defining its subject-matter in ways that differ from the religious reader's understanding. Treating the Bible as a historical source or as a literary artefact will, in a secular culture, yield religious meaning only if these rational approaches are linked (through some theory of religion and reality) to the religious reader's belief-system.

Interpretations which speak of God in the same religious way as the biblical texts require a context in which the word 'God' has its religious meaning. If this can no longer be taken for granted (as it can when the Bible is read in worship or private devotion) then it must be reconstituted by the theological interpreter. Modern readings of the biblical documents can sustain religious belief and practice only if they are related to the larger metaphysical claims implied by Christianity and Judaism. In worship and private devotion believers make these links unreflectively by projecting their own religious understandings on to the text they are hearing. But this is unsatisfactory in a responsible theological interpretation, which must also do justice to the historical meaning of the text. That is why theological interpretation needs a theory of religion and reality which embraces both the original meanings of the text and the self-understanding of contemporary religious readers.

Earlier chapters (2–4) have suggested that historical scholarship has long been associated with various theories of religion in (usually implicit) theological interpretations. Reacting against their respective predecessors, liberals avoided the word 'theology', and the kerygmatic theologians the word 'religion'. But both were engaged in theological interpretations made possible by their views of God and the world. By contrast, *The Bible Designed to be Read as Literature* was religiously offensive because it lacked any theologically acceptable theory of religion and reality, and therefore implied a non-religious view of the world.

But this defect can easily be remedied. As we saw in Chapter 7, the study of literature offers theories of literature, reading, and human existence. It is not difficult to insert theories of religion and reality here. Theologians engaged in the literary criticism of the Bible may, if they wish, join in these theoretical discussions and find allies as well as enemies. Much of this potential seems threatening, but theological interpretation of the Bible in the modern world has often worked with theory that initially seemed hostile.

The strategy is no different from that adopted when the Bible is read as history. In both cases, many theological interpreters today read the Bible as a collection of human documents and ask questions of a historical or literary nature. They do not directly seek revealed information about God, or speak at once about encounter with God. A secular and pluralist culture no longer thinks of the Bible as the

Word of God, and to start out with that claim would be to break off communication with the world outside. The modern world thinks of the Bible primarily as religious literature, like the Koran or *Bhagavadgita*, and in this context 'religious' (rather than 'sacred') reflects a view of the world in which religion is a human option that may or may not mediate a relationship with a transcendent reality. This agnostic attitude is not necessarily hostile to religion, but it rejects the claims of religion to control everything. If theology is still for believers the only possible queen of the sciences, relating all human knowledge to its divine source and goal, she is now at best a constitutional monarch with no real power over her subjects, and at worst an arrogant pretender.

Most modern theology has accepted its change of public status with a good grace. It does not presume to arbitrate in foreign fields, and is acutely aware of its own incapacity to orchestrate the sum of human knowledge into a divine symphony. Its attempts to speak the truth of God today can only be fragmentary stutterings, following attentive listening. But if it makes fewer claims for the Bible, it says no less about the reality of God. Where such a claim is acknowledged it remains absolute, however inadequately expressed in theological formulations. The theological interpreter today accepts the human character of the biblical word, reflects on it in the light of other relevant knowledge, and hopes that the resulting interpretation might become a vehicle through which some today will hear God's voice. This is not very different from what actually happened when the Bible was thought of as Word of God in a more direct and literal sense.

The new feature in modern theological interpretations is their theory of religion and reality. Religion is the best category for constructing an interpretative framework because it can embrace both the religious meanings of the biblical text and also the beliefs of its religious readers. It facilitates empirical description of the documents and connects this with the believer's appropriation of their religious subject-matter. Only where both are present is theological interpretation successful.

In connection with this, a theory of history is needed by theological interpreters who read the Bible as history of religion, and a theory of literature by those who read it as religious literature. The theory is needed to relate the partial knowledge about the Bible achieved by a particular method or approach, to the wider reality that religious readers claim it discloses. The danger of reductionism is always present when rational methods are applied to the Bible in a way that leaves no place for reflection on its theological content. This can be met by philosophical reflection on the methods being used.

Theologians may, when interpreting the Bible, choose the methods whose corresponding theory offers them the best opportunities for articulating their sense of God. That is why some today prefer a literary paradigm. Baur brought his theory from Hegel, and Bultmann from Dilthey and Graf Yorck von Wartenburg. But constructive philosophy of history has fallen on hard times since the First World War. Literary theory, by contrast, offers possible rational justifications for the Christian interpretative community which reads the Bible on the assumption that it speaks of 'God whom we worship'.

Such justifications are less 'hard' than those claimed by the older forms of metaphysics. Theologians are unlikely to find a theory that will make religious convictions rationally compelling for any unwilling to test them in their own lives and experience. There is nothing self-evident about religious truth today. It has to be discovered afresh by anyone who wants to know.

The literary appreciation of the Bible will support Jewish and Christian faith if a 'user-friendly' theory of literature and religion is presupposed. But reductive theories of religion, and anti-religious theories of human existence and reality, are implicit in some literary criticism. When religion is ignored, or literature seen as an aesthetic substitute, theologians must challenge the resulting interpretations of the Bible by challenging their underlying theory. But they cannot enforce their own theory. Theological interpretations of the Bible, formed by the combination of literary criticism with a more congenial theory of religion and reality, may be more or less persuasive. But in a secular culture they are neither self-evident nor (without intellectual conversion) rationally compelling. They are, however, rationally defensible, and their value and truth may become clear in experience. They are also the kind of interpretations most interesting to the majority of Bible readers.

Faith and reason

A theologically responsible Christian reading of the Bible must include all relevant information drawn from other perspectives and take care not to contradict any truth perceived in any quarter. The kinds of knowledge sought by historians of religion, social scientists, literary critics, moralists, and metaphysicians are clearly important for theological interpreters, or 'biblical theologians'. That phrase includes all (professional and amateur, clerical and lay) who read the Bible intelligently in the expectation of assimilating something of the insight and knowledge of God treasured by their religious community. Theology involves clarifying the relationship of all rational enquiry to the believer's knowledge of God. 'Biblical theology' does this in the field of biblical interpretation. It is better called 'theological interpretation of the Bible', in order to avoid the impression which the other phrase still gives of digging theological information out of these texts. Both theology and interpretation involve the person engaged in them more personally than the digging metaphor suggests. Spinning wool or other yarns provides a closer analogy.

The argument of this book is that the relationship between faith and reason with which theological interpretation is concerned is best secured by means of a 'middle term'. It is possible to connect the rational methods rightly used to interpret the Bible with the religious aims of most of its readers, through a rational theory about religion and reality, including a theory about the methods being used and the knowledge of reality that they disclose. Just as most great historians have held some theory of history, most literary critics some theory of literature, and most social scientists some theory of society, so most theological interpreters of the Bible have held a theory about religion and reality as well as a theory about the methods they use and the knowledge thus gained, even if they have rarely been explicit and not always even aware of this.

Theological interpreters cannot guarantee the truth of their theories about religion and reality, but they can defend them rationally. There is no through-train of argument from their historical conclusions to their Christian theological theories. But if these were not at least *compatible* with what is known by ordinary rational methods, their form of Christian belief would be false.

Biblical scholars, like other historians and literary critics, can leave these larger questions to the philosophers and theologians. But if they want to produce theological interpretations they are dependent on someone doing the theoretical groundwork, and they may (like Baur and Bultmann) choose to do it for themselves. Modern interdisciplinary discussion of 'theory' now offers a promising context for this.

Theological interpretation of the Bible or any other text can be defended as rational only if it allows the underlying theory of religion and reality which it presupposes to be scrutinized, and if necessary criticized. Believers think they have seen in and through their religion some ultimate truth that others have not seen. They therefore choose (or hold) a theory of religion which allows for this possibility, even though it cannot demonstrate the truth of a personal conviction held in an experience that is never fully and publicly communicable.

A religion's claim to revelation goes beyond all reason. In the case of Christianity, this is expressed in the Christological dogma. That cannot be rationally justified, but it can be protected from misunderstanding and attack. It can be explained as well as communicated by showing its place in the Christian religious system of symbols, and defending rationally the theory of religion implied in that explanation. It is important for religions not only that their theologians preserve the foundational claim to revelation ('O Timothy, guard the deposit', 1 Tim. 6: 20), but also that they patrol the frontiers with the shared knowledge of the contemporary culture. Without the preservation of boundaries, Christian identity would be lost. But without this open frontier, no communication with the wider world would be possible. Theologians therefore define such frontier posts as the nature of religion, literature, and history, in terms which command the widest possible agreement. Rational theories of religion provide theology with common ground between its own faith and more generally shared assumptions.

Theology also finds room for itself on the intellectual map of a secular culture through its contributions to the wider discussions about the scope and methods of interpretation. Such reflection is in any case necessary for a theology which wants to keep its methods attuned to contemporary thought. Because the greater part of theology's work consists in interpreting its tradition, every hermeneutical discipline has possible methodological interest. But this interest is not merely in techniques. Philosophical discussions of hermeneutics raise questions about human existence and the nature of reality as such, which are the very stuff of theological reflection. It is extraordinary how much of this conversation is today conducted without significant input from the discipline with the longest experience of exploring these questions, and the richest resources for handling them. That is a comment on the low priority that some forms even of Christianity give to its intellectual needs, and the extent to which a consumer society is unwilling to invest many resources in areas of such fundamental human importance as religion and ethics.

The primary responsibility of theology is to articulate anew the faith of its religious community. But it also has other responsibilities in a pluralist society which it claims is God's world. The perspective of its religious faith has to be brought to bear in all matters of common concern. This application of religious insights takes theology beyond the community's boundary with the wider culture. However, even this public work contributes indirectly to the worship and mission of the community, because its members are also members of the wider secularized culture. Even those who do it every Sunday, or every morning and evening, need help in understanding what it means to speak of God. Theological interpretation of their scriptures is the most natural context in which this can take place. Nobody interested in 'the life of scripture', that is, in the life that scripture mediates to the community, or the life of the community nourished by its scripture, can afford to neglect it.

Scholarship and faith

The secular character of most biblical scholarship is simply a product of the modern Western intellectual situation. Nothing written in earlier chapters has disputed its legitimacy or the value of research that is not intended to serve religious ends. Christians and Jews have benefited from the labours of many historians and linguists who have not been members of their religions. Both religious and non-religious scholars have contributed to this interface between the modern world and traditional religions.

Scholars who are not members of a religion, or interested in the relationship of their work to existing religious communities, have equal rights to interpret the Bible in their own alternative ways, because the Bible is the possession of Western culture as well as being the scripture of its ancient religions. Nevertheless, it is a cultural monument only as a (major) side-effect of its religious significance, and today as always the majority interests in the Bible are religious. It would be curious if the way it is studied even in secular institutions were not largely determined by that fact.

A study of the Hebrew or Christian Bible in order to understand Judaism or Christianity is bound to explore its religious dimensions, whether or not it is members of these religious communions who are engaged in it. But most interpreters of the Bible have a more than intellectual interest in religion. If they are believers they also need what we have called a 'middle term' relating their rational knowledge of the Bible with their religious faith and theology.

The acuteness of this need, however, varies according to how directly their theology is informed by the Bible. Christians whose theology has a foundation in scripture, and whose devotional and liturgical life is nourished by it, may nevertheless be satisfied with mere compatibility between their rational knowledge of the Bible and their religious faith. Old Testament scholarship enriches their reading of the Bible by increasing their historical awareness and literary sensitivity, but without making much direct impact upon their theology. It only shapes this indirectly, through the contribution which an informed understanding of the Bible makes to the religious and intellectual life from which theological reflection springs.

New Testament scholarship also serves some Christians in this way. But others find that their reading of the New Testament is more directly connected with their theology. It determines the whole shape of their Christian understanding, and not only by influencing their religious response but by defining the doctrinal and moral character of their religion. Such a biblically shaped Christianity needs a theological interpretation of its scripture more urgently than the other, and is compelled to draw into its understanding of the Bible the wider theological and philosophical dimensions which both precede and go beyond the necessary historical exegesis.

Without presuming to choose between these different degrees of religious dependence upon the Bible, it may be noted that in a secularized culture much that once preserved the identity of Christianity no longer does so. Believers must therefore lay greater stress on what is 'given' within their religion itself, and that points primarily to participation in the community's worship and a thorough knowledge of its scriptures. This is turn underlines the need for theological interpretations which enable Christians to understand the Bible in Christian ways.

The uses of methods

Our emphasis upon the readers' interests or interpreters' aims has shifted attention away from the customary preoccupation with methods. But of course any interpreter of any text has to ask what methods are appropriate. The answer given throughout this book is that in biblical interpretation a variety of methods is necessary, but that these need to be organized to correspond both to the texts under consideration and to the aims of the interpreters. Beyond that formal proposal, three material suggestions have been made in Chapters 1, 6, and 7 on the basis of our quite narrowly focused account of biblical scholarship and theological interpretation over the past two centuries.

First, the *study of religion* occupies a nodal position in biblical interpretation, both because it provides a field in which all the various scholarly disciplines that are appropriate to biblical study can meet, and also because it links these *rational methods* with the *religious interests* which largely motivate it. On the one hand, study of the biblical religions uses a variety of methods—linguistic, historical, literary, and social-scientific; on the other, the results of this study are useful also to those who read the Bible as their scripture. Believers in some ways identify with the religion their scripture contains and expresses. Clarifying this by rational methods can assist this partial identification even as it highlights the historical distance.

Secondly, the different methods used in the study of biblical religion have to be organized in a way that allows them to answer the questions of the interpreters as clearly as possible. Even then they do not lead directly to the theological interpretation which most readers seek. Our most emphatic material suggestion has been that if that is what is wanted, then a *theory of religion and reality* has to be attached to the rational methods used. This constitutes a middle term linking the religion perceived in the texts with the interpreter's own religious understanding of reality. It holds the position occupied by the notion of 'pre-understanding' in Bultmann's hermeneutics.

Our third suggestion has been that a *literary* framework, which includes the results of historical and linguistic research, is today more promising for the study of religion and for theology than the *historical* framework (which includes literary study) that has dominated New Testament studies in particular since the 1830s.

The main reason for this preference is that literary approaches offer more scope for making connections with a theory of religion. That is because they allow a large range of legitimate interpretations of the Bible. Historical study is a valuable control against the chaos of arbitrary interpretations, but its passion for the single correct answer, were it attainable, would leave the Bible looking more fragmented than ever. It would offer from the distant past various pieces of information with little relation to the present. Some theologians have accepted this consequence, and argued for reducing the weight of the Bible in Christianity. But this has been resisted by most. A valuable resource is to be properly used, not relinquished.

The historical framework that has dominated much biblical scholarship remains legitimate, and will continue to orchestrate some of its tasks. History of religions research, enriched by social-scientific perspectives, remains the backbone of the scientific study of religion. Schleiermacher called 'historical theology', which he saw as also part of the modern study of history, 'the actual corpus of theological study' (*Brief Outline*, §28). Nothing said in Chapters 6 and 7 was intended to denigrate historical-critical scholarship or question its importance for theology. As a critical discipline which explores a religious tradition, theology needs a strong historical-critical component.

Nevertheless, some relativization of historical research has been implied at several points: historical investigation has been made relative to the aims for which it is undertaken. Where those aims are historical, as they sometimes are (even in theology), the historical framework of research co-ordinates all the methods used. Where the aims of biblical interpretation are religious or theological, it is necessary to consider exactly how historical study is important for this, and to recognize its proper place, which may be a subordinate one.

The polemic implied here is directed only against the uncritical assumption that the inevitable prominence of historical *methods* in studying these ancient texts means that historical *aims* are the only ones that are respectable. Interpreters choose their own aims, and the reasons why most people read the Bible are religious. Religions need theology, and both religions and theologies need history. But the uses of history are varied. Historical information about origins and classical periods contributes to a religion's sense of its identity; historical *criticism* can also serve a more negative function, because it makes independent claims to truth about the tradition. These different uses of history sometimes conflict. It may then be wise to limit the damage that historical criticism can inflict upon religious identity by recalling that in Christianity and Judaism, even the historical narratives that the Bible contains are more often read as literature than as sources for modern critical history. This suggests that as far as religious identity is concerned, literary approaches have a natural priority in the interpretation of these texts.

But theology is concerned with religious truth, not simply religious identity. It cannot evade the hard questions posed by the historical criticism of the Bible. The history of theology is a constant history of readjustment—not tampering with the faith (as its enemies assert), but modifying its culturally conditioned formulations. Biblical interpreters have made significant contributions to this process in every age, though never so dramatically as in the Churches' coming to terms with modern thought. The critical historical study of the Bible is a relative newcomer to the conversation of Church and Synagogue with their scriptures, but its impact has been powerful, and in one area (Gospel criticism) epoch-making. The present shape of Christianity is partly determined by its accommodation of and resistance to modernity.

Historical-critical study forced a theology committed more deeply to truth than to tradition to restate the traditional faith. This was achieved by forging its new historical knowledge into alliances, notably with idealist philosophy in the nineteenth century and kerygmatic theology in the twentieth. That produced some valuable modern theology and some effective theological interpretation of the Bible.

But neither the negative theological role of historical criticism in destroying formulations which no longer rang true, nor its positive contributions to constructive theological restatement, should obscure its everyday task of making possible Christians' appropriation of their scriptures. The new accommodations between faith and reason directly benefited only an educated minority in Western Christianity. The majority were still nourished on a much less critical diet of theological interpretation. As with school meals, the memory of this has given some scholars a lifelong aversion to religious equivalents of tapioca. Reaction against all theological interpretation is well documented among biblical scholars from conservative religious or theological backgrounds.

This disease can now be avoided, or its incidence reduced. The historical training and skills of modern theological interpreters enable them to provide a more healthy diet, so that other believers may benefit indirectly from the theological renewal of contemporary Christianity. This everyday task of theological interpretation today involves articulating the new insights of modern study in the daily and weekly task of saying what some portion of the Bible means, and saying it in a way that illuminates the interpreter's own Christianity or Judaism, yet without doing violence to the text itself. The question of which methods to use is answered by reference to that aim, which includes reference to the character of the texts.

Theology today

There is no reason to suppose that all truth has been on one side in the bitter disputes of the past 200 years. It is as important for contemporary theology to do justice to what the conservatives were rightly struggling to retain as to welcome the critical insights of more independent scholars. One of the attractions of the new literary paradigm in some recent biblical scholarship is that it allows these two theological tendencies to work together in a less confrontational way. That has its attendant dangers. The very openness of literary study to all kinds of interpretations means that the question of truth, which is always central to theology, can disappear from view. The greater the toleration of diverse interpretations in a theologically pluralist Church, the more there is need for the critical eye of well-trained historians and linguists.

But it is not sufficient for religious communities to train critical or theologically perceptive teachers who are ready to call rubbish by its name. Religious teachers also need the more constructive skills of expressing their message in relation to the shared Bible. The scriptures are a source of authority for religious life. Their interpreters need to be both critical and constructive. Historical study remains the best school for critical theologians. Doubts arise only over its capacity (in isolation) to generate constructive theological interpretations.

In view of these doubts, there is much to be said theologically for the new moves in biblical interpretation, which give its literary qualities fuller recognition. The words 'interpretation' and 'hermeneutics' actually suggest a literary, rather than a historical, frame of reference, without in the least underestimating the contribution of history and language to literary study. In some ways this 'literary turn' is a *re*turn to more traditional models of biblical study after a period in which the new historical impulses led to some one-sidedness in European biblical scholarship.

Theology tomorrow

Because the focus of this book has remained within the ambit of modern Western scholarship, some of the larger dimensions of biblical interpretation have not been discussed. The cluster of hermeneutical problems springing from the historical and literary work represented by the other volumes in the Oxford Bible Series is matter enough for one dense book. Nevertheless, such a practical topic as biblical interpretation calls for at least a glance out of the study window, and into the wider world.

Everywhere we look, people are using texts. Despite some decline in literacy in the age of the microchip, and economic pressures which squeeze education at every level, the interpretation of culturally significant texts remains the hallmark of civilization. But literary study itself has clearly yielded ground to other forms of education and training. Calculation is more obviously characteristic of modern life than reflection. The study and performance of texts remains central in law, the theatre, and religion, but only small minorities are actively engaged in these vital cultural enterprises. Even within the humanities, with their dedication to this interpretation of significant texts, scholars are not agreed about how to read those texts which they agree are significant.

The fragmentation and lack of consensus which this represents poses a challenge to all who work with ideas in the hope of affecting social realities. Various minority groups are offering remedies for the cultural crisis, among them larger and smaller religious communities. Some of these are united in a family resemblance by their intended loyalty to the witness of the Christian Bible. They carry a heavy burden of history, but precisely that tradition contains hopeful possibilities of development. Part of the fascination of biblical interpretation lies in the astonishing range of possible meanings this collection of writings contains. That potential is bound up with the communities which use it as scripture and their contributions to a culture which needs to rediscover the founts and motivations of its moral tradition.

The ambiguous character of this culture's central text shows how much depends upon interpretation. Different denominations of Jews and Christians all appeal to the Hebrew Bible, and understand it somewhat differently. The Christians usually prefer one or another translation—which is already an interpretation, and not necessarily any worse for that. Extra links in a religious chain can strengthen as well as weaken it. St Jerome had his reasons for preferring the 'Hebrew truth', but his contemporaries had their reasons for preferring the Septuagint. There is much to be said for new translations referring back (so far as possible) to the originals, but also much to be learned from attending to the whole tradition of interpretation.

If knowledge of God is located in the community's dialogue with its scriptures, rather than in the Bible alone, even the tradition's errors gain significance. In any case, a community that has lived with one translation of the Bible or a Prayer Book for centuries ought not lightly to abandon them. It would be religiously foolish to sacrifice 'the valley of the shadow of death' in Psalm 23, or 'I know that my redeemer liveth' in Job 19, to the scruples of philologists.

Newer versions have to be welcomed, because the past is always receding. Most believers echo the sentiment in Luke 5: 39 that 'the old is good' (or even, as in some manuscripts, 'better'). But they have to admit that the old must be constantly reinterpreted if it is to be preserved alive. Tradition is only tradition, and not to be confused with the event of revelation or guidance of the Spirit in the present. If Timothy 'guards the deposit', it is so that this holy tradition may, like a solid flint, be a means of future sparkings.

The actual decisions about which versions of the Bible to use, and which interpretations to admit, are partly political decisions. That makes human authority necessary, even in the religious institutions most resistant to the structures of power found elsewhere. But religious truth is far removed from such exercise of ecclesiastical authority. It is discovered through participation in the religious life. New interpretations or developments are therefore to be judged partly by the quality of religious life that they help bring about.

The value of any theological interpretation is thus acknowledged gradually, in the long course of religious life. But the political decisions of a religious community or its leaders cannot wait upon this gradual recognition of religious truth. They therefore need theological arguments, and these too are a part of the community's life. Arguments are marshalled to justify existing practices, or to persuade other believers to share an opinion, or to change a practice. The reason why, in this context also, appeals are made to the Bible despite its notorious ambiguity is that scripture is important for the community's self-definition. Scripture helps preserve a religious community's identity by being constantly read and reread within a tradition of interpretation. Innovations are always possible, but need to establish some claim to continuity with the tradition, and if possible with its scriptural foundations.

This can sometimes be done by appeal to particular texts. Contrary to the impression created by some theological argument, that does not settle the truth or falsity of a proposal, only its continuity with the tradition. But this is important in a community that is always thinking, arguing, and seeking agreement and unity.

However difficult it is to get clear answers out of such an infinitely flexible resource as the Bible, it is evident that there would be even less chance of securing agreement without such a shared, respected, and heavily used set of foundational traditions. It is a common experience that studying the Bible together often brings believers to a common mind. The rabbinic saying that 'when two sit and there are between them words of Torah, the Shechinah [divine presence] rests between them' reflects this experience, as does Matthew 18: 20. This common mind effected by the 'near Word' may well be quite different from anything that the distant human author intended, and yet discussion of what was intended forms part of the process of securing agreement.

The reason that both Christians and Jews find as much agreement as they do in the interpretation of their scriptures is that the tradition and life of their communities provide some guidance about what meanings are appropriate, and also provide the motivation to seek agreement. A community that does not live from 'the unity of the Spirit in the bond of peace' is unlikely to find strong agreement simply by reading the same canonical documents. On the other hand, even a community actively seeking unity would be less likely to find it without a collection of respected documents which are already agreed to provide some kind of norm.

The spectacle of a divided Christianity appealing to a shared scripture, and yet remaining divided, shows that interpretation alone does not solve all a religion's problems. But if unity is truly desired, new interpretations of the tradition can dissolve many of the barriers.

A second issue is also important. The fact that Jews and Christians use some of the same writings as scripture remains as instructive a phenomenon in contemporary biblical interpretation as it was during the first and second centuries of the common era. This again shows that what is ultimately decisive is not the text in isolation, but the principle or centre by which it is interpreted. 'Scripture alone' always means 'scripture interpreted', because the concept of scripture itself implies a religious community with its own revelational claim guiding theological interpretation. Judaism and Christianity are different religions because, although they agree about the identity of God who is worshipped and share some of the same scriptures, they disagree about whether the decisive revelation of God is in Torah or in the Lord and Messiah Jesus who was crucified.

In a generation in which many find the old denominational divisions of little interest, and even the differences between religions small in comparison with what unites religious people, a third issue has overshadowed the preceding chapters. This is the phenomenon of the same collection of writings functioning in partly different ways for two overlapping constituencies—a religious and a secular one.

The secularization of Western culture brought non-religious assumptions into biblical scholarship. That created a dangerous situation for the religions which read the Bible on a different (though overlapping) set of assumptions. But earlier chapters have shown that the threat was at the same time an opportunity. The new approaches provided a context for the theological task of engaging with contemporary thought.

In the eighteenth and nineteenth centuries the new intellectual situation in Europe triggered some rationalist attacks upon traditional Christian doctrine. But behind these rowdy scenes of religious controversy, theologians and others were quietly making the necessary adjustments, and teaching the faith accordingly. They claimed allegiance to the same Lord, and held the same faith, and held it in the same community. But they learned to understand it rather differently, taking account of the new knowledge. The Churches' integration of the new rational methods and results into their own thinking about God and the world represents a major, if unfinished, theological achievement.

Loss and gain

Taking up modern knowledge into Christian understandings of God and the world was and is a revolutionary process. But revolutions are destructive, costly, and painful. The price that the Western Churches are now paying for their theological revolution is some considerable variety of belief among their members, with all the weakness, uncertainty, and controversy this brings with it.

Another, and related, result of the secularization of Western culture is that in a post-Christian society it is impossible to draw clear lines of demarcation between those inside and those who are outside. Many Christians share assumptions with their non-Christian neighbours that would have shocked another generation, and still shock some of their co-religionists. Different ways of reading the Bible are both a symptom and a product of this religious and theological pluralism.

Such a confused situation places the identity of religious communities at risk, and this partly explains the neo-conservative reactions which cling to the Bible (or Koran) in traditional ways. They should not be too easily dismissed for their evident irrationalities. The sectarian impulse belongs to the essence of Christianity, and rightly fastens upon the Bible. Theological liberals are wise to remain in close communication with their conservative friends, not only because that is where power in the Church usually resides, but because the conservatives usually preserve (amidst much that might well be abandoned) something of value that the avant-garde would lose.

Much has already been lost in a rapidly changing world. The principle enunciated by Ninian Smart, of making the most of your tradition, is often neglected in a consumer society that stands Luke 5: 39 on its head. But the new situation has also brought real gains. Where the modern virtue of tolerance has been adopted by Christianity (and religions generally relate positively to the best moral thinking of the age), it has been transfigured by Christian love that 'rejoices in the truth' (1 Cor. 13: 6), and has so been freed of indifferentism. This deepening of moral sensibility and tempering of religious fanaticism offers hope to a divided world. A religion whose scriptures proclaim that 'the earth is the Lord's and all that therein is' can combine the depth and intensity of an absolute and exclusive commitment with the breadth and generosity of a social and cultural responsibility. As well as contributing to boundary preservation, biblical interpretation sustains this wider vision.

Our sharp distinction between religious and non-religious uses of the Bible, or aims in its interpretation, was an attempt to explain and justify the diversity in contemporary biblical interpretation. It implied, for the sake of analysis, a clarity which rarely exists in reality. Religious and non-religious aims are usually intertwined and are bound to overlap, both because religion encompasses all of human life, and because members of religious societies may also share in the other interests of their culture.

The tangled situation of religious belief and unbelief today is the obvious explanation of the variety in contemporary biblical interpretation. The preceding discussions have pressed the claims of one kind of interpretation. A theological interest was confessed in the Preface, and not suppressed in any of the succeeding chapters. But the argument remains open-ended. It makes space for non-theological, even anti-theological, interpretations of the Bible. So long as the Bible is read and understood, it is likely to do good, even if the theological keys which unlock religious interpretations go rusty and need renewal.

Christians and Jews can welcome any serious study of the Bible. A spiritual heritage is to be shared. But believers have firm ideas of their own about what the Bible means, and seek to persuade others that their theological interpretations are not only valuable, but true. One way of doing this is by supplementing their ancient formulations, sanctified by centuries of use, with language drawn from contemporary experience.

When these new ideas are brought into the interpretation of the Bible, there is a high risk of unacceptable developments. Theological discrimination is necessary. We may balance the high profile given to David Friedrich Strauss in earlier chapters with the caution of Robert Browning's Bishop Blougram:

> Then add there's still that plaguy hundredth chance
> Strauss may be wrong.

Subsequent Christianity has preferred Browning to Strauss, hard though that is for biblical interpreters to accept. But the theological errors of Strauss were worth making, and clarified the boundaries of Christianity as well as advancing our understanding of the Gospels. The risk of getting it wrong is a condition of all interpretation and all communication. Believers are true to their trust in God when they accept the risk and even the loss involved in sowing their seed with abandon.

Some interpreters spread the word so that it yields fruit thirty, sixty, or a hundredfold. Others keep it in the culture's intellectual banks, where at least it creates interest—and at present interest rates are high. Yet others (according to St Paul) hawk it about for their own profit—a salutary warning to all who make a profession out of the Bible and its interpretation. The warning is well taken, but St Paul himself was a master theological interpreter, on one occasion apparently being mistaken for Hermes (Acts 14: 12).

Books about interpretation are no more a substitute for interpreting than recipes are a substitute for cooking. They may need correcting, but the final test is not whether they stimulate further methodological reflections: it is whether they encourage good cooking. As the aim of cooking is to promote nourishment, so the Bible is to be heard, read, marked, learned, and inwardly digested. That involves interpretation, whether this task is performed by the reader who appropriates the Bible, or by some intermediary like Philip, who offered help to the Ethiopian eunuch.

Annotated Index of Names

These notes provide further information on some major scholars whose work has featured in this book. Page-references are given after each entry, bold type indicating the main discussions. Some significant figures not mentioned by name in the text are also included, with references in parentheses to the chapters or pages where they could have been discussed. At the end of some entries the author and date of a monograph on the scholar is indicated; where this is in German it is given in square brackets. More detail will shortly be available in the major *Dictionary of Biblical Interpretation*, ed. J. H. Hayes. *The Oxford Dictionary of the Christian Church*, and *A New Dictionary of Christian Theology*, ed. A. Richardson and J. Bowden (1983), and *A Dictionary of Biblical Interpretation*, ed. R. Coggins and J. L. Houlden (1990), contain information on the subject and on some interpreters.

ALBRIGHT, WILLIAM FOXWELL (1891–1971). Leading bib. archaeol., son of Methodist missionaries. Director of American School of Oriental Research in Jerusalem (1920–9, 1933–6). Prof. Sem. Langs. Johns Hopkins Univ. (1929). Aimed to restore confidence in reliability of OT. *The Archaeol. of Palestine and the Bible* (1932–5), *From the Stone Age to Christianity* (1940–6). L. Finkelstein (ed.), 1948. (ch. 4)

ALT, ALBRECHT (1883–1956). OT prof. Basle (1914), Leipzig (1922). Major contributions to hist. of Israel (cf. M. Noth) based on deep knowledge of Egyptian documents and land of Palestine ('historico-geog. method'). 'The Origins of Israelite Law' (1934; ET 1966 in *Essays in OT Hist. and Relig.*) distinguished case law (e.g. Ex. 20: 22–23: 19) from apodictic law (e.g. Decalogue), proposing a cultic origin for latter. (ch. 4)

ALTER, ROBERT (b. 1935). Ph.D. Harvard (1962). Prof. Heb. and comp. lit ., Univ. Cal. Berkeley (1969).   **224–7**, 235, 266

ANDERSON, BERNHARD WORD (b. 1916). Ph.D. Yale (1945). OT theol. prof. Princeton Theol. Sem. (1968). *The Living World of the OT* (Am. title *Understanding the OT*) (1957), *Creation versus Chaos* (1967), ed. *The OT and Christian Faith* (1963), ed. *Creation in the OT* (1984).

129

ANNET, PETER (1693–1768). Schoolmaster, last of Deists. 'The Resurrection of Jesus examined by a moral philosopher' (1744) antcipates Reimarus's fraud hypothesis.   56, (175)

ASTRUC, JEAN (1684–1766). Prof. anatomy Toulouse, Montpellier, Paris. On basis of two divine names (Elohim and Jehovah) suggested in 1753 that Moses composed Genesis by combining older sources: *Conjectures sur les mémoires originaux dont il paraît que Moïse s'est servi pour composer le livre de Genèse.*   77

AUERBACH, ERICH (1892–1957). German lit. hist. Prof. Romance langs. Marburg (1929–35), Istanbul (1936–47), Yale (1950). *Mimesis: The Representation of Reality in Western Lit.* (1946; ET 1953), *Dante, Poet of the Secular World* (ET 1961).   222 f., 227, 230

AUGUSTINE, ST (353–430). Bishop Hippo (395), father of Western Christianity, Cath. and Prot. Voluminous writings on Bible include sermons, tracts, comms., a *Harmony of the Evangelists* (c.400; ET 1873), and *On Christian Doctrine* (final form 427), a hermeneutical classic. Introduced typical Western enthusiasm for, understandings and misunderstandings of, St Paul, *On the Spirit and the Letter* (412) anticipating Luther. P. Brown, 1967; H. Chadwick, 1985.

15, 29, (48), 206

BACON, BENJAMIN WISNER (1860–1932). NT prof. Yale (1897–1927). Many books on Gospels, notably Mark (1919, 1925) and *Studies in Matt.* (1930)—'five books of'. R. A. Harrisville, 1976.   (ch. 4)

BARCLAY, WILLIAM (1907–78). Prof. div. and bib. crit., Glasgow (1963–74). Prolific and widely read popularizer (NT). C. L. Rawling, 1984.   (ch. 1)

BARR, JAMES (b. 1924). Prof. NT Montreal (1953); OT Edinburgh (1955), Princeton (1961); Sem. langs. and lit. Manchester (1965); Oriel (1976) and Heb. (1978) prof. Oxford. Leading British writer on bib. interp. In addition to works listed, see *The Semantics of Bib. Lang.*

(1961), *Explorations in Theol. 7: The Scope and Authority of the Bible* (1980), *Fundamentalism* (1977). P. R. Wells, 1980.   42, 130, 200

BARRETT, CHARLES KINGSLEY (b. 1917). Inspired by Hoskyns and taught by Davey at Cambridge. Methodist theol. and most substantial British NT scholar since Lightfoot. Prof. Durham (1958–82), Comms. *John* (1955, 1978²), *Rom.* (1957), *1 and 2 Cor.* (1968, 1973, *Pastorals* (1963, popular), and (forthcoming) *Acts*. Other monographs include *The Holy Spirit and the Gospel Tradition* (1947), *From First Adam to Last* (1962), *Jesus and the Gospel Tradition* (1967), *The Signs of an Apostle* (1970), *The Gospel of John and Judaism* (1975). See also *NT Essays* (1972), *Essays on Paul* (1982), *Essays on John* (1982).   (ch. 4)

BARTH, KARL (1886–1968). Studied at Tübingen, Berlin, Marburg (under Herrmann). Pastor at Safenwil (1911). Prof. Göttingen (1921), Münster (1925), Bonn (1930), Basle (1935). Greatest theol. of century, revitalized theol. interp. of Bible through *The Epistle to the Romans* (1919, 1921²; ET 1933). Comms. *1 Cor.* (1924; ET 1933), *Phil.* (1928; ET 1962). Later vols. of *Church Dogmatics* now inspiring narrative approaches to Bible. D. Ford, 1981; E. Jüngel, ET 1986.

32, 37, **90, 94**, 108 f., 118, 146, 217

BAUER, BRUNO (1809–82). 'Right-wing', then radical, 'young Hegelian' theol. in Berlin. Taught Marx. Dismissed from Bonn lectureship in 1842. From 1840 wrote increasingly radical crit. of NT, finally denied hist. existence of Jesus. Later became politically conservative. A. Schweitzer, *Quest*; [G. Lämmermann, 1979].   233

BAUER, GEORG LORENZ (1755–1806). Prof. orient. langs. etc. Altdorf (1789), and Bib. exeg. Heidelberg (1805). Applied Heyne's work on myth in a bib. hermeneutics (1799), a theol. of OT (1796), and a bib. theol. of NT (4 vols., 1800–2), the first to separate the Testaments. [O. Merk, 1972.]   (ch. 6)

BAUER, WALTER (1877–1960). NT prof. Göttingen (1916–45). Revised Preuschen (1928²) into the now standard NT Greek dictionary (1937³, 1952⁴; ET Arndt and Gingrich, 1957). Comm. *John* (1912, 1933³) and influential *Orthodoxy and Heresy in Earliest Christianity* (1934; ET 1971).   (ch. 4)

BAUR, FERDINAND CHRISTIAN (1792–1860). NT, church hist., hist. of dogma, symbolics, prof. Tübingen (1826). Founded mod. Prot. 'Tübingen school' of radical hist. crit. Found in Hegel's phil. of relig. and hist. a theory enabling him to interp. NT and hist. of Christian

doctrine theologically. P. Hodgson, 1966.   32, 56, **62–76,** 88–94,
          104, 107, 113–15, 126, 140, 147, 152, 188 f., 196, 208,
                212, 228, 244, 276, 280, 282, 286, 322

BELO, FERNANDO (b. 1933). Engineer. Portuguese Marxist Christian.
                                                      156 f., 252

BENTLEY, RICHARD (1662–1742). Classicist, pioneer of crit. method,
Master Trinity, Cambridge (1700). *A Confutation of Atheism* (1692).
Demolished Collins in *Remarks upon a Late Discourse of Freethinking*
(1713). R. J. White, 1965.   (ch. 2)

BENTZEN, AAGE (1894–1953). Pupil of Pedersen, influenced also by
Mowinckel. OT prof. Copenhagen (1923). Continued cultic approach
to OT. *Introduction to OT* (1941; ET 1948). Comm. *Dan.* (1937).
                                                            (ch. 4)

BERGER, PETER L. (b. 1929 in Vienna). Ph.D. New School for Social
Research (1954). Sociol. of relig. and culture, made phenomenol.
sociol. of A. Schultz (1899–1959) on social worlds fruitful for relig.
thought. Prof. social ethics Hartford Sem. (1958), New School (1963),
Rutgers (1969), Boston Coll. (1979) and Univ. (1980). Strong theol.
interest, e.g. *A Rumour of Angels* (1969), *The Heretical Imperative*
(1979), but most imp. for bib. interp. are *The Social Construction of
Reality* (with T. Luckman 1966), *The Sacred Canopy: Elements of a
Sociol. Theory of Relig.* (1967; Eng. title: *The Social Reality of Relig.*).
R. Wuthnow *et al.*, 1984.   162

BEST, ERNEST (b. 1917). Leading Irish NT scholar, prof. Glasgow
(1974–8). Several monographs on Mark and Paul. Comms. *Rom.*
(1967), *1 Peter* (1971), *1 and 2 Thess.* (1972).   (ch. 4)

BETZ, HANS-DIETER (b. 1931). Pupil of Braun in Mainz (Dr. theol.
1957), prof. Claremont (1963), Chicago Div. Sch. (1978). Authority on
Graeco-Roman background to NT and application of classical
rhetorical categories to NT. Comm. *Gal.* (1979), *2 Cor. 8–9* (1985), and
(forthcoming) *Matt. 5–7*. Other works on Lucian, Plutarch, Paul, NT
ethics, Greek magical papyri.   **216**

BILLERBECK, PAUL (1853–1932). Village pastor and rabbinic scholar.
His *Kommentar zum Neuen Testament* (4 vols., 1922–8) is wrongly
known as 'Strack-Billerbeck'.   (ch. 4)

BLEEK, FRIEDRICH (1793–1859). Pupil of Schleiermacher and de Wette,
but moved in conservative direction. OT and NT prof. Bonn (1829).

Intro. to OT (1860; ET 1869), *Intro. to NT* (1862; ET 1869–70), *Lectures on Apocalypse* (1862; ET 1874). Extensive works on Gospels (esp. John 1846) and epistles (esp. Heb. 1828–40) not trans. 59

BOFF, LEONARDO (b. 1938). Pupil of Karl Rahner at Munich, doctorate on the Church as Sacrament (1972). Franciscan Liberation theol. in Petropolis, Brazil. *Jesus Christ Liberator* (1972; ET 1978). Has written on the Resurrection, narrative theol., ecclesiology—and clashed with Curia. (ch. 5)

MÍGUEZ BONINO, JOSÉ (b. 1924). Prot. Liberation theol. and ecumenist. Studied at Emory Univ. and Union Theol. Sem., NY. Prof. theol. and ethics in Buenos Aires, Argentina. *Doing Theol. in a Revolutionary Situation* (1975). (ch. 5)

BORNKAMM, GÜNTHER (1905–90). Pupil of Bultmann. NT prof. Heidelberg (1949–71). *Jesus of Nazareth* (1956; ET 1960) chief work of 'new quest'. Pioneered redaction crit. of Matt. and wrote a standard textbook on *Paul* (1969; ET 1971). Comm. *Matt.* forthcoming.
70, 72, 117 f., 120, 130

BOUSSET, WILHELM (1865–1920). Founding member of Göttingen 'hist. of relig. sch.' NT prof. Giessen (1916). Founded *Theol. Rundschau* (with Heitmüller). Major works on *Judaism* (1902), *Apocalyptic* (1903), *Gnosticism* (1907) never trans., but popular *Jesus* (1904; ET 1906), *What is Religion?* (1903; ET 1907), and classic *Kyrios Christos* (1913, 1921²; ET 1970). Comm. *Rev.* 1896. [A. F. Verheule, 1973.] 76, 125, 127

BOWDEN, JOHN STEPHEN (b. 1935). Ed. SCM Press (1966). Prolific translator, imported German bib. schol. 1960s and 1970s. 297

BROWN, RAYMOND EDWARD (b. 1928). Sulpician priest and leader of American Cath. schol. Pupil of Albright at Johns Hopkins Univ. NT prof. Union Theol. Sem., NY (1971). Anchor Comm. *John* (2 vols, 1966, 1970), *Johannine Epistles* (1982). Co-ed. *Jerome Bib. Comm.* (1968). *The Crit. Meaning of the Bible* (1981). G. A. Kelly, 1983.
37, 228

BRUCE, FREDERICK FYVIE (1910–90). Rylands prof. Manchester (1959–78). Leading evang. NT schol. Comms. *Acts* (1953), *Heb.* (1964), *Rom.* (1969), *1 and 2 Cor.* (1971), *Col., Phm., Eph.* (1984), and many monographs. (128)

BUDDE, KARL (1850–1935). OT prof. Bonn (1879), Strasburg (1889),

Marburg (1900–21). Source crit., extended Wellhausen's hypothesis beyond Pentateuch. Comms. *Judges* (1897), *Samuel* (1902), *Isaiah 40–66* (1922). *Hist. of Israel's Relig. to the Exile* (1899) contains 'Kenite hypothesis' that Israel's Yahwism came from Moses' marriage. (ch. 3)

BULTMANN, RUDOLF KARL (1884–1976). Pupil of Herrmann, Gunkel, Weiss, Heitmüller. NT prof. Marburg (1921–51), commanding figure in mod. bib. interp. In addition to works discussed, see esp. *Jesus and the Word* (1926; ET 1934), essays in *Faith and Understanding* (1933; ET 1969), and *Existence and Faith* (1961). *NT Mythology and Other Writings* (1984) includes S. M. Ogden's retrans. initial 'demythologizing' (1941) and 'Problem of hermeneutics' (1950) essays. *Hist. and Esch.: The Presence of Eternity* (1957) and *Primitive Christianity* (1949; ET 1959) also characteristic. Comms. *Johannine Eps.* (1967²; ET 1973), *2 Cor.* (1976; ET 1985). C. W. Kegley (ed.), 1966; W. Schmithals, ET 1968; J. Painter, 1987.   32, 37, 50, 68, 72, 75 f., 90, 94, 103, **104–20**, 122, 126 f., 130 f., 146 f., 152, 172, 188 f., **190** f., 196, 243, 245, 247, 253, 257, 280, 282, 286

BUNSEN, (BARON) CHRISTIAN CARL JOSIAS VON (1791–1860). Prussian diplomat in Rome (1823–39), London (1841–54), OT schol. In close contact with Eng. theol. and 'Broad Church'. Patron of Max Müller. Wrote on bib. schol. for church people (9 vols. 1858–70), and *Egypt's Place in Universal Hist.* (1846–57; ET 1848–67), *God in Hist.* (3 vols., 1857–8; ET 1868–70). R. A. D. Owen (Wisconsin diss.), 1924; J. Rogerson, *OT Crit.*, 1984; [W. Hocker, 1951].   (ch. 2)

BURNEY, CHARLES FOX (1868–1925). Oriel prof. (OT) Oxford (1914). *Notes on the Hebrew Text of the Book of Kings* (1903), *Israel's Settlement in Canaan* (1918), comm. *Judges* (1918), *Aramaic Origin of the Fourth Gospel* (1922), *The Poetry of our Lord* (1925).   222, 240

CADBURY, HENRY JOEL (1883–1974). Hollis prof. div. (NT) Harvard (1934–54); Quaker hist. and activist. Nobel peace prize (1947). *The Making of Luke–Acts* (1927) a pioneer work of stylistic analysis. Contributions to *The Beginnings of Christianity*, iv and v (1933). *The Peril of Modernizing Jesus* (1937), *The Book of Acts in Hist.* (1955). (ch. 4)

CALVIN, JOHN (1509–64). French reformer in Geneva. *Institutes of the Christian Relig.* (1536, 1559). Comms. on every NT book except Rev. F. Wendel, ET 1963; T. H. L. Parker, 1971.   30, 94

CARLYLE, THOMAS (1795–1881). Scottish hist., biographer, and

essayist. A bridge between England and Germany. J. A. Froude, 1882
(2 vols.).   84

CASE, SHIRLEY JACKSON (1872–1947). NT prof. Chicago Div. Sch.
(1908–38) (1917–25 combined with Early Church Hist.); leading
member of 'Chicago school' of social hist. Main works 1923 and 1933.
Also *The Evolution of Early Christianity: A Genetic Study of First-
century Christianity in Relation to its Relig. Environment* (1914), *Jesus:
A New Biography* (1927; rp. 1968 and 1969), *Jesus through the Centuries*
(1932). W. J. Hynes, 1981.   141, 149, 165

CHARLES, ROBERT HENRY (1855–1931). Prof. Bib. Greek Dublin
(1898), 1906–13 resident in Oxford. Canon (1913) and Archdeacon
(1919) Westminster. Leading British student of apocalyptic lit. Eds. of
pseudepigraphic writings (1893–1908). Ed. *The Apocrypha and
Pseudepigrapha of the OT* (2 vols., 1913). Comms. *Rev.* (2 vols., 1920)
and *Dan.* (1929).   (109), 128

CHILDS, BREVARD SPRINGS (b. 1923). OT prof. Yale Div. Sch. (1966)
and Reformed (Calvinist) theol. Recognizing *Bib. Theol. in Crisis*
(1970), explored new paths in comm. *Exodus* (1974) and 'canonical
crit.' (1979), also *The NT as Canon: An Intro.* (1984), *OT Theol. in a
Canonical Context* (1985). J. Barr, *Scripture*, 1983.   42, 130, 213 f.

CHUBB, THOMAS (1679–1749). Salisbury glovemaker, self-taught
English deist, hostile to doctrine and ritual. *The True Gospel of Jesus
Christ, Asserted* (1738) sees the moral teaching of hist. Jesus as law of
Christians and as coinciding with law of reason. T. L. Bushell, 1967;
H. Graf Reventlow, ET 1984.   56, (175)

COLENSO, JOHN WILLIAM (1814–83). Mathematician, fellow St John's,
Cambridge (1837), first bishop of Natal (1853). Comm. *Rom.* (1861)
denied eternal punishment. Pentateuchal crit. (1862–79). Declared
deposed by Bishop Gray of Cape Town in 1863, and 'excommunicated'
in 1866, causing schism. P. Hinchliff, 1964.   57–9, 61

COLERIDGE, SAMUEL TAYLOR (1772–1834). English romantic, poet,
intellectual, father of 'Broad Church'. Helped German phil. and bib.
crit. into England. *Aids to Reflection* (1825), *Confessions of an Inquiring
Spirit* (1840; rp. 1956). J. D. Boulger, 1961; E. S. Schaffer, *Kubla
Khan*, 1975.   (ch. 2)

COLET, JOHN (*c.*1467–1519). Oxford humanist, Neoplatonist, friend of
Erasmus, Thomas More, and Thomas Linacre. Lectured on Paul

1496/7 (ET 1873–4) and wrote on *Mosaic Account of the Creation* (ET 1876). Dean St Paul's (1504), refounded the school (1509/10). F. Seebohm, 1867; E. W. Hunt, 1956; L. Miles, 1961.   (ch. 1)

COLLINS, ANTHONY (1676–1729). English deist, friend and disciple of Locke, influenced by Chillingworth and Tillotson. *Essay Concerning the Use of Reason* (1707) opposed distinction between what is above and what is against human reason. *A Discourse of Freethinking* (1713; rp. Stuttgart, 1965) was anti-clerical and drew powerful replies from Berkeley, Bentley, Swift (rp. 1957), Hoadly, and Whiston. *Inquiry Concerning Human Liberty* attacked by S. Clarke. *Discourse of the Grounds and Reasons of the Christian Relig.* (1724), *The Scheme of Literal Prophecy Considered* (1727) denied OT contains prophecies of Christ. Proposed Maccabean date for Daniel. J. O'Higgins, 1970; H. Frei, *Eclipse*, 1974.   56, (175)

CONZELMANN, HANS (1915–89). Pupil of Bultmann. NT prof. Zurich (1954), Göttingen (1960). Pioneer redaction crit.: *The Theology of Saint Luke* (1956; ET 1960). Comms. *Acts* (1963), *1 Cor.* (1969; ET 1975). *RGG*[3] article 'Jesus Christ' (1959; ET 1973) contributed to 'new quest'. *An Outline Theol. of the NT* (1968, 1977[6], ET 1969).   117, 120

CREED, JOHN MARTIN (1889–1940). Fellow Caius (1914), Dean St John's (1919), Ely prof. (1926) Cambridge, Anglican modernist theol. Comm. *Luke* (1930), *The Divinity of Jesus Christ* (1938; rp. 1964). *Relig. Thought in the 18th Century* (with J. S. Boys-Smith) (1934).
                                                                (chs. 1–4)

CROSSAN, JOHN DOMINIC (b. 1934). Irish NT scholar. Chicago Servite 1951–68, Ph.D. Maynooth 1957, prof. De Paul Univ., Chicago (1969). Sensitive lit. crit. of parables and aphorisms of Jesus (1973, 1983). *The Dark Interval* (1975), *Finding is the First Act* (1979), *Cliffs of Fall* (1980), also suggestive. *Four Other Gospels* (1986) represents new fringe in relig. studies.   240, 245, 247 f., 256, 267

CUMONT, FRANZ (1868–1947). Belgian archaeol. and hist. of religs. Pupil of Usener, prof. Ghent (1896), museum director Brussels (1899), private schol. Rome and Paris (1913). *The Mysteries of Mithra* (1902; ET 1903), *The Oriental Religions in Roman Paganism* (1906, 1909²; ET 1911), *Astrology and Religion among the Greeks and Romans* (1912).
                                                                (ch. 4)

DAHL, NILS ALSTRUP (b. 1911). Outstanding Norwegian student of Bultmann and Odeberg. NT prof. Oslo (1946), Yale (1965–82). Diss.

on 'The People of God, an Investigation of Early Christian Consciousness of the Church' (German, 1941). Essays collected in *The Crucified Messiah* (1974), *Jesus in the Memory of the Early Church* (1976), *Studies in Paul* (1977). These include one on hist. Jesus (1953; ET 1955, rp. 1974) anticipating 'new quest', and classic review of Bultmann's *Theol. NT* (1954; ET 1974). (ch. 4)

DALMON, GUSTAV HERMANN (1855–1941). Pupil of Franz Delitzsch. Director of archaeol. institutes in Jerusalem (1902–17, 1925–41), OT prof. Greifswald (1925). Aramaist and specialist on Palestine. *The Words of Jesus* (1898; ET 1902), *Jesus–Jeshua* (1921; ET 1929, rp. 1971), *Sacred Sites and Ways* (1919; ET 1935). Saw himself 'In the Footsteps of John Lightfoot' (*Exp. Times*, 35 (1923–4)). 128

DAVIES, WILLIAM DAVID (b. 1911). Welsh NT schol., prof. Union Theol. Sem., NY (1949), Duke Univ. (1950), Princeton (1955), Union Theol. Sem. NY (1959), Duke Univ. 1967). Sympathetic student of Jewish context. *Paul and Rabbinic Judaism* (1949), *The Setting of the Sermon on the Mount* (1964), *The Gospel and the Land* (1974). Ed. *Cambridge History of Judaism* (1984–), forthcoming comm. *Matt.* 128

DEISSMANN, ADOLF (1866–1937). NT prof. Heidelberg (1897), Berlin (1908). Began debate on 'in Christ' formula (1892). *Bible Studies* (1895; ET 1901 includes *New Bible Studies*, 1897), *Light from the East* (1908; ET 1910) assessed linguistic imp. of new discoveries of papyri in Egypt. *Paul* (1911; ET 1926) typical of lib. Prot. interp. Ecum. contacts with England, cf. *Mysterium Christi*, ed. Bell and Deissmann (1930). 88

DELITZSCH, FRANZ JULIUS (1813–90). Pietistic Lutheran of Jewish descent. Prof. theol. Rostock (1846), Erlangen (1850), Leipzig (1867). Rabbinist, linguist, bib. theol. with salvation-hist. orientation; colleague and friendly critic of von Hofman, hostile to hist.-crit. research. Translated NT into Heb. (1878), engaged in mission to Jews, and combatted anti-Semitism. Many pop. and practical comms.: *Hab.* (1843), *Song of Songs and Eccles.* (1875; ET 1877), *Gen.* (1852), *Psalms* (1869; ET 1871), *Heb.* 1857; ET, 2 vols., 1868–70), *Job* (1864; ET, 2 vols., 1866), *Isaiah* (1866; ET, 2 vols., 1867), *Prov.* (1873; ET, 2 vols., 1875). Also wrote on hist. of post-OT Jewish poetry (1836) and Eucharist (1844), bib. psychol. (1855; ET 1867), *Jesus and Hillel* (1866; ET in *Jewish Artisan Life*, 1877), mod. theol. (1888), messianic prophecy (1890). [S. Wagner, 1978]; J. Rogerson, 1984. (ch. 3)

DELITZSCH, FRIEDRICH (1850–1922). Son of Franz. Assyriologist, prof.

Leipzig (1877), Breslau (1893), Berlin (1899). Wrote Assyrian (1889) and Sumerian (1914) grammars. *The Heb. Lang. Viewed in the Light of Assyrian Research* (English, 1883), *Babel and Bible* (1902–3; ET 1903) claimed much OT had Babylonian origin ('Panbabylonism'). Further polemic against Christianity followed.   126

DE WETTE, WILHELM MARTIN LEBERECHT (1780–1849). Pupil of Herder, Griesbach, Gabler, Paulus. Greatest bib. schol. and interp. (OT and NT) of century. Prof. Heidelberg (1807–8), Berlin (1810 until dismissal in 1819), Basle (1822). Used philosophy of Fries for theol. interp. Contributions to NT (1805) and OT (2 vols., 1806–7) Intro. Textbooks on OT (1817) and NT (1826; ET 1858) Intro. Comm. *Psalms* (1811), a dogmatics (1846), *Ethics* (3 vols., 1819–33). Edited Luther's letters (5 vols., 1825–8). Wrote novels (1822, 1829), poems, a drama, published sermons (5 vols.). His theory of relig. remains suggestive. [R. Smend, 1958]; J. W. Rogerson, 1988.

39, 59, 78–81, 93

DIBELIUS, MARTIN FRANZ (1883–1947). Pupil of Harnack and Gunkel, NT prof. Heidelberg (1915), continuator of hist. of religs. school and pioneer form crit. of Gospels (1919; ET 1934) and epistles. Comms. on shorter Paulines (1912), *Pasts.* (1913; ET 1966–72), *James* (1921; ET 1976). Popular works on *Jesus* (1939; ET 1949) and *Paul* (1951; ET 1953). *Studies in the Acts of the Apostles* (1951; ET 1956) advanced style crit.   68, (ch. 4)

DILTHEY, WILHELM (1833–1911). Prof. phil. Berlin (1882). Influential in hermeneutics and the human sciences. Major life of Schleiermacher (vol. i, 1870). Selections from other writings ed. H. P. Rickman, *Pattern and Meaning in Hist.* (1961). H. A. Hodges, 1944; M. Lamb, 1978; H. P. Rickman, 1979.   43, 280

DIONYSIUS OF ALEXANDRIA (d. *c.*264). Pupil of Origen. Led catechetical school (*c.*233). Bishop (*c.*247). Persecuted by Decius and Valerian, readmitted the lapsed. [W. A. Bienert, 1978.]   207

DODD, CHARLES HAROLD (1884–1973). Greatest British (Welsh) NT schol. and interp. of century. Rylands prof. Manchester (1930), Norris–Hulse Cambridge (1935–49). Comms. *Rom.* (1932), *Johannine Eps.* (1946). *The Bible and the Greeks* (1935) liberalized 'wrath of God'. *The Parables of the Kingdom* (1935, 1961³ (rev.)) advocated 'realized esch.' *The Apostolic Preaching and its Developments* (1936) popularized the word 'kerygma' in a non-Bultmannian sense. Greatest book *Interp.*

of the Fourth Gospel (1953). Also *Hist. Trad. in the Fourth Gospel* (1963), *The Founder of Christianity* (1967), and other books, some on interp. F. W. Dillistone, 1977. 37, **240**, **246** f.

DOUGLAS, MARY (b. 1921). Pupil of Evans-Pritchard at Oxford. Social anthropologist at Univ. Coll. London (1951), New York (Russell Sage Foundation, 1977), Northwestern (1981). *Purity and Danger: An Analysis of the Concepts of Pollution and Taboo* (1966) and *Natural Symbols: Explorations in Cosmology* (1970) have helped bib. schols. R. Wuthnow *et al.*, 1984. 162

DRIVER, SAMUEL ROLLES (1846–1914). Followed Pusey as Regius prof. Heb. Oxford (1883), helped establish crit. schol. in Church of England. *Intro. to the Lit. of OT* (1891). Comms. *Deut.* (1895), *Joel and Amos* (1897), *Daniel* (1900), *Genesis* (1904). (chs. 2–3)

DROYSEN, JOHANN GUSTAV (1808–84). Pupil of Humboldt, prof. Berlin (1850). Hist. of 'Hellenism' who (1836–43, 1877–8[2]), dist. Hellenistic age (Alexander to Augustus) from classical Greece. Work on theory of hist. (1858, rp. 1958[3]; ET 1893) and ed. of Aristophanes (1835) show poetic sensibility. [K. H. Spieler, 1970.] 74

DUHM, BERNARD (1847–1928). Pupil of Ewald (with friend Wellhausen), de Lagarde, and Ritschl. OT prof. Göttingen (1877), Basle (1888). Outstanding psychol., ethical idealist, and neo-Romantic interp. of the prophets. *Theology of the Prophets* (1875—accepting Graf's view that the law came later), *Israel's Prophets* (1916), comm. *Isaiah* (1892) rediscovered Lowth's view of the prophets as poets, and stressed their ecstatic experience. Established theory of J. G. Eichhorn identifying chs. 40–55 as 'Deutero-Isaiah' (*c*.540) and saw chs. 56–66 (against Eichhorn) as unitary 'Trito-Isaiah'. Comms. *Job* (1897), *Psalms* (1899), *Jeremiah* (1901). 83

DURKHEIM, ÉMILE (1858–1917). Pioneer French sociol. *The Elementary Forms of the Religious Life* (1912; ET 1915) saw relig. as symbolic representation of social bond, expressed in ritual. S. Lukes, 1973; W. F. S. Pickering, 1975 and 1983. 140, 146, 154, 162 f.

EBELING, GERHARD (b. 1912). Syst. and hist. theol., NT interp. Prof. interchangeably from 1946 at Tübingen and Zurich. Leading figure on German hermeneutical scene in 1960s, including 'new quest'. *Word and Faith* (1960; ET 1963), *The Nature of Faith* (1959; ET 1961), *The Truth of the Gospel* (on Galatians) (1981; ET 1985). Outstanding

Dogmatics (3 vols., 1979) ET forthcoming. [P. Knauer, 1970.]
130, 192, (196)

EICHHORN, JOHANN GOTTFRIED (1752–1827). Imp. in origins of hist. crit. of Bible. Student of Michaelis and Heyne at Göttingen, influenced also by Semler and Herder. Prof. oriental langs. Jena (1775) and phil. Göttingen (1788). Intro. concept of myth into bibl. study (*Urgeschichte*, 1779). Cf. R. Browning, 'Christmas Eve'. *Intro. to OT* (1780–3) and NT (1804–12), a 3-vol. work on the prophets (1816–9), and many works of hist. C. Hartlich and W. Sachs, *Myth*, 1952; E. S. Schaffer, *Kubla Khan*, 1975.   (ch. 6)

EICHRODT, WALTHER (1890–1978). OT prof. Basle (1922). *Theol. OT* (1933–9; ET 1959–67) reacted against historicism and centred on covenant in search for unity and revelatory meaning of OT. *Man in the OT* (1944; ET 1951). D. G. Spriggs, *OT Theols.*, 1974.   (ch. 4)

EISSFELDT, OTTO (1887–1973). Pupil of Wellhausen and Gunkel. Leading lit. (source) crit. OT prof. Halle 1921–57. Produced a synopsis of Hexateuch. *The OT: An Intro.* (1934; ET of 3rd. (1964) ed. 1965). Also hist. of oriental religs.   130

ELLIOTT, JOHN HALL (b. 1935). Dr. theol. Münster (1963), Prof. Theol. Univ. San Francisco (1975). Sociol. interp. of NT. Comm. *1 and 2 Peter and Jude* (1986).   148, 165

ENGNELL, IVAN (1906–64). OT prof. Uppsala (1947), crits. of Wellhausen's source crit., emphasized oral trad., over-pressed traditio-hist. method. *Crit. Essays on the OT* (ET 1970) contains essay on 'The Pentateuch', and work on the prophets. *The Call of Isaiah* (1949). *Studies in the Divine Kingship in the Ancient Near East* (1943, 1967²) prominent in the 'myth and ritual' debate (S. H. Hooke, A. R. Johnson).   (ch. 4)

ERASMUS, DESIDERIUS (1465/9–1536). Greatest Renaissance humanist, influenced by Valla's *Adnotationes* on NT. Prof. Greek Cambridge (*c.*1509–14). From 1521 lived in Basle. Published first printed Greek ed. of NT (1516). Paraphrased Gospels and epistles (1522–4). Eds. of Church Fathers, methodological treatises. J. W. Aldridge, 1966; R. H. Bainton, 1969; J. H. Bentley, 1983.   (ch. 6)

ERNESTI, JOHANN AUGUST (1707–81). Prof. classics (1742), rhetoric (1756), theol. (1759) Leipzig. *Institutio interpretis Novi Testamenti*

(1761, 1809⁵; ET *The Biblical Interpreter*, 1826), *Lectures on Hebrews* (1795). W. G. Kümmel, *Hist.*, 1972; H. Frei, *Eclipse*, 1974. (ch. 6)

EVANS, CHRISTOPHER FRANCIS (b. 1909). Pupil of Hoskyns at Cambridge, colleague and ed. of R. H. Lightfoot at Oxford. Lightfoot prof. Durham (1958), NT prof. King's London (1962). Notorious for phrase 'the curse of the canon'. *Is 'Holy Scripture' Christian?* (1971), *Resurrection and the NT* (1970). Comm. *Luke* forthcoming. (ch. 8)

EVANS-PRITCHARD, SIR EDWARD EVAN (1902–73). Oxford social anthropol., trained by Malinowski at LSE. Field-work in S. Sudan. Prof. Oxford (1946). *Witchcraft, Oracles and Magic among the Azande* (1937) and trilogy on Nuer (1940, 1951, 1956). His theoretical work changed direction following conversion in 1944. M. Douglas, 1980.

139, 143 f., 162

EWALD, HEINRICH GEORG AUGUST (1803–75). Pupil of Eichhorn, outstanding Orientalist (Sem. linguist), teacher of Wellhausen, Duhm, Reuss. OT prof. Göttingen (1827, dismissed 1837, among 'Göttingen seven'), Tübingen (1838), back in Göttingen (1848–67, dismissed as anti-Prussian). Opposed Baur, hotly. *Hist. of Israel* (5 vols., 1843–55; ET 7 vols., 1864–8). Wrote on OT poetry (1835–9) and prophecy (1840–1)—idealist interp. T. Witton Davies, 1903; J. Rogerson, *OT Crit.*, 1984. (ch. 3)

FARLEY, WILLIAM EDWARD (b. 1929). Ph.D. Union Theol. Sem., NY 1952. Prof. Theol. Vanderbilt (1969). *Ecclesial Man: A Social Phenomenology of Faith and Reality* (1974), *Ecclesial Reflection* (1982), *Theologia* (1983) all imp. for theol. interp. 43, (ch. 6)

FARMER, WILLIAM R. (b. 1921). NT prof. Southern Methodist Univ., Dallas (1964). Energetic advocate of Griesbach hypothesis (1964 and subsequent conferences, colloquia, etc.). Ed. a *Synopticon* (1969). *Jesus and the Gospel* (1982). C. M. Tuckett, *Griesbach*, 1983. 237

FIORENZA, ELIZABETH SCHÜSSLER (b. 1938). NT prof. Notre Dame (1970, 1975, 1980), Episc. Div. Sch., Cambridge, Mass. (1984). Leading feminist interp. of NT. *In Memory of Her* (1982), *Bread not Stone* (1984). Earlier writings in German on women's ministry (1964), Priesthood, and Book of Rev. (1972), and in English, *Invitation to the Book of Revelation* (1981). **157–9**, 200, **246**

FITZMYER, JOSEPH AUGUSTINE (b. 1920). Studied at Louvain, Ph.D. Johns Hopkins Univ. (1956). Jesuit NT prof. Bib. Langs. and Lit.

Cath. Univ. of America, Washington (1976). Outstanding comm. *Luke* (2 vols., 1981, 1985). Co-ed. *Jerome Bib. Comm.* (1968). Important contributions on Qumran and on Aramaic philology.   (ch. 4)

FRAZER, SIR JAMES GEORGE (1854–1941). Scottish 'armchair' anthropologist at Cambridge, friend of Robertson Smith. Psychol. and evolutionary reductionist, saw relig. as primitive science, stage after magic. *The Golden Bough* (1890, 1911–15²), *Totemism and Exogamy* (1910), *Folklore in the OT* (1918). Influenced Cambridge classicists, D. H. Lawrence, and T. S. Eliot, rather than anthropologists. R. A. Downie, 1940; R. Ackermann, 1987.   144 f.

FREI, HANS WILHELM (1929–89). Prof. relig. studies Yale (1957, 1963, 1974). *The Eclipse of Biblical Narrative* (1974), *The Identity of Jesus Christ* (1975), and article on Strauss in *Camb. Hist. of Relig. Thought in West*, i (1985).   61, 189, 200, 211

FREUD, SIGMUND (1856–1939). Founder of psychoanalysis and maker of modern culture. Eccentric on Bible and relig., but other work fundamental for bib., as for all, interp. P. Ricœur, 1970.

5, 43, 60, 139

FUCHS, ERNST (1903–83). Pupil of Bultmann. NT prof. Berlin (1955), Marburg (1961–70). Wrote deeply but obscurely on hermeneutical themes, e.g. *Studies of the Hist. Jesus* (1960; ET 1964) in 'new quest'. J. M. Robinson and J. Cobb (eds.), *New Herm.*, 1964; A. C. Thiselton, *Horizons*, 1980.   246

FULLER, REGINALD HORACE (b. 1915). English NT schol. Lampeter (Wales) (1950), Prof. Seabury-Weston (Chicago) (1955), Union Theol. Sem., NY (1966), Virginia Sem. (Washington) (1972–86). *The NT and Current Study* (1962), *The Foundations of NT Christology* (1965), *The Formation of the Resurrection Narratives* (1971). Translated Bultmann and others.   (ch. 4)

FUNK, ROBERT WALTER (b. 1926). Prof. NT Vanderbilt (1966), relig. studies Montana (1969). Trans. and ed. Blass–Debrunner, *Grammar of NT Greek and other Early Christian Lit.* (1961). *Language, Hermeneutics and Word of God* (1966), *Jesus as Precursor* (1975), *Parables and Presence* (1982). Academic entrepreneur, founded Scholars Press, *Journal for Theol. and the Church* (1965–70). Operates polls, opposes 'the fiction of revelation', and calls for 'a new narrative of Jesus, a new gospel' (1985), creating a new fringe in American academe.

247 f., 268

GABLER, JOHANN PHILIPP (1753–1826). Pupil of Eichhorn and Griesbach. Prof. Theol. Altdorf (1785), Jena (1804). Followed Eichhorn in applying Heyne's concept of myth to OT. His 1787 lecture 'On the proper distinction between biblical and dogmatic theology and the specific objectives of each' (ET *Scottish Journal of Theology*, 1980, discussion in *Expos. Times*, 1987) taken as birth-hour of modern OT and NT theol. [O. Merk, 1972]; H. Boers, *NT Theol.*, 1979. (ch. 6)

GADAMER, HANS-GEORG (b. 1900). Pupil of Heidegger and Bultmann. Prof. phil. Heidelberg (1949–68). Hermeneutical classic *Truth and Method* (1960; ET 1975) as influential in lit. crit. and social sciences as in theol. R. E. Palmer, *Hermeneutics*, 1969; A. C. Thiselton, *Horizons*, 1980.   43, 111

GEDDES, ALEXANDER (1737–1802). Enlightenment Scottish RC priest, pioneer of OT textual and lit. crit. Bible translations led to suspension in 1792. Contributions to mythol. interp. of Genesis, influenced by Eichhorn. R. C. Fuller, 1984.   (ch. 6)

GOPPELT, LEONHARD (1911–73). NT prof. Hamburg (1954), Munich (1967). *Typos: The Typological Interp. of the OT in the New* (1939, 1969²; ET 1982), *Apostolic and Post-apostolic Times* (1962; ET 1970). Incomplete posthumous *Theol. NT* (2 vols., 1975–82; ET 1981–2) best critical-conservative balance to Bultmann. Comm. *1 Peter* (1978).
                                                                (ch. 4)

GOTTWALD, NORMAN KAROL (b. 1926). OT Prof. Andover Newton (1955), Grad. Theol. Union (1965), NY Theol. Sem. (1980). Outstanding Christian Marxist interp. of OT.   152–4, 156, 164 f.

GRAF, KARL HEINRICH (1815–69). Pupil of Reuss at Strasburg; schoolteacher. Recognized (cf. Wellhausen 1878) that 'basic document' (later called Priestly Code) was late, i.e. post-exilic, therefore prophets preceded law: Graf–Wellhausen hypothesis. *The Historical Books of the OT* (1866).   79

GRIESBACH, JOHAN JAKOB (1745–1812). Studied and taught at Halle. Lived with Semler (1771), prof. Jena (1775). Epoch-making textual critic, first to challenge the 'received text'. Published a *Synopsis of the Gospels of Matt., Mark and Luke* (1774–6). For 1783 solution to the 'synoptic problem' (priority of Matt., Mark dependent on Matt. and Luke) see W. R. Farmer 1964. B. Orchard and T. R. W. Longstaff (eds.), 1978.   67

GUNKEL, HERMANN (1862–1932). Founder member of Göttingen 'hist. of religs. school'. Taught at Halle and Berlin, prof. Giessen (1907), Halle (1920). Father of form criticism. Programmatic statement of NT crit. (1903; ET *The Monist* (1903), 388–455). See also *Expos. Times*, 38 (1926–7), 532–6. A part ET of *Creation and Chaos* (1895) in B. W. Anderson (ed.), *Creation in the OT* (1984). Intro. to comm. *Genesis* (1901; ET as *The Legends of Genesis* (1901; rp. 1964)). 1930 encyclopedia article on 'Prophets of Israel since Amos' (ET, ed. J. Pelikan, 1969). [W. Klatt, 1969.]   76,**96–8**, 100, 103–5, **124**, **127**, 130, 146 f., 201, **209** f., 211, 215, 217

GUTIERREZ, GUSTAVO (b. 1928). Liberation theol., prof. Cath. univ., Lima, Peru. 1951–5 studied phil. and psychol. at Louvain, 1955–9 at Lyon. *A Theology of Liberation* (1971; ET 1973) sees the Exodus-liberation, Jesus, and poverty in political terms.   (ch. 5)

HARNACK, ADOLF VON (1851–1930). Leading liberal Church hist., prof. Giessen (1879), Marburg (1886), Berlin (1889–1921). Much of vast output in ET. *Hist. of Dogma* (1886–9; ET, 7 vols., 1894–9), monographs on Luke, Acts, Q, *The Mission and Expansion of Christianity* (1902, 1924²; ET, 2 vols., 1904–5). Lectures on the essence of Christianity (ET *What is Christianity?* 1901) a best-seller. W. Glick, 1967; H. Rumscheidt, 1972.   69, 76, 84, 88, 93 f., 96, 113, 189, 195, 243

HATCH, EDWIN (1835–89). Greatest Oxford NT and early Church hist. Also univ. administrator and poet. Combined Readership with parish (Purleigh) from 1882. Opposed by Anglo-Catholics (Gore, Liddon), admired and translated by Harnack. 1880 Bampton Lectures: *The Organization of the Early Christian Churches* (1881), *Essays in Bib. Greek* (1889), *The Influence of Greek Ideas and Usages upon the Christian Church* (1890; rp. New York, 1957), *A Concordance to the Septuagint and the Other Greek Versions of the Old Testament, Including the Apocryphal Books*, ed. with H. A. Redpath (1897). N. F. Josaitis, 1971; I. Ellis, forthcoming.   141

HEGEL, GEORG WILHELM FRIEDRICH (1770–1831). German phil. of absolute idealism, most imp. thinker of century for theol. and for social thought. *Lectures on the Phil. of Relig.* (1832, 1840; ET 1895) now re-ed. by P. C. Hodgson (new ET, 3 vols., 1984–8). *Life of Jesus* (1795; ET Notre Dame, 1984). H. S. Harris, 1972; B. M. Reardon, 1977.   32, 47, 50, **62** f., 68, 71, 79, 83, 102, 107, 110, 126, 280

HEIDEGGER, MARTIN (1889–1976). Prof. phil. Marburg (1923), Freiburg (1928). *Being and Time* (1927; ET 1962) helped Bultmann by its analysis of human existence, influenced by Augustine, Luther, Kierkegaard. He remains a key figure in hermeneutics. J. Macquarrie, 1955; G. Steiner, 1978; A. C. Thiselton, *Horizons*, 1980.

32, 43, 104, 110, 115

HEITMÜLLER, WILHELM (1869–1926). NT prof. Marburg (1908), Bonn (1920), Tübingen (1924). Member of 'hist. of religs. school'. Set sacraments in context of Hellenistic religs. (1903, 1911). Co-founder of *Theol. Rundschau* (with Bousset). Bultmann's teacher and predecessor. Comm. *John* (1907).   127

HENGEL, MARTIN (b. 1924). NT prof. Erlangen (1967), Tübingen (1971). Leading German hist. of Jewish context of NT. *Judaism and Hellenism* (1969, 1973²; ET 1974) opposed over-sharp distinction between Palestinian and Hellenistic Jewish elements in NT. *The Charismatic Leader and his Followers* (1968; ET 1981) his best monograph.   130

HENGSTENBERG, ERNST WILHELM (1802–69). OT prof. Berlin (1828). Leading opponent of crit. bib. schol.; influential ed. of *Evangelische Kirchen-Zeitung* from 1827. *Christology of the OT* (1829–35; ET 1835–9, rp. 1854–8), comm. *Psalms* (1842–7; ET 1844–8), *Contributions to the Introduction of the OT* (1831–9; ET 1847–8). He also wrote on freemasonry and duelling. [Bachmann, 1876–9.]   59, 79

HERDER, JOHANN GOTTFRIED (1744–1803). Pupil of Kant and Hamann at Königsberg, with Goethe at Weimar from 1776. Aimed to grasp 'The Spirit of Hebrew Poetry' (1782) by sympathetic understanding, psychological intuition, or empathy ('Einfühlung' is his coinage). His aesthetic approach did not exclude an interest in hist. factuality: 'Whoever turns a gospel of Christ into a novel has wounded my heart . . .' See also *Reflections on the Phil. of the Hist. of Mankind* (1784–91; ET 1800, abridged 1968). He recognized the imp. of Mark and partial non-hist. of John. [T. Willi, 1971]; H. Frei, *Eclipse*, 1974.

83, 97, 208

HEYNE, CHRISTIAN GOTTLOB (1729–1812). Göttingen classicist, first to analyse and classify myth by hist. crit., distinguishing it from the poetry in which Homer and Hesiod had given it shape. His researches stimulated Eichhorn's *Urgeschichte* (1779; rev. by Gabler, 3 vols., 1790–3) which overcame older deist and rationalist interps. that claimed deliberate deceit by the bib. authors. This approach led to

Strauss (1835). [C. Hartlich and W. Sachs, *Myth*, 1952]; Fuller, *Geddes*, 1984.   211

HILGENFELD, ADOLF (1823–1907). Follower, but not pupil, of Baur. NT associate prof. Jena (1850), founded *Zeitschrift für wissenschaftliche Theol.* (1858–1914). Wrote widely on Canon (1863), apocalyptic (1857), apostolic fathers, extra-canonical and heretical writings (1884). [H. Pölcher, diss. Erlangen 1961.]   128

HILLEL (*fl. c.*20 BCE–15 CE). Leading liberal pharisaic scribe in Jerusalem, founder of ultimately victorious school of rabbis. Wrote seven rules (Middoth) for scriptural interp. (Halakhah). N. N. Glatzer, 1956; J. Neusner, 1971.   (ch. 1)

HOBBES, THOMAS (1588–1679). Epoch-making political phil. at dawn of mod. world, when the subject still involved bibl. interp. Used OT typologically to provide basis for authority of monarchy. Subordinated Church to State. Exile in Paris 1640–51. *De Cive* (1642), *Leviathan* (1651). Clergy son, Magdalen, Oxford, proposed univ. reform, writings burned by univ. (1682). F. C. Hood, 1964; D. P. Gauthier, 1969; H. Graf Reventlow, ET 1984.   78

HOLTZMANN, HEINRICH JULIUS (1832–1910). NT prof. Heidelberg (1865), Strasburg (1874–1904). Classic on Synoptic Gospels (1863) established two-source hypothesis. His *NT Theology* (1896/7, 1912²) criticized by Wrede (1897; ET 1973). *NT Introduction* (1885), *Jesus' Messianic Self-Consciousness* (1907), on Eph. and Col. (1872), comms. on *Pastorals* (1880), *Synoptics and Acts* (1889), *John* (1891). W. G. Kümmel, *Hist.*, ET 1972.   67, 69, 76, 93, 96

HORT, FENTON JOHN ANTHONY (1828–92). Cambridge theol. and NT textual scholar, prof. (1878) with Lightfoot and Westcott. Wrote intro. for famous ed. of Greek NT (Westcott and Hort 1881). Influential in revision of Authorized Version (Revised Version 1881, esp. margin). *Judaistic Christianity* (1874), *The Christian Ecclesia* (1897). *The Way the Truth and the Life* (1893). Part comms. *1 Peter* (1898), *Rom. and Eph.* (1895), *James* (1909). G. Rupp, 1970.   (chs. 2–3)

HOSKYNS, SIR EDWYN CLEMENT (1884–1937). Dean of Corpus Christi, Cambridge (1919). Anglo-Cath. NT theol., contrib. to *Essays Catholic and Critical*, ed. E. G. Selwyn (1926). As a teacher, contrib. to 'bib. theol.' movement. Trans. Barth's *Romans* (1933), friendly with German theol. Contrib. to *Mysterium Christi* (1930). With F. N. Davey, *The Riddle of the NT* (1931), *The Fourth Gospel* (2 vols., 1940),

Crucifixion—Resurrection (1981). G. Wakefield, *Cruc.—Res.*, 1982; R. E. Parsons, 1985.   (ch. 6)

HOULDEN, JAMES LESLIE (b. 1929). Anglican NT theol., pupil of Nineham. Taught NT and doctrine at Oxford (1960) and King's, London (1977), supervises Church theol. educ. *Ethics and the NT* (1973), *Patterns of Faith* (1977), *Explorations in Theol.* (1978), *Connections* (1986), comms. *Captivity Eps.* (1970), *Johannine Eps.* (1973). *Pastoral Epistles* (1975).   201, 297

HUME, DAVID (1711–76). Empiricist phil. of Scottish Enlightenment. Wrote *Essay on Miracles*, criticizing supernatural revelation, as part of *Treatise of Human Nature* (1739) in 1735–7, but delayed publishing till 1747. *Natural Hist. of Religs.* (1757). *Dialogues concerning Natural Relig.* (*c.*1751, pub. 1779)—Hamann showed his German trans. to Kant (1780), waking him up. *Hist. of England* (1754–62). A. Leroy, 1930.   48, 56

IRENAEUS, ST (*c.*115–*c.*190). Disciple of Polycarp (in Asia Minor) and missionary. Bishop of Lyons from 177. Wrote against heretics (esp. Valentinian gnostics). Made formation of NT canon an interpretative event securing Catholic orthodoxy. See von Campenhausen, *The Formation of the Christian Bible* (1968; ET 1972).   (ch. 1)

JEREMIAS, JOACHIM (1900–79). NT prof. Greifswald (1929), Göttingen (1935). Specialist on *Jerusalem in the Time of Jesus* (1962[3]; ET 1969) and the *verba ipsissima* of Jesus. Theologically committed to continuing 'quest'. *The Eucharistic Words of Jesus* (1935; ET 1966), *The Parables of Jesus* (1947, 1970[8]; ET 1954, 1963[2]), *Theology of the NT* (1971; ET 1971).   123 f., 189, 222, 246

JEROME, ST (331 or 342–420). Ascetic monk at Bethlehem (386). Greatest bib. schol. of ancient Western Church. Translator of Vulgate and author of many commentaries and letters. Controversalist, not popular today either. J. N. D. Kelly, 1975.   78, 290

JOSEPHUS, FLAVIUS (*c.*37–*c.*100). Jewish renegade and hist. *Jewish War* (77–8) and *Antiquities of the Jews* (94) best primary sources for Palestine in NT period. L. H. Feldman, 1984.   (ch. 4)

JOWETT, BENJAMIN (1817–93). Underpaid Regius prof. Greek, Oxford (1855), Master of Balliol (1870). Comm. *Eps. of St Paul* (2 vols., 1855), trans. Plato (4 vols., 1871; 5 vols., 1892) and Aristotle's *Politics* (2 vols., 1885). Theol. and academic liberal, but storm over his essay 'The

Interpretation of Scripture' in *Essays and Reviews* (1860) put him off publishing theology. G. Faber, 1957; P. Hinchliff, 1987.   207

JÜLICHER, ADOLF (1857–1938). NT prof. Marburg (1888–1923), almost blind from 1925, textual critic. Classic on parables (2 vols., 1888–9) refuted allegorical understandings. *Intro. to NT* (1894; ET 1904). Comm. *Rom.* (1907). [H.-J. Klauck, in G. Schwaiger (ed.), 1980.]

94

JÜNGEL, EBERHARD (b. 1932). Pupil of Fuchs, outstanding interp. of Barth and Bultmann, prof. syst. theol. Zurich (1967), Tübingen (1969). Theol. interp. of NT includes *Jesus und Paulus* (1962) and several essays. *God as the Mystery of the World* (1977; ET 1983). J. B. Webster, 1986.   192, (196), 246

KÄHLER, MARTIN (1835–1912). Conservative Lutheran syst. theol., prof. Halle (1860). Spirited attack on liberal life of Jesus research, *The So-called Hist. Jesus . . .* (1892, 1896²; ET 1964), classic of the 'faith and history' debate, in which he also argued fruitfully with W. Herrmann. [H.-G. Link, 1975.]   109, 115, 118, 189

KÄSEMANN, ERNST (b. 1906). Pupil and penetrating crit. of Bultmann. NT prof. Mainz (1946), Göttingen (1951), Tübingen (1959–71). Instigator of 'new quest' (1953). Stirred up discussion of the canon, unity, and diversity in early Christianity, Johannine interp., 'early catholicism', apocalyptic as 'the mother of Christian theology', the righteousness of God in Paul. Comm. *Rom.* (1973; ET 1980). In 1930s opposed Hitler, in 1980s nuclear weapons. P. Gisel, 1977; [P. Ehler, 1986]; D. Way, 1989.   94, 111, 113, 115, 118, 120, **123**, 130, **191**

KAUTSKÝ, KARL (1854–1938). Czech Marxist intellectual, friend of Engels, lived in Vienna, London, Germany. Wrote widely, including *Foundations of Christianity* (1908; ET 1925), a Marxist interp. of Christian origins. G. P. Steenson, 1979.   148

KECK, LEANDER E., (b. 1928). Ph.D. Yale 1957, NT prof. Vanderbilt (1959), Emory (1972), Dean of Yale Div. Sch. (1980). *A Future for the Hist. Jesus* (1971).   165

KITTEL, GERHARD (1888–1948). NT prof. Tübingen (1926). Founder and ed. of *Theol. Dict. of NT* (1933–74; ET 1964–76), student of 1st-cent. and rabbinic Judaism, became a Nazi. R. P. Erickson, 1985.

128

KNOX, JOHN (b. 1900). Methodist and Episc. theol., NT prof. Union

Theol. Sem., NY (1943–66). *Philemon among the Letters of Paul* (1935 Chicago Ph.D., rev. 1959), *Christ the Lord* (1945), *Chapters in a Life of Paul* (1950), comm. *Rom.* (1954), *The Death of Christ* (1958), *The Church and the Reality of Christ* (1962), *The Humanity and Divinity of Christ* (1967). (ch. 6)

KNOX, WILFRED LAWRENCE (1886–1950). Cambridge Anglo-Catholic NT and Philo scholar. *St Paul and the Church of Jerusalem* (1925), *St Paul and the Church of the Gentiles* (1939), *Sources of the Synoptic Gospels*, ed. H. Chadwick (1953–7). (ch. 4)

KOESTER, HELMUT (b. 1926 at Hamburg). Pupil of Bultmann, Bornkamm, and Käsemann. NT prof. Harvard Div. Sch. (1959, 1964). *Introduction to NT* (1980; ET, 2 vols., 1982). Transplanted Bultmannian hist. of religs. trad. to N. America. 131

KRAUS, HANS-JOACHIM (b. 1918). Student of von Rad and Noth. Prof. OT Hamburg (1954). Reformed theol. Göttingen (1968). Wrote a hist. of OT schol. (1956) and on hist. and problem of bib. theol. (1970). (ch. 6)

KUENEN, ABRAHAM (1828–91). Prof. Leiden NT (1853), ethics (1860), OT (1877). *The Pentateuch and Book of Joshua* (ET, ed. Colenso, 1865), *The Religion of Israel to the Fall of the Jewish State* (3 vols., ET 1874), *The Prophets and Prophecy in Israel* (2 vols., 1875; ET 1877), *National Religions and Universal Religion* (English 1882). Followed Graf on Pentateuchal crit. 59

KÜMMEL, WERNER GEORG (b. 1905). NT prof. Zurich (1932), Mainz (1951), Marburg (1952). Refuted biog. interp. of Rom. 7 (1929), celebrated *Intro. to NT* (1963; ET rev. 1975), best hist. of mod. NT schol. (1958; ET 1973), and a popular *NT Theol.* (1972; ET 1974). Revised some older works (Lietzmann, Dibelius). 61, 92, 131, 244

KURTZ, JOHANN HEINRICH (1809–90). Conservative Lutheran prof. theol. Dorpat (1850–70). *The Bible and Astronomy* (1842; ET 1857), *Manual of Sacred Hist.* (1843; ET 1855), *Bible Hist.* (1847; ET 1867), *Hist. of the Old Covenant* (1848–55; ET, 3 vols., 1860), *Text-book of Church Hist.* (1849; ET, 2 vols., 1860), *Hist. of Christian Church* (1853–4; ET 1863), *Sacrificial Worship of the OT* (1862; ET 1863), *Church Hist.* (1890[11]; ET of 9th ed., 3 vols., 1890). 59

LACHMANN, KARL (1793–1851). Prof. German and classics Berlin

(1827). Produced (1831, 1847–50 with large apparatus) first ed. of NT based entirely on most ancient (i.e. fourth-century) manuscripts. Proposed Mark as earliest Gospel (1835), because agreement in order is always Matthew and/or Luke agreeing with Mark, who therefore best preserved order of (supposed) earlier Gospel on which all depended. N. H. Palmer, *NTS* 3 (1966/7).   67

LEACH, SIR EDMUND RONALD (1910–90). Prof. social anthropol. Cambridge and Provost of King's College (1966–79). Interested in structuralism, hostile to relig. and theol. *Rethinking Anthropol.* (1961) objected to 'butterfly hunting'.   144, 163 f.

LESSING, GOTTHOLD EPHRAIM (1729–81). Father of German lit., key figure in Enlightenment, strong theol. background and interests. Artfully published *Fragments* of Reimarus (1774–8) and stirred up discussion and controversy (with Pastor Goeze). Thought Synoptic Gospels all derived from an Aramaic Gospel of the Nazarenes (1776), and treated evangelists as 'merely human historians' (1778)—both published posthumously. Influenced Eichhorn and Herder. H. Chadwick, 1956; W. Pons, 1961; J. K. Riches, *JTS*, 1978.

47, 53, 62

LÉVI-STRAUSS, CLAUDE (b. 1908). Prof. social anthropol. Collège de France. Fashionable theoretician from 1950s through 1970s; see esp. his structuralist study of myth, based on S. American ethnography, and *The Savage Mind* (1962; ET 1966). *Tristes tropiques* (1955; ET 1973) a great intellectual autobiography. E. Leach, 1970.   143, 163, 218, 251

LIETZMANN, HANS (1875–1942). Early Church hist. prof. Jena (1908), Berlin (1924, succeeding Harnack). Founded NT comm. series, *Handbuch zum NT* (*Rom.* 1906, *1 and 2 Cor.* 1907). *Mass and Lord's Supper* (1926; ET 1979.). His correspondence (ed. K. Aland, 1979) reveals German Prot. theol. life over 50 years.   94

LIGHTFOOT, JOHN (1602–75). Master of St Catharine's, Cambridge (1650), and Vice-Chancellor (1654), canon of Ely. Pioneer rabbinicist. *Horae Hebraicae et Talmudicae* (1658–74; ET 1822) made Jewish studies fruitful for NT schol. D. M. Welton, 1878.   (ch. 4)

LIGHTFOOT, JOSEPH BARBER (1828–89). Fellow of Trinity (1852), prof. Cambridge (1861), Bishop Durham (1879). Outstanding NT historian and exegete of century. Comms. *Gal.* (1865), *Phil.* (1868), *Col.* (1875), and above all *Clement of Rome* (1869, Appx. 1877, 1890², and *Ignatius*

(1885, 1889²), which showed seven epistles genuine. G. R. Eden and F. C. Macdonald, 1932; C. K. Barrett, 1972. 46, 72

LIGHTFOOT, ROBERT HENRY (1883–1953). NT prof. Oxford (1934). Introduced form crit. sympathetically to England in *History and Interpretation in the Gospels* (1935). Impressed also by Lohmeyer. Forerunner of redaction crit. *Locality and Doctrine in the Gospels* (1938), *The Gospel Message of St Mark* (1950), comm. *John* (1956, ed. C. F. Evans). D. E. Nineham, *Studies in Gospels*, 1955, and *Theol.*, 1983. (ch. 4)

LINDBECK, GEORGE ARTHUR (b. 1923 in China). Ph.D. Yale 1955. Lutheran syst. and hist. theol., ecumenist. Prof. Yale (1967). *The Nature of Doctrine* (1984) important for theol. interp. of Bible. 148

LOCKE, JOHN (1632–1704). Oxford Whig phil., expelled from studentship at Christ Church after Exclusion Controversy (1684). Combined Christian rationalism and empiricism. *Letters concerning Toleration* (1689–92) wanted a broad national Church (Latitudinarian). *Essay concerning Human Understanding* (1690) opposed Platonist innate ideas. *The Reasonableness of Christianity as Delivered in the Scriptures* (1695) gives reason the last word, while accepting miracles. Wrote *A Paraphrase and Notes on the Epistles of St Paul* (1705–7, rp. 1988) and *A Discourse on Miracles* (1706). H. MacLachlan 1941; H. Graf Reventlow, ET 1984. (ch. 6)

LOHMEYER, ERNST (1890–1946). Outstanding NT scholar, prof. Breslau (1920–35, dismissed because anti-Nazi), Greifswald, where, as Rector-elect, he organized its reopening (1946) but in the same night was arrested by Russians and presumably murdered. Comm. *Rev.* (1926), *Phil., Col., Phm.* (1930), *Mark* (1937), *Matt.* (1956). Platonist interp. of Pauline theol. Anticipated redaction crit. *Lord of the Temple* (1942; ET 1961), *The Lord's Prayer* (1952; ET 1965). [E. Esking, 1951.] (chs. 4, 6)

LOISY, ALFRED (1857–1940). French RC modernist, prof. exegesis Institut Catholique (Paris) (1889–93), Collège de France (1904–26), excomm. 1908 for bib. crit. *The Gospel and the Church* (1903; ET 1904), a reply to Harnack's *What is Christianity?* Comms. on *Synoptic Gospels* (1907–8) and *Acts* (1920) masterly, others less so. P. Klein, 1977; A. H. M. Jones, 1983; S. W. Sykes, *Identity*, 1984. (ch. 4)

LOWTH, ROBERT (1710–87). Wykehamist, Oxford prof. poetry (1741–50), Bishop St Davids, Oxford (1766), London (1777), but refused Primacy, despite personal visit and entreaty from George III. *Praelectiones de sacra poesi Hebraeorum* (1753), ed. J. D. Michaelis with notes and additions in 1758–62 (1769/70). *Isaiah, a New Translation with Notes* (1778, 1842[13]). M. Pattison, 1889.   97, **210** f., 221, 217–19, 226

LUTHER, MARTIN (1483–1546). Prof. scripture Wittenberg (1511), hymn-writer. Greatest interp. of Paul and Bible translator, NT 1522, complete 1534, revisions 1541 and 1546. Comms. *Rom.* (lectures 1515/16, rediscovered 1908; ET 1961), *Gal.* (1535; modern ET 1953). ET of *Complete Works*, Augsburg ed. (1955–). G. Rupp, 1947; G. Ebeling, ET 1970; H. Bornkamm, ET 1983.

29 f., 32, 44, 88, 94, 103 f.

LUZ, ULRICH (b. 1938). Pupil of Schweizer and Ebeling. Taught in Japan (1970), prof. Göttingen (1972), Berne (1980). Comm. *Matt.* (3 vols., 1985–), translation forthcoming.   (chs. 4, 6)

MALHERBE, ABRAHAM JOHANNES (b. 1930 in S. Africa). NT prof. Dartmouth (1969), Yale (1978), Buckingham Prof. (1981). *The Cynic Epistles* (1977), *Social Aspects of Early Christianity* (1975, 1983[2]).

165

MALINA, BRUCE (b. *c*.1939). NT prof. Creighton Univ. Theoretician of anthropol. approaches to NT.   145, 165

MANSON, THOMAS WALTER (1893–1958). English Presbyterian NT scholar, Dodd's successor at Mansfield, Oxford (1932) and in Rylands chair, Manchester (1936). *The Teaching of Jesus* (1931), *The Sayings of Jesus* (1939). Firm opponent of Wrede and of form crit.

(ch. 4)

MARCION (d. *c*.160). Native of Sinope in Pontus, bishop's son. Greatest heretic, interp. and mutilator of St Paul in early Church. Tried to recall Church to Pauline antithesis of Gospel to law, but excomm. Rome 144. Dualist but not gnostic. His canon of NT (expurgated Luke and Paul) may have been a catalyst in formation of Catholic canon. Irenaeus, Tertullian, and others responded. [Harnack, 1921]; J. Knox, 1942; H. von Campenhausen, ET 1972.   (ch. 1)

MARTYN, JAMES LOUIS (b. 1925). Ph.D. Yale 1957, prof. NT Union Theol. Sem., NY (1959, 1967–86). *Hist. and Theol. in the Fourth Gospel* (1968, 1978[2]) marks an epoch in Johannine schol. Comm. *Gal.* forthcoming.   (ch. 4)

MARX, KARL HEINRICH (1818–83). Influential economist and pol.

scientist, maker of modern culture. Opposed to relig. but imp. for theol., including bib. interp. D. McLellan, 1973; N. Lash, 1981.

5, 12, 45, 60, 139, 153, 161

MATHEWS, SHAILER (1863–1941). Baptist turned liberal. As prof. NT (1894), hist. theol. (1906), and Dean (1908–33) of Chicago Div. Sch., presided over 'Chicago School'. *The Social Teachings of Jesus* (1897), *A Hist. of NT Times* (1899). In *The Messianic Hope in the NT* (1905) he changed from social ideal to esch. interp. of 'the kingdom of God'. *The Social Gospel* (1910), *The Faith of Modernism* (1924), *Jesus on Social Institutions* (1928; rp. 1971, ed. K. Cauthen), *Atonement and the Social Process* (1930), *The Growth of the Idea of God* (1931). K. Cauthen in 1971 reprint. (ch. 5)

MEEKS, WAYNE ATHERTON (b. 1932). Ph.D. Yale 1965. Prof. rel. studies Indiana (1966, 1969), Yale (1973). Outstanding social hist. of early Christianity. *The Writings of St Paul* (1972), *The Prophet-King: Moses Traditions and the Johannine Christology* (1967), *The First Urban Christians* (1983), *The Moral World of the First Christians* (1986). Influential essays on John (cf. J. Ashton, 1986).

131, 147–51, 153, 165

METZGER, BRUCE MANNING (b. 1914). Polymath, textual crit., bibliographer. Prof. NT Princeton Sem. (1938), member of RSV panel. *Chapters in the Hist. of NT Textual Crit.* (1963), *The Text of the NT* (1964), *A Textual Comm. on the Greek NT* (1971). (ch. 1)

MICHAELIS, JOHANN DAVID (1717–91). Prof. oriental langs. Göttingen (1750). Studied in England (1741–2), revised Lowth (1768²). *Paraphrases of OT* (13 vols., 1769–86). First part of unfinished *OT Introduction* (1787). Influential in England through Bishop Marsh's translations of *Introduction to NT* (1750, 2 vols.; 1788⁴; ET, 6 vols., 1826). Also *Comms. on the Laws of Moses* (1770; 1775², 6 vols.; ET, 4 vols., 1810). [H.-J. Kraus, 1956]; W. G. Kümmel, *History*, ET 1972.

211

MOMMSEN, THEODOR (1817–1903). Outstanding Roman hist. and jurist, prof. Leipzig (1848–50; dismissed for pol. activity), Berlin (1858, prof. from 1861). *Hist. of Rome*, i–iii (1854–6; ET 1862–6), v (1885). Vol. iv never written, possibly because he disliked Christianity. His study of Roman law touched on NT studies and he illuminated relations of early Church and Roman State during persecutions. Founded *Corpus Inscriptionum Latinarum* (1861–). Attacked

Treitschke's anti-Semitism. G. P. Gooch, 1913; [L. Wickert, 3 vols., 1959–69].   80 f.

MOORE, GEORGE FOOT (1851–1931). Studied at Yale and Union Theol. Sem., NY. Presbyterian pastor (1878) and Heb. prof. Andover Seminary (1883), Fotheringham prof. hist. of religs. Harvard (1904–21). *Judaism in the First Centuries of the Christian Era* (3 vols., 1927) a classic, and his article 'Christian Writers on Judaism', *Harvard Theol. Review* (1921) anticipated and stimulated K. Stendhal and E. P. Sanders.   128

MORGAN, THOMAS (1680–1743). Deist opponent of NT. *The Moral Philosopher* (1737) criticized David's morals (cf. Bayle, Voltaire) and called for a moral Christianity purged of Jewish national relig. Anticipated Semler and Baur on divisions in early Christianity. H. Graf Reventlow, ET 1984.   (175)

MOULE, CHARLES FRANCIS DIGBY (b. 1908). NT prof. Cambridge (1952–76). Leading Anglican NT theol. Comms. *Mark* (1965), *Col.* (1957). *The Birth of the NT* (1962, rev. 1981) a fine introduction to NT study. Also *The Phenomenon of the NT* (1967), *The Origin of Christology* (1977).   (chs. 4, 6)

MOWINCKEL, SIGMUND (1884–1966). Norwegian pupil of Gunkel (at Giessen), OT prof. Oslo (1922). Continued Gunkel 'type' (*Gattung*) or form-crit. and cultic work on *Psalms* (1921–4), having early applied it to *Jeremiah* (1914). *Servant of Yahweh* (1921), *Isaiah* (1925), *Decalogue* (French, 1927). Also *Prophecy and Trad.* (English, 1946). *The Psalms in Israel's Worship* (1951; ET 1962, 1982) a classic.   (ch. 4)

NEILL, STEPHEN CHARLES (1900–84). English polymath, missionary bishop in South India (1938–44), and ecumenist. Many popular works on NT, including a readable if tendentious hist. of its mod. (1861–1961) interp. (1964). Prof. missions, Hamburg (1962–7), relig. studies, Nairobi (1969). Retirement in Oxford, writing *History of Christianity in India* (1980–).   (ch. 6)

NEUSNER, JACOB (b. 1932). Ph.D. Columbia 1960. Controversial prof. rel. studies (Judaism) Brown (1968), productive rabbinic scholar.

163

NIEBUHR, BARTHOLD GEORG (1776–1831). Prussian civil servant and Ambassador in Rome 1816–23 (concordat 1821). Founder of crit. use of sources in ancient hist. Lectured on Roman hist. in Berlin 1810–12.

Hist. of Rome, i, ii (1811/12; ET 1828–31), iii (1832; rp. 1873/4). J. C. Hare, 1829. 65, 80

NIETZSCHE, FRIEDRICH WILHELM (1844–1900). Philosopher, friend of Overbeck, critic of Christianity, maker of modern culture, father of deconstructionism. Prof. Greek lang. and lit., Basle (1869–79). Wrote *The Antichrist* in 1888, went insane 1889. W. Kaufman, 1950, 1974[4].

5, 43, 60, 181, 324, 331

NINEHAM, DENNIS ERIC (b. 1921). Prof. London (1954), Cambridge (1964), Warden of Keble, Oxford (1969), prof. Bristol (1979–86). Writes widely on hermeneutics. *The Church's Use of the Bible* (ed. 1963) encouraged other bibl. scholars to specialize on 'the modern end of the problem' (168). Associated with 'cultural relativism' thesis. His popular Penguin comm. *Mark* (1963) made impact on English theol. education. 43, (ch. 6)

NOCK, ARTHUR DARBY (1902–63). Fellow of Clare, Cambridge (1923–30) and univ. lecturer in classics (1926). Fotheringham prof. hist. of religs., Harvard (1930). Ed. *HTR* (1933–63). *Early Gentile Christianity and its Hellenistic Background* (in Rawlinson, 1928), *Conversion* (1933), *St Paul* (1938), and (with Festugière) ed. hermetic literature (1945–54). Selected essays, 2 vols. (Oxford, 1972). (ch. 4)

NOTH, MARTIN (1902–68). Pupil of Alt, OT prof. Königsberg (1930) and Bonn (1946). *Hist. of Israel* (1950; ET of 1960 ed. 1965) advanced hist. of trad. research. Suggested Israel's tribal structure similar to Greek amphictyonies (union of independent communities united by common worship at a central shrine, the ark). Comms. *Exod.* (1959; ET 1962), *Lev.* (1962; ET 1965), *Joshua* (1938), *Numbers* (1966; ET 1968). *A Hist. of Pentateuchal Trads.* (1948; ET 1972). (ch. 4)

ORIGEN (*c.*185–254). Greatest bib. interp. and father of syst. and myst. theol. Threefold sense of scripture: literal, moral, allegorical. Succeeded Clement at catechetical school in Alexandria. Ordained in Palestine (230) despite impediment. J. Daniélou, ET 1955; R. P. C. Hanson, 1959; Trigg, 1983. 15, 207

OTTO, RUDOLF (1869–1937). Prof. syst. theol. Göttingen (1897), Breslau (1914), Marburg (1917–29). Concerned with essence and truth of relig. Combined Kant and Luther, and drew on Fries, de Wette, Schleiermacher, in his phenomenol. of relig. *The Idea of the Holy* (1917; ET 1923, rev. 1929) provided a vocabulary for the non-rational and numinous in relig. He also ed. Kant on morals (1930) and

Schleiermacher's *Speeches on Relig.* (1899). Main bib. work *The Kingdom of God and the Son of Man* (1934; ET 1938). R. F. Davidson, 1947.   (chs. 1, 4, 6)

OVERBECK, FRANZ (1837–1905). Unbelieving prof. NT and early Church hist. Basle (1870–97). Close friend and neighbour of Nietzsche, critical follower of Baur. Forerunner of form crit. Revised de Wette's comm. *Acts* (1870; part ET in Zeller's *Acts*, 1875). Sharp crit. of theol. scene (1873 and 1919), influenced Barth. Aimed to write a 'profane' history of Church. Wrote on hist. of canon (1880) and beginnings of patristic lit. (1882; rp. 1954) and on *Fourth Gospel* (1911). But most of his icy writings remain in Basle unpublished. K. Löwith, ET 1967; [A. Pfeifer, 1975; J. C. Emmelius, 1975].   38, 323

PANNENBERG, WOLFHART (b. 1928). Leading German syst. theol. Prof. Mainz (1961), Munich (1968). In *Revelation and Hist.* (1961; ET 1969) he led Heidelberg young theols. attacking dominant 'theol. of Word', and built on hist. of trads., owing much to von Rad. *Jesus God and Man* (1964; ET 1968) claims resurrection of Jesus a hist. event. *Basic Questions in Theol.* (1967–70; ET, 3 vols., 1970–3), *The Apostles' Creed* (1972; ET 1972), *Theol. and Phil. of Science* (1973; ET 1976), *Anthropol. in Theol. Perspective* (1983; ET 1985). A. Galloway, 1973; F. Tupper, 1973.   (ch. 6)

PAULUS, HEINRICH EBERHARD GOTTLOB (1761–1851). Rationalist prof. oriental langs. (1789), exegesis (1793) at Jena, theol. Würzburg (1803), Church. hist. Heidelberg (1811). Ed. Spinoza (1802–3). Comms. *Psalms* (1791), *Isaiah* (1793), *NT* (1800–4), *Synoptics* (3 vols., 1830–3), and *Life of Jesus* (2 vols., 1828) which explained away miracles as natural events ('created exegetical miracles in order to do away with the bib. miracles').   48 f.

PEDERSEN, JOHANNES (1883–1977). Danish OT schol., Arabist, Islamicist. Prof. Sem. philol. Copenhagen (1916–50). Influenced by Danish anthropologist Grønbech. *Israel* (4 vols., 1920, 1934; ET 1926, 1940) a classic of more phenomenol., anthropol., and psychol. approach to Israelite relig. than Wellhausen's. His suggestion that Ex. 1–15 took shape as Passover liturgy (1934 and 1940, pp. 728–37) doubtful. 141

PERRIN, NORMAN (1921–76). NT prof. Emory (1958), Chicago (1964, 1969). Pupil of Manson and Jeremias, thesis on *The Kingdom of God in the Teaching of Jesus* (1963). *Rediscovering the Teaching of Jesus* (1967) more sceptical. *Jesus and the Language of the Kingdom* (1976) advocated lit. approaches. R. C. Mercer, 1987.   131, 268

PFLEIDERER, OTTO (1839–1908). Last pupil of Baur (1857–60), liberal, phil. idealist. Prof. syst. theol. Jena (1870), Berlin (1875). Wrote on *Fichte* (1877), *Paulinism* (1873; ET, 4 vols., 1877), *Primitive Christianity* (1887; ET 1906), *The Influence of the Apostle Paul on the Development of Christianity* (English, 1885), *Phil. of Relig. on Basis of its Hist.* (1878; ET, 4 vols., 1886–8), *Development of Theol. in Germany since Kant and its Progress in Great Britain since 1825* (ET 1890). [R. Leuze, 1980.]   (ch. 4)

PHILO OF ALEXANDRIA (*c*.20 BCE–*c*.50 CE). Jewish theol. and bib. interp. His allegorical interp. influenced Clement and Origen. H. A. Wolfson, 1947.   (ch. 1)

PUSEY, EDWARD BOUVERIE (1800–82). Studied Göttingen and Berlin (1825). Regius prof. Heb. Oxford (1828–82). Wrote on theol. in Germany (1828–30) but 1833 became a tractarian. Conservative theol., univ. politician, spiritual leader. H. P. Liddon, 1893–7.   (ch. 2)

RAD, GERHARD VON (1901–71). Pupil of Alt. OT prof. Jena (1934), Göttingen (1945), Heidelberg (1949). 'The Form Critical Problem of the Hexateuch' (1938; ET in *The Prob. of the Hexateuch and other Essays*, 1965) a pioneering work of redaction crit. of J source. Thought credal summaries in Deut. 6: 20–4; 26: 5*b*–9; Josh. 24: 2*b*–13 very early. His trad.-hist. approach to the prophets illuminated their theol. In addition to *OT Theol.* (1957–60; ET 1962–5), comm. *Genesis* (1953; ET 1972). *Wisdom in Israel* (1970; ET 1972) argued that apocalyptic owed more to wisdom than to prophecy. D. G. Spriggs, 1976; J. L. Crenshaw, 1978.   98–104, 105, 113, 130 f., 146 f.

RAMSEY, ARTHUR MICHAEL (1904–88). Pupil of Hoskyns. Bib. theol. and 'last of the Church Fathers'. Prof. div. Durham (1940), Cambridge (1950), Bishop Durham (1952), Archbishop York (1956), Canterbury (1961–74). *The Gospel and the Catholic Church* (1936), *The Resurrection of Christ* (1945), *The Glory of God in the Transfiguration of Christ* (1949), *From Gore to Temple* (1960), and many devotional and catechetical works.   (chs. 6, 8)

RANKE, LEOPOLD VON (1795–1886). Prof. hist. Berlin (1834), founder of mod. crit. hist. and leading 'historicist'. *Hist. of the Popes* (3 vols., 1834–6, 1874⁶; ET 1847³). *German Hist. in the Times of the Reformation* (6 vols., 1839–47; ET 1905). G. P. Gooch, 1913).   65, 80, 86, 231

REIMARUS, HERMANN SAMUEL (1694–1768). Deist, philologist, influenced by Wolff's rationalism. Taught in schools, Weimar (1723), Hamburg (1729). Pub. two works on natural relig. (1745, 1762), Dio Cassius (1750–2). *Apology or Defence for the Rational Worshippers of God*, part pub. by Lessing (1774–8), authorship remaining secret till 1814, finally pub. in 1972. Part ET 1879, reissued 1962, expanded 1970 (*Fragments*). A. Schweitzer, *Quest*, ET 1910.   52–7, 60 f.,
                    65, 68, 70, 108, 119, 121, 173, 175, 177, 241, 298

REITZENSTEIN, RICHARD (1861–1931). Classics prof. Giessen (1892), Strasburg (1893), Freiburg (1911), Göttingen (1914). Influenced Bousset and Bultmann and so gave NT hist. of religs. research a non-Jewish twist, and advanced the study of early gnosticism. *Poimandres* (1904) suggested Hermetic influences on NT. *The Hellenistic Mystery Religions* (1910, 1927³; ET 1978) saw Christianity, esp. Paul, as dependent on Hellenistic, Mandean, and Iranian ideas. Also wrote on *Goddess Psyche* (1917), on *The Iranian Mystery of Redemption* (1921), and on the pre-history of Christian baptism (1929). [C. Colpe, 1961.]
                    127

RENAN, (JOSEPH) ERNEST (1823–92). Ex-seminarian, NT schol., littérateur. Romantic *Life of Jesus* (1863), first of a 7-vol. *Hist. of the Origins of Christianity* (1863–82; ET, 7 vols., 1888–9) started fashion. 5-vol. *Hist. of the People of Israel* (1887–93; ET, 3 vols., 1889–91). Popularized bibl. schol. for French public, influenced Loisy. Schweitzer, *Quest*, ET 1910; H. W. Wardman, 1964.   47

REUSS, EDUARD (1804–91). Outstanding Strasburg bib. schol., NT prof. (1838), OT (1864). First dean (1872–88) when it became a proper German univ. Established crit. schol. in French Prot. Pentateuchal crit., first to see the law later than prophets (1834 lectures). *Hist. of NT Writings* (1842, 1887⁶; ET, 2 vols., 1884) and *Johannine Theol. (1847)*, *Hist. of Christian Theol. in Apostolic Age* (French, 1852, 1864³; ET 1872) corrected Baur. Comm. *Job* (1869). *Crit. Intro. to OT* (1881; ET 1890). Ed. Calvin.   72

RITSCHL, ALBRECHT (1822–89). Prof. Bonn (1852) Göttingen (1864). Leading syst. theol. of 1870s, shaped liberal Prot. until 1920s. As NT pupil of Baur suggested (1846) canonical Luke based on Marcion's; but more conservative after 1850. *The Origin of the Early Catholic Church* (1850, 1857²) a classic, 2nd ed. broke with Baur. Vol. ii of *Justification and Reconciliation* (1874) a memorable example of older bib. theol.

Hist. of Pietism (1880–6; ET of Prolegomena 1972), *Theol. and Metaphysics* (1881; ET 1972). P. Hefner, 1966; J. Richmond, 1978; D. Jodock, 1978.   72, 88, 109, 125 f., 244

ROBINSON, JAMES McCONKEY (b. 1924). Studied with Barth and Cullmann in Basle (Dr. theol. 1952, thesis on Herrmann), Th.D. Princeton (1955), prof. NT Emory (1952), Claremont (1958), and Director of Institute of Antiquity (1971). Popularized 'new quest' of hist. Jesus (1959) and collaborated with R. W.. Funk and G. Ebeling to propagate Bultmannian hermeneutical theol. in N. America through *Journal for Theol. and the Church* (1965–70) and (with J. B. Cobb) *New Frontiers in Theology* (1963–7). Later became representative of the American secular Prot. turn from NT theol. and Church. Managerial skills most effective in achieving publication of *The Nag Hammadi Library* (1977).   131

ROBINSON, JOHN ARTHUR THOMAS (1919–83). Pupil of Dodd. Dean of Clare and NT lecturer Cambridge (1951), Bishop Woolwich (1959), Dean of Trinity, Cambridge (1969). When young, wrote stimulating monographs on bib. (NT) theol. Testimony on *Lady Chatterley's Lover* (1961) and *Honest to God* (1963) made him a symbol of the 1960s, but independent mind and innate Anglican conservatism evident in *Redating the NT* (1976) (all pre-70) and *The Priority of John* (1985) which emphasized its hist. components. R. P. McBrien, 1966.   124

SANDAY, WILLIAM (1843–1920). Dean Ireland's (NT) (1882) and Lady Margaret (1885) prof. Oxford. Reported on German Gospel crit. to Church of England. Bampton Lectures on *Inspiration* (1893), comm. *Rom.* (with A. C. Headlam) (1895). From 1894 led a seminar in Christ Church on synoptic problem, which produced *Oxford Studies* (1911). *Outlines of the Life of Christ* (1905), *The Life of Christ in Recent Research* (1907), *Christologies Ancient and Modern* (1910).   (ch. 2)

SANDERS, ED PARISH (b. 1937). NT prof. McMaster (1966), Oxford (1984). *Paul and Palestinian Judaism* (1977, German trans. 1985) revised assessment of 1st cent. Judaism. *Paul, the Law and the Jewish People* (1983) completed a major reorientation in understanding of Paul. *Jesus and Judaism* (1985) proposed stimulating theory of Jesus as prophet, 'restoration eschatology'.   115, 121, 124, 128, 131, 242–4

SANDERS, JAMES ALVIN (b. 1927). Ph.D. Heb. Union Coll. (1955). OT prof. Colgate Rochester Div. School (1954), Union Theol. Sem., NY (1965), Intertestamental and Bib. studies Claremont (1977). *The*

Psalms Scroll of Qumran Cave 11 (1965), *Torah and Canon* (1970, 1972²), 'Hermeneutics' (*Interp. Dict. of Bib.*, Supp., 1976), *Canon and Community: A Guide to Canonical Crit.* (1984), *From Sacred Story to Sacred Text* (1987).   213

SCHLATTER, ADOLF (1852–1938). Giant among conservatives, appreciated by Bultmann, Käsemann, and pietists. Prof. NT Greifswald (1888), Berlin (1893), Tübingen (1898). Popular comms. on every book of NT, major ones on *Matt.* (1930), *John* (1930), *1 and 2 Cor.* (1934), *James* (1932), *Rom.* (1935). *NT Theol.* (1910), monographs on Jewish context of NT, dogmatics, and hist. of phil. Methodological essay on NT theology (1909; ET 1973). [W. Egg, 1968; I. Kindt, 1978.] 128

SCHLEIERMACHER, FRIEDRICH DANIEL ERNST (1768–1834). Pietist background, met crit. thought at Halle. Preacher at Berlin Charité (1796), friend of Schlegel, trans. Plato (ET of *Introductions to Dialogues* 1836). *Speeches on Relig.* (1799; ET 1893), *Soliloquies* (*Monologen*) (1800; ET 1926), *Christmas Eve* (1805; ET 1967). Associate prof. Halle (1804 till it closed in 1806), back to Berlin, prof. 1810. *Brief Outline on the Study of Theol.* (1811, 1830²; ET 1966). *The Christian Faith* (1821/2, rp. 1985, 1830/1²; ET 1928). 'Father of modern theol.', lectured regularly on NT. Questioned authenticity of 1 Tim. (1807) and had doubts about Eph. (cf. *Introduction to NT*, 1845). Lectures on hermeneutics (1838, crit. ed. 1959; ET 1977). Monograph on *Luke* (1817; ET 1825). From 1819, first to lecture on *Life of Jesus* (1832, but 1819 pub. 1864; ET 1975) and severely criticized by Strauss (1865; ET 1977). Thought Papias's Matt. a collection of sayings (cf. Q). R. R. Niebuhr, 1964; [H. Weisweiler, 1972]; B. A. Gerrish, 1984.

31–3, 39, 43, 57, 63 f., 89, 113, 119, 135, 188, 286

SCHLIER, HEINRICH (1904–82). Pupil of Peterson and Bultmann, prof. Bonn (1946), became Rom. Cath. Comms. *Gal.* (1949), *Eph.* (1957), *Rom.* (1977). Wrote on Pauline theology (1978) and on problem of interp.   (chs. 4, 6)

SCHMIDT, KARL LUDWIG (1891–1956). Theol. engaged NT prof. Giessen (1921), Jena (1925), Bonn (1929–33, quickly dismissed by Nazis), Basle (1935–53). After pioneering work on the framework of the (Synoptic) Gospels (1919) and their lit. character (1923) wrote for Kittel's *Theol. Dict. of NT* (esp. arts, *basileia* (1933) and *ecclesia* (1938)) on Church and State, and on Jewish–Christian relations. Ed. *Theol. Blätter* (1922–37) and *Theol. Zeitschrift* (1945–53).   68, 217

SCHÜRER, EMIL (1844–1910). NT prof. Giessen (1878), Kiel (1890), Göttingen (1895). Pioneer student of early Judaism, but called it 'late Judaism'. Influential as founding ed. *Theol. Lit. Zeitung* (1876–80, 1888–1910). Wrote on Schleiermacher's concept of relig. (1868), and on preaching of Jesus (1882). *Hist. of the Jewish People in the Age of Jesus Christ* (1874, 1886–7, 1901–9⁴; ET of 2nd ed. 1895–91; rev. vols. i (1973), ii (1979), iii (1986)).   128

SCHÜRMANN, HEINZ (b. 1912). RC prof. Münster and NT Erfurt, East Germany (1952). Profound theol. and outstanding hist. of trads. investigator of Gospels. Comm. *Luke* (1969–) incomplete.   37, 194

SCHWEITZER, ALBERT (1875–1965). NT lecturer in Strasburg (1902), musician (Bach book, 1905; ET 1911), medical missionary in W. Africa (1913), relig. thinker. Nobel peace prize 1952, warned against atomic weapons. *The Mystery of the Kingdom of God* (1901; ET 1925) and *The Quest of the Hist. Jesus* (1906; ET 1910) popularized and corrupted J. Weiss's thesis on esch. of Jesus. *Paul and his Interps.* (1911; ET 1912) prepared for *The Mysticism of Paul the Apostle* (1930; ET 1931). *The Lord's Supper* (1901; ET 1982). [E. Grässer, 1979.]   45, 48 f.,
53, 61, 64, 108 f., 120 f., 241–5

SCHWEIZER, EDUARD (b. 1913). Pupil of Bultmann, studied also with Barth and Brunner. NT prof. Zurich (1949–78). Comms. *Mark* (1967; ET 1970), *Matt.* (1973; ET 1975), *Luke* (1982; ET 1984), *Col.* (1976; ET 1982) and books on *Lordship and Discipleship* (1955; ET 1960, rp. 1986). *Church and Church Order in NT* (1959; ET 1961, rp. 1978), *The Church as the Body of Christ* (English, 1965), *Jesus* (1968; ET 1971).
(ch. 4)

SEGUNDO, JUAN LUIS (b. 1925). Jesuit liberation theol. at Montevideo, Uruguay. Studied in Argentina, Louvain, Paris. *A Theol. for Artisans of a New Humanity* (1973–4). Has written on *The Hist. Jesus* (1986) and *Paul* (1986).   (ch. 5)

SEMLER, JOHANN SALOMO (1725–91). Pietist roots, prof. theol. Halle (1752), 'neologist', father of hist. crit. of Bible. Dist. between theol. and relig., and between Bible and Word of God. Influenced by English deists, trans. and/or commented on them, but remained pious, and in 1779 opposed Reimarus's *Fragments*. Prolific writer, style difficult. His *Free Research on the Canon* (4 vols., 1771–5) epoch-making, breaking with doctrine of inspiration. Anticipated Baur's distinction between Jewish and Pauline Christianity in NT. He thought Jesus and the apostles 'accommodated' themselves to thought of their day. Comms. *Rom., John, 1 and 2 Cor.*, etc., and works in the hist. of doctrine. [G. Hornig, 1961]; W. G. Kümmel, *Hist.*, ET 1972.　　(chs. 2, 3), 322

SHAMMAI (*fl. c.*20 BCE–15 CE). Leading conservative and rigorist pharisaic scribe in Jerusalem, opponent of Hillel, and founder of school.　　(ch. 1)

SIMON, RICHARD (1638–1712). French priest, expelled from Oratory for *Histoire critique du Vieux Testament* (1678), which denied Mosaic authorship of Pentateuch. Also wrote on NT textual crit. (1689) and hist. of interp. (1693); 'the founder of the discipline of NT Introduction' (cf. Kümmel, *Hist.*, 40–7). [K. H. Graf, 1847]; J. Steinmann, 1960.　　(ch. 2)

SMART, NINIAN (b.1926). Oxford-trained phil., was taught Chinese by army intelligence and sent to Ceylon. Lecturer in Wales and London. Prof. theol. Birmingham (1962), relig. studies at Lancaster (1967) and Santa Barbara (1976), establishing new trend in British univ. and schools. Prolific writer on phil., phenomenol., and hist. of relig.

61, 294

SMITH, WILLIAM ROBERTSON (1846–94). Studied at Aberdeen, Edinburgh, Bonn, Göttingen. Prof. OT and oriental langs., Free Church College, Aberdeen (1870), dismissed (1881) for bib. crit. Fellow of Christ's, Cambridge (1885). Friend of Frazer, prof. Arabic (1886–9), Univ. Librarian (1889). *The OT in the Jewish Church* (1881) popularized Wellhausen's pentateuchal crit. *The Prophets of Israel* (1882), *Kinship and Marriage in Early Arabia* (1885). *The Religion of the Semites* (1889) saw the point of sacrifice as communion with the Deity, not propitiation. J. W. Rogerson, *OT Crit.*, 1984.　　95, 140, 143

SPINOZA, BARUCH/BENEDICT DE (1632–77). Dutch Jewish phil. *Tractatus Theologico-politicus* (1670) pioneered bib. crit.　　(ch. 2)

STENDAHL, KRISTER (b. 1921). Pupil of Fridrichsen. NT prof. Uppsala (1954), Harvard Div. Sch. (1958, 1963) and Dean (1968–79). Bishop Stockholm (1980). *The School of Matt.* (1957) illuminated NT use of OT with help from Qumran. *Paul among the Jews and Gentiles* (1976) includes reprint of 'The Apostle Paul and the Introspective Conscience of the West' (1963), contributed to the anti-Lutheran turn in recent non-German study. Concerned for better Jewish–Christian relations. His essays on 'Bibl. Theol., Contemporary' in *Interp. Dict. of Bib.*

(1962, rp. 1980) and 'The Bible and the Role of Women' (1966) also imp. 43, 115, 179, 322

STRAUSS, DAVID FRIEDRICH (1808–74). Part of his reply to critics of *The Life of Jesus* is now in ET (1983, ed. M. C. Massey). *Critical Hist. of Doctrine* (2 vols., 1840–1). *Life of Jesus for the German People* (1864; ET, 2 vols., 1865), *The Christ of Faith and the Jesus of Hist.* (1865; ET 1977). *The Old Faith and the New* (1872; ET 1873) is politically and socially conservative, religiously weak, and deservedly buried by Nietzsche in *Untimely Meditations* (1873; latest ET 1983). [J. Sandberger, 1972]; H. Harris, 1973; H. Frei, *Eclipse*, 1974, and *Nineteenth-century Relig. Thought*, 1985; [F. W. Graf, 1982]. **44–54**, 56 f., 60–8, 70, 75, 79, 90, 93, 107, **114–16**, 126, 172, 188 f., 207, **210** f., 228, 295 f.

STRECKER, GEORG (b. 1929). NT prof. Göttingen (1964). Leading redaction critic of Matt. *The Sermon on the Mount* (1984; ET 1988).
(ch. 4)

STREETER, BURNET HILLMAN (1874–1937). Student, fellow (1905), and Provost (1933) of Queen's, Oxford, and (1915) canon of Hereford. Textual critic, Gospel critic, English modernist theol. *The Four Gospels* (1924) occupied a central place in English study of synoptic problem until 1960s, despite earlier German advances. First major theol. to die in plane crash. W. R. Farmer, 1964.
(ch. 3)

STUBBS, WILLIAM (1825–1901). Medieval hist., established crit. mod. hist. Oxford. Bishop Chester (1884), Oxford (1889). *Select Charters of English Constitutional Hist.* (1870), *The Constitutional Hist. of England* (1873–8). W. H. Hutton, *Letters*, 1904.
46

TANNEHILL, ROBERT C. (b. 1934). Ph.D. Yale (1963), NT prof. Methodist Theol. Sch., Ohio (1974). *Dying and Rising with Christ* (1967). *The Sword of His Mouth* (1975) pioneered lit. approaches. *The Narrative Unity of Luke–Acts: A Lit. Interp.* (1987–). Essay on 'The Disciples in Mark' (1977; rp. Telford 1985) also noteworthy.
242 f., **244** f., 268

TAYLOR, VINCENT (1887–1968). Methodist NT theol., tutor (1930), principal (1936) Headingley College, Leeds. Wrote on Synoptics, Q, Luke, comm. *Mark* (1952), and on NT theology; *Jesus and his Sacrifice* (1937), *The Atonement in NT Teaching* (1940), *Forgiveness and Reconciliation* (1941), *The Person of Christ in NT Teaching* (1958), *The*

Passion Narrative of St Luke (1970). C. L. Mitton (in Taylor's *NT Essays*), 1970. (ch. 3)

THEISSEN, GERD (b. 1944). NT prof. Copenhagen (1978) and Heidelberg (1980). Pioneer of mod. sociol. and psychol. interp. In addition to works discussed and listed, see *On Having a Crit. Faith* (1978; ET 1979), *The Shadow of the Galilean* (1986; ET 1987), and *Essays* (1979, 1983²; ET 1988).   37, 143, 148, **150** f.,
153, 163, 166, **253**

THEODORE OF MOPSUESTIA (*c*.350–428). Leader of Antiochene school of bib. interp., rejected Alexandrian use of allegory. R. A. Greer, 1961; R. A. Norris, 1963. (ch. 1)

THIRLWALL, CONNOP (1797–1875). Fellow (1818) and tutor (1832) of Trinity, Cambridge. Dismissed over compulsory chapel (1834). Bishop St Davids (1840–74). Translated Schleiermacher's *Luke* (1825) and (with J C. Hare) Niebuhr's *Hist. of Rome* (1828–31). Wrote a classic crit. *Hist. of Greece* (8 vols., 1835–40). Opposed *Essays and Reviews*. J. C. Thirlwall, 1936. 46, 57 f.

TINDAL, MATTHEW (1655–1733). Leading deist, Fellow of All Souls, Oxford (1678). Erastian. *A Defence of the Rights of the Christian Church* (1709) burned by hangman. *Christianity as Old as the Creation, or The Gospel a Republication of the Religion of Nature* (1730; rp. 1967) became 'the Bible of the Deists'. H. Graf Reventlow, ET 1984. 56, (175)

TOLAND, JOHN (1670–1722). 'English' (Irish) Deist. *Christianity not Mysterious* (1696; rp. 1964) opposed reason to revelation. *Tetradymus* (1720) includes a rationalist interp. of Mosaic hist. Coined the word 'pantheist' in 1705 and in *Pantheisticon* (1720) became one. R. E. Sullivan, 1982. (56, 175)

TRIBLE, PHYLLIS (b. 1932). Pupil of J. Muilenberg. OT prof. Wake Forest (1963), Andover Newton Theol. Sch. (1971) and Union Theol. Sem., NY (1979). Leading feminist interp. of OT. 159, 267

TROELTSCH, ERNST (1865–1923). Hist. and phil. of relig., ethicist, prof. syst. theol. Heidelberg (1894), phil. Berlin (1915). Friend of Bousset and 'systematic theol. of the hist. of religs. school', saw imp. of esch. for early Christianity. Reflections on hist. method and its significance for theol. Friend and colleague of Max Weber, introduced a sociol. dimension into hist. of Christianity: *The Social Teachings of the Christian Churches* (1912; ET, 2 vols., 1930). Improved by B. Wilson, his church-sect typology has become influential in NT schol. W. Wyman, 1983; S. Coakley, 1988.   39, 125, 129, 145 f., 163

TYCONIUS (d. *c*.400). Donatist, wrote *c*.380 a 'book of [seven] rules' for interp. scripture (*Liber Regularum*, Texts and Studies 3, 1894), influenced St Augustine and so medieval exegesis.   (ch. 1)

VATKE, (JOHANN KARL) WILHELM (1806–82). Hegelian historian of OT relig. and theol. Lecturer (1830), junior prof. (1837) Berlin. [L. Perlitt, 1965.]   62 f., 68 f., 73, 75, **79** f., 83, 89 f., 93 f., 101, 104, 188

VAUX, ROLAND DE (1903–71). OT hist. and archaeol. Dominican prof. at École Biblique, Jerusalem. *Ancient Israel* (1958; ET 1961), *The Early History of Israel to the Period of Judges* (1973; ET 1976). Moved away from defence of historicity on appeal to archaeol. (*The Bible in Modern Scholarship*, ed. J. P. Hyatt, 1965) and 'On Right and Wrong Uses of Archaeol.' (*Near Eastern Archaeol.*, 1970).   141

VIA, DAN OTTO (b. 1928). Pupil of W. D. Davies. NT prof. Wake Forest (1956), Univ. Virginia (1968), Duke (1985). Pioneering lit. crit. and theol. interp. NT.   37, **237** f., **246**–8, **254** f., **258** f.

VOLTAIRE (pseudonym of François Marie Arouet) (1694–1778). French deist and littérateur. Wrote scurrilously about Bible and Church, in the interests of social justice, and was nice about England. Opposed atheism. *Phil. Dict.* (Penguin, 1967) bed-time reading. R. Pomeau, 1956.   60

WEBER, MAX (1864–1920). Prof. pol. economy Freiburg (1894), Heidelberg (1897). Breakdown 1898–1903. A founding father of mod. social theory and key figure in sociol. of relig. Shared house with Troeltsch in Heidelberg and so was informed about theol., and used term 'charisma'. His work on different forms of authority has been used in bib. schol. (e.g. Schütz, Holmberg, Wilson). See also *The Prot. Ethic and the Spirit of Capitalism* (1905; ET 1930), *Ancient Judaism* (1922; ET 1952), *The Sociol. of Relig.* (1922; ET 1963). R. Bendix, 1960.
                139 f., 146, 153, 163 f.

WEDER, HANS (b. 1947). Pupil and successor of E. Schweizer at Zurich. Theol. interp. of parables (1978) and Paul (1981), and hermeneutical theorist (1986).   (chs. 4, 6)

WEISS, BERNHARD (1827–1918). Conservative NT prof. Kiel (1863), Berlin (1877). Father of Johannes. Meyer Comms. *Matt.* (1883), *Mark*

(1878), *Luke* (1878), *John* (1880), *Rom.* (1881), *Past.* (1885). His *Bib. Theol. of NT* (1868; ET 1882–3), *Life of Jesus* (1882; ET, 3 vols., 1883–4), and *Intro. to NT* (1889²; ET, 2 vols., 1889) once widely read.

(ch. 3)

WEISS, JOHANNES (1863–1914). Son of Bernhard, pupil and son-in-law of Ritschl. Associated with hist. of religs. school. NT prof. Marburg (1895), Heidelberg (1908). Pioneer of form crit. (*RGG¹*, 1912). *Jesus' Proclamation of Kingdom of God* (1892; ET 1971), comms. *Luke* (1893), *1 Cor.* (1910; rp. 1970, 1977), *Primitive Christianity* (1914/17; ET 1937, 1959) and several popular works. 76, 108, 125–7, 242

WEISSE, CHRISTIAN HERMANN (1801–66). Prof. phil. Leipzig (1845). Idealist phil. and theol. *Gospel Hist.* (1838) advocated two-source hypothesis: priority of Mark, and use of another source by Matt. and Luke. H.-H. Stoldt, *Marcan Hyp.*, 1977 (ET 1980). 67

WEIZSÄCKER, KARL HEINRICH VON (1822–99). Baur's successor at Tübingen (1861). Ed. *Jahrbücher für deutsche Theol.* (1856–78). *The Apostolic Age* (1886; ET, 2 vols., 1894–5). 72

WELLHAUSEN, JULIUS (1844–1918). Pupil of Ewald. Leading OT lit. (source) critic. Prof. OT Greifswald (1872–82: resigned because his bib. crit. seemed incompatible with Protestantism). Prof. Semitics Marburg (1885), Göttingen (1892). *Hist. of Israel* (1878), *Prolegomena* (1883; ET 1885). Wrote also on *Composition of Hexateuch and Hist. Books* (1885), on *Pharisees and Sadducees* (1874). His short comms. to and Intro. on Synoptics (1903–5) and Acts (1914) are gems. J. W. Rogerson, *OT Crit.*, 1984. [L. Perlitt, 1965.] 62, 69, 76–88, 92–7, 100, 103 f., 111, 113, 125, 127, 147, 171, 189, 208

WESTCOTT, BROOKE FOSS (1825–1901). Fellow of Trinity, Cambridge (1849), teacher at Harrow (1852), Regius prof. Cambridge (1870), Bishop Durham (1890). Christian socialist, Platonist theologian. *Intro. to the Study of the Gospels* (1851) helped establish bib. crit. in Church of England, *Hist. of Canon* (1855) also imp. Crit. ed. of NT (with Hort) 1881, and NT Reviser 1870–81. Comms. *John* (1881), *Eps. of John* (1883), *Heb.* (1889). 228

WESTERMANN, CLAUS (b. 1909). OT prof. Berlin (1949), Heidelberg (1958). *Basic Forms of Prophetic Speech* (1967), *Creation* (1974), comms. *Isaiah 40–66* (1966; ET 1969), *Gen.* (1974–82; ET 1984–7). Ed. *Essays in OT Interp.* (1960; ET 1963). 132

WILDER, AMOS NIVEN (b. 1895). Congregationalist, studied at Yale, Brussels, and Mansfield, Oxford. Served in Great War. Prof. Chicago Theol. Seminary (1943) and Harvard (1954), retd. 1963. Secular lit. crit. and poet. Father of North American lit. study of NT. Important contributions on relig. lang., including *Eschatology and Ethics in the Teaching of Jesus* (1939, 1950²). J. D. Crossan, 1981. **245**, 247 f., 266

WILKE, CHRISTIAN GOTTLOB (1786–1854). Dismissed from parish in Erz Mountains, converted to Rom. Cath. *Der Urevangelist* (1838) on relationship between Synoptic Gospels: priority of Mark, and Matt. dependent on Luke. Also published a NT dictionary and work on NT rhetoric and hermeneutics. H.-H. Stoldt, *Marcan Hyp.*, 1977 (ET 1980). 67

WINDISCH, HANS (1881–1935). Outstanding German NT schol., lit. crit., hist. of religs. approach and theol. NT prof. Leiden (1914), Kiel (1929), Halle (1935). Answered Bultmann on teaching of Jesus (*Sermon on the Mount*, 1929; ET 1950) and on Paul's ethics. Comms. *Cath. eps.* (1911), *Heb.* (1913), *Barnabas* (1920), *2 Cor.* (1924). [K. Prumm, 1961–2.] 215, 217, 228

WOOLSTON, THOMAS (1670–1733). Deist, Fellow of Sidney Sussex, Cambridge (1691, dismissed 1721). Origen enthusiast, claimed Virgin Birth and Resurrection allegories. His (six) *Discourses on the Miracles of our Saviour* (1727–30) led to a £100 fine and, since he could not pay, to prison, where he died. L. Stephen, 1886; G. Rupp, 1986. 56, (175)

WREDE, WILLIAM (1859–1906). Brilliant NT critic, prof. Breslau (1896). Friend of A. Eichhorn and co-founder of Göttingen 'hist. of religs. school'. In addition to *The Messianic Secret* (1901; ET 1971) his work on *The Task and Methods of 'NT Theol.'* (1897; ET 1973), *Paul* (1904; ET 1907, rp. 1962), and *John* (1903) remain provocative. [G. Strecker, 1960]; H. Rollmann, 2 vols., forthcoming.
67, 76, **107** f., 109, 116, 121, 125–7, 171, 233

ZAHN, THEODOR VON (1838–1933). Conservative NT prof. Kiel (1877), Erlangen (1878, 1892–1909), Leipzig (1888–92). Historian of the canon (1888–92 and 11 vols. 1891–1916). *Intro. to NT* (1897–9; ET 1909) and many NT comms. in his own series (1903–26). 72

ZIMMERLI, WALTHER (1907–83). OT prof. Göttingen (1951). Comms. *Eccles.* (1962), *Ezekiel* (1969; ET 1979–83). *Outline OT Theol.* (1972; ET 1978). (ch. 4)

INDEX OF OTHER NAMES

SUBJECT INDEX